Mass Migration to the United States

Classical and Contemporary Periods

Edited by
PYONG GAP MIN

ALTAMIRA
PRESS

A Division of Rowman & Littlefield Publishers, Inc.
Walnut Creek • Lanham • New York • Oxford

ALTAMIRA PRESS
A Division of Rowman & Littlefield Publishers, Inc.
1630 North Main Street, #367
Walnut Creek, CA 94596
www.altamirapress.com

Rowman & Littlefield Publishers, Inc.
A Member of the Rowman & Littlefield Publishing Group
4720 Boston Way
Lanham, MD 20706

12 Hid's Copse Road
Cumnor Hill, Oxford OX2 9JJ, England

British Library Cataloguing in Publication Information Available

Library of Congress Cataloging-in-Publication Data

Mass migration to the United States : classical and contemporary periods / edited by
Pyong Gap Min.
    p. cm.
Includes bibliographical references and index.
    ISBN 0-7591-0231-7 (hc: acid-free)—ISBN 0-7591-0232-5 (pb: acid-free)
    1. United States—Emigration and immigration—History. 2. Immigrants—United
States—Social conditions. I. Min, Pyong Gap, 1942–
JV6450 .M367 2002
304.8'73—dc21   2002000707

Printed in the United States of America

♾™ The paper used in this publication meets the minimum requirements of American
National Standard for Information Sciences—Permanence of Paper for Printed Library
Materials, ANSI/NISO Z39.48-1992.

CONTENTS

CONTENTS

TABLES AND FIGURES

ACKNOWLEDGMENTS

F ive of the nine chapters included in this book were significant or moderate revisions of the articles published in a special issue (fall 1999) of the *Journal of American Ethnic History*. I wish to thank Ronald Bayor, the editor of the journal, for inviting me to serve as the guest editor for the special issue and for subsequently allowing me to use the articles for this book. I also would like to thank seven contributors for writing and revising their papers to make them suitable for the special issue and/or for this book. My thanks also go to Rosalie Robertson, the editor of AltaMira Press, for recognizing the significance of this book project and coordinating with me efficiently and Erin McKindley, the production editor at Rowman & Littlefield Publishers, for editing the manuscript professionally and expediting publication of the book. Also, I should not forget to express thanks to Dean Savage, my colleague at the Queens College Department of Sociology, for his unflinching support of my research activities for this book and other research projects over the past several years. Finally, I feel grateful to Young Oak for her loving support of my research and careful editing and proofreading of the manuscript.

INTRODUCTION

Pyong Gap Min

Classical and Contemporary Mass Migration Periods

During the five-decade period between 1880 and 1930, approximately twenty-eight million people immigrated to the United States, with an average of 560,000 per year. These fifty years are known as the "mass migration" period in American history. This period is interesting to researchers not only because of the massive scale of immigration flow but also because of the differences in the immigrants' origins, their religious backgrounds, and socioeconomic characteristics from those admitted before 1880. While an overwhelming majority of immigrants admitted before 1880 were drawn from northwestern European countries—the United Kingdom, Germany, and Ireland, in particular—the proportion of southeastern European immigrants began to increase in the 1880s, immigration reaching its peak during the next decade. In the peak decade of the 1900s, Italy, Russia, Hungary, and Poland were among the top source countries of immigrants, with the first two replacing the United Kingdom and Germany as the top two source countries.

Most of the immigrants from these economically underdeveloped European countries were Catholic, Jewish, or Eastern Orthodox Christian. Their language, religious, "racial," and other differences, along with nativism, led native-born Protestants to consider their mass migration a threat to the very foundation of American cultural and political systems. The negative attitudes toward new immigrants resulted in racial violence and the development of "scientific racism," the belief in the biological differences in intelligence and behavioral traits among different racial

1

groups. The racist ideology that emphasized the biological superiority of the "Teutonic race" ultimately led to the passage of restrictive immigration laws in the early 1920s.

The majority of southern and eastern European immigrants in the "mass migration" period were farmers and unskilled workers who were illiterate, although there were significant national origin differences in the immigrants' class background. As a result, most of them, with the exception of Jews, who had largely urban and higher educational backgrounds, were at the bottom of the occupational hierarchy in American society (Lieberson 1980: 171; Steinberg 1983). Partly because of their class disadvantages and partly because of the industrial structure of the time (prevalence of factory jobs), even many of their second-generation descendants remained in blue-collar occupations.

As elaborated in *The Polish Peasant* by Thomas and Znaniecki (1918), the earlier southern and eastern European immigrants of a heavily rural background kept their "old-world traits" in urban America. Many working-class immigrants who settled in ethnic enclaves were able to transmit their ethnic language and customs to their children. However, these "unassimilable" white ethnic groups also experienced an inexorable march toward acculturation. Beyond the second generation, they lost their ethnic language and much of their ethnic customs. By the 1970s, their third and fourth generations had achieved cultural and social assimilation to the extent that they maintained their ethnicity loosely, using only ethnic symbols such as ethnic food and ethnic festivals (Alba 1990; Gans 1979; Waters 1990).

Discriminatory immigration laws of 1921 and 1924, along with the Great Depression and World War II, led to a drastic reduction of the immigration flow in the next four decades beginning in 1930. However, the liberalization of the immigration laws in 1965 (see Reimers 1992); the U.S. government's military, political, and/or economic involvement in many Third World countries; and other structural factors have accelerated immigration flow since 1965, ushering in the second mass migration period. More than nine million immigrants were admitted to the United States in the 1990s, slightly outnumbering the 8.8 million immigrants admitted in the peak decade of the first mass migration period in the 1900s.

Interestingly, a vast majority of post-1965 immigrants have originated from Latin America, the Caribbean basin, and Asia. While nearly 90 percent of immigrants admitted between 1880 and 1930 were drawn from Europe and Canada, only about 12 percent of post-1965 immigrants have originated from these regions (see chapter 2 for other differences in immigration patterns between the two periods). Even this relatively small proportion of European immigrants came largely from the former Soviet Union and other eastern European, former communist countries. Mexico, the Dominican Republic, Jamaica, El Salvador, Cuba, Haiti, the Philippines, China, India, Vietnam, and South Korea are major source countries of post-1965 immigrants, with Jews from the former Soviet Union and the Middle East being the only major contemporary white immigrant group.

The overrepresentation of nonwhite, Third World people among contemporary immigrants is something policymakers neither intended nor expected when they liberalized the immigration law. In 1965, when Congress passed the liberal immigration law, only small numbers of Latino, Asian, and Caribbean black immigrants were naturalized citizens. Thus, policymakers never imagined the possibility of the multiplier effects of the family-based immigration (Liu et al. 1991). However, an increasing number of Third World immigrants who came to the United States as beneficiaries of the new immigration law have become naturalized citizens and thus have been able to invite their immediate family members and relatives through the "family reunification" preferences. Since family reunification has been the major mechanism for legal immigration to the United States during recent years, new immigrant groups from Third World countries have been able to bring more and more immigrants here from their countries. In addition, the legalization of some 2.7 million former undocumented immigrants and "special agricultural workers" under the amnesty provisions of the 1986 Immigration Reform and Control Act contributed to the record number of annual immigrants beyond one million between 1989 and 1992 (see table I.1).

As discussed in chapter 4, it is unlikely that the U.S. government will revise the current immigration law to reduce the number of immigrants in the foreseeable future. Moreover, researchers have warned that once social networks between American destination cities and places of origin have been firmly established in this global period, the U.S. government cannot stem the tide of the current immigration flow through restrictive measures (Massey 1995; Portes and Rumbaut 1996: 272–284). Thus, the current

TABLE 1.1. Immigration to the United States by Decade, Region, and Race, 1841–1996

Decade	Total N (in 1,000s)	Northern and Western Europe	Southern and Eastern Europe	Eastern Canada and Newfoundland	Total White	Latin America and Caribbean Islands	Asia and The Middle East	Year	% Foreign Born	% White
1841–1850	1,713	93.0	0.3	2.4	95.7	1.2	0.0	1850	9.7	84.3
1851–1860	2,598	93.6	0.8	2.3	96.7	0.6	1.6	1860	13.1	85.6
1861–1870	2,315	87.8	1.5	6.7	96.0	0.6	2.8	1870	14.0	87.1
1871–1880	2,812	73.6	7.7	13.6	94.9	0.7	4.4	1880	13.3	86.5
1881–1890	5,247	72.0	18.2	7.5	97.7	0.7	1.3	1890	14.7	87.5
1891–1900	3,688	44.6	51.9	0.1	96.6	1.0	2.0	1900	13.6	87.9
1901–1910	8,795	21.7	69.9	2.0	93.6	2.1	3.7	1910	14.6	88.9
1911–1920	5,763	25.3	50.0	12.9	88.2	6.0	4.3	1920	13.1	89.7
1921–1930	4,107	32.5	27.5	22.2	82.2	14.4	2.7	1930	11.5	89.8
1931–1940	528	38.7	27.2	20.5	86.4	9.7	3.0	1940	8.6	89.8
1941–1950	1,035	49.9	10.1	16.6	76.6	17.7	3.1	1950	6.9	89.3
1951–1960	2,516	38.2	14.5	15.0	67.7	24.6	6.1	1960	5.4	88.6
1961–1970	3,322	18.3	15.5	12.4	46.2	39.3	12.9	1970	4.7	87.6
1971–1980	4,493	11.6	10.0	23.8	45.4	40.3	35.3	1980	6.2	79.6
1981–1990	7,338	4.6	5.2	1.8	11.6	46.8	38.0	1990	8.0	75.6
1991–1998	7,605	3.3	10.2	1.5	15.0	47.7	31.9	2000	11.0	70.0

Sources: U.S. Bureau of the Census (1960), Series A 9-22, A 34-50, C 23-38, and C 228-295; (1975), Series A 9-22, A 44-50, C 23-28, and C 228-295; (1983a); table 39; (1983b); table 253; (1993a); table 25; (1993b); table 143. U.S. Immigration and Naturalization Service (1950–1978, 1979–1998).

level of immigration is likely to continue in the near future. As the contemporary mass migration period takes shape, the original mass migration period is often referred to as the "classical mass migration period."

As shown in table I.1, until the 1960s, the white population had maintained its numerical supremacy at almost 90 percent. Of course, Asian and Pacific Islander Americans have a long history in Hawaii, California, and other West Coast states, while Mexicans are natives to California, Texas, Arizona, and other southwestern border states. Yet before the 1960s, Latino, Asian, and Pacific Islander populations still composed very small fractions of the U.S. population. Even in 1970, Latinos and Asian Americans composed 4.5 and 0.7 percent of the U.S. population, respectively. The only significant racial minority group before the 1960s was the African American. However, the influx of immigrants from Latin America, Asia, and the Caribbean islands since the late 1960s has led to a phenomenal increase in minority populations, with a concomitant reduction of the proportion of the non-Hispanic white population. During the period between 1970 and 2000, the non-Hispanic white population decreased from 88 to 70 percent, while the Latino and Asian/Pacific Islander populations rose to 13 and 4.5 percent, respectively.

According to population projections, the non-Hispanic white population will be reduced to 53 percent in 2050, while the Latino, black, and Asian American populations will grow to 25, 14, and 8 percent, respectively (U.S. Bureau of the Census 1996: 19). Assuming that the current immigration trend continues even after 2050, non-Hispanic whites are likely to be a numerical minority, although they are expected to maintain their political and economic dominance well after the year. As immigrants are heavily concentrated in large metropolitan cities, especially in central cities, already in the year of 2000, minority members outnumber whites in nearly half (forty-eight) of the one hundred largest cities in the United States (Schmitt 2001).

Research on Immigrants and Their Descendants

The influx of large numbers of immigrants to the United States in each mass migration period led scholars to conduct research on immigrants and their descendants, but the two periods significantly differ in the time lag between migration and research. Researchers began to systematically study the 1880–1930 immigrants and their descendants only in the 1920s, about forty years after the mass migration had started (Gans 1997). In fact, most significant books that examined major immigrant groups in the classical mass migration period and their descendants, such as Thomas Kessner's *The Golden Door* and Stephen Steinberg's *The Ethnic Myth*, have been published since the 1970s. Since the immigrants and their descendants in the classical mass migration period were studied several decades after the period, they were largely historical in nature, written by historians and historically oriented social scientists (Bodnar 1985; Higham 1974; Kessner 1977; Perlmann 1988; Steinberg 1983; Thernstrom 1973).

By contrast, social scientists began to conduct research on post-1965 immigrants immediately after the contemporary mass migration started. As a result, hundreds of articles and numerous books dealing with the adjustments of post-1965 immigrants were published by the early 1990s, only twenty-five years after the contemporary mass migration started. While the first book on the second generation of the immigrants in the classical mass migration period was published in 1943 (Child 1943), contemporary researchers began to examine the "new second generation" in the late 1980s. As of 2002, several books focusing on the second generation have already been published (Gibson 1988; Hirschman et al. 1999; Min 2002; Min and Kim 1999; Portes 1996; Portes and Rumbaut 1996; Rumbaut and Cornelius 1995; Rumbaut and Portes 2001; Waters 1999; Zhou and Bankston 1998).

It is not difficult to understand why it took much longer (several decades) for the researchers in the earlier period to start research on the immigrants and their descendants than for today's scholars to start studying post-1965 immigrants and their descendants. Today, hundreds of sociologists and other social scientists focus on research on contemporary immigrants and their children. Contemporary immigrants include many professionals who initially came to the United States as foreign students and have subsequently changed their status to permanent residents. As a result, immigrant scholars who represent the immigrant groups under investigation have often studied their own groups (Gans 1997). By contrast, there were few social scientists in the beginning of the twentieth century who could conduct research on immigrants because most social science disciplines were just beginning to develop at that time.

The other important reason that contemporary social scientists could develop theoretical models to predict not only post-1965 immigrants' but also their children's adjustments even before the children became adults is that they had conceptual and theoretical frameworks derived from studies of the earlier immigrant groups. For example, Portes and his associates developed segmented assimilation theory without collecting empirical data to predict the prospects of the socioeconomic adjustment of the "new second generation" (Portes 1995; Portes and Zhou 1993; Zhou 1997). As summarized in chapter 2, the theory posits that the descendants of the new immigrants will adopt three different modes of adaptation, depending on their race, parents' socioeconomic status, residential locale, and family/community structure: 1) incorporation into the white middle class with a high level of social mobility through education, 2) incorporation into the minority youth culture with no opportunity for social mobility, and 3) retention of ethnic culture with social mobility found within the ethnic community. By predicting the three different modes of adaptation for different groups of immigrants, it rejects the one-way path of adaptation theorized by the classical assimilationist theory associated with Warner and Srole (1945) and Gordon (1964). They developed the segmented assimilation theory largely by examining the differences in the characteristics of immigrants and the economic structure of American society between the two mass migration periods. Thus, they could not have been able to develop the theoretical model without the benefit of the classical assimilation theory (based on the second, third, and even fourth generations of the earlier immigrants) they intended to challenge. By contrast, scholars at the turn of the twentieth century did not have the similar vantage points in theory and information about the immigrants' and their children's modes of adaptation, as there had been no comparable massive migration of people entirely different from the native-born population in origin, religion, and even physical characteristics.

Herbert Gans has made educated speculations about "second generation decline" (Gans 1992) and the possibility of a black and nonblack bimodal racial hierarchy in the twenty-first century United States (Gans 1999). Other sociologists (Alba and Nee 1997; Massey 1995; Min 1999), too, have made speculations about contemporary immigrants' and their children's adjustment patterns by examining the differences between the two periods in immigrants' characteristics and structural factors. However, many social scientists and historians have cautioned against making "hasty predictions" (inferences) about what will happen to contemporary immigrants and their children before we get enough evidence (DeWind and Kasinitz 1997; Perlmann and Waldinger 1997). As an anonymous reviewer (a historian) of the manuscript of this book put it, "The impact of the turn of the century (1900) immigration has taken decades to work its way through American society. We have only a few indications of the next seventy-five years." Even Herbert Gans, who, as cited previously, made his own "speculative analyses," cautioned against making a prediction about the new second generation's identity as follows (Gans 1997: 882):

> It is too early to tell what forms today's major expressions of identity—personal, group, or both—will take among the new immigrants and the second generation since most members of the latter are still too young for college or the workplace—and also because identities may change in the passage from adolescence to adulthood.

The Importance of Comparing Two Mass Migration Periods

Historians usually try to describe or explain historical events on the basis of historical documents. Thus, they are generally not interested in making predictions about what modes of adaptation the children of post-1965 immigrants are likely to take until they have access to data regarding second-generation children's labor market outcomes. However, social scientists, especially sociologists, tend to make speculations using inferences without empirical data, as Portes and his associates did with regard to the new second generation. As suggested previously, today's social scientists have advantage in studying the post-1965 immigration because they are equipped with concepts, theories, and information about the adjustments of immigrants and their descendants derived from studies of turn-of-the-century immigrant groups. Of course, some old concepts and theories might not be effectively applicable to the context of the contemporary immigration. But we can revise an old concept and/or theory or provide an alternative theoretical model to fit the experiences of contemporary immigrants and their children.

The predictions that Portes and his associates made regarding the new second generation's labor market outcomes are based on historical insights derived from comparing two mass migration periods in immigrants' characteristics and the industrial structure of American society. But their predictions are based partly on untested assumptions and thus can be proved wrong by empirical data in the future. This is why some scholars have cautioned against making "hasty predictions" about the new second generation before we get enough data. However, social scientists can effectively use historical insights by comparing the two mass migration periods with regard to what has already happened. Analyzing the similarities and differences between the two mass migration periods with regard to what has already happened would help us better understand both the issues in the contemporary period and those in the earlier period (Hirschman et al. 1999).

On cursory observation, there are many similarities between the two mass migration periods. To give a few examples, because of the massive immigration scale and the differences in characters between immigrants and the native-born population, both waves of immigrants encountered similar anti-immigrant attitudes and actions. Nativism and anti-immigrant movements, in turn, strengthened the internal solidarity of many immigrant groups in both periods. In the 1920s and 1930s, the Ivy League schools set quotas to restrict the increasing number of Jewish students. In the 1980s, Asian American faculty members and community leaders claimed that Asian American students were subjected to discrimination similar to Jewish students in the early twentieth century. Similarly, Korean merchants in black neighborhoods encountered boycotts and riots in the 1980s and 1990s, just as Jewish merchants in black neighborhoods experienced hostility earlier in the century (see chapter 9).

On closer examination, however, there are significant differences between the two mass migration periods. In the early twentieth century, many influential social scientists emphasized the moral and intellectual inferiority of southern and eastern Europeans on "scientific" grounds in order to support a measure to restrict their immigration. But few social scientists today would make such unscientific claims. Because of their alleged differences in religion, "race," and "intelligence," southeastern European immigrants were subjected to high levels of prejudice, discrimination, and even racial violence. But their descendants have assimilated into American society progressively over generations to the extent that they are no longer distinctive from descendants of northwestern European ancestry. Because of their differences in origin and physical differences, however, the descendants of contemporary, Third World immigrants are not likely to follow this straight-line assimilation path.

Historical comparison is an important component of social science research methods. Thus, in addition to the previously cited studies, several other social scientists have already used insights derived from comparing two mass migration periods. We have already witnessed enough nativist reactions to the post-1965 immigration wave comparable to the massive wave of immigrants at the turn of the twentieth century. Thus, as cited in chapter 1, a few books and a few articles focusing on comparing the two mass migration periods in nativist movements have already been published (Bennett 1988; Higham 1999; Perea 1997; Reimers 1998). Lopez (1999) analyzed the 1990 U.S. census to examine Latinos' and Asian Americans' linguistic and social assimilation. He discussed the linguistic and social assimilation of the two largest immigrant groups, mainly with reference to the earlier white immigrant groups. Glick-Schiller and others have compared two mass migration periods in transnational ties (Foner 1997; Glick-Schiller 1999; Goldberg 1992). Waldinger and Bozorgmehr (1996a) have compared two mass migration periods in terms of the largest immigrant cities. Finally, in her most recent book, Foner (2000) has compared turn-of-the-century and contemporary immigrants in New York City in settlement patterns, economic adjustments, and other aspects of immigrant experiences.

Collection of Nine Essays
Comparing Two Mass Migration Periods

This book contributes to the growing literature comparing classical and contemporary mass migration periods. It includes nine chapters, each of which has systematically compared two mass migration periods with regard to the topic under consideration. The topics covered are anti-immigrant attitudes and action, immigrants' settlement patterns, Asian immigrant entrepreneurship, the effects of ethnic diversity on ethnic conflicts, naturalization laws and trends, settlement patterns of immigrants in New York City, immigrant women's work, intergenerational transmission of culture, and Jewish immigrants. This book probably has covered more topics using the comparative framework than any other book available now. As such, I expect that this book, along with a few other recently published ones (Foner 2000; Hirschman et al. 1999; Waldinger and Bozorgmehr 1996b), provides deep insights for both historians and social scientists interested in either or both of the two mass migration periods.

It would be helpful to describe to the readers the genesis of this book. In 1998, Ronald Bayor, the editor of the *Journal of American Ethnic History*, and I discussed the importance of the historical comparison between the two mass migration periods. Bayor decided to organize a special issue on the topic for the journal and invited me to serve as the guest editor. Five of the articles submitted for the special issue were selected and published in the *Journal of American Ethnic History* in the spring of 1999. Although ethnic historians comprise the majority of the subscribers to the journal, all five articles were written by social scientists, four by sociologists and one by an anthropologist. This reflects the divergence of interest between ethnic historians and social scientists studying ethnicity and immigration. As suggested previously, ethnic historians, while focusing on particular historical periods or historical events, usually do not compare the contemporary period with the earlier historical period to examine their similarities and differences. But social scientists studying American immigration and ethnic history have great interest in analyzing similarities and differences in different issues between the two mass migration periods.

Since social scientists are not likely to have read the special issue of the historical journal, I decided to publish the special-issue articles in an edited book to make it available to both social scientists and historians. Thus, four chapters of this book (1, 3, 7, and 8) were originally published in a special issue of the *Journal of American Ethnic History*. All of them were revised and updated in the summer of 2001 to be included in this book. My own chapter, which focuses on intergenerational transmission of culture (chapter 4), is a significant modification of the chapter originally published in the spring 1999 special issue of the journal. I have collected four more papers for this book, three by sociologists (chapters 2, 6, and 9) and one by a historian (chapter 5). The latter was published in the summer 2001 issue of the *Journal of American Ethnic History*.

To stimulate the readers' interest and expectations, let me summarize the nine substantive chapters. In chapter 1, Charles Jaret has examined the similarities and differences between the anti-immigrant phenomena and nativism in the two mass migration periods by comprehensively synthesizing the existing literature. He concludes, "Nativism and other anti-immigrant phenomenon today, as in the past, arise from both an age-old unsettled debate over what 'American identity' really is . . . and from persistent fears that mass migration will harm the nation's economy, culture, political system, and/or a subset of its people." But he also sees the basic differences in nativism and other anti-immigrant phenomena between the two periods. In his view, "compared to the earlier era, some realignment, reformulation, and diminution of anti-immigrant attitudes have occurred." Some rightists have relaxed or lost their suspicion and antipathy toward immigrants. Moreover, public officials and the mass media today are less explicit in referring to race in discussing immigration issues. In addition, organized labor, historically anti-immigrant, has taken a new stance most recently, speaking out for illegal immigrants and asking them to join unions. Many other researchers examined nativism with an a priori assumption that it was associated with "illegitimate discourse or irrational beliefs." Unlike these researchers, Jaret focuses on "its core substantive fears and concerns, explicating and comparing the central ideas found in today's nativism and that of the 1880–1924 era" without trying to "dispute or give credence to each nativist claim."

In chapter 2, Min Zhou covers a number of issues relating to the post-1965 migration period by loosely comparing it with the classical mass migration period. Zhou specifically examines the historical trends of immigration to the United States, the settlement patterns of new immigrants in America's largest metropolitan regions, the nature of racial and ethnic relations in areas of high immigration, and the key determinants of social mobility for new immigrants and their offspring. As previously indicated, Portes and Zhou argue that the children of new immigrants will not follow the linear assimilation path the children of the immigrants in the classical migration period took. She intends the chapter to help us to "understand how contemporary immigration differs from the immigration at the turn of the twentieth century and how such differences may affect our approach to the issues and concerns over the changing face of America."

In chapter 3, Suzanne Shanahan and Susan Olzak examine the relationship among immigration, diversity, and racial and ethnic collective mobilization in urban America in the two mass migration periods. Susan Olzak, along with her colleague Joane Nagel, developed competitive theory of ethnic mobilization and used it in explaining many empirical cases (Olzak 1992; Olzak and Nagel 1986). This study is also built on the same competitive perspective. The authors' event history analysis shows that the ethnic diversity of immigration flows, rather than immigration per se, raised the rates of ethnic and racial conflict in both periods. They suggest that the diversity of immigrants raised racial conflict by increasing the salience of the boundary between whites and nonwhites.

In chapter 4, I have examined several structural factors that give contemporary immigrants advantages over the earlier white immigrants in transmitting their culture to their children. Contemporary immigrant groups have higher residential concentration in a few or several cities than the earlier white immigrant groups and higher segregation within each city. The greater residential concentration and segregation of contemporary immigrant groups and their proximity and transnational ties to their home countries give them advantages in maintaining their cultural traditions. Moreover, the changes in minority policies from Anglo conformity to multiculturalism and permanence of contemporary migration flows are additional structural factors that help them maintain their cultural traditions. Moreover, the descendants of post-1965 immigrants will be subject to color-based prejudice and discrimination, which will be a major structural source of their ethnic identity.

In chapter 5, Dorothee Schneider reviews naturalization policies and trends in the United States from the nineteenth century to the contemporary period with a focus on two mass migration periods. Throughout the nineteenth century, naturalization procedures remained without the supervision of the federal government and subject to local governments' corruption and irregularities. But since the Naturalization Act of 1906, the federal government has enforced the centralized system of naturalization, making naturalization procedures uniform for the entire country. According to Schneider, this is one of the major differences in naturalization policy between the nineteenth century and the later period, including the contemporary period. In the late nineteenth and early twentieth centuries, women were not eligible for naturalization, while some racial minority groups, especially East Asian groups, were eliminated from naturalization until the early 1950s. Another major difference between the classical and contemporary mass migration periods is that these racial and gender restrictions in naturalization were abolished in the interim period. In the earlier period, the distinction between a naturalized citizen and a noncitizen was important because nonnaturalized residents were not eligible for many social programs. However, the distinction is not important in the contemporary period, as permanent residents can obtain most social programs created for American citizens, which is, according to Schneider, another major difference between the two periods.

In chapter 6, Andrew Beveridge analyzes census data in 1910 and 1990, the key years of the two mass migration periods, to compare residential patterns of major immigrant groups in New York between the two periods. His analysis shows that the immigrants in New York City in 1910 originated largely from Russia, Italy, and a few other European countries and were heavily concentrated in Manhattan. By contrast, his analyses of 1990 census data reveal that New York's immigrants consist of many different racial and ethnic groups, originating from all four areas of the world (Latin America, the Caribbean, Asia, and Europe), settled throughout the New York metropolitan area. They also show that contemporary immigrants in the city are more concentrated in enclaves and are more residentially segregated from both the native-born population and other immigrant groups than the turn-of-the-century immigrants.

Chapter 7 analyzes major differences in immigrant women's economic activities in New York City between two mass migration periods. Nancy Foner's analysis shows that at the turn of the century, few Jewish and Italian immigrant wives worked outside the home because of a stigma attached to working wives at that time. Although many immigrant wives earned money, all their income-producing activities were done at home. Consequently, these activities did not help reduce their responsibility for housework and childcare, thus rigidifying the traditional gender division of labor. By contrast, the majority of today's immigrant wives participate in the labor force, many working long hours—many more hours than they did in their home countries. Foner devotes a great deal of space to discussing the implications of contemporary immigrant wives' increased economic role for their marital relations. As a result of their economic contribution, today's immigrant women can enjoy their independence and power in the marriage to a greater extent than Jewish and Italian immigrant women did at the turn of the century. However, she also emphasizes the negative side to women's increased economic role, characterized by their overwork, role strain, and marital discord.

Chapter 8 compares Jewish immigrants in the two mass migration periods. It is meaningful to compare Jewish immigrants in the two periods because Jews are one of the major (top ten) immigrant groups in both periods. One major difference, according to Steven Gold, is that the European component remains less significant among today's Jewish immigrants than among the earlier Jewish immigrants, as many of today's Jews originated from Israel and other Middle Eastern countries. Gold's comparison shows two other significant differences. While the American Jewish community tried to Americanize the earlier highly religious eastern European Jewish immigrants, the contemporary American Jewish community has attempted to Judaize the secularized eastern European Jewish immigrants. Gold considers a big reduction of anti-Semitism as another difference between contemporary and the earlier Jewish immigrants. Jewish immigrants at the turn of the century were concerned mainly with economic survival and avoiding anti-Semitism. By contrast, the main concern of Jewish immigrants today is cultural preservation, as they do not encounter anti-Semitism and get extra services from the U.S. government as refugees.

In chapter 9, I delineate three major differences in Asian immigrants' business patterns between the pre-1965 and the post-1965 periods. The first major difference has to do with the differential degrees of the involuntary nature of Asian immigrants' entry into small business. The earlier Chinese and Japanese immigrants were forced to enter small business for economic survival because white male workers did not allow them to compete in the labor market. By contrast, contemporary Korean and other Asian immigrants enter small business semi-involuntarily mainly because of their language barrier and other disadvantages for employment in the general labor. The second major difference is that middleman minority theory is far more useful for understanding the experiences of contemporary Korean business owners than for understanding those of the Chinese and Japanese shopkeepers in the pre-1965 period. Korean produce, grocery, and liquor retail shopkeepers in black neighborhoods as middleman merchants have had serious conflicts with black customers and white suppliers, while neither the earlier Chinese nor Japanese business owners had conflicts with either party. The third major difference pertains to the significance of ethnic resources and ethnic solidarity for business establishment and operation. The earlier Asian immigrants heavily depended on rotating credit associations for business establishment, while contemporary Asian immigrants depend mainly on their own class resources. Moreover, ethnic employees are less important for Asian-owned businesses and less loyal to the business owners in the post-1965 period than they were in the pre-1965 period.

References

Alba, Richard. 1990. *Ethnic Identity: Transformation of White America.* New Haven, CT: Yale University Press.

Alba, Richard, and Victor Nee. 1997. "Rethinking Assimilation Theory in a New Era of Immigration." *International Migration Review* 31: 875–892.

Bennett, David H. 1988. *The Party of Fear: From Nativist Movements to the New Right in American History.* Chapel Hill, NC: University of North Carolina Press.

Bodnar, John. 1985. *The Transplanted: A History of Immigrants in Urban America.* Bloomington, IN: Indiana University Press.

Child, Irvin L. 1943. *Italian or Americans? The Second Generation in Conflict.* New Haven, CT: Yale University Press.

DeWind, Josh, and Philip Kasinitz. 1997. "Everything Old Is New Again? Processes and Theories of Immigrant Incorporation." *International Migration Review* 31: 1096–1111.

Foner, Nancy. 1997. "What's New about Transnationalism? New York Immigrants Today and at the Turn of the Century." *Diaspora* 6: 355–376.

———. 2000. *From Ellis Island to JFK: New York's Two Great Waves of Immigration.* New York: Columbia University Press.

Gans, Herbert. 1979. "Symbolic Ethnicity: The Future of Ethnic Groups and Cultures in America." *Ethnic and Racial Studies* 2: 1–20.

———. 1992. "Second-Generation Decline: Scenarios of the Economic and Ethnic Futures of the Post-1965 Immigrants." *Ethnic and Racial Studies* 15: 173–192.

———. 1997. "Toward a Reconciliation of 'Assimilation' and 'Pluralism': The Interplay of Acculturation and Ethnic Retention." *International Migration Review* 31: 875–892.

———. 1999. "The Possibility of a New Racial Hierarchy in the Twenty-First Century United States." In *The Cultural Territories of Race: Black and White Boundaries,* edited by Michele Lamont. Chicago: University of Chicago Press.

Gibson, Margaret. 1988. *Accommodation without Assimilation: Sikh Immigrant Children in an American High School.* Ithaca, NY: Cornell University Press.

Glick-Schiller, Nina. 1999. "Transmigrants and Nation-States: Something Old and Something New in the U.S. Immigrant Experience." In *The Handbook of International Migration: The American Experience,* edited by Charles Hirschman, Philip Kasnitz, and Josh DeWind. New York: Russell Sage Foundation.

Goldberg, Barry. 1992. "Historical Reflections on Transnationalism, Race, and the American Immigrant Saga." In *Toward a Transnational Perspective on Migration,* edited by Nina Glick Schiller, Landa Basch, and Cristina Blanc-Szanton. New York: New York Academy of Science.

Gordon, Milton. 1964. *Assimilation in American Life: The Role of Race, Religion, and National Origins.* New York: Oxford University Press.

Higham, John. 1974 [1955]. *Strangers in a Strange Land: Patterns of American Nativism, 1960–1925.* New York: Atheneum.

———. 1999. "Instead of a Sequel, or, How I Lost My Subject." In *The Handbook of International Migration: The American Experience,* edited by Charles Hirschman, Philip Kasinitz, and Josh DeWind. New York: Russell Sage Foundation.

Hirschman, Charles, Philip Kasinitz, and Josh DeWind. 1999. *The Handbook of International Migration: The American Experience.* New York: Russell Sage Foundation.

———. 1999. "International Migration and Immigration Research: The State of the Field." In *The Handbook of International Migration: The American Experience,* edited by Charles Hirschman, Philip Kasinitz, and Josh DeWind. New York: Russell Sage Foundation.

Kessner, Thomas. 1977. *The Golden Door: Italian and Jewish Immigrant Mobility in New York City 1880–1915.* New York: Oxford University Press.

Lieberson, Stanley. 1980. *A Piece of the Pie: Blacks and White Immigrants since 1880.* Berkeley: University of California Press.

Liu, John, Paul Ong, and Carolyn Rosenstein. 1991. "Dual Chain Migration: Post-1965 Filipino Migration." *International Migration Review* 25: 487–513.

Lopez, David. 1999. "Social and Linguistic Aspects of Assimilation Today." In *The Handbook of International Migration: The American Experience,* edited by Charles Hirschman, Philip Kasinitz, and Josh DeWind. New York: Russell Sage Foundation.

Massey, Douglas. 1995. "The New Immigration and Ethnicity in the United States." *Population and Development Review* 21: 631–652.

Min, Pyong Gap. 1999. "A Comparison of Post-1965 and Turn-of-the Century Immigrants in Intergenerational Mobility and Cultural Transmission." *Journal of American Ethnic History* 18: 65–94.

———, ed. 2002. *The Second Generation: Ethnic Identity among Asian Americans.* Walnut Creek, CA: AltaMira Press.

Min, Pyong Gap, and Rose Kim. 1999. *Struggle for Ethnic Identity: Narratives by Asian American Professionals.* Walnut Creek, CA: AltaMira Press.

Olzak, Susan. 1992. *The Dynamics of Ethnic Competition and Conflict.* Stanford, CA: Stanford University Press.

Olzak, Susan, and Joane Nagel, eds. 1986. *Competitive Ethnic Relations.* Orlando, FL: Academic Press.

Perea, Juan F., ed. 1997. *Immigrants Out: The New Nativism and the Anti-Immigrant Impulse in the United States.* New York: New York University Press.

Perlmann, Joel. 1988. *Ethnic Differences: Schooling and Social Structure among the Irish, Italians, Jews, and Blacks in an American City, 1880–1935.* New York: Cambridge University Press.

Perlmann, Joel, and Roger Waldinger. 1997. "Second Generation Decline? Children of Immigrants, Past and Present—A Reconsideration." *International Migration Review* 31: 893–922.

Portes, Alejandro. 1995. "Segmented Assimilation among New Immigrant Youth: A Conceptual Framework." In *California's Immigrant Children: Theory, Research, and Implications for Educational Policy,* edited by Ruben Rumbaut and Wayne Cornelius. San Diego: Center for U.S.-Mexican Studies, University of California at San Diego.

———. 1996. *The New Second Generation.* New York: Russell Sage Foundation.

Portes, Alejandro, and Ruben Rumbaut. 1996. *Immigrant America: A Portrait.* 2nd ed. Berkeley: University of California Press.

Portes, Alejandro, and Min Zhou. 1993. "The New Second Generation: Segmented Assimilation and Its Variants among Post-1965 Immigrant Youth." *Annals of the American Academy of Political and Social Science* 530: 74–98.

Reimers, David. 1992. *Still the Golden Door: The Third World Comes to America.* 2nd ed. New York: Columbia University Press.

———. 1998. *Unwelcome Strangers: American Identity and the Turn against Immigration.* New York: Columbia University Press.

Rumbaut, Ruben G., and Wayne A. Cornelius, eds. 1995. *California's Immigrant Children: Theory, Research, and Implications for Educational Policy.* San Diego: Center for U.S.-Mexican Studies, University of California at San Diego.

Rumbaut, Ruben, and Alejandro Portes, eds. 2001. *Ethnicities: Coming of Age in Immigrant America.* Berkeley: University of California Press.

Schmitt, Eric. 2001. "Whites Are Minority in Largest Cities, the Census Shows." *New York Times,* April 30, A1, 12.

Steinberg, Stephen. 1983. *The Ethnic Myth: Race, Ethnicity, and Class in America.* New York: Atheneum.

Thernstrom, Stephan. 1973. *The Other Bostonians: Poverty and Progress in the American Metropolis, 1880–1970.* Cambridge, MA: Harvard University Press.

Thomas, William I., and Florian Znaniecki. 1918. *The Polish Peasants in Europe and America.* Chicago: University of Chicago Press.

U.S. Bureau of the Census. 1960. *Historical Statistics of the United States, Colonial Times to 1957.* Washington, DC: U.S. Government Printing Office.

———. 1975. *Historical Statistics of the United States, Colonial Times to 1970.* Washington, DC: U.S. Government Printing Office.

———. 1983a. *1980 Census of Population, Detailed Population Characteristics, United States Summary.* Washington, DC: U.S. Government Printing Office.

———. 1983b. *1980 Census of Population, General Population Characteristics, United States Summary.* Washington, DC: U.S. Government Printing Office.

———. 1993a. *1990 Census of Population, General Population Characteristics, United States Summary.* Washington, DC: U.S. Government Printing Office.

———. 1993b. *1990 Census of Population, Social and Economic Characteristics, United States.* Washington, DC: U.S. Government Printing Office.

———. 1996. *Statistical Abstracts of the United States, 1996.* Washington, DC: U.S. Government Printing Office.

U.S. Immigration and Naturalization Service. 1950–1978. *Annual Report.* Washington, DC: U.S. Government Printing Office.

———. 1979–1998. *Statistical Yearbook.* Washington, DC: U.S. Government Printing Office.

Waldinger, Roger, and Mehdi Bozorgmehr. 1996a. "The Making of a Multicultural Metropolis." In *Ethnic Los Angeles.* New York: Russell Sage Foundation.

———, eds. 1996b. *Ethnic Los Angeles.* New York: Russell Sage Foundation.

Warner, Warner Lloyd, and Leo Srole. 1945. *The Social Systems of American Ethnic Groups.* New Haven, CT: Yale University Press.

Waters, Mary. 1990. *Ethnic Options: Choosing Identities in America.* Berkeley: University of California Press.

———. 1999. *Black Identities: West Indian Immigrant Dreams and American Realities.* New York: Russell Sage Foundation.

Zhou, Min. 1997. "Growing Up American: The Challenge Confronting Immigrant Children and Children of Immigrants." *Annual Review of Sociology* 23: 63–95.

Zhou, Min, and Carl Bankston III. 1998. *Growing Up American: How Vietnamese Children Adapt to Life in the United States.* New York: Russell Sage Foundation.

CHAPTER ONE

TROUBLED BY NEWCOMERS: ANTI-IMMIGRANT ATTITUDES AND ACTIONS DURING TWO ERAS OF MASS MIGRATION

Charles Jaret

This chapter examines anti-immigrant attitudes and actions during our two eras of heaviest immigration, 1880 to 1924 and 1970 to 2001. The goal is to describe the similarities and differences between anti-immigrant phenomena in both eras and examine the central fears and threats that many Americans feel when the United States undergoes mass immigration.

Two cautions are given. First, looking at anti-immigrant phenomena without also considering pro-immigrant actions and attitudes is like listening to just one side of a conversation and can produce a distorted sense of what is going on. The thrust and parry of praise and blame, welcome and restriction, are integral parts of America's dialogue on immigration. More attention, however, is given here to the anti-immigrant side because of space limitations and because fear and animosity aimed at newcomers are serious problems. Second, this chapter does not attempt to show all the twists and turns in anti-foreign sentiment transpiring in the 1880–1924 era or the current period. The anti-immigrant phenomena discussed in each era are not constant—they rise, recede, and may rise again within or across decades (Bennett 1988; Higham 1975; Simon and Alexander 1993).

This chapter reaches two conclusions. First, in several respects, recent years have seen anti-immigration attitudes and behavior undergo some significant realignment, reformulation, and diminution. Second, despite these changes, many of the core beliefs and fears that created and sustained anti-immigrant perspectives in the past are still widely held; thus, many of today's anti-immigrant phenomena resemble those of the earlier era. Despite some positive changes, it does not appear that, in general, Americans have made a clean and permanent break either with their concerns regarding foreign newcomers or from older nativist sentiments.

Shortly after passage of the 1924 Johnson–Reed Act that led to national origin quotas and sharply reduced immigration to the United States, historian Roy Garis said, "The amazing thing about the immigration problem is the likeness of the arguments of one generation to the contentions of another" (cited in Williamson 1996: 8). It remains true that today's claims, fears, and views about immigration are similar in many respects to those of past eras. Despite some new issues, many manifestations of anti-immigrant sentiment in the United States over the past two decades resemble those of the earlier peak period of American immigration, 1880 to 1924. Indeed, some scholars and activists suggest that current anti-immigrant legislation and attitudes are like that of "the bad old days."

Both periods have a widely read "classic text" that fuses nativist fears and accusations with racist notions of white supremacy (Grant's [1921] *The Passing of the Great Race* and Brimelow's [1995] *Alien Nation: Common Sense about America's Immigration Disaster*). In both eras, certain political-economic interests line up in a similar way: Business organizations favor high immigration, and immigrants create lobbying groups and use their own political power to defend their interests. Moreover, on certain indicators, the same region (the South) in the 1920s and in the 1980s seems to take the strongest anti-immigrant positions (Tatalovich 1995: 83). Each era saw its "problems of mass immigration" studied in detail by prestigious government commissions (the U.S. Immigration Commission [Dillingham Commission] appointed in 1907; the Select Commission on Immigration and Refugee Policy [Hesburgh Commission] appointed in 1978; and the U.S. Commission on Immigration Reform [Jordan Commission] appointed in 1992). These commissions gave most attention to economic consequences of immigration, and Congress later adopted some of their recommendations. Now, as then, immigrants' waving the flag of their homeland often draws criticism.[1]

Fears about or precautions against immigrants bringing in and transmitting contagious diseases today (e.g., concerning Haitians and HIV infection in the 1990s) have numerous counterparts in the 1880–1924 period (Kraut 1994; Markel and Stern 1999). Even the practice of trying to figure the dollar value to our economy by the presence of immigrants is not as new as many might think. In 1886, Andrew Carnegie estimated the average monetary value of an immigrant at $1,500 (Higham 1975: 17); today, data from the National Research Council study suggest that the average immigrant worker produces a $278 annual net gain to the U.S. economy (Smith and Edmonston 1997).

But are these similarities more apparent than real? Do they mask deeper historical differences and transformations? The following section discusses the most striking similarities and differences in anti-immigrant phenomena in the 1880–1924 era and the present period.

Similarities in Anti-Immigrant Attitudes and Action

Concern over Changes in Immigrants' National and Racial Origins

By 1912, politicians, scholars, and the public were alarmed over shifts in immigrants' national origins. The Dillingham Commission and scholars of that era emphasized the diminution of the "old" immigration from northern and western Europe and the rise of the "new" immigration from southern and eastern Europe (Jenks and Lauck 1911: 24–25) . They cite 1883 as a dividing point, noting that before 1883, 95 percent of the immigrants to the United States came from England, Ireland, Scotland, Wales, Belgium, Denmark, France, Germany, Norway, Sweden, the Netherlands, and Switzerland, but that from 1883 to 1907, 81 percent of the European immigrants came from Austria–Hungary, Bulgaria, Greece, Italy, Montenegro, Poland, Portugal, Rumania, Russia, Serbia, Spain, Syria, and Turkey.

This change was seen as more than a mere geographic shift; it was widely accepted that the "new" immigrants from southern and eastern Europe differ "much more radically in type from the earlier American residents than did the old immigration, and that in consequence the problem of assimilation has become much more difficult" (Jenks and Lauck 1911: 25).[2] Asian immigrants were considered to be much harder to assimilate than the various southern and eastern European "races." Those groups that were perceived to be unable to adapt to the customs or institutions of America were said to bring discord and undesirable traits into the community, and it was recommended that they be excluded (Jenks and Lauck 1911: 200, 265–266). Asian, Mexican, and southern and eastern European immigrants were declared to be racially different from the native-born whites, who were said to be of "Nordic" racial stock. Although Jenks and Lauck (1911: 200) indicate that the Dillingham Commission did not consider these other races inferior, many other Americans certainly did. Most outspoken on the East Coast were Madison Grant (a naturalist affiliated with the American Museum of Natural History and the New York Zoological Society and vice president of the Immigration Restriction League), Lothrop Stoddard (a Harvard University graduate and an advocate of "Nordic" racial superiority), and Kenneth Roberts (a writer whose work was featured in the *Saturday Evening Post*), who spoke of "worthless," "weak, broken, and mentally crippled" races from the Mediterranean, Balkans, and Poland bringing crime and lowering or vulgarizing American life. Summing up these sentiments in 1921, as the United States was reducing the number allowed to enter from these countries, the words of James V. McClintic (a congressman from Oklahoma) rang out in the House of Representatives, "I say the class of immigrants coming to the shores of the United States at this time are not the kind of people we want as citizens of this country" (Reimers 1998: 6). Earlier, on the West Coast, men such as labor leader Dennis Kearney and historian Hubert H. Bancroft said similar degrading things about Asian immigrants.

Similarly, most articles written today on American immigration emphasize the dramatic shift in national origins since the late 1960s. That shift shows much less European emigration and an upsurge in immigration from Asia, Latin America, and the Caribbean. Here, too, the concern is more than geographic, and, as shown later in this chapter, many Americans fear that our current immigration is causing terrible difficulties in assimilating the newcomers. For example, Lawrence Auster, a writer affiliated with an anti-immigration group called the American Immigration Control Foundation, claims that immigration is "turning America into a nonwhite country, dispossessing white America and its culture" (1995: 204). He describes current policy on immigration as "the path to national suicide," contending that a rapid change from "an historically European-majority country into a multiracial, white-minority country must result in a breakdown of the common culture" and that the large influx from the Third World in California and Brooklyn pose a great threat to American intellectual life, the arts, museums, and symphony music (Auster 1990, 1992: 173, 174).

Many of today's foes of immigration are more reticent than were those of the 1880–1924 era to object on racial grounds to immigrants' presence. Many restrictionists believe that it is morally wrong to use racial or ethnic criteria to decide who may enter the United States. For example, Bouvier (1992: 7) says that "under no circumstances should a prospective immigrant's race, ethnic background, or religious preference be a factor in determining if that person should be admitted," and he urges a policy of reduced immigration for different reasons. Other immigration opponents believe that tactically it is wise to avoid being labeled a racist and is smarter to argue for less immigration on the grounds of alleged economic and social costs (Bosniak 1997). However, this taboo for "respectable" writers was broken by Peter Brimelow, who proclaimed the need for the United States to defend and preserve its white European heritage and demographic profile. According to Brimelow (1995: 264),

> Race is destiny in American politics. . . . Any change in the racial balance must obviously be fraught with consequences for the survival and success of the American nation. It is simply common sense that Americans have a legitimate interest in their country's racial balance. It is common sense that they have a right to insist that their government stop shifting it. Indeed, it seems to me that they have a right to insist that it be shifted back [to nearly 90 percent white].

Among Americans who do not care the least about "racial sensitivity," no reticence to protest against "racially inferior" immigrants exists. Some of today's most extreme nativists think of themselves as "Aryan" whites and fear the growing influx by foreigners of color. A striking example of their anti-immigrant attitudes comes in the form of a map drawn by an ardent white separatist, showing settlement patterns of Cubans, Haitians, Jews, Pakistanis, Laotians, and other immigrant groups in the United States, with the caption,

> "Alien Invasion of North America": In all the world's history never has a strong, productive, advanced Racial Nation of people, occupying a geographical territory, separated in the main by great oceans from the earth's diverse, primitive peoples, been invaded and occupied by these regressive alien hords [sic] with such impunity! Aryan technology (Fulton's steamboat, Wright brother's airplane) plus Aryan treason made possible

what was impossible for these mongrel peoples to accomplish. They, who have never dreamed of steam or jet power, land on our shores daily. Skilled Aryan captains, piloting Aryan-conceived craft, bring the alien hords to our shores in 747 luxury beyond the wildest imagination of ancient kings. (Dobratz and Shanks-Meile 1997: 101)

Reimers (1998: 110) suggests that the groups now advocating such extreme views play "no significant role in the immigration battles in Congress or in the public discussions." Yet even in more moderate quarters, concerns about current immigrants' racial-ethnic mix were raised, with enough impact to result in Congress authorizing in 1990 a new category, "diversity immigrants" (up to 40,000 entrants annually), mainly for people in parts of Europe (such as Ireland) that in recent years have not been sending many immigrants to the United States.

Public Opinion

The public's attitudes on immigration today resemble those of the earlier era in several ways. Opinion polls on immigration using modern survey methods began in the 1940s, but Higham found one done in Wisconsin in the 1880s. Respondents were workers in varied occupations, and about half of them said that "immigration was injuring their trade" (Higham 1975: 46). Today, survey data from Los Angeles show quite similar results: 56.8 percent of blacks and 46.7 percent of whites said that they would have less economic opportunity if immigration continues at the present rate (Johnson et al. 1997: 1061). More important, Higham shows a dramatic shift in American public opinion from the late 1890s to the 1920s. Fresh from victory in the Spanish–American War and buoyed by the reform spirit of the Progressive movement, American sentiments near the start of the twentieth century were relatively friendly and open to foreigners (except Asians). They showed faith in immigrants' potential to make positive contributions to America and confidence in the nation's ability to assimilate them. But over the next two decades, public opinion shifted to a negative attitude characterized by the belief that the newcomers to America were unassimilable and a danger to the nation. By 1921, much of the American public was very anti-immigrant; invidious distinctions were made between old immigrants (northern/western Europeans) and the racially and culturally "different and inferior" new immigrants (southern/eastern Europeans and Asians). Public opinion strongly supported the restrictive and selective immigration laws of 1921 and 1924.

From 1965 through the mid-1990s, there was a similar shift toward more hostility to immigration. Americans felt most favorable about immigration in the early 1960s. Huber and Espenshade (1997: 1038) show that the percentage of Americans who want *fewer* immigrants entering has *risen* from about one-third in 1965 to half in the 1990s. Other surveys in the 1990s find even higher opposition (e.g., between 60 and 70 percent favoring laws to reduce the number of immigrants entering the United States [*Time* 1993]). Moreover, just as before, the public makes invidious comparisons among different immigrant groups. Surveys done in the 1980s show that the groups rated as being "good for this country" are mainly European, while those rated "bad for this country" are the Cubans, Haitians, Puerto Ricans, Vietnamese, Koreans, and Mexicans (DeSipio and de la Garza 1998: 129; Simon and Alexander 1993: 45).

The attitudes of blacks toward immigrants, now and in the 1880–1924 era, are an interesting aspect of public opinion. From 1880 to 1924, blacks' views grew more negative toward immigrants, and they supported restriction. The most common complaint was that immigrants displaced American blacks from jobs. Italian, Greek, Mexican, Filipino, and Chinese immigrants were said to take jobs that blacks once held in the railroad industry, on farms, in laundries, and as cooks, waiters, barbers, domestic workers, and restaurant operators (Fuchs 1990; Shankman 1982). Blacks were upset that immigrants' competition would lower workers' wages and reduce the standard of living. In addition to this economic-based antipathy, they also accused foreigners of "divided interests and allegiances" and of holding customs that were bizarre or despicable.[3] They also resented immigrants for having rights and privileges that were denied to blacks and for adopting the anti-black stereotypes, attitudes, and behaviors of native-born whites. While attitudes of blacks were generally unfavorable toward immigrants and supported the restriction laws of the 1920s, a significant segment of the black community spoke out and said that it was wrong to single out Chinese or Japanese immigrants on racial grounds and to put more onerous restrictions on them than on European immigrants (Hellwig 1977).

Current attitudes of blacks on immigration show continuity over time. Morrison (1993) objects to immigrant advancement coming "on the backs of blacks" and is angered that assimilation from "charming" immigrant to "entitled white" involves learning to feel superior to and contemptuous of blacks. Opinion polls show that most American blacks think that immigrants, especially illegals, displace the native-born from jobs and help keep wages low. Recently, some local and state-level black leaders have voiced their concerns, but many national and congressional black leaders hesitate to take anti-immigration positions, partly because they do not want to jeopardize the support they receive on other issues from Asian American and Hispanic American leaders (Jackson 1988; Reimers 1998: 34–37).

Nativist Fears

In calling today's nativism "old poison in new bottles," sociologist Joe Feagin (1997) shows several similar themes in "old" and "modern" nativism. In both eras, a common nativist fear is that the use of languages other than English by immigrants or their children threatens the nation's unity. In the 1890s, some Americans felt that "a secure modern state rested on a community of language and proposed therefore to limit immigration to English-speaking applicants" (Higham 1975: 92). That idea lacked the support necessary to become the law. Later, during the Americanization movement's campaign for patriotism and national unity (1914–1920), intense efforts were made to teach and require immigrants to speak English (Baron 1990). Similarly, today's outspoken proponents of English as the "true language" of the United States want immigrants to adopt English very quickly. Groups have formed in support of proposals that would require the use of English in all or most settings where public or civic business takes place. One such organization, called U.S. English, circulated a letter in 1988 that said, "I am concerned that our traditional language [English] is becoming irrelevant as foreign languages become more and more widely accepted in our country. And I believe that if this trend is not challenged promptly and forcefully, it will destroy the very fabric of our country." This movement has not received enough support to amend the Constitution to make English the nation's official language, but it has been successful at lower government levels (e.g., more than twenty states have declared English their official language [Baron 1990; Tatalovich 1995, 1997]).

Feagin (1997) notes other similarities between nativism then and now. One is that at both times, people charged immigrants with having below-average intelligence. Early IQ data and anecdotal accounts of foreigners' poor mental powers caused many prominent Americans to fear that heavy immigration from southern/eastern Europe was causing a decline in the nation's intelligence (Grant 1924). That worry is less visible in current nativism but was raised by Herrnstein and Murray (1994: 360–361) and alluded to by Brimelow (1997: 56), who say that "Latino and black immigrants are, at least in the short run, putting some downward pressure on the distribution of intelligence"; they suggest that immigration law should be changed to reduce the number of people with low cognitive ability who enter the United States (Herrnstein and Murray 1994: 549).

Violence

Physical violence against immigrants is a reality of the 1880–1924 and present eras. Beatings and murders of Chinese miners were frequent in the West in the late 1800s, with atrocities in Rock Springs, Wyoming (1885), and Hell's Canyon, Idaho (1887) (Kitano and Daniels 1995: 24). Violent mob attacks against Greek immigrants took place in Nevada (1908), in Utah (1917 and the early 1920s), and most notably in South Omaha (1909), where they were beaten and their homes burned (Moskos 1980: 16–17). In New Orleans, eleven Italian immigrants accused of murder were declared not guilty by a jury but were killed by a lynch mob in 1891. Also in the 1890s, Pennsylvania militia killed and wounded dozens of Slavic and Polish coal miners during labor disputes. Hundreds of Italian immigrants were burned out of their homes, clubbed, and expelled from West Frankfort, Illinois, in 1920 (Higham 1975).

Today, violence against immigrants, sometimes recorded as "hate crimes," is a serious problem. But unlike the earlier era, it does not consist of mobs descending on immigrant communities and driving them out of town, nor is it associated with the struggles of organized labor; instead, there are outbursts of anger and intimidation aimed at local scapegoats. In the cases of Vincent Chin in 1982 and Jim Loo in 1989, hostility toward Asian foreigners was misdirected tragically and ended with the murder of American-born men of Chinese ancestry (Espiritu 1992), while in 1992, racial-ethnic hostility was directly implicated in the murder of Luyen Phan Nguyen, a Vietnamese American teenager in Coral Springs,

Florida. Immigrants from India and Southeast Asia have been shot at, stabbed, and purposely hit by automobiles. During the 1992 Los Angeles riots, more than two dozen Latinos and Asians were caught on the street or pulled from cars and savagely beaten (Sanchez 1997). In 1988, racist skinheads murdered an Ethiopian immigrant in Portland, Oregon, and in the summer of 1999, a man linked to white supremacist groups shot and killed a Filipino American postal worker because the killer did not think that he looked like he belonged in America.

Differences in Anti-Immigrant Attitudes and Action

Illegal Immigration

An important difference between today and the past is the prominence of illegal immigration. Actually, foreigners entering and residing in the United States in violation of existing laws and treaties is not new. Early in the twentieth century, immigrant women were illegally brought in for prostitution ("the white slave trade") by importers who lied and said that the women were their wives and relatives (Jenks and Lauck 1911: 62–64). In the 1880s, Americans on the West Coast were angry that Chinese laborers barred from entering the United States were sneaking in through British Columbia. Others complained that Chinese men in the United States who had documents allowing them to go to China and then return here were illegally selling them "to parties shipping fresh loads" of Chinese to America (Shankman 1978: 10). After the 1924 Johnson–Reed Act gave small quotas to immigrants from nations in southern and eastern Europe, people from those countries evaded the law by first going to Canada and then entering the United States. Little is known about those earlier illegal immigrants, but it seems that they were a relatively small part of the stream of newcomers, and nationwide the public did not become very agitated about them or see it as a high-priority problem.

In contrast, many people today fixate on the "illegal alien" as the main part of the "crisis" in immigration policy. Most Americans think that the number of illegal immigrants is much larger than it really is; more than 60 percent incorrectly think that a majority of those entering the country do so illegally (*Time* 1993). The public also thinks that virtually all of it is of Mexican origin, but a significant portion of it is Asian, European, Latin

American, and Middle Eastern. Much of the inflammatory rhetoric about immigrants and job competition, crime, welfare, and the angry charge that the United States "has lost control of its borders" attacks and blames illegal immigrants. California's Proposition 187 was explicitly aimed at illegal immigrants, and surveys indicate that 85 percent of the public favors changing federal law to reduce the number of illegal entries (*Time* 1993). All this special attention aimed at this single component of the foreign-born population is a key feature distinguishing the present era from 1880–1924.

Organized Labor's Position

During 1880–1924 and for many decades after, the labor movement had a mixed record in terms of incorporating immigrants. Great numbers of German, Irish, Jewish, Italian, Polish, Slavic, and Finnish newcomers created or joined labor unions, but other immigrants, from Asia and Mexico (along with black migrants who moved from the South to the North), were unwelcome in and not allowed to join those unions. Organized labor advocated that they be restricted from immigrating to the United States and tried to prevent them from working in the same occupations that union members held. In 1882, largely at the urging of white workers in western states, Congress passed the Chinese Exclusion Act to prevent immigration by Chinese laborers. The reason given by the unions typically involved the idea that union members needed to protect "their" jobs or the wage levels they struggled so hard to obtain and that these other immigrant workers (often perceived in a racialized way as "nonwhite," hence inferior) were job competitors who drove down wages and working conditions and were used by business owners as strikebreakers.

For most of the current era, labor unions held a similar attitude toward illegal immigrant workers. Union leaders and members thought that the presence of illegal workers in a labor market hurt the wages and bargaining position of union members, and they believed that most illegal workers were either uninterested in joining unions or afraid to join because it might anger employers who could fire them, withhold their pay, or have them deported. As a result, much of the organized labor movement supported policies aimed at minimizing employers' access to and use of illegal immigrant workers (e.g., it supported penalties on employers who hired illegal immigrants). This began to change in the late 1990s, when, after years of declining membership, some union organizers revised their thinking and saw illegal immigrants as a potential source of new members. In 2000, the AFL-CIO reversed its longstanding position and came out in favor of an amnesty program that would allow millions of illegal immigrants to become legal permanent residents. Other labor organizations now have adopted that position and call for an end to raids by the Immigration and Naturalization Service (INS) on businesses that employ illegal workers; they want to protect those illegal workers from abuse and exploitation by employers and invite illegal immigrants to become union members (Osinski 2000). The new union logic is that as long as these workers have illegal status, they will be underpaid, be poorly treated, and have no recourse, but if they become legal, they can be more assertive and might join unions, thereby revitalizing the labor movement's numbers and political clout. As one labor leader put it, "We don't care about green cards. We care about union cards" (Roosevelt 2001: 69; see also Greenhouse 2001).

If the labor movement's current move to embrace illegal immigrants and advocate on their behalf remains on course, it will be a dramatic change from their prior hostile stance toward immigrants, whom they perceived as job competitors and surplus labor. The potential effect of this shift is becoming visible in California and New York (where immigrants are responsible for increases in union membership and where union-supported political candidates have won local elections) and at the national level, where, at the time of this writing, organized labor has joined with certain business interests, political leaders, and immigrant advocacy organizations to support a proposal to grant legal status to several million illegal immigrants currently in the United States and to create a new temporary labor ("guest worker") program (Foskett 2000; Moscoso 2001).

Discriminatory Laws

From 1917 to 1924, "state and national governments legislated almost ceaselessly against the successive dangers that seemed to arise from America's foreign population" (Higham 1975: 300). Earlier, state and local governments singled out all immigrants or categories of them (e.g., aliens ineligible for citizenship [i.e., those born in Asia] or those who had not

declared their intent to become naturalized citizens) and passed laws giving them fewer rights and privileges than native-born Americans. People
today do not realize the extent of these laws, and their abundance in the
1880–1924 era is another difference between these periods of mass immigration. For instance, certain states had licensing laws that explicitly prevented aliens from practicing medicine, surgery, chiropractic, pharmacy,
architecture, engineering, surveying, or driving buses. Some states required attorneys to be American citizens, Michigan prohibited aliens from
obtaining a barber's license, a few had laws barring foreigners from jobs on
state or local public works construction projects, and Idaho "prohibited
private corporations from hiring aliens who had not declared their intention to become citizens" (Higham 1975: 301; see also 46, 72, 161). In a
move aimed at Japanese immigrant farmers, California and several other
western states made it illegal for immigrants ineligible for citizenship to
own agricultural land.

Today some occupational prohibitions against legal immigrants exist,
especially for jobs in the federal government, but they are permitted to
work in most private-sector jobs. As for illegal immigrants, according to
the 1986 Immigration Reform and Control Act, employers are not allowed to knowingly hire them (though clearly many do so despite this
law). Getting licensed to work in some occupations remains a problem for
many legal immigrants, not because of an explicit anti-immigrant prohibition but because immigrants' educational credentials and work experience often are not accepted by licensing boards or because limited English
skills make it hard to pass examinations. Industries vary in their employment of immigrants. It is well known that many are recruited for work in
low-skill services, but many also are employed in medicine (in 1990, 20
percent of all physicians were immigrants) and high-tech industries. In
fact, one of the lesser-known differences between the present immigration
and that of 1880 to the 1920s is that many more today come with advanced education and technical job skills. *Business Week* (1992: 50) pre-
dicted that "the next generation of scientists and engineers at U.S. high-
tech companies will be dominated by immigrants," but critical reactions to
this trend have emerged. Some object to the stereotypical view in business,
industry, and academia that highly educated immigrants are excellent
technicians and engineers but do not make good managers or executives.
Other critics suggest that the heavy reliance on foreign-born scientists,

doctors, nurses, and engineers allows American schools to do a poor job teaching science to native-born children (especially minorities and women) and that so many foreigners in technology and science puts American engineers and technicians out of work or may create a national security risk (Beck 1996; North 1995; Simcox 1996).

Restriction

Calls for reducing the number of immigrants and changing the kinds of people allowed in are very common in both eras. A very important difference, however, is that in the 1880–1924 era, restrictionists succeeded in passing laws that greatly reduced the numbers and changed immigrants' national origins (e.g., the 1882 Chinese Exclusion Act, a 1917 law banning immigration from almost all of Asia, and the 1924 Johnson–Reed Act), but in the present era, restriction advocates have tried but, so far, have been unable to pass laws that lower the numbers and have made only minor changes in the kinds of immigrants admitted. In fact, in late 2000, Congress acted to enable many more people to gain immigrant status, and by mid-2001, a new amnesty policy that would shift several million people's status from illegal to legal immigrant seemed likely to be adopted. However, the September 11 attacks on America have shifted public and congressional sentiment and put the amnesty program on hold for the near future.

During the earlier period, requiring immigrants to pass a literacy test before they were allowed to enter the United States was seen by its supporters as a means of upgrading the quality of new arrivals. Literacy test supporters thought that it would screen out most southern/eastern Europeans, who they believed were inferior immigrants. After a political battle that lasted more than twenty years, Congress enacted a literacy test for immigrants in 1917. However, it was not very successful in reducing the flow of southern and eastern Europeans into the United States (Higham 1975: 308), so Congress created the restriction and national quota laws of 1921 and 1924. These laws reflected a massive loss of faith in the idea of the country as a melting pot. After World War I, most Americans believed that the nation could not assimilate the large numbers and kinds of foreigners and felt that the newcomers created serious problems for society. Leading the drive to restrict immigrants were the American Federation of

Labor and organizations claiming to be "patriotic and 100 percent American," such as the Immigration Restriction League's successors, the National Civic Federation and the American Defense Society (Higham 1975).

The present era also has outspoken individuals and groups lobbying for laws to reduce immigration or to change its composition (e.g., former Colorado Governor Richard Lamm, former presidential candidate Patrick Buchanan, the Federation for American Immigration Reform, and the American Immigration Control Foundation), and in 1995 the Jordan Commission recommended lowering immigration numbers. So far, however, these efforts have not been successful. The 1990 Immigration Act actually increased the number of preference immigrants by 40 percent, to 675,000 per year (DeSipio and de la Garza 1998). In 1996, a strong attempt at reducing immigration was mounted in Congress but did not succeed, resulting mainly in efforts that try to cut illegal immigration (e.g., more resources for the Border Patrol) or to speed up deportations. It is true that many people suspect that congressional and state efforts in the 1990s to limit immigrants' access to social services or to prohibit bilingual education (e.g., California Propositions 187 and 227, respectively) were designed to discourage and reduce immigration (Chavez 1997). But even if that was their motivation, there is no evidence yet that they are any more successful in lowering immigration than was imposing a literacy test on immigrants back in 1917, and, if anything, the trend in the early 2000s seems to be toward increasing immigration.

The U.S. Position in the World

The U.S. position in the world and its relationship with the rest of the world is very different in the two eras examined here. These differences strongly affect immigration policy and attitudes. Briefly, from 1880–1924, the United States became a major commercial and military power. It involved itself in high-level international diplomacy, won a war that gave it overseas possessions, entered World War I and with its allies was victorious, and tried to establish the League of Nations and stabilize a world order. Most of these political and military efforts increased the flow of immigrants. But then America changed its mood, and by 1920 it felt "a general revulsion against European entanglements" (Higham 1975: 270) and disillusionment with international contacts. It adopted a defensive isolationist position, hoping to avoid the rest of the world's problems by erecting walls (e.g., high trade tariffs and tight immigration quotas), and it experienced "purifying" movements (e.g., eugenics, Prohibition, and the Ku Klux Klan) that were laced with nativism.

In contrast, it is an understatement to say that from the mid-1960s to the present the United States has played an active and powerful international role. The military, economic, political, and cultural ties between the United States and other nations stimulate immigration, and whenever anti-immigrant rhetoric or calls for restriction have appeared in recent years, people and organizations that benefit from those international relationships speak out to dampen and oppose those sentiments. Consistent with this, Americans who favor an active international role on economic and foreign policy issues are more likely to have favorable attitudes toward high immigration levels than are Americans who hold isolationist attitudes (Espenshade and Hempstead 1996). On the other hand, the ideology of the most extreme nativist (white separatist) groups in the United States, not surprisingly, contains vitriolic attacks on the "new world order," is anti-immigrant, claims that international organizations and treaties (the United Nations and the North American Free Trade Agreement) are part of a secret Jewish plot to take over the world, and tries to sway people to an isolationist position (Dobratz and Shanks-Meile 1997). As long as the United States continues to play a leading international role, it is unlikely to adopt the kind of anti-immigrant restrictions that it instituted in the 1920s.

Two New Attitudes

Opponents of immigration now have two arguments that were unavailable in the 1880–1924 era. One claims that with hindsight we can now see that the restriction laws of the 1920s were successful and good because they gave American society time to recover from the impact of millions of newcomers and allowed a "digestion" or "cooling-off" period during which assimilation, economic adjustment, and creation of a common culture did in fact occur (Beck 1996). Using that premise as precedent, today's critics of immigration argue that we are now at a similar historical juncture as in 1920, desperately in need of a recovery period after three decades of mass immigration.

The other new argument is that the 1965 immigration law was not intended to increase immigration dramatically; moreover, opinion surveys show that most Americans are unfavorable to the existing high levels, so anti-immigrant groups claim that current policy is an anti-democratic violation of the will of the people. Simon and Alexander (1993) note that millions more people have immigrated than the public desires and call it "the miracle of immigration." But others who are more wary of or hostile to immigration complain that this proves that powerful but illegitimate elites and special interests are controlling federal policy in defiance of what the majority wants and are implementing policies that hurt the nation.

Nativism Then and Now

Anti-immigrant attitudes and actions are based on several common fears that generate unease, mistrust, and conflict. Those associated with nativism center on the belief that foreign-born newcomers pose a serious threat to the nation or to American people and their way of life at the community level. This section compares nativist fears in the earlier era with those of the present day. The material is organized by dividing these fears into four accusations about immigrants: 1) threats to the political order, 2) threats to our economic system, 3) threats to social and cultural components of "the American way of life," and 4) threats to the natural environment.[4]

Immigrants as Political Threats

Nativist fears about immigrants as political threats take three forms. One is that immigrants may work as agents of a foreign power that wants to weaken, destroy, or conquer the United States. Foreigners are accused of disloyalty to or subversion of the nation. Such charges are common in times of international conflict when it is not clear that the United States will prevail. Several cases stand out in the years 1880–1924. Most severe was the rampant anti-German wave that swept the country during World War I. Before the United States entered the war, German Americans who tried to get the government to adopt policies favorable to Germany were accused of being "un-American," and when sabotage was linked to the German embassy in Washington, D.C., an "image of the German-American community riddled with treason and conspiring under orders from Berlin" spread in the public's mind (Higham 1975: 197). After the United States entered the war, rumors about German American spies and subversive activity abounded, and hatred of all things German grew. Schools stopped teaching the German language, newspapers written in German were banned, and German music was boycotted. Many American people, businesses, and places "Americanized" their German names. Congress revoked the charter of the largest German American organization, and physical attacks on German Americans were frequent (Higham 1975: 208–209).

American nativists also attacked Catholic, Jewish, and Japanese immigrants as agents of foreign powers. Anti-Catholic activity peaked in the years 1893–1894 and 1910–1915. The central accusation was that the Catholic Church and the pope are reactionary anti-democratic forces, enemies of Protestant America, seeking to gain control over the country and the entire world. Irish, Italian, and Polish Catholic immigrant priests, nuns, and congregants were accused of being loyal "soldiers" of the pope, and fraternal groups, such as the Knights of Columbus, were suspected of plots against America's democratic political, social, and economic institutions (Higham 1975).

Immigrant Jews were also depicted as a political threat and were accused of being unruly radical agents of foreign revolutionary parties and ideologies (anarchism, socialism, and communism) or of being operatives of an international Jewish conspiracy to get control of the United States and the rest of the world. Nativists feared that foreign Jews and their native-born Jewish allies had no real national patriotism but instead were loyal to international causes (e.g., communism or Zionism) and were trying to either tear down the government or infiltrate and take it over in hopes of dominating and exploiting Christian Americans (Higham 1975).

Nativist attacks on Japanese immigrants as "fifth-column" agents of the emperor of Japan were common after Japan proved its military prowess by defeating Russia in 1905. The phrase "Yellow Peril" became associated with the view that Japan would become a military threat to West Coast security and American interests in the Pacific. These fears arose in the late 1800s and the first decades of the twentieth century. Hearst newspapers said that Japanese immigrants were actually military men in disguise who were awaiting orders from the emperor (Ringer and Lawless 1989: 181). After World War I, nativists contended that Japan was engaged in, over previous decades, a "diabolical scheme" to gain living space and resources on the West Coast. It involved sending Japan's "surplus population" to the United States as immigrants but retaining their loyalty and the loyalty of their American-born children. They charged that when the Japanese government gave the order, these immigrants and their children[5] would try to disrupt and weaken the United States to aid Japan's expansionist plans (Ringer and Lawless 1989: 182).

Fear of aliens as agents of hostile nations has not been as prominent in our current high-immigration era as it was from 1880 to 1924. Rather than viewing newcomers from communist nations as potential subversives, they often are depicted and welcomed as freedom-loving opponents of the Kremlin, Castro, or Ho Chi Min. A high-profile exception, however, occurred in 1996. Wen Ho Lee, a Taiwanese-born scientist working for the United States at the Los Alamos National Laboratory, was accused, arrested, and prosecuted for letting secret information about nuclear weapons be transferred to the People's Republic of China. Most charges against him were dropped in 2000. It seems that his handling of classified material was no different than other scientists and officials, but he was singled out and suspected of "spying" for China merely because he was "Chinese." Many Asian American organizations complained that he was treated unjustly and that his arrest fueled unwarranted suspicions of other Asian-born immigrants.

In two other cases—Arab and Mexican immigrants—contemporary nativists have accused aliens of aiding a foreign nation. Suspicion and fear that Arab immigrants engage in terrorism on behalf of Arab nationalism or Islamic fundamentalism was strong during the Iran–U.S. hostage crisis of the late 1970s, the Persian Gulf War, and after the bombing of the World Trade Center in 1993 (Novick 1995). After the deadly explosion at the Oklahoma City federal building in 1995, the immediate assumption by many Americans was that it was the work of foreign Arab fanatics. Most recently, in the wake of September 11, there was a rise in verbal and physical aggression against Arab and Muslim immigrants and foreigners as well as widespread government interrogation and detention of them.

Contemporary nativist charges about Mexican immigrants serving the interests of their homeland resemble accusations made earlier against the Japanese. The claim is that under cover of immigration, a large section of the United States (the Southwest) has quietly been "invaded" by Mexico's "surplus population" with the goal being eventually to "liberate" and reclaim land that was Mexico's prior to the Mexican–American War. Brimelow (1995: 194) says that "groups like the campus-based MEChA, the Movimiento Estudiantil Chicano de Aztlan, are openly working for Aztlan, a Hispanic-dominated political unit to be carved out of the Southwest and (presumably) reunited with Mexico," and that Mexico has opened "cultural institutes" and political party offices in American cities and donated textbooks to Los Angeles schools to gain a strong foothold in the Southwest. In California, Glenn Spencer (founder of a pro–Proposition 187 organization called Voice of Citizens Together) claims that illegal Mexican immigration is "part of a reconquest of the American Southwest by foreign Hispanics. . . . It boils down to this: Do we want to retain control of the Southwest more than the Mexicans want to take it from us?" (Chavez 1997: 68). Lamm and Imhoff (1985: 94–95) warn about separatist groups that threaten other nations with partition (e.g., Canada and India) and then say that a Mexican American group (National Council of La Raza) has a plan of "revolutionary nationalism" for bringing "independence" to Aztlan (the southwestern United States).

The second type of nativist fear about aliens as political threats to America is a belief that most foreign-born people do not have the qualities needed to be good citizens in a democratic republic. In the 1880–1924 era, this charge was directed at immigrants from Asia (who were not allowed to become naturalized citizens) and at immigrants from southern and eastern Europe and from Mexico. One version of this complaint was that since these immigrants came from homelands ruled by kings, emperors, and political institutions antithetical to democracy, they must lack the socialization and experiences needed to understand how to act as responsible citizens in a democracy. Nativists said that these immigrants could not overcome their nondemocratic heritage or the circumstances of immigrant life, which allegedly made them politically unruly, prone to extremism and violence, or susceptible to bribery and misguided leadership by corrupt political bosses (Bancroft 1890; Gossett 1965: 298–309; Morgan 1890).

During the heyday of the Americanization movement (1914–1920), nativists and progressives felt that immigrants could be made into good naturalized citizens by having them listen to patriotic speeches, attend classes to learn American history and government, and get instruction about American citizenship, customs, and how to speak English. However, by 1920, many Americans lost hope and concluded that most of the immigrants could not be "remade" into good citizens. The prevailing beliefs were that their old ways were just too deeply ingrained or that the immigrants' political defects could not be corrected because they were inborn "racial" traits. By the 1920s, this latter view, that certain immigrants were racially flawed and inferior, was powerful and widely held and contributed to the immigration restriction laws.

Today it is easy to find nativists who make similar charges about new immigrants' inability to become good American citizens. Writing about recent immigrants from the Third World in *The New American*, Thornton (1994: 28) says,

> By their very nature, [they] are temperamentally different from the European Christians who settled North America, fashioned the United States, devised its system of laws, and fathered its free institutions. For those who doubt that temperament plays any role in these things, I suggest they compare life in Calcutta with that in Edinburgh, Hong Kong with that in Frankfurt, Mogadishu with that in Brussels, or pre-1960 Los Angeles, New York, and Boston with those same cities now. In other cases it is not so much temperament that distinguishes people as it is the persistence of age-old cultures. Beliefs in paternalism and, sometimes, despotism are deeply ingrained in many of the world's cultures, going back millennia, and culture, as we know, is one of the most powerful forces in the world.

Thornton (1994: 28) then quotes Thomas Jefferson, Alexander Hamilton, and other American leaders on the undemocratic character and perils of dual loyalty that most foreigners allegedly bring. Similarly, Williamson (1996: 143–144) claims that Third World immigrants lack the essential qualities that are the foundation for a democracy, such as a capacity for working together for the common good, and he says that

> there is cause to fear that non-European immigration may lead in time not just to radical changes in the composition of the American people, but to a dissolution of what remains of the laws and institutions they have enjoyed for centuries. Freedom, it begins to seem, may not be compatible with a multicultural society.

Immigrants from Mexico face similar charges today. Nativists who do not seriously think that immigrants are agents of Mexico trying to reclaim the Southwest accuse them of the opposite sin—of being too apolitical and indifferent. These critics complain that Mexican Americans naturalize at a lower rate than other immigrants because they lack "feelings of identity as Americans" and "think of themselves as Hispanics first, and Americans second" (Graham 1988: 133). Bikales and Imhoff (1988: 144) embellish this line of attack by saying Mexican Americans are indifferent to responsible political participation because they think that "politics is too complicated," rarely discuss political issues or vote, and, unless they speak English well, do not identify with the two major parties. The conclusion today's nativists draw from Mexican American political inactivity is that it is another indication of their unwillingness or inability to join the "American mainstream." The perceived threat to the nation arises with the idea that a rapidly growing politically alienated population that is unattached to established political processes and institutions creates an unhealthy, potentially dangerous situation.

The third political fear associated with immigrants in nativists' minds is that even if they are not agents of a hostile foreign power and even if they can and do learn to participate in the political process, the immigrants' political interests and values will be vastly different from and at odds with those of the rest of "us." They fear that immigrant citizens will vote for or support political positions or candidates that diverge from what "we" define as desirable, thereby causing divisiveness, polarization, or wholesale disruption of the existing order.

The struggle to outlaw alcoholic beverages provides a good example from the 1880–1924 era. The strongest supporters of Prohibition, particularly groups such as the Anti-Saloon League (ASL), came from old-stock Protestants in the less urbanized Midwest and South. On the other hand, most southern/eastern European immigrants and the largest groups from the previous wave of immigration (Irish and German) were against Prohibition; indeed, as producers and consumers, they were very involved with beer, wine, and liquor. The ASL argued that alcoholic drinks harmed the nation's economy; contributed to crime, political corruption, and the destruction of families; and generally lowered morality in America. Immigrants, they claimed, were both victims of alcohol's evils and the worst supporters of this vice since immigrants usually opposed Prohibition and profited from its sale (as owners, managers, and workers in wineries, breweries, and distilleries). As a result, the ASL used harsh anti-immigrant rhetoric, supported restricting immigration, and depicted foreigners as a serious menace to the nation's health (Goldberg 1991).

Today, too, we see nativist charges that immigrants' political positions and actions are misguided and bad for the nation. The language issue is a good example. Americans who fear that language diversity excessively strains school or other agencies' budgets or that it undermines national unity have castigated non-English-speaking immigrants as a whole (often with little or no data other than personal anecdotes) for supporting bilingual education or opposing "English as the official language" initiatives. Nativists feel that they know what is best for the nation, and political opposition or mobilization in disagreement by immigrants is not acceptable, so this leads nativists to want to reduce the number of foreigners. This tendency is found on other issues, too. For instance, immigrants get it from both sides on the question of affirmative action. Those who believe that affirmative action is a bad policy for the nation often take a nativist position if they think that most immigrants strongly favor it. On the other hand, many advocates of affirmative action criticize immigrants if they believe that immigrants do not support it strongly enough or if they believe that immigrants have lobbied for and undeservingly receive benefits that are supposed to go only to native-born disadvantaged groups (Beck 1996: 187–191; Muller 1993: 262).

Immigrants as Economic Threats

Unlike fears of foreigners as political dangers, fears about immigration as an economic problem for the nation have a positive counterpart. This positive view is that immigrants spark economic growth—as productive inexpensive workers willing to work hard; as business entrepreneurs expanding commerce; as essential contributors to industries reliant on science, engineering, or computer technology; and as consumers serving as new markets for goods and services. Many researchers laud the economic benefits of immigration (Muller 1993; Simon 1989; Wattenberg and Zinsmeister 1990), and a recent National Academy of Science report finds that "as a nation, on net, we gain economically from immigration" (Smith and Edmonston 1997: 164).

However, in times of economic difficulty or among groups mired in disadvantaged positions, intense negative sentiments arise over the possible economic harm caused by immigrants. In the current period, a desire to reduce immigration has a strong positive correlation with the unemployment rate (Espenshade and Hempstead 1996), and in the earlier era, economic depressions gave rise to hostile movements against immigrants (Higham 1975). A common economic accusation hurled at immigrant workers by native-born Americans in or below the middle class is that when many foreign workers are in a labor market, they take jobs away from native-born workers because they accept employers' offers of lower pay and worse working conditions, resulting in native-born workers being unemployed or having to accept jobs with poorer wages and working conditions. Thus, immigrants are blamed for driving down native-born Americans' standard of living below acceptable, previously attained levels. For instance, Beck (1996: chap. 6) argues that recently a few large corporations in the meat slaughter and packing industry used available cheap immigrant labor to break labor unions and restructure the entire industry, changing it from one that gave native-born Americans good wages to one that now offers low-paying dangerous jobs mainly to immigrants.

Although many labor organizations made this claim in the 1880–1924 era, the Dillingham Commission saw it slightly differently, indicating that "there is no evidence to show that the employment of southern and eastern European wage-earners has caused a direct lowering of wages . . . in mines and industrial establishments." Instead, they believed the harm was that

> the availability of the large supply of recent immigrant labor prevented the increase in wages which otherwise would have resulted during recent years from the increased demand for labor. The low standards of the southern and eastern European, his ready acceptance of a low wage and existing working conditions . . . have rendered it extremely difficult for the older classes of employees to secure improvements in conditions or advancement in wages. (Jenks and Lauck 1911: 195–196)

Fears that foreigners were a subversive economic threat did exist in the years 1880–1924. The best example is a wave of anti-Catholic protest in 1893–1894, sparked by a major depression. The American Protective Association (APA) and the Junior Order United American Mechanics were the largest anti-Catholic organizations, with more than 600,000 members. Speakers for the APA said that the economic collapse was started by

Catholics in the United States who withdrew their money from banks, on orders from the pope, to disrupt the American economy. They claimed that this plan to destroy the United States included having Catholic workers start labor strikes and promote more class conflict. Anti-Catholic groups circulated bogus documents, allegedly from the Vatican, ordering Catholics to take jobs from Americans and form secret military units for a bloody uprising when the pope gave the command. To combat the threat, APA members vowed never to vote for a Catholic and were told to boycott Catholic-owned businesses and not hire Catholics (Higham 1975: 79–86).

Other anti-immigrant acts of that era reflect economic fears and other motives. Such is the case with the alien land laws passed in California in 1913 and 1920[6] to prevent Japanese immigrants from owning agricultural land. White farmers lobbied for laws that would rid them of competition with Japanese farmers, accusing them of taking the best land or working it in ways that gave Japanese farmers unfair advantages. Some of these anti-Japanese attitudes arose from white farmers' own economic self-interest, not from a perceived threat to the nation's economic well-being, but other "national" fears contributed to passage of the alien land laws: anxiety about the Japanese being an "alien race" unable to fit into a white Anglo-Saxon nation and concern that Japanese Americans' attempts to "rise above" their "lower station" in life would disrupt the "natural order" of American society. This latter concern was stated frankly in a 1910 *San Francisco Chronicle* editorial:

> Had the Japanese laborer throttled his ambition to progress along the lines of American citizenship and industrial development, he probably would have attracted small attention of the public mind. Japanese ambition is to progress beyond mere servility to the plane of the better class of American workman and to own a home with him. The moment that this position is exercised, the Japanese ceases to be an ideal laborer. (Kitano 1976: 18)

Speaking just as bluntly about the Japanese in the United States and the motive behind the alien land laws, California's attorney general said in 1913,

> The fundamental basis of all legislation . . . has been, and is, race undesirability. It seeks to limit their presence by curtailing their privileges

which they may enjoy here, for they will not come in large numbers and long abide with us if they may not acquire land. And it seeks to limit the numbers who will come by limiting the opportunities for their activity here when they arrive. (Kitano 1976: 18)

Moving to the present era, we see reiteration of earlier fears about jobs being taken by immigrants and wages or working conditions worsening because of them. Long ago, Warne (1913: chap. 9) identified numerous industries in which southern/eastern European immigrants were displacing native-born whites and blacks, as has Bodnar (1976). Today, Beck (1996: 138–144) says that the same thing is happening in the computer industry, engineering, and movie production as businesses seek lower labor costs. Many argue that just as European immigrants took away jobs from blacks in earlier eras, blacks are again seeing immigrants get hired instead of them (Miles 1992; Waldinger 1997), exacerbating already high black poverty and unemployment rates. On this issue, Steinberg (1995: 201) says, "It is difficult to escape the conclusion that present immigration policy not only subverts the cause of racial justice, but, given the immense human and social costs of the racial status quo, it is also antithetical to the national interest."

A newer form of nativism, rooted in anger over economic disadvantage and exploitation, targets some immigrants (today mainly those from Korea, India, or the Middle East) who own businesses in poor minority neighborhoods. People who analyze the situation from a racial-ethnic "nationalist" perspective (e.g., black nationalism) and draw on internal colonialism theory often view businesses owned by an out-group (e.g., "middleman" immigrants) as hurting the economic development of "the community" (Min 1996: 23). For example, Korean store owners are accused of overcharging customers, not hiring black workers, and parasitically profiting at the expense of local residents while taking the money out of the neighborhood without investing any of it in the community. Immigrants' businesses in certain neighborhoods are said to help immigrants and America's corporate elite prosper but prevent the development of a class of black entrepreneurs who, if they could establish themselves, would bring some economic opportunity and prosperity to the black community. In some poor minority neighborhoods, anti-immigrant boycotts and violence have arisen.

On the other hand, a few old fears about immigrants as economic threats may be waning. Some Americans reject the idea that immigrants take jobs away from "us" and think they mainly take bad jobs that "we" do not want. Many policy planners consider immigrants as a part of a solution to two economic problems. One is the coming crisis of the Social Security system. Analysts such as Francese (1990) say that in twenty years, because of the aging of the population, there will be too few working-age people to support our vast number of retirees, so we must admit more immigrants who are younger workers and will therefore pay Social Security taxes. The other economic problem is lack of capital for starting or expanding businesses. Instead of fearing or resisting newcomers' investment in and ownership of American economic resources, the framers of the 1990 Immigration Act thought that attracting rich immigrant investors would help the economy. They reserved 10,000 permanent resident slots per year for immigrants who invest large sums in businesses employing at least ten workers (Steinberg 1995: 260).

Immigrants as Social and Cultural Threats to the "American Way of Life"

Another nativist fear is that when certain immigrants settle in America, they do not simply blend in and become assimilated; instead, the way "they" live puts "us" and "our way of life" at risk. This worry, that they will change us for the worse more than we can change them for the better, was expressed in 1753 by Benjamin Franklin as he pondered the arrival of many German immigrants:

> Why should the Palatine Boors be suffered to swarm into our settlements, and by herding together, establish their language and manners, to the exclusion of ours? Why should Pennsylvania, founded by the English, become a colony of Aliens, who will shortly be so numerous as to Germanize us instead of our Anglifying them? (Olson 1979: 26)

But Franklin had faith in the assimilative power of the nation, and the solution he favored was not to keep out German immigrants but rather to have them reside in a dispersed pattern and attend English schools, which would put them in more contact with Anglo-Americans and lead to their use of English and to social and cultural assimilation (Baron 1990: 65–67; Gordon 1964: 89).

That dilemma, "Americanization" or restriction, arose regarding other groups in the 1880–1924 and the present eras. Discussing the former period, Garcia (1978) shows how Anglos in the Southwest saw Mexicans' alleged "cultural liabilities" as a threat to modernization and progress in the region.[7] They charged Mexicans with deficiencies (e.g., lacking ambition, not being industrious, living in a filthy manner, and menacing public health) and sought to change them by transforming their values and behavior with an Americanization program.

A harsher nativist reaction, tinged with racism, came from people such as Madison Grant, who felt that there was something inherently different and wrong with Asian or southern and eastern European immigrants that prevented them from ever becoming "real" Americans no matter how hard they might try. Speaking of the influx of Polish Jews in New York City, Grant (1921: 91) said, "These immigrants adopt the language of the native American; they wear his clothes; they steal his name, and they are beginning to take his women, but they seldom adopt his religion or understand his ideals," and they elbow the white Anglo-Saxon American out of his home. Similarly, the eugenics movement of that era stimulated fear that those foreigners would "out-reproduce" the Anglo-Saxon Americans, creating an "evolution in reverse" pattern in which an allegedly "lower or inferior" culture would replace a "superior" one.

A fear of being pushed aside, overrun by people who take parts of the culture but distort it and cannot grasp its essence or central values, was quite evident in the 1880–1924 era. But is that fear alive today? It is among nativists associated with journals such as *Chronicles: A Magazine of American Culture* and *Social Contract* (both of which are ardently anti-immigration) who espouse the idea that many immigrant groups are not suitable for "the American way of life." Thomas Fleming, for instance, contends that only immigrants from ethnic groups of northern Europe are adapted by nature to live in and positively contribute to American society and culture. Williamson (1996: 99) revives Madison Grant's ideas in saying that immigrants can be taught United States history, its literature and its customs, but they

> cannot, however, experience its past in the way that [a] native, whose ancestors fought in the American Revolution, pioneered the West, or attended Princeton with Scott Fitzgerald and Edmund Wilson, can expe-

rience it. Nor can they, in the degree that their countries of origin differ
from the [United States], appreciate the meaning of that past.

He goes on to claim that earlier immigrants such as Irving Berlin, George
Gershwin, Frank Capra, and Billy Wilder did more to vulgarize and
commercially exploit "Anglo-American" culture than they did to revise
and re-create American culture in a positive way, and he implies that today's immigrants will also undermine American culture by distorting it
further or imposing alien cultural forms on it.

Perhaps the most explicit nativist tirade on social-cultural shortcom-
ings and the threat embodied in current immigrants comes from James
Thornton. He contends that the great civilization of Rome declined because of "thorough-going displacement of Romans by non-Romans"—
foreign slaves and strangers who were incorporated into Roman society
but lacked the virtues, temperament, and traditions needed to keep Rome
great. He warns that the United States today "is being overwhelmed, as
Rome was overwhelmed, by populations permeated with cultures, religions, folkways, ideals of government, and patterns of life radically different from, and often in conflict with, our own" (Thornton 1994: 28).[8]
He calls for Americans to stand up and defend their "Greco-Roman-
Christian heritage" from being undermined by the other cultures brought
in by aliens and not to permit "outrages" against American culture (e.g.,
using taxpayers' money for a statue honoring a pagan Aztec god, Quetza-
coatl[9] or revising the meaning of the Alamo from a symbol of American
courage to a symbol of American racism).

While many Americans who are worried about immigration do not
hold such extreme sentiments, similar attitudes expressed in less con-
frontational terms are common. They feel that large numbers of immigrants settling in a community causes erosion of cherished local norms
and symbols. This disinclination to accept certain "odd" immigrant customs or new cultural changes allegedly caused by immigrants goes beyond
a rebellion against non-English-language use (Horton 1995). Some hostility grows out of the feeling that the newcomers do not sufficiently respect or conform to modes of behavior that are deemed "typically American" or have become local community behavioral standards. This
includes, for instance, people who are afraid that so many foreigners will
make soccer replace baseball as the national sport, neighbors who are

appalled by seeing immigrants add the slaughter of a goat to the rituals of the suburban family barbecue, and people who feel that some foreign cultural norms and practices have no place in America and should not be tolerated here (e.g., Albanian, African, and Caribbean immigrant customs of blood revenge, female circumcision, and Santeria, respectively).

Of the social problems that immigrants are accused of causing or exacerbating, one of the most common pertains to crime and violence in the community. In 1908, New York's police commissioner said that half the city's criminals were immigrant Jews. Immigrants from southern Italy had an even worse public image. They were widely regarded as habitual criminals, quick with a stiletto knife, and as bringing organized crime (i.e., the Black Hand and the Mafia) to America. Given the many charges about immigration and crime, the Dillingham Commission made it part of its inquiry. It drew an interesting conclusion: "Immigrants are no more inclined toward criminality, on the whole, than are native Americans, although these statistics do indicate that the children of immigrants commit crime more often than the children of natives" (Jenks and Lauck 1911: 51–52; see also Orebaugh 1922). Allegations of immigrant criminality were prominent among supporters of the 1920s restriction laws (Steinberg 1981).

As in the past, we now hear a litany of charges contending that immigrants are heavily involved in crime. Lamm and Imhoff (1985: 53) claim that "most immigrant groups commit crimes at a higher rate than the general population," and they cite many violent acts by criminals from the 1980 Cuban Mariel arrivals. Others speak about immigrant Russian, Jamaican, Nigerian, Vietnamese, and Chinese gangs involved in robbery, drug smuggling, prostitution, and fraud (Brimelow 1995: 182–186). However, despite anecdotal evidence of high immigrant involvement in crime, current research indicates that for most crimes, they have lower rates than do the native-born and that influxes of recent immigrants in American communities are not associated with higher crime rates (Smith and Edmonston 1997: 388–389).

On the other hand, one old accusation about immigrants' alleged socially harmful effects is rarely heard today: that immigrants bring about the lowering of American morality and the spread of sexual lust. In the 1880s, Anthony Comstock, a crusader against vice and an advocate for censorship of literature with sexual themes, contended that working-class immigrants were corrupting American morals because they spread obscenity and pornography (Beisel 1992: 113–114). A little later, the charge of corrupting the morals of the nation and leading youth astray was common among people who disliked Jewish immigrants and condemned their activity in the entertainment and movie industries. Today, however, this charge apparently is not credible, and immigration foes rarely try to blame immigrants for lowering America's moral-sexual standards.

Another harmful social problem frequently related to immigrants is the charge that their poverty and other social needs place too large a burden on society. Some of the first categories of people prevented from entering the United States, by an 1882 immigration law, were those who the directors of private urban charities felt would strain the charities' financial resources—"persons likely to become public charges, lunatics, and idiots" (Higham 1975: 43–44). Again, in 1903 and 1907, efforts were made in immigration laws to protect the country from individuals who might be unproductive and need charity. These laws allowed deportation of immigrants who became public charges within two years of their arrival and prohibited the entry of "imbeciles, feebleminded persons, persons with physical or mental defects, children unaccompanied by their parents, and women coming into the United States for immoral purposes" (DeSipio and de la Garza 1998: 26). Today, unlike 1880–1925, when most assistance came from private charity funds, immigration critics now contend that the money to pay for costly welfare, health, and schooling assistance mainly and unfairly comes out of local taxpayers' pockets. The strongest resentment growing from this charge falls on illegal and/or female immigrants, as demonstrated by the passage of Proposition 187 in California in 1994 (Chavez 1997; Sanchez 1997), but efforts have also been made to prevent legal immigrants from obtaining certain kinds of social service and welfare benefits (e.g., 1996 changes in federal welfare law and immigration law).

The broadest contemporary nativist complaint based on sociocultural fears, however, is a two-part criticism: 1) the new immigration is bringing in too many people with cultures and values that differ from and conflict with that of the "American mainstream" or its established lifestyle groups, and 2) this plethora of diversity will create a disaster in the form of cultural strife and fragmentation that may weaken or destroy one of history's greatest civilizations. This idea is articulated most often by people who advocate making

English the "official" or the only language used for public affairs in the United States. Lamm and Imhoff (1985) worry that American society is "splintering" or will become "balkanized." They see excessive diversity and preference for cultural pluralism rather than assimilation (epitomized by the retention of foreign language) and wonder what commonalities will unify and keep the nation together. Their answer is that "English is the glue. It holds our people together; it is our shared bond" (Lamm and Imhoff 1985: 100). They feel that all immigrants should learn and use English in public conversations, for reasons both symbolic (signifying identification with and commitment to the American nation) and practical (making communication easier), even if it means "giving up part of oneself." Passage of California's Proposition 227 in 1998 (ending bilingual education in that state's public schools) and successful efforts by "English-only" advocates to have states or counties declare English as their "official language" show that this movement is strong (Tatalovich 1995, 1997).

Immigrants as Threats to the Natural Environment

Unlike the perceived threats previously discussed, the idea that mass immigration has a negative impact on the U.S. ecosystem is a new fear. Only a few American writers in the 1880s, seeing the frontier close, said that the country should not be letting in more immigrant settlers because there was no longer enough habitable open land (Higham 1975). Most people at the turn of the century did not see limited environmental resources as a problem, and those who did felt that it was an issue separate from that of immigration. President Theodore Roosevelt saw them as two unrelated matters when he said that the "immigration problem" was the nation's most important problem, "with the possible exception of that of the conservation of the natural resources of the country" (Jenks and Lauck 1911: xv). The Dillingham Commission said nothing about the impact of immigration on the nation's natural environment. Americans certainly did not worry about overpopulation as a problem in that earlier era, nor were they concerned about immigrants polluting the environment or decimating wildlife; as Glazer (1995: 54) notes, "It was not the immigrants who wiped out the buffalo." While it is true that some in the anti-immigrant movement of that era worried that the foreigners had higher birthrates than the native born, that concern led to fears about "race suicide" and replacement by "inferiors" (and actions designed to prevent it), and it was not based on fear that American society was becoming overpopulated.

Today, however, immigration opponents often make a connection between millions of immigrants, the natural environment, and the well-being of the nation and even the entire world. Several relatively small environmental organizations concerned about overpopulation and ecological deterioration want drastic cutbacks in immigration (e.g., Population-Environment Balance, Negative Population Growth, and the Carrying Capacity Network) because they think that its contribution to increasing the U.S. population adds to an already excessive burden on the supply of fuel, clean air and water, forests, and farmland and exacerbates problems of housing and waste disposal (Reimers 1998: 48–49). The Carrying Capacity Network proposes no more than 100,000 immigrants per year. They claim that most serious problems, such as pollution, traffic congestion, resource depletion, cultural fragmentation, overcrowded schools, and welfare dependency, "have deep roots in our unsustainable population growth" and that most of this new growth comes from immigration. By cutting back on immigration, they claim that the population growth can be cut at least in half and that it must be done to avoid overpopulation and its attendant problems.

Beck (1996) links the tragic decline of Chesapeake Bay to overpopulation mainly from net immigration in the area. Grant and Bouvier (1994) say that Americans' consumption habits make the United States the most destabilizing entity in earth's fragile ecosystem and that population growth here has the worst impact on it. They argue that immigrants coming to the United States and adopting our high-consumption living exacerbates an already serious problem. DinAlt (1997) puts it more bluntly, saying that every mile immigrants drive in the United States pollutes the air and depletes resources that might not have been affected if they had remained in their native lands. He adds that crossing the border "enables them to make lifestyle changes that adversely affect the environment; by becoming Americans they adopt the consumption and pollution patterns of the world's most environmentally destructive lifestyle." In contrast to the previously discussed nativists who think that today's immigrants cannot or do not want to move into the "American mainstream," nativists holding these environmental fears make the opposite argument, saying that "within a few years, most immigrants adopt the American way of life, including all the environmental warts" (DinAlt 1997). Immigrants seem damned if they do and damned if they do not join the mainstream.

A recent vote by members of the Sierra Club[10] tested how strong these anti-immigration sentiments are among people in the ecology movement. Two statements were sent to all members in a vote taken in April 1998. "Position A," representing a new policy for the Sierra Club, said that the club should reverse its earlier stance and advocate an end to U.S. population growth by reducing natural increase and also reducing net immigration. "Position B" reaffirmed the club's prior stance, namely, to take no position on United States immigration levels and policies and to seek a comprehensive approach to solve global population problems. When the ballots were counted, 60 percent of those who voted chose position B, and 40 percent chose position A, so the Sierra Club's official position remains neutral, neither supporting nor opposing a change in immigration levels. The vote, however, created much internal bitterness and division within the club, and the matter will arise again, either in the Sierra Club or in other environmental groups. Up to this point, as Reimers (1998) notes, these environmental groups and their concerns have had negligible influence on the public debate on immigration or on congressional action.

Conclusion

Nativism and other anti-immigrant phenomena today, as in the past, arise both from an age-old unsettled debate over what "American identity" really is (and who that label rightfully embraces) and from persistent fears that mass immigration will harm the nation's economy, culture, political system, and/or a subset of its people. Some observers, such as George Sanchez (1997), argue that a "new racial nativism" has emerged marked by antipathy toward non-English languages, hostility toward multiculturalism and affirmative action, and worry that immigrants are a drain on public welfare, education, and health services. But as we have seen in this analysis of the 1880–1920 era, most of these are long-standing concerns among people hostile toward immigrants.

In contrast, other observers contend that recent immigration reform policies represent a decisive break with America's earlier nativist traditions and indicate that an "ideological convergence in favor of sustained immigration" has been reached, at least among those in influential positions in business and government (Miller 1998a; Tichenor 1998: 403). That view, to a large extent, was shaped by the prosperous economy of the mid- and late 1990s. As the economy slowed down in the early 2000s, we now hear other observers warning that if a recession occurs, immigrants will be blamed for stealing jobs, straining school budgets, and bringing unwanted changes to neighborhoods; still others predict that immigrants will become targets for protests and ethnic violence (Badie 2001; Bixler 2001).

In my opinion, it is valid to say that compared to the earlier era, some realignment, reformulation, and diminution of anti-immigrant attitudes have occurred. Chavez (1997: 1021) notes that today people with anti-immigration views "stretch across the political spectrum, from rightwingers like Pat Buchanan, to political 'moderates' like Pete Wilson, to self-proclaimed liberals like Michael Lind." As Bennett (1988) and Lind (1995) observe, some on the right have relaxed or lost their suspicion and antipathy toward immigrants (especially if the newcomers are conservative, "pro-family," devoutly religious, and seen as part of a hard-working "model minority" group [Fukuyama 1993]), and they are now more concerned with the harm they think certain native-born political opponents are doing to the nation. In addition, public officials today are less explicit in referring to race in discussions of immigration; the racist rhetoric in the mass media also has been toned down and has been eliminated in the two major political parties' presidential campaign platforms, compared to what it was like in the 1880–1924 era. Surprisingly, even the organized labor movement, in the past two or three years, has taken a new stance, speaking out on behalf of illegal immigrants and encouraging them to join unions. But we also see that some people associated with the black struggle against racism and some in the environmental movement have become ardent opponents of high immigration, believing it responsible for other national problems (e.g., black unemployment and environmental deterioration).

Despite these changes, in many respects we see that current fears and perceptions of immigrants as threats resemble those of the past. They are rooted in concerns—some outlandish, others realistic—that the arrival of foreign newcomers leads to unwanted or undesirable social, political, cultural, and economic changes and a widening of cleavages that exist at the national, regional, or local community levels. In that sense, I do not think it is correct to say that Americans in general have made a decisive break with the nativist tradition or have firmly embraced an ideology favoring sustained immigration. Some researchers explain the spread of these fears in the 1980s and 1990s as due more to economic anxiety than to ethnic prejudice, arguing that Americans associated twenty years (1975–1995) of wage stagnation and poor job opportunities with high immigration rates. But isn't that often a form of scapegoating, and isn't it very hard to know who or what really is to blame for one's troubles? This suggests yet another resemblance to the earlier era, as the last time the United States had very low economic growth coupled with high immigration was 1911–1920, a time of severe anti-immigrant beliefs and behaviors (Bean et al. 1997).

Rather than equating nativism with illegitimate discourse or irrational beliefs (i.e., as xenophobia), this chapter focuses on its core substantive fears and concerns, explicating and comparing the central ideas found in today's nativism and that of the 1880–1924 era. Ultimately, those fears and concerns must be evaluated and given a response, though this is not the forum for that. In some cases, anti-immigration positions grow from a defensive nationalistic "America and Americans first" mentality associated with opposition to job displacement and other harsh consequences of economic restructuring and globalization rather than with personal antipathy toward immigrants. In other cases, the anti-immigrant mentality and rhetoric of both eras resemble the terms and tone of discourse generated in debates over who is or is not worthy of inclusion in "civil society" (Alexander 1992). It is often, but not always, a matter of unfamiliarity with foreign newcomers, mean-spirited ethnocentrism, or racism. As Higham (1958) noted in a "second look" at nativism, its more "irrational" elements are not necessarily the main source of anti-immigrant phenomena; real intergroup competition over status and other resources plays an important role. Those who take a more positive view of immigration must become aware of the multiple faces of nativist and anti-immigrant phenomena and become adept at responding honestly and convincingly.

Notes

I wish to thank Miriam Boeri and Kevin Cohen for helpful research assistance on this chapter.

1. The Irish in New York discovered this in 1888, when the mayor scolded them for flying a shamrock flag at City Hall by saying that they should go back

to where they came from if they prefer it over the American flag (Higham 1975: 41). So did Mexican immigrants in 1994; after waving Mexican flags during rallies against California's Proposition 187, they were criticized by people who said, "They don't want to be Americans" (Miller 1998b: 3–5).

2. This was the Dillingham Commission's conclusion; for a discussion and critique of that commission's evidence and conclusions, see Handlin (1957: chap. 5).

3. For instance, African Americans were repulsed by the Chinese immigrant practice of sending the bones of their dead back to China for burial and scorned them for the "barbarous custom of binding the feet of women" (Shankman 1978: 3, 11). African Americans also believed that Italian immigrants had filthy sanitary habits that caused them to spread disease and that they were inherently violent and criminal (Shankman 1978: 92).

4. Two more threats can be formulated: immigrants as 5) a threat to the "racial order" of the United States (see Pavalko 1980) and 6) a threat to the physical health of the general public (see Kraut 1994). Immigration as a "racial threat" is not treated separately in this chapter; instead, it is interwoven with material on related issues. The fear that immigrants have and will spread deadly communicable diseases (e.g., cholera, tuberculosis, and AIDS) has led to entire groups of foreign-born people being stigmatized as a contaminating element. A few scholars mention this issue (Lyman 1974 and Garcia 1978 on Chinese and Mexican immigrants, respectively), but the key sources are Kraut (1994) and Markel and Stern (1999). Space limitations prevent discussion of immigration as a medical or health problem in this chapter.

5. Nativists claimed that Japan defined American-born children of Japanese immigrants (who therefore had U.S. citizenship) to be Japanese citizens subject to Japanese military service.

6. Also in Arizona (1917); Louisiana (1921); New Mexico (1922); Idaho, Montana, and Oregon (1923); and Kansas (1925) (Petersen 1971: 52).

7. While many of these Mexicans were immigrants, a large portion of them were descendants of much earlier settlers and natives of the Southwest, and from their perspective, the Anglos were the new immigrants to this region.

8. In making this claim about the decline of the Roman civilization, Thornton is repeating a warning originally made by a nativist writer of the 1920s, Kenneth L. Roberts (1924).

9. Lest readers think that this is an isolated instance, Horton (1995: 127) reports that a nativist political leader in Monterey Park, California, chastised his opponents by saying that it is shameful that a statue honoring Confucius stands on a nearby college campus while his plan to erect a statue of George Washington in a local park failed because of resistance from recent Chinese immigrants in the city.

10. The Sierra Club is one of the largest and most influential organizations in the United States devoted to environmental preservation, conservation of natural resources, and reduction of population growth.

References

Alexander, Jeffrey C. 1992. "Citizen and Enemy as Symbolic Classification: On the Polarizing Discourse of Civil Society." In *Cultivating Differences*, edited by Michele Lamont and Marcel Fournier. Chicago: University of Chicago Press.

Auster, Lawrence. 1990. *The Path to National Suicide: An Essay on Immigration and Multiculturalism*. Monterey, VA: American Immigration Control Foundation.

———. 1992. "The Forbidden Topic." In *Arguing Immigration*, edited by Nicolaus Mills. New York: Touchstone Books, 1994.

———. 1995. "Immigration and Multiculturalism." In *Discrimination: Opposing Viewpoints*, edited by Bruno Leone. San Diego: Greenhaven Press, 1997.

Badie, Rick. 2001. "Economy May Fuel Opposition to Immigration." *Atlanta Journal-Constitution*, April 3, B3.

Bancroft, Hubert H. 1890. *Essays and Miscellany*. San Francisco: The History Company.

Baron, Dennis. 1990. *The English-Only Question*. New Haven, CT: Yale University Press.

Bean, Frank D., Robert G. Cushing, Charles W. Haynes, and Jennifer V. W. Van Hook. 1997. "Immigration and the Social Contract." *Social Science Quarterly* 78: 249–268.

Beck, Roy. 1996. *The Case against Immigration*. New York: W. W. Norton.

Beisel, Nicola. 1992. "Constructing a Shifting Moral Boundary: Literature and Obscenity in Nineteenth-Century America." In *Cultivating Differences*, edited by Michele Lamont and Marcel Fournier. Chicago: University of Chicago Press.

Bennett, David H. 1988. *The Party of Fear: From Nativist Movements to the New Right in American History*. Chapel Hill: University of North Carolina Press.

Bikales, Gerda, and Gary Imhoff. 1988. "A Kind of Discordant Harmony: Issues in Assimilation." In *U.S. Immigration in the 1980s*, edited by David E. Simcox. Boulder, CO: Westview Press.

Bixler, Mark. 2001. "Illegal Immigrants at Risk When Economy Weakens." *Atlanta Journal-Constitution*, March 5, B3.

Bodnar, John E. 1976. "The Impact of the 'New Immigration' on the Black Worker: Steelton, Pennsylvania, 1880–1920." *Labor History* 17 (spring): 214–229.

Bosniak, Linda S. 1997. "'Nativism' the Concept: Some Reflections." In *Immigrants Out!*, edited by Juan F. Perea. New York: New York University Press.

Bouvier, Leon F. 1992. *Peaceful Invasions*. Lanham, MD: University Press of America.

Brimelow, Peter. 1995. *Alien Nation: Common Sense about America's Immigration Disaster.* New York: Random House.

BusinessWeek. 1992. "The Immigrants: How They're Helping to Revitalize the U.S. Economy." July 13, 114–120, 122.

Chavez, Leo R. 1997. "Immigration Reform and Nativism: The Nationalist Response to the Transnationalist Challenge." In *Immigrants Out!*, edited by Juan F. Perea. New York: New York University Press.

DeSipio, Louis, and Rodolfo O. de la Garza. 1998. *Making Americans, Remaking America: Immigration and Immigrant Policy.* Boulder, CO: Westview Press.

DinAlt, Jason. 1997. "The Environmental Impact of Immigration into the United States." *Carrying Capacity Network Focus* 4 (2): 1–9.

Dobratz, Betty A., and Stephanie L. Shanks-Meile. 1997. *"White Power, White Pride!" The White Separatist Movement in the United States.* New York: Twayne Publishers.

Espenshade, Thomas J., and Karen Hempstead. 1996. "Contemporary American Attitudes toward U.S. Immigration." *International Migration Review* 30: 535–570.

Espiritu, Yen Le. 1992. *Asian American Panethnicity.* Philadelphia: Temple University Press.

Feagin, Joe R. 1997. "Old Poison in New Bottles: The Deep Roots of Modern Nativism." In *Immigrants Out!*, edited by Juan F. Perea. New York: New York University Press.

Foskett, Ken. 2000. "Immigrants Strengthening Big Labor's Political Clout." *Atlanta Journal-Constitution,* June 18, B1, 6.

Francese, Peter. 1990. "Aging American Needs Foreign Blood." *Wall Street Journal,* March 27, A20.

Fuchs, Lawrence H. 1990. "The Reactions of Black Americans to Immigration." In *Immigration Reconsidered,* edited by V. Yans-McLaughlin. New York: Oxford University Press.

Fukuyama, Francis. 1993. "Immigrants and Family Values." *Commentary* 95 (May): 26–32.

Garcia, Mario T. 1978. "Americanization and the Mexican Immigrant, 1880–1930." *Journal of Ethnic Studies* 6: 19–32.

Glazer, Nathan. 1995. "Immigration and the American Future." *The Public Interest* (winter): 45–60.

CHARLES JARET

Goldberg, Robert A. 1991. *Grassroots Resistance.* Belmont, CA: Wadsworth.

Gordon, Milton M. 1964. *Assimilation in American Life.* New York: Oxford University Press.

Gossett, Thomas F. 1965. *Race: The History of an Idea in America.* New York: Schocken Books.

Graham, Otis. 1988. "Immigration and the National Interest." In *U.S. Immigration in the 1980s,* edited by David E. Simcox. Boulder, CO: Westview Press.

Grant, Lindsey, and Leon F. Bouvier. 1994. "The Issue Is Overpopulation." *Los Angeles Times,* August 10, B7.

Grant, Madison. 1921. *The Passing of the Great Race.* 4th rev. ed. New York: Charles Scribner's.

———. 1924. "The Racial Transformation of America." *North American Review* 219 (March): 343–352.

Greenhouse, Steven. 2001. "In U.S. Unions, Mexico Finds an Unlikely Ally on Immigration." *New York Times,* July 19, A1.

Handlin, Oscar. 1957. *Race and Nationality in American Life.* New York: Doubleday Anchor.

Hellweg, David J. 1977. "Afro-American Reactions to the Japanese and the Anti-Japanese Movement, 1906–1924." *Phylon* 38: 93–104.

Herrnstein, Richard J., and Charles Murray. 1994. *The Bell Curve.* New York: The Free Press.

Higham, John. 1958. "Another Look at Nativism." *Catholic Historical Review* 44: 147–158.

———. 1975 [1955]. *Strangers in the Land: Patterns of American Nativism, 1860–1925.* New York: Atheneum.

Horton, John. 1995. *The Politics of Diversity.* Philadelphia, PA: Temple University Press.

Huber, Gregory A., and Thomas J. Espenshade. 1997. "Neo-Isolationism, Balanced-Budget Conservatism, and the Fiscal Impacts of Immigrants." *International Migration Review* 31: 1031–1054.

Jackson, Jacquelyne Johnson. 1988. "Seeking Common Ground for Blacks and Immigrants." In *U.S. Immigration in the 1980s,* edited by David E. Simcox. Boulder, CO: Westview Press.

Jenks, Jeremiah W., and W. Jett Lauck. 1911. *The Immigration Problem.* New York: Funk & Wagnalls.

Johnson, James H., Walter C. Farrell, and Chandra Guinn. 1997. "Immigration Reform and the Browning of America: Tensions, Conflicts, and Community Instability in Metropolitan Los Angeles." *International Migration Review* 31: 1055–1096.

Kitano, Harry H. L. 1976. *Japanese Americans*. 2nd ed. Englewood Cliffs, NJ: Prentice Hall.

Kitano, Harry H. L., and Roger Daniels. 1995. *Asian Americans: Emerging Minorities*. 2nd ed. Englewood Cliffs, NJ: Prentice Hall.

Kraut, Alan M. 1994. *Silent Travelers: Germs, Genes, and the "Immigrant Menace."* New York: Basic Books.

Lamm, Richard D., and Gary Imhoff. 1985. *The Immigration Time Bomb: The Fragmenting of America*. New York: Truman Talley, E. P. Dutton.

Lind, Michael. 1995. *The Next American Nation*. New York: The Free Press.

Lyman, Stanford M. 1974. *Chinese Americans*. New York: Random House.

Markel, Howard, and Alexandra Minna Stern. 1999. "Which Face? Whose Nation? Immigration, Public Health, and the Construction of Disease at America's Ports and Borders, 1891–1928." *American Behavioral Scientist* 42: 1314–1331.

Miles, Jack. 1992. "Blacks vs. Browns." *Atlantic Monthly*, October, 41–45, 48, 50–55, 58–60.

Miller, John J. 1998a. "The Politics of Permanent Immigration." *Reason* 30 (October): 34–40.

———. 1998b. *The Unmaking of Americans*. New York: The Free Press.

Min, Pyong Gap. 1996. *Caught in the Middle: Korean Communities in New York and Los Angeles*. Berkeley and Los Angeles: University of California Press.

Morgan, Appleton. 1890. "What Shall We Do with the Dago?" *Popular Science Monthly* 38 (December): 172–179.

Morrison, Toni. 1993. "On the Backs of Blacks." *Time* (special issue, fall): 57.

Moscoso, Eunice. 2001. "Unions Seek Broader Amnesty." *Atlanta Journal-Constitution*, July 30, B1, 5.

Moskos, Charles C. 1980. *Greek Americans*. Englewood Cliffs, NJ: Prentice Hall.

Muller, Thomas. 1993. *Immigrants and the American City*. New York: New York University Press.

North, David. 1995. *Soothing the Establishment: The Impact of Foreign-Born Scientists and Engineers on America*. Lanham, MD: University Press of America.

Novick, Michael. 1995. *White Lies, White Power*. Monroe, ME: Common Courage Press.

Olson, James S. 1979. *The Ethnic Dimension in American History*. New York: St. Martin's Press.

Orebaugh, David A. 1992. *Crime, Degeneracy, and Immigration: Their Interrelations and Interactions*. Boston: Gorham Press.

Osinski, Bill. 2000. "Labor Forum Backs Illegal Immigrants." *Atlanta Journal-Constitution*, April 30, G1, 2.

Pavalko, Ronald M. 1980. "Racism and the New Immigration: A Reinterpretation of the Assimilation of White Ethnics in American Society." *Sociology and Social Research* 65: 56–77.

Petersen, William. 1971. *Japanese Americans*. New York: Random House.

Reimers, David M. 1998. *Unwelcome Strangers: American Identity and the Turn against Immigration*. New York: Columbia University Press.

Ringer, Benjamin B., and Elinor R. Lawless. 1989. *Race-Ethnicity and Society*. New York: Routledge.

Roberts, Kenneth L. 1924. "Slow Poison." *Saturday Evening Post* 196 (February 2): 8–9, 54, 56, 58.

Roosevelt, Margot. 2001. "Illegal but Fighting for Rights." *Time*, January 22, 68–70.

Sanchez, George J. 1997. "'Face the Nation': Race, Immigration, and the Rise of Nativism in Late Twentieth Century America." *International Migration Review* 31: 1009–1030.

Shankman, Arnold. 1978. "Black on Yellow: Afro-Americans View Chinese-Americans, 1850–1935." *Phylon* 39: 1–17.

———. 1982. *Ambivalent Friends: Afro-Americans View the Immigrant*. Westport, CT: Greenwood Press.

Simcox, David. 1996. "Importing and Nurturing a Professional Elite." *Immigration Review* 24: 13–15.

Simon, Julian L. 1989. *The Economic Consequences of Immigration*. Oxford: Basil Blackwell.

Simon, Rita J., and Susan H. Alexander. 1993. *The Ambivalent Welcome: Print Media, Public Opinion and Immigration*. Westport, CT: Praeger.

Smith, James P., and Barry Edmonston, eds. 1997. *The New Americans: Economic, Demographic, and Fiscal Effects of Immigration*. Washington, DC: National Academy Press.

Steinberg, Allen. 1981. "The History of Immigration and Crime." Appendix A in *U.S. Immigration Policy and the National Interest*. Washington, DC: Select Commission on Immigration and Refugee Policy.

Steinberg, Stephen. 1995. *Turning Back: The Retreat from Racial Justice in American Thought and Policy*. Boston: Beacon Press.

Tatalovich, Raymond. 1995. *Nativism Reborn? The Official English Language Movement and the American States*. Lexington: University of Kentucky Press.

———. 1997. "Official English as Nativist Backlash." In *Immigrants Out!*, edited by Juan F. Perea. New York: New York University Press.

Thornton, James. 1994. "The Threat from Immigrants" (original title: "Multicultural Invasion"). In *Ethnic Conflict*, edited by C. P. Cozic. San Diego: Greenhaven Press.

Tichenor, Daniel J. 1998. "Inclusion, Exclusion, and the American Civic Culture." In *The Immigration Reader*, edited by D. Jacobson. Malden, MA: Blackwell.

Time. 1993. "Not Quite so Welcome Anymore." Special issue (fall): 10–12, 14–15.

Waldinger, Roger. 1997. "Black/Immigrant Competition Re-Assessed: New Evidence from Los Angeles." *Sociological Perspectives* 40: 365–386.

Warne, Frank Julian. 1913. *The Immigrant Invasion*. New York: Dodd, Mead.

Wattenberg, Ben J., and Karl Zinsmeister. 1990. "The Case for More Immigration." *Commentary*, April, 19–25.

Williamson, Chilton. 1996. *The Immigration Mystique: America's False Conscience*. New York: Basic Books.

CHAPTER TWO

THE CHANGING FACE OF AMERICA: IMMIGRATION, RACE/ETHNICITY, AND SOCIAL MOBILITY

Min Zhou

Contemporary immigration refers to the period of large-scale, non-European immigration to the United States that has begun to accelerate since the late 1960s after a long hiatus of restricted immigration (Massey 1995). Between 1971 and 1995, the United States admitted approximately 17.1 million immigrants, including 1.6 million formerly unauthorized aliens and 1.1 million "special agricultural workers" (SAWs) who were granted permanent resident status under the provisions of the Immigration Reform and Control Act of 1986 (IRCA). The scale of contemporary immigration almost matched that during the first quarter of the century (17.2 million admissions between 1901 and 1925), when immigration to the United States was at its peak. Although similar in numbers, the annual admission trends in these two peak periods looked quite different. During the first twenty-five years of the century, annual admission numbers fluctuated drastically with several noticeable ebbs and flows. In contrast, during the twenty-five years near the end of the millennium, the inflows were fairly steady, which had been kept under the half-million mark until 1978 and then gradually increased from 1978 to 1988. The year 1989 witnessed a sudden surge beyond the one-million mark that lasted for the next three consecutive years. This surge was almost entirely represented by the legalization of the formerly undocumented population permitted by IRCA. Clearly, had it not been for IRCA, immigration trends would have been stable, though heading in a gradual, upward direction.[1]

Just as the turn-of-the-century immigration dramatically transformed America, contemporary immigration has repeated history, changing the face of America in ways that are unique and challenging the traditional views of immigrant incorporation. In this chapter, I specifically examine the following issues: 1) the historical trends of immigration to the United States, 2) the settlement patterns of contemporary immigrants in America's largest metropolitan regions, 3) the nature of racial and ethnic relations in areas of high immigration, and 4) the key determinants of social mobility for new immigrants and their offspring. The chapter aims at understanding how contemporary immigration differs from turn-of-the-century immigration and how such differences may affect our approach to the issues and concerns over the changing face of America in the new millennium.

Distinctive Features of Contemporary Immigration

Trends

Several distinctive features of contemporary immigration are noteworthy in historical perspective. First, despite a similarity in the absolute numbers, the rate of contemporary immigration relative to the total U.S. population is much lower than that of the earlier period since the U.S. population has more than tripled during the course of the twentieth century (3.9 vs. 11.7 per thousand) (Smith and Edmonston 1997). The comparatively low rate of contemporary immigration implies a more modest overall impact on the U.S. population today than in the past. However, such an impact is disproportionately localized in areas of high immigration, not only in historic gateway cities but also in smaller urban or suburban areas in which few immigrants had settled in the past. Second, the rate of contemporary emigration is considerably lower today than in the past. It was estimated that, for every one hundred immigrants during the first two decades of high immigration, thirty-six had returned to their homelands. In contrast, between 1971 and 1990, less than a quarter had returned (U.S. Immigration and Naturalization Service 1997; Warren and Kraly 1985). This trend suggests a more steady growth today than in the past, indicating that contemporary immigrants are more likely than their earlier counterparts to stay in the United States permanently. Third, unlike immigration then, contemporary immigration is accompanied by a much larger number of undocumented immigrants because of historical patterns of reliance on Mexican labor migration, especially in agriculture, as well as the operation of migration networks that has facilitated undocumented immigration through backdoor channels (Massey 1995; Massey et al. 1987). Fourth, compared to immigration then, today's inflows are made up of a much more visible proportion of refugees and asylees.[2] During past thirty-five years (1961–1995), annual admission of refugees averaged 68,150, compared to the average annual admission of 47,000 over the fifteen-year span immediately after World War II. The admission of refugees today implies a much enlarged base for later immigration through family reunification.

Last but not least, the all-time high presence of nonimmigrants arriving in the United States temporarily each year also bears a broad implication for potential immigration, both legal and illegal. Statistics from the Immigration and Naturalization Service (INS) showed that 22.6 million nonimmigrant visas were issued in 1995: 17.6 million (78 percent) were tourists who came for short visits for business or pleasure; the rest were on long-term nonimmigrant visas, including 395,000 foreign students (along with their spouses and children), 243,000 temporary workers or trainees (along with their immediate relatives), and a smaller number of traders and investors. These latter groups of nonimmigrants contain a significant pool of potential immigrants. The majority of those who initially entered as students can freely seek employment in the United States after the completion of their studies, which in turn increases the probability of later adjusting to permanent resident status. Among those who entered as tourists, the great majority will depart on time. However, a relatively small proportion, but a quantitatively large number, of those who might qualify for family-sponsored immigration may overstay their visas and wait in the United States to have their status adjusted. In 1995, almost half the legal immigrants admitted had their nonimmigrant visas adjusted in the United States. About 40 percent of the total undocumented immigrant population was "nonimmigrant overstays" (U.S. Immigration and Naturalization Service 1997).

In sum, a lower rate of emigration, greater numbers of undocumented immigrants and refugees or asylees, and the larger pool of potential immigrants among nonimmigrants imply the complexity of contemporary immigration. Another significant implication for immigrant America is that it is a more challenging task than ever before to accurately measure the scale and impact of immigration and to manage or control the inflows.

Diversity

Compared with the turn-of-the-century immigrants, contemporary immigrants are markedly different in national origins, types of admission, spatial distribution, and socioeconomic characteristics. The newcomers are predominantly from non-European countries. Since the 1980s, more than 85 percent of the immigrants admitted to the United States come from Asia and the Americas (excluding Canada) and only 10 percent from Europe compared to more than 90 percent at the earlier peak. In particular, the share of immigrants from the Americas as a proportion of total legal immigrant admissions has risen substantially from 25 percent in the 1950s, moving to 39 percent in the 1960s, and jumping up to 50 percent since the 1980s. Similarly, the share of immigrants from Asia as a proportion of the total admissions grew from a tiny 5 percent in the 1950s, to 11 percent in the 1960s and 33 percent the 1970s, and stayed at 35 percent since 1980, except for 1991, when the Asian share dropped to 18 percent because of the sudden increase in the legalizees under IRCA, most of whom were of Latin origins (U.S. Immigration and Naturalization Service 1997). The top five sending countries during the period between 1981 and 1995 were Mexico, the Philippines, China/Taiwan, the Dominican Republic, and India, compared to Italy, Austria–Hungary, the Soviet Union, Canada, and the United Kingdom during the first two decades of the century. Mexico alone accounted for more than one-fifth of the total legal admissions since the 1980s. In fact, Mexico was on the INS list of the top five countries of last residence between 1921 and 1960 and was number one after 1960 (U.S. Immigration and Naturalization Service 1997).

The composition of contemporary immigration has a lasting effect on the growth and composition of the general U.S. population. During the past thirty years, immigration accounted for more than a third of the total population growth. Asian- and Latin-origin populations grew particularly fast in both absolute and relative sizes. Some groups—Salvadorans, Guatemalans, Dominicans, Haitians, Jamaicans, Asian Indians, Koreans, Vietnamese, Cambodians, and Laotians—grew at spectacular rates, mainly as a result of immigration. It is estimated that, at the current levels of net immigration, intermarriage, and ethnic affiliation, the size of the Asian population will grow from nine million in 1995 to thirty-four million in 2050 (growing from 3 to 8 percent of the total U.S. population) and that the Hispanic population will grow from twenty-seven million in 1995 (about 9 percent of the population) to ninety-five million (or 25 percent of the population) in 2050 (Smith and Edmonston 1997).

Spatially, the turn-of-the-century immigrants were highly concentrated along the northeastern seaboard and the Midwest. For them, the top five most-preferred state destinations were New York, Pennsylvania, Illinois, Massachusetts, and New Jersey, and the top most-preferred immigrant urban destinations were New York, Chicago, Philadelphia, St. Louis, and Boston (Waldinger and Bozorgmehr 1996). In contrast, today's newcomers are highly concentrated, not simply in states or urban areas traditionally attracting most immigrants, but also in states or urban areas that had few immigrants in the past. Since 1971, the top five states of immigrant-intended residence have been California, New York, Florida, Texas, and New Jersey, accounting for almost two out of every three newly admitted immigrants. California was the leading state of immigrant destination since 1976. In 1995, the five leading urban areas of high immigrant concentration were New York, Los Angeles–Long Beach, Chicago, Miami–Hialeah, and Orange County (U.S. Immigration and Naturalization Service 1997).

The new immigrants also differ from the turn-of-the-century inflows in their diverse socioeconomic backgrounds. The image of the poor, uneducated, and unskilled "huddled masses," used to depict the turn-of-the-century European immigrants, no longer applies to today's newcomers. The 1990 U.S. census attests to the vast differences in levels of education, occupation, and income by national origins. For example, more than 60 percent of foreign-born persons (aged twenty-five years or older) from India reported having attained college degrees, three times the proportion of average Americans, but less than 5 percent of those from El Salvador and Mexico so reported. Among employed workers (aged sixteen years or older), more than 45 percent of the foreign-born persons from India held managerial or professional occupations, more than twice the proportion of average American workers, but less than 7 percent of those from El Salvador, Guatemala, and Mexico so reported. Moreover, immigrants from India reported a median household income of $48,000, compared to

$30,000 for average American households; those from the Dominican Republic and the Soviet Union reported a median household income below $20,000. Poverty rates varied, ranging from a low of 5 percent for Indians and Filipinos to a high of 33 percent for Dominicans and an extreme high of more than 40 percent for Cambodians and 60 percent for Hmongs, compared to about 10 percent for average American families.

The New Second Generation

Spatial concentration, diverse origins, and socioeconomic status of new immigrants hinge not only on the fate of immigrants but also on their children. Because of the recency of contemporary immigration, a new generation of immigrant children and children of immigrant parentage is just coming of age. This new second generation is not only disproportionately young but also ethnically diverse. The Current Population Survey (CPS) for the period 1994–1998 shows that almost 40 percent of the second generation are under eighteen years of age, in contrast to 28 percent of the U.S. population. In the second generation, more than a third are of Latin American ancestry and 7 percent of Asian ancestry, compared with 12 and 4 percent, respectively, in the total U.S. population reported in the 2000 census. If it were distributed randomly across America's urban landscape, the new second generation would not be of great interest since it is relatively small in absolute numbers. However, historical and contemporary patterns of immigrant settlement suggest that immigrants and their children are highly concentrated in just a handful of metropolitan regions. For example, California alone accounted for some 45 percent of the nation's immigrant student population, more than one out of ten school-aged children in the state were foreign born, and more than a third of the state's school-aged children spoke a language other than English at home (Cornelius 1995). In Los Angeles County, two-thirds of the public schools have a numerical majority of nonwhite students, and 39 percent are represented by more than three-quarters of U.S.- or foreign-born minority students. In major immigrant-receiving cities, such as Los Angeles, San Francisco, New York, and Miami, more than a third of the students in the entire school system speak a language other than English at home.

These changes, impacted by a massive immigration during the past three decades, along with the changes in local cultures, economies, and neighborhoods, have created diverse receiving contexts quite different from the ones in which European immigrants entered a century ago. The challenge for the adaptation of immigrant offspring into postindustrial America is profound. Differing from their immigrant parents, immigrant children lack meaningful connections to their "old" world. Thus, they are unlikely to consider a foreign country as a place to return to or as a point of reference. Instead, they are prone to evaluate themselves or to be evaluated by others by the standards of their new country (Gans 1992; Portes 1995; Portes and Zhou 1993). Nonetheless, the encounter in any metropolitan context is likely to invoke one of two, if not more, scenarios: The child either succeeds in school and moves ahead or falls behind (or remains the same as) the modest, often low status of the parents' generation. The latter scenario is labeled by the sociologist Herbert Gans (1992) as "second-generation decline." Thus, a more pressing issue is whether the new second generation will be able to incorporate into middle-class America, following the path taken by the "old" second generation arriving at the turn of the century, and to advance beyond their parents' generation.

Transforming Urban America: Old and New Immigrant Metropolises

Like earlier waves of European immigrants, contemporary immigrants are overwhelmingly urban bound, but they differ from their earlier counterparts in geographic distribution. While about 94 percent of immigrants from Asia and close to 90 percent of Latin American immigrants live in urban areas (compared to just over 70 percent of the native-born U.S. population), they are concentrated not only in metropolitan areas in the West and Northeast but also in the Southeast and the Southwest. New immigrants, like their fellow Americans, are spatially distributed not only by social class and race but also by social networks and family or kinship ties. The settlement patterns of contemporary immigrants are characteristic of dispersion and concentration. New immigrants are more spread out than ever before, yet they continue to be highly concentrated within the metropolitan region of settlement. Next, I focus on describing the particular patterns of spatial concentrations in selected metropolitan areas—New York, Los Angeles, Miami, San Francisco, and Chicago[3]—and

71

examine how different national origin groups converge on particular urban centers and how these urban centers are in turn impacted by the arrival of newcomers.

The Old and New "Ellis Islands"

Ellis Island, where the Statue of Liberty stands, has been the historic gateway to immigrant America. Seeking a better life or an alternative means of livelihood in a new land, millions of European immigrants entered the United States through this gateway in the late nineteenth and early twentieth centuries. Many made New York City their new home, even though thousands returned to their homelands after a lengthy period of sojourning (Moch 1992; Morawska 1990). Since the 1970s, immigration has transformed the "old" Ellis Island and given rise to new ones. While New York remains the most popular immigrant-receiving center, Los Angeles has surpassed it as the largest immigrant metropolis in absolute and relative terms. In absolute numbers, Los Angeles metropolitan region had 600,000 more foreign-born persons than New York as of 1990. Relatively, a third of Los Angeles' residents are immigrants, compared to 27 percent in New York, whose immigrant share was as high as 40 percent at the turn of the century (Waldinger and Bozorgmehr 1996). Miami and San Francisco, though much smaller in size, have become more densely populated by new immigrants than any other U.S. metropolitan area, with a share of 34 and 27 percent, respectively. In contrast, Chicago, the second-largest immigrant metropolis in 1910, dropped a few places down the list in 1990 when measured by the immigrant share of the total population (13 percent).

Compared to the old urban centers, new immigrant-receiving centers take a much larger share of the country's foreign-born population. In 1910, the foreign-born shared 15 percent of the U.S. total population. About a quarter of them lived in the top five largest metropolises— New York, Chicago, Philadelphia, St. Louis, and Boston (Waldinger and Bozorgmehr 1996). As shown in figure 2.1, the foreign stock's (immigrants and their children's) share of the total population in 1990 was much smaller, less than 9 percent. However, a much higher proportion (37 percent) of the immigrants were concentrated in the top five largest metropolitan areas—Los Angeles, New York, San Francisco, Miami, and

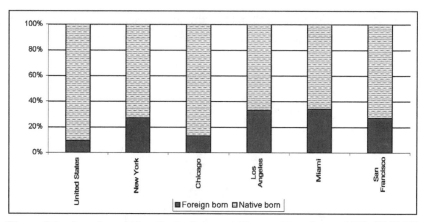

Figure 2.1. Immigrant Density in Selected Metropolitan Areas, 1990 (PMSAS)
Source: U.S. Census of Population (1990).

Chicago. In addition, the majority of urban immigrants lived in the central city.

Preferred Destinations

Different immigrant urban centers today attract immigrants from different countries. Table 2.1 displays the top ten national origin groups in each of the selected metropolitan areas. As shown, immigrants of different national origins are not evenly distributed across the urban landscape. New York, an urban center that received primarily European immigrants across the Atlantic Ocean at the turn of the century, has become the center for Caribbean immigrants. The three main Caribbean groups comprise almost a fifth of the area immigrant population. What is more striking is that none of these groups outnumbered others by an overwhelming margin and that none, except for the Chinese, appeared on the national top ten list, an indicator of extremely high concentration in just one area. In fact, 66 percent of Dominican immigrants, 36 percent of Haitian immigrants, and 39 percent of Jamaican immigrants in the United States lived in New York alone.

The picture in Los Angeles is drastically different. Mexican immigrants are the largest national origin group, comprising 40 percent of the area's foreign stock, 5.5 times larger than the second-largest group on the metropolis' top ten list and on the national top ten list. Also noticeable are

Table 2.1. Top-Ten Foreign-Born, National Origin Groups by Selected PMSAs, 1990 (in 1,000s)

Number	United States	N	New York	N	Los Angeles	N	Miami	N	San Francisco	N	Chicago	N
1	Mexico	4,298	Dominican Republic	232	Mexico	1,167	Cuba	429	China[1]	95	Mexico	238
2	Philippines	913	China[1]	166	El Salvador	213	Nicaragua	67	Philippines	60	Poland	76
3	China[1]	774	Jamaica	129	Philippines	161	Haiti	45	Mexico	48	Philippines	43
4	Canada	745	Italy	122	China[1]	136	Columbia	43	El Salvador	26	India	34
5	Cuba	737	Soviet Union	84	Korea	114	Jamaica	31	Vietnam	17	Italy	28
6	Germany	712	Haiti	80	Guatemala	108	Dominican Republic	16	Nicaragua	14	Germany	28
7	United Kingdom	640	Guyana	77	Vietnam	76	Honduras	16	United Kingdom	14	Korea	25
8	Italy	580	Columbia	71	Iran	67	Peru	15	Germany	11	China[1]	24
9	Korea	568	Poland	66	Soviet Union	51	Mexico	10	Soviet Union	11	Greece	18
10	Vietnam	543	Ecuador	64	Japan	40	Spain	10	Canada	9	Yugoslavia	18
Top Ten		10,510		1,092		2,102		682		300		532
Total		19,767		2,286		2,895		875		441		797

[1]Includes Hong Kong and Taiwan.
Source: U.S. Census Bureau (1993).

immigrants from El Salvador and Guatemala, making up 11 percent of the area's immigrant population. Although these two Central American groups are not on the national top list, they are disproportionately concentrated in Los Angeles, which is home to 48 percent of Guatemalan immigrants and 46 percent of Salvadoran immigrants in the United States. Compared to immigrant New York, Los Angeles appears to be less diverse ethnically, though it may have as many national origins groups as one can count. It is also less diverse in class status because of the strong correlation between national origins and the skill levels of the newcomers.

The dominance of Cubans in Miami is a different story. Though Miami is a much smaller metropolitan area, not only does it have the highest proportion of immigrants, but it is also a metropolis with the largest presence of Cuban Americans. More than half of Miami's foreign stock is of Cuban origin, and the group is 6.5 times larger than the second-largest group on the metropolitan top ten list. Unlike Mexicans in Los Angeles, Cubans in Miami are not simply the largest group in size, but also socioeconomically diverse with a significantly large middle class and strong influence in the areas' political and economic matters.

Like Miami, San Francisco is also a much smaller metropolis. Though no single national origin group is dominant, the Asian presence is impressive, making up more than 40 percent of the foreign stock. In contrast, Chicago is a much larger metropolis, but its foreign-born stock is only 13 percent. Interestingly, Mexican immigrants form the largest national origin group, three times larger than the second group on the metropolitan top ten list. However, their visibility is blurred by the area's relatively large native-born population.

Demographic Transformation in Immigrant-Receiving Urban Centers

The diversity of contemporary immigrants and their geographic concentration, combined with recent trends of deindustrialization and suburbanization, have reshaped the demographic profiles of both old and new immigrant-receiving centers. Figure 2.2 illustrates the racial composition of the three largest metropolitan areas 1980 and 2000. During the last two decades of the twentieth century, demographic transformation is drastic: The proportions of the "colored" components other than "black" in the general population increased corresponding to the decreasing dominance

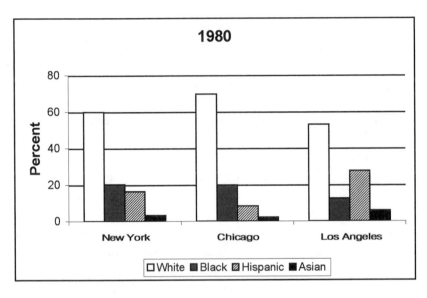

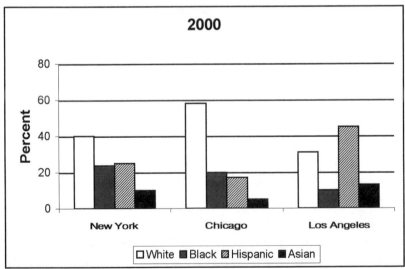

Figure 2.2. Population Growth by Race/Ethnicity, Selected Metropolitan Areas, 1980–2000 (PMSAS) Source: U.S. Census of Population (2000).

of the "white" component. In both New York and Los Angeles, non-Hispanic white populations had become a numerical minority by the year 2000. Even in Chicago, the diminishing dominance of the white population is significant. What have altered the racial composition in these metropolises are the obvious influxes of Asians and Latinos. Past research on internal migration patterns in the United States has also shown consistent findings that, in high-immigration metropolitan areas, there is a significantly large out-migration and that out-migrants are predominantly non-Hispanic whites (Frey 1995). At the metropolitan level, therefore, the demographic impact of immigrant influx is singularly on whites. But whether whites are pushed out by new immigrants or by other economic forces is debatable and may be a topic for yet another chapter.

Just thirty years ago, America's urban landscape, including the areas with high immigrant density, was predominantly white. The racial hierarchy was dictated by a black–white dichotomy with an unquestionable, all-encompassing white dominance. Although there were various immigrant groups coexisting within the urban social structure, these immigrants were expected to eventually become assimilated into the dominant white Anglo-Saxon Protestant (WASP) culture. Immigrant enclaves or ghettos did exist, mostly in the central city, but they did not constitute a permanent problem because they were considered transitional stops or springboards and would eventually die down with time. Indeed, with the span of only two or three generations and a long hiatus of low immigration, the white ethnics, such as the Irish, Jews, and Italians, who were once designated as inferior "races," have now become indistinguishably "white" (Alba and Nee 1997). Meanwhile, the majority of second- and third-generation Asian and Latin Americans also quietly dispersed into the white middle class without much public notice because they represented only a tiny fraction of the population.

Figure 2.3 shows the patterns of ethnic change by immigrant generations, using more current CPS data. In the first generation, the racial composition in major immigrant-receiving centers reflects the patterns of contemporary immigrant settlement I have just discussed: American cities have now become less "white" (but no less "black") and more "colored" than ever before. Los Angeles and Miami have turned into "Latin-dominant" cities, a description that can be detected from the top chart of figure 2.3. The middle chart displays racial/ethnic composition of the children of immigrants.

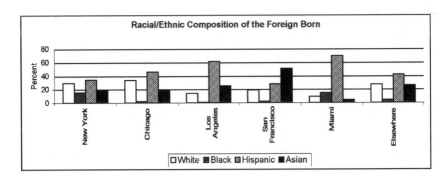

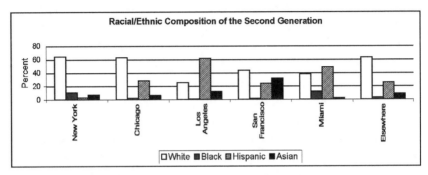

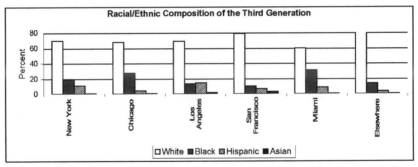

Figure 2.3. Distribution of Major Ethnic Groups by Generational Status in Selected Metropolitan Areas (PMSAS) Source: Current Population Survey (1994–1998).

Only Los Angeles contains a "Latin-dominant" second generation, with the same shift in Miami slowed down by its large concentration of white second-generation retirees, making Miami's second-generation population an ethnically diverse group. New York and Chicago contain a second-generation population that can only be described as "white dominant," a reflection of the impact of these regions' earlier immigration histories. San Francisco, the singularly "Asian-dominant" region, stands out as different, boasting the greatest variety in the ethnic composition of its second generation as well as the most pronounced Asian tilt.

As for the third-plus generation described in the lower chart in figure 2.3, this turns out to be the one characteristic around which there is the least regional variation. The whites comprise 60 percent of the third-plus generation population in every region, and the black–white dichotomy is quite striking while other ethnic groups are barely visible across regions. Noteworthy is the absence of third-generation Asian Americans in San Francisco. Because of various Asian exclusion acts that barred immigration from Asia since the 1880s and much of the twentieth century, only the Japanese-ancestry group (and Chinese to a lesser extent) has a noticeable third generation. Nonetheless, third-generation non-Mexican Latin Americans (mostly Puerto Ricans who have citizenship rights by birth) in New York and Mexican Americans (who are mostly descendants of native-born Mexicans rather than Mexican immigrants) in Los Angeles are visibly represented.

It should be noted that changes in racial composition that were impacted by immigration have occurred also in areas historically receiving relatively few immigrants. The U.S. census data shows that, between 1990 and 2000, Hispanic and Asian populations grew at 631 and 172 percent, respectively, in Raleigh–Durham–Chapel Hill; 388 and 197 percent in Atlanta; and 189 and 111 percent in Minneapolis–St. Paul. These recent demographic trends suggest that new immigrants are more dispersed across America than earlier waves.

The Changing Dynamics of Race and Ethnicity

What is more striking about these demographic changes is that the arrival of new immigrants and the concurrent trend of rapid out-migration of non-Hispanic whites in immigrant metropolitan areas significantly alter the dynamics of race and ethnicity. They make ethnicity more salient and pose new challenges to all Americans—native-born whites, blacks, Asian and Latin Americans alike, as well as the newcomers themselves.

Non-Hispanic Whites

The non-Hispanic white population comprises primarily of the grandchildren or great-grandchildren of European immigrants. Decreasing numbers notwithstanding, non-Hispanic whites still hold dominant political and economic power in immigrant-receiving centers, and the shift of the black–white paradigm does not change this dominance. How, then, have non-Hispanic whites been affected by immigration? Perhaps the most significant impact has involved the notion of American identity, as many fear that newcomers would overtake America and that Americans would be un-Americanized by them. The hotly contested issues of multiculturalism, bilingualism, and immigration reform in the political arena reflect some of these deeply rooted fears. In areas of immigrant concentration, many whites are confronted with a new dilemma of becoming a minority with a majority mentality in a multiethnic society (Horton 1995). In affluent suburban communities with a large and sudden influx of middle-class newcomers, such fears are more pronounced. For example, in Monterey Park, California, whites used to be able to drop their hyphens as unqualified Americans. But in the wave of a large influx of affluent Asian immigrants, they find themselves on the defensive without an ethnic culture of resistance and empowerment to express their fears (Horton 1995). However, nativist fears manifest themselves differently in different metropolitan settings. For example, in Mexican Los Angeles, the Spanish language is stigmatized and is being banned from instruction in schools, whereas in Cuban Miami, the same language is considered an important marketable skill, and bilingualism is celebrated as the American way.

Non-Hispanic Blacks

The foreign-born component of non-Hispanic blacks is relatively small, though migration from the Afro-Caribbean region has been on the rise, and Afro-Caribbean immigrants tend to concentrate in New York and Miami. As essentially a native-born population and the most American of the Americans, non-Hispanic blacks have been socially affected by the influx of other "colored" immigrants in different ways. In the wake of immigration's surge, non-Hispanic blacks have experienced increasing differentiation in socioeconomic characteristics at the individual level and bifurcation between the middle class and the poor (Grant et al. 1996; Oliver and Shapiro 1995). These patterns of differentiation and bifurcation are caused primarily by the drastic economic restructuring of America's urban labor markets that is simultaneous with rapid growth in immigration. Uneducated and poor blacks have been trapped in the inner city, where ladders of social mobility have disappeared and where the entry to low-skilled jobs is barred by employer discrimination and immigrant employment networks (Waldinger 1996; Wilson 1996). Middle-class blacks have experienced unprecedented social mobility, yet many have continued to face racial discrimination, especially in the housing market that constrains their residential mobility (Clark 1996; Massey and Denton 1987).

The arrival of large numbers of nonwhite immigrants has significantly changed the racial composition of the urban population, rendering the black–white paradigm outdated. However, such a change has not moved blacks up the racial hierarchy. Instead, blacks' racial caste status has been pushed down further by the internalization of other colored immigrants into, unfortunately, the "moral problem in the hearts and minds of Americans" (Myrdal 1962). For example, the widely publicized black–Korean conflicts in America's inner cities and the 1992 Los Angeles civil unrest were not caused by economic competition but rather by the realignment of race relations, manifested in the tension over "turf," which has continued to constrain blacks in virtually every aspect of their lives (Min 1996; Morrison and Lowry 1994). In their struggle for racial equality, many native-born blacks are confronted with a daunting dilemma: how to deal with being a minority competing with other new minorities whose members have come from different backgrounds and headed for many directions.

Native Americans of Asian and Latin Origin

The children and grandchildren of Asian and Latin immigrants have also felt the powerful social impact of contemporary immigration. Almost overnight, native-born Americans of Asian and Latin origin, especially those already "assimilated" or "melted" into white middle-class suburban communities, are confronted with the renewed image of "foreigners." Their American identity is constantly questioned because they look like the newcomers who do not fit the old characterization of an American as "either an European or the descendant of an European" (De Crevecouer 1904) or as an "immaculate, well-dressed, accent-free Anglo" (Zangwill

1914). These phenotypical definitions of "American," widely and often unconsciously held, make it harder for some native-born people to feel fully American if they happen to be Native Americans or Mexican Americans, whose ancestors settled on this land long before the *Mayflower* reached shore.

Stereotyping images of an "American" create special problems for native-born Americans of non-European ancestry whose national origin groups contain a disproportionately large number of recent arrivals. Incidents of harassing a native-born Mexican American suspected of being an undocumented immigrant or comments about a third-generation Japanese American's "good English" are frequently heard. The children, U.S.-born and similar to other American children, have found to suffer from persistent disadvantages merely because they look "foreign" (U.S. Commission on Civil Rights 1988, 1992).

While they are infuriated by the unfair treatment as foreigners, native-born Hispanic and Asian Americans are also caught in a dilemma of inclusion versus exclusion in their struggle for racial equality. Similar to other Americans in speech, thought, and behavior, native-born Hispanic and Asian Americans and their foreign-born counterparts often hold contradictory values and standards over labor rights, individualism, civil liberty, and ultimately the ideology of assimilation. These differences, intertwined with the acculturation gap between immigrant and native-born generations, have impeded ethnic coalition and ideological consensus. For example, the picketing of restaurants in New York's Chinatown in 1994 and Los Angeles' Koreatown in 1998 was a conscious effort mostly by second-generation Asian Americans fighting for immigrant rights. But it was perceived by the ethnic community as a group of "whitened" kids trying to "destroy their parents' businesses" and the ethnic community. Ironically, the parent generation consciously struggles to push children to become "white" by moving their families into white neighborhoods, sending their children to white schools, and discouraging their children to play basketball and mimic hip-hop culture. For Afro-Caribbean immigrants, the parents even push their children to adopt certain strategies, such as invoking their accents or other references to French or British colonial culture to differentiate themselves from native-born blacks and to avoid the stigma of "blackness" (Portes and Stepick 1993; Waters 1994, 1996). But becoming "white" is politically incorrect and thus unacceptable for the native-born generation.

The Newcomers

The social impact of contemporary immigration is perhaps most intense on the newcomers themselves. Earlier labor migrants of Asian or Latin American origin were mostly sojourners with an intention of eventually returning to their homelands. In contrast, most new immigrants are permanent settlers, even though there is a significantly visible presence of transnationals who have maintained their homes or lead their regular lives simultaneously in their countries of origin and destination. Most permanent settlers have made concerted efforts to assimilate first economically and then culturally. No matter how much they want to be like other Americans, however, the newcomers often find themselves facing an ambivalent public that questions their willingness to assimilate and doubts their assimilability. They also face the unrealistically high expectation that they should assimilate quickly. It took earlier European immigrants two or three generations to assimilate into the middle class, and such a pace was facilitated by economic expansion, industrialization, and a long hiatus of restricted immigration (Alba 1985; Alba and Nee 1997; Perlmann and Waldinger 1997). Today, the second generation of contemporary immigrants is just coming of age, and predictions about their future outcome of assimilation are only estimates.

Today's immigrants also encounter various structural constraints that limit their chances of integration. On the one hand, the continuous high volume of immigration has affected new arrivals in ways similar to their native-born coethnics. However assimilated they may have become, they are still likely to be viewed as foreigners "fresh off the boat." On the other hand, many newcomers, especially the low-skilled poor, lack contact with and exposure to the segment of American society into which they aspire to assimilate. In this case, they may either allow themselves and their children to assimilate into the inner city or build ethnic communities to help shield coethnic members from being trapped in the inner city (Portes and Zhou 1993). Either way, the process is viewed as a rejection to assimilation.

In real life, immigrants must first deal with the issue of economic survival. New immigrants arrived in cities where economic restructuring and globalization have created bifurcated labor markets with numerous labor-intensive and low-paying jobs on the one end and a growing sector of knowledge-intensive and well-paying jobs on the other. This bifurcated labor market renders many immigrants underemployed with substandard wages or occupational overqualification (Zhou 1997a). The 1990 census data reveal that immigrant men of all groups displayed fairly low rates of labor force nonparticipation (below 8 percent), except for Southeast Asians (16 percent) (Rumbaut 1995; Zhou and Bankston 1998).[4] In particular, Mexican men, who were most handicapped of all immigrant groups by the lack of skills and English proficiency, showed the lowest labor force nonparticipation rate, probably because of the fact that most of Mexican immigrant workers arrived through extensive employment and migrant networks (Massey 1996). Among those who were in the labor force, all male immigrants, except for the Europeans, were more likely than native white workers to be underemployed, with over half the immigrants—more than 60 percent of the Asians among them—experiencing underemployment measured by partial employment, low-wage employment, and overqualified employment. Mexicans were almost twice as likely as other groups to be underemployed by low wages. By contrast, Africans, Asians, and Europeans were more likely to be underemployed by being educationally overqualified for the jobs they held. It is clear that disadvantages in labor market status do not necessarily affect immigrant groups in the same manner. For those who are not able to obtain adequate employment, Mexican immigrants are more likely to be absorbed in partial or low-wage employment, while African and Asian immigrants are more likely to be occupationally overqualified in occupations.

The underemployment patterns among employed men were similar to those among employed women. Overall, however, gender expectations about employment are different. For example, male workers who are discouraged to seek work may be viewed as being forced to detach themselves from the labor market. But the same view may not be applicable to unemployed women because they may voluntarily withdraw from the labor force because of marriage or childbearing. By the same token, partial employment among men may be viewed as an imposed disadvantage, but partial employment among women may be voluntary or a strategy for supplementing husbands' underpaid family wages. Whether all forms of underemployment accrue to economic disadvantages remains a matter of debate. I would argue that unemployment is an absolute disadvantage. Partial employment or low-wage employment does not help much because their jobs are usually inadequate for sustaining a decent living, much less for moving up the socioeconomic ladder. This disadvantage affects

Mexican immigrants disproportionately. Although Mexican immigrants have relatively easy access to the U.S. labor market, their employment stability is heavily affected by the uncertain demands of the highly competitive, volatile industries in which they work. These conditions in turn constrain Mexican immigrants' ability to achieve economic success commensurate with their high rate of labor force participation.

While many immigrant workers start out as low-wage workers and gradually move up in the labor market, others may be "stuck" in dead-end jobs. Of course, whether one can successfully move out of their underemployment depends not simply on individual human capital or incentive because the effects of human capital may be intervened by factors beyond the control of individual group members. Immigration selectivity is one such factor. Immigrants who have arrived with strong human capital may be able to overcome labor market disadvantages by overqualification. Those who have arrived with little human capital are likely to be employed in low-wage and "bad" jobs. They usually have few economic resources and cannot afford the time for the kind of reeducation and retraining that can possibly move them up in the labor market. However, it would be premature to conclude that those who initially hold entry-level, low-wage jobs are necessarily "trapped" at the bottom of the labor market. In fact, as immigrants gain labor market experience, many are able to advance within and across industries to better-paying positions and even to self-employment (Portes and Zhou 1992, 1996; Zhou 1992). Thus, the long-term outcomes of underemployment as an alternative means to upward social mobility or as a dead-end street trapping immigrants in their starting point or pushing them further down toward the bottom are speculative but not mutually exclusive scenarios.

The Impact of Race/Ethnicity on Immigrant Incorporation

Classical sociological theories about immigrant adaptation predicts a linear trajectory in which immigrants, starting their American life at disadvantaged positions, eventually converge toward the mean and become indistinguishable Americans (Alba 1985; Gordon 1964; Park 1928; Warner and Srole 1945). This conclusion is based on two assumptions. One is that there is a natural process by which diverse and initially disadvantaged ethnic groups come to share a common culture and to gradually gain equal access to the opportunity structure of the host society. The other is that this process consists of gradually deserting old cultural and behavioral patterns in favor of new ones and that, once set in motion, this process moves inevitably and irreversibly toward assimilation (Warner and Srole 1945).

Immigrants' intergenerational mobility has been empirically measured by the extent to which immigrant groups achieve parity with the society's dominant group in education, occupation, income and wealth, and political power, which is, in Gordon's (1964) term, "secondary structural assimilation." Looking back in history from the present standpoint, the experiences of the children and grandchildren of earlier European immigrants appear to confirm the assimilationist prediction about structural assimilation. Between the 1920s and the 1950s, when America experienced a long hiatus of restricted immigration, the host country seemed to have absorbed the great waves of immigrants who had experienced significant upward mobility across immigrant generations, as determined by the length of stay since immigration, the mastery of the English language, the acquisition of human capital, and increasing exposure to American culture (Alba 1985; Chiswick 1977; Greeley 1976; Sandberg 1974; Wytrwal 1961).

However, it remains an open question whether new immigrants and their offspring will follow the path of their European predecessors. In terms of the direction of intergeneration mobility, the distinctions between yesterday's European immigrants and today's newcomers may not be as sharp as they appear to be. However, with regard to the rate of structural assimilation—the degree to which immigrant groups achieve parity with the dominant group—the classical assimilationist paradigm shows its constraints. The historiography of the turn-of-the-century European immigrants reveals divergent rather than convergent outcomes among different national origin groups (Perlmann 1988). Past studies on intergenerational mobility have found persistent interethnic differences in the rate of progress even after controlling for measurable human capital characteristics and contextual factors. In a study of the Irish, Italian, Jewish, and African Americans in Providence, Rhode Island, Perlmann (1988) found that, with family background factors held constant, ethnic differences in levels of schooling and economic attainment persisted in the second and later generations. He also found that schooling did not equally commensurate with occupational advancement for African Americans as for other European Americans across generations. Recent studies have also indicated that the distance between immigrant offspring and the native-born population in key socioeconomic measures varies among different national origin groups and that for some it continues to remain substantial (Model 1991; Tang 1993; Tienda and Lii 1987; Zhou and Kamo 1994). Even the direction of intergenerational mobility does not appear to be linear, and research has found both general and group-specific trends of second- or third-generation decline (Gans 1992; Landale and Oropesa 1995). These findings about past and present immigrant experiences have suggested that the direction and the rate of social mobility are two distinct dimensions of the adaptational outcomes and that what determines the direction may not necessarily be what determines the rate. Next, I highlight the ways in which race and ethnicity impact the prospects of immigrant incorporation.

Ethnicity and Class

Ethnicity, which is intrinsically linked to national origin, has been found to be one of the most salient factors influencing social mobility of new immigrants. Classical assimilationist theories often treat ethnicity as a measure of old-country ways and consider it an impediment to structural assimilation, but acknowledge that ethnicity does more in predicting the rate than in predicting the direction of mobility (Park 1928; Warner and Srole 1945). Yet empirical research indicates significant differences in the magnitude of progress across different ethnic or national origin groups. Steinberg (1996) revealed a surprisingly prominent and strong role that ethnicity played in structuring the lives of adolescents, both in and outside of school. He found that students of Asian origin outperformed non-Hispanic white students, who in turn outperformed black and Hispanic students by significantly large margins. He also found that the ethnic differences remained marked and consistent across nine different high schools under study after controlling for social class, family structure, and place of birth of parents. He also found similar ethnic effects on other important predictors of school success, such as the belief in the payoff of schooling, attribution styles, and peer groups. A study reported in *Ethnic Los Angeles*, conducted by a research team at the University of California,

MIN ZHOU

Los Angeles, and headed by Roger Waldinger and Mehdi Bozorgmehr, showed significant intergroup differences in the rate of intergenerational progress while revealing trends of upward mobility for all immigrant groups. This study found that native-born Mexicans and Central Americans experienced greater earnings and educational disparities with non-Hispanic whites relative to their Asian and Middle Eastern counterparts (Bozorgmehr et al. 1996; Cheng and Yang 1996; Lopez et al. 1996; Ortiz 1996). Portes and Rumbaut (1996) attributed these differences to the interplay of premigration conditions, individual characteristics, host reception, and group adaptational patterns. They argue that the diverse socioeconomic characteristics on arrival among new immigrants give rise to varied modes of incorporation that in turn affect the rate as well as the direction of progress among second and later generations.

Ethnicity and the Ethnic Hierarchy

While ethnicity is intrinsically intertwined with national origin, it is deeply rooted in America's ethnic stratification system, exerting positive as well as negative effects on adaptational outcomes. What makes ethnicity favor some groups while penalizing others? One way to interpret the varied effects of ethnicity is to examine its interaction with class. Socioeconomic status has an independent effect on mobility outcomes because it influences where people lives, where they go to school, with whom they are in close contact, and what kind of family and community resources are available. Wealthier and skilled immigrants are able to integrate into better sectors of the host economy with relative ease and settle directly in suburban middle-class communities, albeit with temporary downward mobility. Poorer and unskilled immigrants have few options but take up low-wage jobs and settle in declining urban areas, starting their American life either in poverty or on welfare. Becker (1963) found that early and insignificant differentials in class status can result in substantial differences in educational and occupational mobility in later years. The strong correlation between national origins and skill levels of contemporary immigrants also has a significant bearing on the varied effects of ethnicity. For example, the children of Mexican immigrants lag far behind their peers of Asian origins in academic performance and educational attainment, partly because of socioeconomic differences (Perlmann and Waldinger 1997) and partly because of differential resources generated in the family and the ethnic community (Caplan et al. 1989; Gibson 1989; Rumbaut and Ima 1988; Zhou and Bankston 1998).

However, controlling for the interactive effect between class and national origin does not seem to reduce the significance of ethnicity. Recent studies on the new second generation are a case in point. Using language proficiency as a proxy for the nativity or immigration status in a large-scale study in the San Diego School District during the 1986–1987 and 1989–1990 school years, Rumbaut found that first-generation Chinese, Korean, Japanese, Vietnamese, and Filipino students had the highest grade-point averages of all students in the district. More remarkable, even the Hmong, who came from preliterate peasant background, and the more recently arrived Cambodians outperformed all native-born English-only American students (Rumbaut 1995). Given the drastic differences in socioeconomic backgrounds of these Asian national origin groups, this finding complicates the effect of class. Portes and his associates reported findings from the Children of Immigrants Longitudinal Survey (CILS) showing that parents' socioeconomic status, length of U.S. residence, and homework hours significantly affected academic performance but that controlling for these factors did not eliminate the effect of ethnicity. More systematic analyses of the educational progress of children of immigrants using the CILS data generally confirmed these findings (Rumbaut and Portes 2001).

The fact that ethnicity continues to shape the American experience of immigrant groups implies that ethnicity also interacts with broader structural factors that produce and reinforce specific advantages or disadvantages in ethnic group membership and that the outcomes of adaptation may be segmented with potential and real risks of downward mobility (Portes and Zhou 1993). Portes and MacLeod (1996), using the National Educational Longitudinal Survey, reported that the negative effect of disadvantaged group memberships among immigrant children was reinforced rather than reduced in suburban schools but that the positive effect of advantaged group memberships remained significant even in inner-city schools. Using the same data set but employing a two-stage least-squares method, Hao and Bonstead-Bruns (1998) found that immigrant status increases educational expectations for Chinese, Koreans, and Filipino families more than for Mexican families. They also found that Chinese background consistently exerted positive effects on educational achievement, while Mexican background showed significantly negative effects, and that the ethnic effects persisted after controlling for important individual and contextual factors.

Why is it that ethnicity exerts opposite effects on the same outcome measures for different national origin groups? Existing literature has suggested that the advantages and disadvantages of ethnic group membership lies not merely in the class status and the corresponding modes of incorporation from which the first generation start life in America, but also in different levels of the social structures in which individuals and groups participate. At the macro level, the system of ethnic stratification functions to provide different ethnic groups with unequal access to economic resources and political power. At the micro level, the networks of social ties, which are often ethnically based, prescribe different strategies to cope with structural disadvantages and mobilize different types of social capital to provide support for group members. Either the members of disadvantaged ethnic groups accept an inferior status and a sense of basic inferiority as part of their collective self-definition or they create a positive view of their heritage on the basis of cultural and ethnic distinction, thereby establishing a sense of collective dignity (Ogbu 1974). If a socially defined ethnic group wishes to assimilate but finds that normal paths of integration are blocked on the basis of ethnicity, the group may be forced to take alternative survival strategies that enable its members to cope psychologically with structural barriers but that do not necessarily encourage structural assimilation. The group may also react to structural disadvantages by constructing resistance to assimilation (Fordham 1996; Kohl 1994). In this case, symbolic expressions of ethnicity and ethnic empowerment hinder rather than facilitate social mobility among group members.

As immigrants and their children are absorbed into different segments of American society, becoming American may not always be an advantage. When immigrants enter middle-class communities directly or after a short transition, they may find it advantageous to acculturate and assimilate. If the social environment surrounding immigrant children is rich in resources and if its goals are consistent with those of the immigrant family, then ethnic resources may be relatively less important, but those ethnic resources may still count. For example, many middle-class immigrant parents move into affluent white neighborhoods and send their children to schools attended mainly by white students from similar or more affluent socioeconomic backgrounds. But they still insist on enrolling their children in ethnic institutions during after-school hours and weekends or involving them in religious or cultural activities. The children then benefit both from privileged socioeconomic contacts with members of the dominant group in mainstream American society and from the group-specific expectations of and opportunities for intellectual development.

Thus, when immigrant children enter the bottom of the ethnic hierarchy, where the forces of assimilation come mainly from the underprivileged, acculturation and assimilation are likely to result in distinct disadvantages, viewed as maladjustment by both mainstream society and the ethnic community. Immigrant children from less fortunate socioeconomic backgrounds have a much harder time than middle-class children succeeding in school. A significant number of the children of poor, especially dark-skinned, immigrants can be trapped in permanent poverty in the era of stagnant economic growth, for in the process of Americanization, these immigrant children "will either not be asked, or will be reluctant, to work at immigrant wages and hours as their parents did but will lack job opportunities, skills and connections to do better" (Gans 1992: 173–174). The prospects facing children of the less fortunate may be high rates of unemployment, crime, alcoholism, drug use, and other pathologies associated with poverty and the frustration of rising expectation.

This new reality defines the world that confronts the children of new immigrants. Children growing up in households headed by poor, low-skilled immigrants face uncertain prospects for moving ahead through school success. The parents, of course, have few of the economic resources that can help children do well in school. The environment does not help when neighborhoods are poor and beset by violence and drugs and local schools do not function well. To add to this difficulty, immigrant children receive conflicting signals, hearing at home that they should achieve at school while learning a different lesson on the street—that of rebellion against authority and rejection of goals of achievement. At the same time, both real life and television expose children to the wage and consumption standards of U.S. society, and children come to expect more than their parents ever had. As a result, children of the foreign born are unwilling to work the low-paying, low-status jobs of their parents, but they do not have the education, skills, or opportunities to do better (Gans 1992). This mismatch between rising aspirations and shrinking opportunities will either lead to second-generation decline or provoke "second-generation revolt" (Perlmann and Waldinger 1997). However, young immigrants or children of immigrants may benefit from cultivating social ties within ethnic communities to develop forms of behavior likely to break the cycle of disadvantage and to lead to upward mobility. The extent to which young people are integrated into this community also becomes a major determinant of school adaptation, especially when the social environment otherwise places children at risk (Zhou and Bankston 1998).

Conclusion

The significant differences between contemporary and turn-of-the-century European immigration necessitate a reconceptualization of the phenomenon and the development of alternative theories. Because of the diverse socioeconomic backgrounds of new immigrants, the pathways toward integration into American society may be as rugged as they are segmented. Many new immigrants continue to follow the traditional rugged route, starting from the bottom rungs of the socioeconomic ladder and gradually working their way up. A visible proportion of them, however, manage to bypass the bottom starting line, incorporating directly into mainstream professional occupations and dispersing into suburban middle-class communities. Still, a significant number may be permanently "trapped" at the bottom, either unable to find work or working at "dead-end" jobs with little hope for social mobility.

Increasing diversity also poses challenges for Americans as they experience the drastic changes in the dynamics of race and ethnicity in an era of rapid social and economic transformations. Again, the old framework of assimilation has become outmoded. In multiethnic metropolises today, all native-born racial/ethnic groups are facing the challenge of adjustment to the new reality. Growing tensions are arising from an urgent need to negotiate the culture of diversity and to redefine oneself in the new racial/ethnic stratification system.

Finally, the future of new immigrants and their children is intrinsically linked to the diversity of immigration and to the current social stratification system into which today's immigrant children are assimilating. The American public still seems to allude to the idea that all immigrant children should move up and melt into the middle class. Because there are poor whites who have never assimilated into the white middle class, it is natural that some immigrant children may not make it, either, as immigrants are incorporating into a highly stratified society that accords individuals with varied life chances. Gans (1992) questions the American faith that mystifies an eventual immigrant success, particularly in regards to the new second generation. While children of the middle class have a better chance for success, the poor, especially the darker skinned, may not fare equally well. Consequently, assimilation as a widespread outcome for contemporary immigrant groups is possible for some but questionable for others. Indeed, for most Europeans, assimilation did not take place until the third or even the fourth generation. Thus, while the new second-generation immigrants may not assimilate, their children or grandchildren may. But with scenarios of second-generation decline still a matter of speculation, it seems clear that assimilation no longer means that everyone will eventually succeed.

Notes

The original version of this chapter was presented at the Research Conference on Racial Trends in the United States, National Research Council, Washington, DC, October 15–16, 1998. Some of the main ideas were drawn from my previously published work (Zhou 1997b, 2001). I thank Roger Waldinger and Mary Waters for their helpful comments and Vincent Fu and Diana Lee for their research assistance.

1. In theory, all the IRCA legalizees should have been residing in the country for a considerable period of time prior to 1989, though a substantial portion of those legalized under the SAW program turned out to be relatively recent arrivals.

2. Refugees and asylees can be anyone with a well-founded fear of prosecution on the basis of race, religion, membership in a social group, political opinion, or national origin. Refugees are those seeking protection outside the United States, while asylees are those seeking protection once already in the United States.

3. These are Census Bureau–designated principal metropolitan statistical areas rather than cities proper.

4. African immigrants also include a significant component of refugees from Ethiopia who had a higher labor force participation rate than Southeast Asian refugees. African refugees, as well as European refugees, tend to have higher educational attainment, more fluent English proficiency, and better access to community-based employment networks than Southeast Asian refugees.

References

Alba, Richard D. 1985. *Italian Americans: Into the Twilight of Ethnicity.* Englewood Cliffs, NJ: Prentice Hall.

Alba, Richard D., and Victor Nee. 1997. "Rethinking Assimilation Theory for a New Era of Immigration." *International Migration Review* 31 (4): 826–874.

Becker, Howard S. 1963. *Outsiders: Studies in the Sociology of Deviance.* New York: The Free Press.

Bozorgmehr, Mehdi, Claudia Der-Martirosian, and Georges Sabagh. 1996. "Middle Easterners: A New Kind of Immigrant." In *Ethnic Los Angeles,* edited by Roger Waldinger and Mehdi Bozorgmehr. New York: Russell Sage Foundation.

Caplan, Nathan, Marcella H. Choy, and John K. Whitmore. 1989. *The Boat People and Achievement in America: A Study of Family Life, Hard Work, and Cultural Values.* Ann Arbor: University of Michigan Press.

Cheng, Lucie, and Philip Q. Yang. 1996. "Asian: The 'Model Minority' Deconstructed." In *Ethnic Los Angeles,* edited by Roger Waldinger and Mehdi Bozorgmehr. New York: Russell Sage Foundation.

Chiswick, Barry R. 1977. "Sons of Immigrants: Are They at an Earnings Disadvantage?" *American Economic Review* 67 (February): 376–380.

Clark, William A. V. 1996. "Residential Patterns: Avoidance, Assimilation, and Succession." In *Ethnic Los Angeles,* edited by Roger Waldinger and Mehdi Bozorgmehr. New York: Russell Sage Foundation.

Cornelius, Wayne A. 1995. "Educating California's Immigrant Children: Introduction and Overview." In *California's Immigrant Children: Theory, Research, and Implications for Educational Policy,* edited by Rubén Rumbaut and Wayne A. Cornelius. La Jolla, CA: Center for U.S.-Mexican Studies, University of California, San Diego.

De Crevecoeur, J. Hector St. John. 1904 [1782]. *Letters from an American Farmer.* New York: Fox, Duffield.

Fordham, Signithia. 1996. *Blacked Out: Dilemmas of Race, Identity, and Success at Capital High.* Chicago: University of Chicago Press.

Frey, William H. 1995. "Immigration and Internal Migration 'Flight' from U.S. Metropolitan Areas: Toward a New Demographic Balkanization." *Urban Studies* 32 (4–5): 733–757.

Gans, Herbert J. 1992. "Second-Generation Decline: Scenarios for the Economic and Ethnic Futures of the Post-1965 American Immigrants." *Ethnic and Racial Studies* 15 (2): 173–192.

Gibson, Margaret A. 1989. *Accommodation without Assimilation: Sikh Immigrants in an American High School.* Ithaca, NY: Cornell University Press.

Gordon, Milton M. 1964. *Assimilation in American Life: The Role of Race, Religion, and National Origins*. New York: Oxford University Press.

Grant, David M., Melvin L. Oliver, and Angela D. James. 1996. "African Americans: Social and Economic Bifurcation." In *Ethnic Los Angeles*, edited by Roger Waldinger and Mehdi Bozorgmehr. New York: Russell Sage Foundation.

Greeley, Andrew M. 1976. "The Ethnic Miracle." *The Public Interest* 45: 20–36.

Hao, Lingxin, and Melissa Bonstead-Bruns. 1998. "Parent-Child Differences in Educational Expectations and the Academic Achievement of Immigrant and Native Students." *Sociology of Education* 71: 175–198.

Horton, John. 1995. *The Politics of Diversity: Immigration, Resistance, and Change in Monterey Park, California*. Philadelphia: Temple University Press.

Kohl, Herbert. 1994. *"I Won't Learn from You" and Other Thoughts on Creative Maladjustment*. New York: The New Press.

Landale, Nancy S., and R. S. Oropesa. 1995. "Immigrant Children and the Children of Immigrants: Inter- and Intra-Group Differences in the United States." Research Paper. Population Research Group, Michigan State University.

Lopez, David E., Eric Popkin, and Edward Tells. 1996. "Central Americans: At the Bottom, Struggling to Get Ahead." In *Ethnic Los Angeles*, edited by Roger Waldinger and Mehdi Bozorgmehr. New York: Russell Sage Foundation.

Massey, Douglas S. 1995. "The New Immigration and Ethnicity in the United States." *Population and Development Review* 21 (3): 631–652.

———. 1996. "The Age of Extremes: Concentrated Affluence and Poverty in the Twenty-First Century." *Demography* 33 (4): 395–412.

Massey, Douglas S., Rafael Alarcon, Jorge Durand, and Humberto Gonzalez. 1987. *Return to Aztlan: The Social Process of International Migration from Western Mexico*. Berkeley and Los Angeles: University of California Press.

Massey, Douglas S., and Nancy A. Denton. 1987. "Trends in Residential Segregation of Black, Hispanics, and Asians: 1970–1980." *American Sociological Review* 52: 802–825.

Min, Pyong Gap. 1996. *Caught in the Middle: Korean Communities in New York and Los Angeles*. Berkeley and Los Angeles: University of California Press.

Moch, Leslie Page. 1992. *Moving Europeans*. Bloomington: Indiana University Press.

Model, Suzanne. 1991. "Caribbean Immigrants: A Black Success Story?" *International Migration Review* 25: 248–276.

Morawska, Ewa T. 1990. "The Sociology and Historiography of Immigration." In *Immigration Reconsidered: History, Sociology, and Politics*, edited by Virginia Yans-McLaughlin. New York: Oxford University Press.

Morrison, Peter A., and Ira S. Lowry. 1994. "A Riot of Color: The Demographic Setting." In *The Los Angeles Riot*, edited by Mark Baldassare. Boulder, CO: Westview Press.

Myrdal, Gunnar. 1962 [1944]. *An American Dilemma: The Negro Problem and Modern Democracy.* New York: Harper & Row.

Ogbu, John U. 1974. *The Next Generation: An Ethnography of Education in an Urban Neighborhood.* New York: Academic Press.

Oliver, Melvin L., and Thomas M. Shapiro. 1995. *Black Wealth/White Wealth: A New Perspective on Racial Inequality.* New York: Routledge.

Ortiz, Vilma. 1996. "The Mexican-Origin Population: Permanent Working Class or Emerging Middle Class?" In *Ethnic Los Angeles,* edited by Roger Waldinger and Mehdi Bozorgmehr. New York: Russell Sage Foundation.

Park, Robert E. 1928. "Human Migration and the Marginal Man." *American Journal of Sociology* 33: 881–893.

Perlmann, Joel. 1988. *Ethnic Differences: Schooling and Social Structure among the Irish, Jews, and Blacks in an American City, 1988–1935.* New York: Cambridge University Press.

Perlmann, Joel, and Roger Waldinger. 1997. "Second Generation Decline? Immigrant Children Past and Present—A Reconsideration." *International Migration Review* 31 (4): 893–922.

Portes, Alejandro. 1995. "Economic Sociology and the Sociology of Immigration: A Conceptual Overview." In *The Economic Sociology of Immigration: Essays on Networks, Ethnicity, and Entrepreneurship,* edited by Alejandro Portes. New York: Russell Sage Foundation.

Portes, Alejandro, and Dag MacLeod. 1996. "The Educational Progress of Children of Immigrants: The Roles of Class, Ethnicity, and School Context." *Sociology of Education* 69 (4): 255–275.

Portes, Alejandro, and Rubén G. Rumbaut. 1996. *Immigrant America: A Portrait.* 2nd ed. Berkeley and Los Angeles: University of California Press.

Portes, Alejandro, and Alex Stepick. 1993. *City on the Edge: The Transformation of Miami.* Berkeley and Los Angeles: University of California Press.

Portes, Alejandro, and Min Zhou. 1992. "Gaining the Upper Hand: Economic Mobility among Immigrant and Domestic Minorities." *Ethnic and Racial Studies* 15: 491–522.

———. 1993. "The New Second Generation: Segmented Assimilation and Its Variants among Post-1965 Immigrant Youth." *Annals of the American Academy of Political and Social Science* 530 (November): 74–98.

———. 1996. "Self-Employment and the Earnings of Immigrants." *American Sociological Review* 61: 219–230.

Rumbaut, Rubén G. 1995. "Vietnamese, Laotian, and Cambodian Americans." In *Asian Americans: Contemporary Trends and Issues,* edited by Pyong Gap Min. Thousand Oaks, CA: Sage Publications.

Rumbaut, Rubén G., and Kenji Ima. 1988. *The Adaptation of Southeast Asian Refugee Youth: A Comparative Study.* Washington, DC: U.S. Office of Refugee Resettlement.

Rumbaut, Rubén G., and Alejandro Portes, eds. 2001. *Ethnicities: Coming of Age in Immigrant America.* Berkeley and Los Angeles and New York: University of California Press and Russell Sage Foundation.

Sandberg, N. C. 1974. *Ethnic Identity and Assimilation: The Polish-American Community.* New York: Praeger.

Smith, James P., and Barry Edmonston, eds. 1997. *The New Americans: Economic, Demographic and Fiscal Effects of Immigration.* Washington, DC: National Academy Press.

Steinberg, Laurence. 1996. *Beyond the Classroom.* New York: Simon & Schuster.

Tang, Joyce. 1993. "The Career Attainment of Caucasian and Asian Engineers." *Sociological Quarterly* 34: 467–496.

Tienda, Marta, and D. T. Lii. 1987. "Minority Concentration and Earnings Inequality: Blacks, Hispanics and Asians Compared." *American Journal of Sociology* 2: 141–165.

U.S. Census Bureau. 1993. *1990 Census of the Population: The Foreign Born Population in the United States.* Washington, DC: U.S. Government Printing Office.

U.S. Commission on Civil Rights. 1988. *The Economic Status of Americans of Asian Descent: An Exploratory Investigation.* Washington, DC: Clearinghouse Publications.

———. 1992. *Civil Rights Issues Facing Asian Americans in the 1990s: A Report.* Washington, DC: U.S. Government Printing Office.

U.S. Immigration and Naturalization Service. 1997. *Statistical Yearbook of the Immigration and Naturalization Service, 1995.* Washington, DC: U.S. Government Printing Office.

Waldinger, Roger. 1996. *Still the Promised City? African-Americans and New Immigrants in Postindustrial New York.* Cambridge, MA: Harvard University Press.

Waldinger, Roger, and Mehdi Bozorgmehr. 1996. "The Making of a Multicultural Metropolis." In *Ethnic Los Angeles.* New York: Russell Sage Foundation.

Warner, W. Lloyd, and Leo Srole. 1945. *The Social Systems of American Ethnic Groups.* New Haven, CT: Yale University Press.

Warren, Robert, and Ellen Percy Kraly. 1985. "The Elusive Exodus: Emigration from the United States." Population Trends and Public Policy Occasional Paper No. 8 (March). Washington, DC: Population Reference Bureau.

Waters, Mary C. 1994. "Ethnic and Racial Identities of Second-Generation Black Immigrants in New York City." *International Migration Review* 28 (4): 795–820.

———. 1996. "Immigrant Families at Risk: Factors That Undermine Chances of Success." In *Immigration and the Family: Research and Policy on U.S. Immigrants,* edited by Alan Booth, Ann C. Crouter, and Nancy Landale. Hillsdale, NJ: Lawrence Erlbaum Associates.

Wilson, William J. 1996. *When Work Disappears: The World of the New Urban Poor.* New York: Knopf.

Wytrwal, J. A. 1961. *America's Polish Heritage: A Social History of Poles in America.* Detroit: Endurance Press.

Zangwill, Israel. 1914. *The Melting Pot: Drama in Four Acts.* New York: Macmillan.

Zhou, Min. 1992. *Chinatown: The Socioeconomic Potential of an Urban Enclave.* Philadelphia: Temple University Press.

———. 1997a. "Employment Patterns of Immigrants in the U.S. Economy." Paper presented at the Conference on International Migration at Century's End: Trends and Issues, International Union for Scientific Study of the Population, Barcelona, Spain, May 7–10.

———. 1997b. "Growing up American: The Challenge Confronting Immigrant Children and Children of Immigrants." *Annual Review of Sociology* 23: 63–95.

———. 2001. "Contemporary Immigration and the Dynamics of Race and Ethnicity." In *America Becoming: Racial Trends and Their Consequences,* edited by Neil Smelser, William Julius Wilson, and Faith Mitchell. Washington, DC: National Academy Press.

Zhou, Min, and Carl L. Bankston III. 1998. *Growing up American: The Adaptation of Vietnamese Adolescents in the United States.* New York: Russell Sage Foundation.

Zhou, Min, and Yoshinori Kamo. 1994. "An Analysis of Earnings Patterns for Chinese, Japanese and Non-Hispanic Whites in the United States." *Sociological Quarterly* 35 (4): 581–602.

CHAPTER THREE

IMMIGRATION AND CONFLICT IN THE UNITED STATES

Suzanne Shanahan and Susan Olzak

T his chapter provides preliminary and suggestive analyses of the effects of immigration and ethnic diversification on racial conflict[1] in American cities in two periods of dramatic immigration. The history of race relations in the United States has been characterized by episodes of conflict: a virulent anti-Chinese movement in the 1880s; significant nativist violence in the 1920s (and more recently in the 1990s); anti-Mexican riots in the 1940s; Korean–black conflict of the 1980s and 1990s; and lynchings, firebombings, and beatings of African Americans by whites in most decades since the nineteenth century. In this study, we ask whether there is a single dynamic or mechanism underlying this diverse array of phenomena. What is the relationship between immigration and racial conflict in urban America? How have specific historical changes—immigration flows, immigration policy, or the economy more broadly—altered this mechanism? There have been countless studies of individual instances of racial unrest.[2] Many of these studies assume an underlying relationship among such individual events. Yet there have been no systematic attempts to collect and analyze data on all ethnic and racial urban conflict over a long historical period or in two very different moments in history. In this chapter, we begin to fill this gap in the literature.

Our Argument: Immigration, Diversity, and Racial Consolidation

Previous research has well demonstrated the link between flows of immigration and episodes of ethnic violence at the turn of the twentieth century (Alba 1985, 1991; Farley and Allen 1987; Higham 1988; Loewen 1988; Olzak 1992; Roediger 1991; Saxton 1990; Sugrue 1996). But a simple correlation between more immigration and more violence against immigrants is complicated by an examination of the targets of conflict from this period. We know that while the majority of immigrants who arrived in the decades around the turn of the century were from Europe (Higham 1988), these same European immigrants were not the central targets of conflict during the peak periods of influx. While immigration may well have led to increased nativism, periods of peak immigration were also associated with periods of intensified violence against African Americans (Olzak 1992; Tolnay and Beck 1995). Indeed, between 1877 and 1914, two-thirds of all racial and ethnic conflict in urban America targeted the African American population, not immigrants. Indeed, African Americans were disproportionately victimized by attacks that included beatings, lynchings, and the firebombing of the houses of black residents. To be sure, African Americans were not the sole victims of ethnic attacks (Bodnar 1985; Higham 1988; Jacobson 1998; Saxton 1990; Smedley 1993). Chinese, Japanese, and other immigrants were attacked and were even more commonly excluded from various citizenship rights, such as the right to own property or to vote. They were also routinely denied union membership and barred from being buried in the United States (Boswell 1986; Fong and Markham 1991; Takaki 1989). How, then, can we explain the relationship between immigration and race relations in twentieth-century America?

We argue that immigration and its attendant ethnic diversification historically generated collective mobilization against persons of color. In particular, we argue that surges in immigration and the diversity of ethnic immigrants initiated competition and collective conflict over existing resources. Such collective action reinforced a white/nonwhite ethnic boundary line as ethnic immigrants gradually joined native whites in their attempts to constrain competition from "nonwhites" (Alba 1985; Farley and Allen 1987; Loewen 1988).

Over time, a highly diversified immigrant population came to identify with (and be identified as) members of the white community. This is not to say that ethnic identities disappeared entirely. It is to suggest that the larger white boundary increased in salience, while the small-scale or national identities declined in importance. Thus, the ethnic *diversity* of immigrants encouraged the process of assimilation into the advantaged "white" population. However, the familiar notion of these groups as distinctly "white ethnics" was not a forgone conclusion in 1890 or even in 1920. Instead, this identity was forged by ongoing changes in the political and national context of race.

Our central argument develops a concept of *racial consolidation,* defined by the increasing salience of a biracial social order.[3] The process of racial consolidation was reinforced by racial violence that increasingly came to target additional groups of immigrants who were viewed as being nonwhite. At the turn of the twentieth century, African, Asian, and Native Americans were the predominant (but not sole) targets of ethnic conflict. To be sure, there were still significant flurries of activity directed against Irish, Italians, and eastern Europeans, but (with the exception of Jews) events against these groups soon declined in number (Jacobson 1998). During the 1930s, as well as more recently, Latinos have become targets of ethnic violence. By the early decades of the twentieth century, it became clear that the there was a growing distinction and debate over which immigrant groups were white and which were not (Jacobson 1998). Many of these debates were accompanied by racial attacks, group conflict, and violence.

In sum, the process of racial consolidation at the end of the nineteenth century was a product of two forces. The first involved the decreasing significance of national and linguistic differences among ethnic immigrants from Europe. The second involved the addition of new groups to the existing nonwhite status. Both processes reinforced a newly drawn boundary line.

We argue that in the first wave (from 1869 to 1924), immigrants reshaped America's ethnic national identity in fundamental ways that reinforced the existing white/nonwhite dichotomy of race. During the second wave of immigration (1965–1993), we argue that the dynamics of ethnic conflict have changed so that immigration by itself is no longer the main precipitant to conflict. Rather, in this second stage, the diversity of incoming immigrants is more of a predictor of conflict than is the sheer size of immigration. Somewhat paradoxically, we are arguing that the diversity of immigration precipitated a renewed importance of the white/nonwhite boundary line. Historical accounts of American race relations anchor their arguments in long-standing Western conceptions of race (Jordan 1968), in the institutional legacy of slavery (Fredrickson 1988), or in Reconstruction (Marx 1998; Woodward 1964). Instead, we argue that ethnic immigration played a pivotal role in organizing and redefining U.S. racial boundaries.

Historical Background

We begin our story of immigration and diversity in 1869, a key moment in the history of American ethnic identity (Saxton 1990; Smedley 1993). Prior to 1869, citizenship had been exclusively reserved for whites, Anglo-Saxon whites in particular. In 1869, however, the United States negotiated the Burlingame Treaty, which encouraged Chinese immigration. The following year, the 1870 Naturalization Act extended the rights of citizenship to persons of African descent. This momentary opening for non-whites began a century-long debate about the racial character of American citizenship and U.S. immigration policy. Together with the Thirteenth Amendment abolishing slavery, these acts raised the possibility that anyone—either white or nonwhite—could become an American. In response, many new immigrants organized their activities around a distinctly white identity.

As white ethnicity came to incorporate more than Anglo-Saxon heritage (Allen 1994; Ignatiev 1995; Jacobson 1998), the distinction between white and nonwhite was reified. The consolidation of the white-American ethnicity boundary is clearly visible in various exclusionary movements that distinguished between "desirable" and "undesirable" racial and ethnic immigrant groups in the decades after 1870 (Higham 1988). The range of these movements is impressive. They included anti-Chinese legislation during the 1880s, anti-foreigner restrictions in the workplace during the 1900s, and violent lynchings, beatings, and attacks against racial and ethnic groups from 1890 through 1930 (Bennett 1988). These late nineteenth- and early twentieth-century reactive social movements disproportionately targeted nonwhites.

Have similar social movements against nonwhites and the foreign born emerged in the late twentieth century? At first glance, the nature of race relations in twentieth-century America seems dramatically changed. Since the 1950s, African Americans have reestablished their right to vote, and the civil rights movement successfully changed behavior, attitudes, and beliefs about the nature and rigidity of racial rules. This liberalization of attitudes is also reflected in the more open and race-neutral immigration policies. More generally, as Wilson has argued, "race" has declined in significance, while class, occupation, and other cleavages have become predominant markers of identity and life chances (Wilson 1978).

At the same time, however, we know that racial politics have not disappeared, nor has violence against nonwhites ceased. Racial protest and unrest are common in many parts of the United States. And certainly, recent race riots in Miami, New York, and Los Angeles seem to undercut the claim that race has diminished in importance (Olzak et al. 1996).

From 1965 to 1999, the United States once again experienced a rise in immigration, second only to the immigrant waves at the turn of the twentieth century. Perhaps not coincidentally, the 1990s have witnessed a rise in anti-immigrant sentiment. Anti-immigrant laws and restrictions surfaced during the 1980s and 1990s in California, Washington, Florida, and New York. This legislation, when coupled with changes in federal welfare legislation, represented a backlash against immigration (Fong and Markham 1991). These facts suggest that heightened racial tensions once again have coincided with increased immigration.

Arguments and Hypotheses

In contrast to views of race and ethnicity as constant and unchanging, we view current racial boundaries as a manifestation of an ever changing process of racial formation (Alba 1990; Omi and Winant 1986). We follow Barth (1969) in defining race and ethnic boundaries as a form of social organization that is based on a set of markers normally demarcated by the in- and out-group membership on the basis of skin pigmentation, language (or dialect), and/or national origin. Furthermore, most scholars suggest that the importance and nature of these identities depend on the context and historical period (Cornell and Hartmann 1998). These views encourage us to explore what conditions might change the makeup and salience of these boundaries. However, changes in ethnic boundaries are difficult to observe directly. Thus, we focus on one observable consequence of these changes in boundaries: conflict. Here, then, we focus on how the diversity of immigrants influenced the likelihood of racial and ethnic violence in urban America.

Competition Theories of Race/Ethnic Relations

We seek to understand these histories of immigration and conflict in terms of sociological theories of ethnic/racial conflict. We rely on competition theory, a perspective that recognizes that ethnic boundaries are socially constructed and inherently reactive. This perspective assumes that the salience of ethnic boundaries rises when formerly separated groups come into contact (Blalock 1967).

Competition theory builds on Barth's (1969) insight that displacement and exclusion are generated by competition. It assumes that initial niche overlap intensifies competition among groups that, in turn, encourages attempts by the historically more powerful groups to exclude the competitors. When targets resist, racial conflict and violence ensue. Racial mobilization can take several forms. Competition can generate waves of protest on the part of disadvantaged minorities over a wide variety of forms, such as symbolic protest, civil disobedience, or race rioting. Alternatively, rising competitive forces can cause reactive mobilization on the part of the dominant groups. Furthermore, the two can be mutually reinforcing, as in the case of movements and countermovements.

Competition theorists also suggest that there are advantages for ethnic groups to realign themselves as part of the dominant language or territorial group (Hannan 1979). As the diversity of a population increases, the relative importance of any one small-scale dialect, nationality, or cultural identity decreases in importance. At the same time, large-scale ethnic group identities may increase, becoming politically and culturally more powerful actors. Here we examine the extent to which these changes were propelled by the size and ethnic diversity of waves of immigration.

This line of thought offers a compelling alternative to conventional theories of ethnic deprivation. These theories hold, first, that poverty and inequality generate ethnic conflict and, second, that integration and the equalization of socioeconomic opportunity and advantage ought to reduce ethnically based grievances and thereby diminish ethnic conflict. Yet recent studies of racial unrest in the United States have not supported these arguments. Instead, they suggest that expansion of economic opportunities is more likely to lead to mobilization among the disadvantaged (Olzak et al. 1996).

Ethnic Inequality and Immigration

Of course, economic opportunities were not equally available to all ethnic and racial groups. African Americans entered the twentieth century severely handicapped by the slavery experience, and many ethnic immigrants arrived penniless, unskilled, and illiterate. Can we explain current racial hostilities in terms of the gaps in racial disadvantages in 1900? Answers to this question vary. For instance, Lieberson (1980) offered a queue model that takes the timing and composition of immigration into account, while Model (1988, 1993), Olzak (1989), and others suggest that competitive exclusion in highly valued occupations played a role in determining occupational mobility rates.

Instead of focusing on the advantages gained by whites, other scholars trace today's race differences in attainment to the apparent decline in rates of upward mobility for African Americans. For example, a major lesson from Lieberson's (1980) pathbreaking research is that African Americans and white immigrants were often equally disadvantaged in 1900. But by 1930, ethnic immigrants from Europe gained in nearly every arena of attainment: education, occupations (especially professional categories), and residential desegregation (Alba 1985, 1990). At the same time, the economic and residential segregation situation of African Americans had worsened. What had happened?

Lieberson (1980: 213–214) provides an answer consistent with our racial consolidation story. He argued that blacks were suppressed because whites mobilized to segregate blacks in low-wage jobs and poor neighborhoods to preserve white dominance. While this explanation seems correct, we believe that it does not go far enough in explaining why white ethnic immigrants assumed a white identity that allowed them to benefit from white dominance while the fortunes of African Americans were actually reversed by 1930. As Lieberson (1980) suggests, something more than the burdens of slavery must have been at work to produce this reversal in fortunes for blacks. Here we emphasize an economic process that encouraged European immigrants to identify as whites.

Split Labor Markets and Competition

When economic differences coincide with racial distinctions, an enduring racial caste system emerges. This existence of a biracial caste system with its legacy of slavery provided strong economic incentives for European immigrants to reject a nonwhite identity. As slavery was abolished in the United States, split labor markets developed along racial caste lines. A split labor market exists to the extent to which different race groups command different wages for similar work (Bonacich 1972). Moreover, split labor markets may encourage racial animosity that is driven by class conflict against a low-wage racial group. Indeed, in Wilson's (1978) view, the peak periods of racial violence that occurred in the North during the period of immigration and industrial expansion can be explained by these arguments.

Does economic contraction also raise rates of conflict? Much of the literature on racial violence, lynching, and other attacks suggests that economic depression, unemployment, and other indicators of economic downturn increase ethnic tensions (Olzak 1992). High unemployment also raises the rate of race riots (Myers 1997). But mobilization also rises during periods of relative prosperity for race/ethnic groups in the disadvantaged niche (Tolnay and Beck 1995). Thus, something in addition to economic subordination must be igniting the violence against subordinated groups.

Perhaps the surge of immigrants who entered the industrial labor market as unskilled workers generated competition within the least-skilled niche. This heightened sense of competition in turn produces a higher rate of ethnic antagonism in an attempt to constrain or even remove the competition. Other factors that create a split labor market should also produce attempts to exclude the competitors. As the proportion of immigrants who are members of racial minorities increases, the growing competitive threat comes to be viewed racially. That is, as the racial consolidation process became entrenched, immigrants, as well as native-born Americans, sought to distinguish themselves from nonwhites.

Split labor markets did not emerge in a vacuum. The establishment of racially divided labor markets was aided by the (mostly white) labor movement, which acted collectively to maintain higher wages for workers (Foner 1974; Mink 1986). Around the turn of the twentieth century, union membership conferred many economic advantages to white ethnic immigrants that were denied to blacks (Model 1993; Wilson 1978). The growth of the labor union movement apparently also raised rates of anti-black conflict (Olzak 1992).

In summary, we argue that increases in immigration, the diversity of immigrant populations, and racial conflict against nonwhites together reinforced the process of racial consolidation around the turn of the twentieth century. Surges in immigration and the diversity of ethnic immigrants intensified competition and conflict over existing resources. In attempting to identify with the advantaged white population, immigrants reinforced the salience of a distinctly dual color caste line by distinguishing themselves apart from nonwhites. Collective violence reaffirmed whiteness as it rejected an out-group identity. In other words, collective action, mobilized along a white boundary line against nonwhites, became a means by which position, power, and prestige could be consolidated (Tolnay and Beck 1995).

Three Hypotheses

We restate these arguments in three key hypotheses:

1. Increases in the ethnic diversity levels of European immigrants raise the rate of collective racial conflict against nonwhites.
2. Increases in the proportion of unskilled European immigrants raises the rate of collective conflict against nonwhites.
3. Increases in the proportion of immigrants who are nonwhite raise the rate of collective conflict against nonwhites.

Research Design

Time Frame

The logic behind our choice of time frame is straightforward. We selected the periods 1869–1924 and 1965–1993, in which the flows of people, money, and ideas across national boundaries were unprecedented. Moreover, in both periods, the effects of immigration were the subjects of considerable popular and public policy debate (LeMay 1987). Both folk and social scientific wisdom has generally posited an important link between these surges in immigration and ethnic unrest. Here we add a counterintuitive notion to this commonsense belief by trying to explain why the proliferation of mainly white immigrants raised rates of attacks on nonwhite residents in urban settings.

The late 1860s was a period of rapid economic expansion, especially in urban centers, where immigration was still promoted in many parts of the United States. During this period, U.S. borders remained tentatively open, and a faith in immigrant assimilation still dominated popular and social scientific beliefs (Cose 1992; Higham 1988; Jacobson 1998).

Between 1869 and 1924, these prevailing ideas would shift dramatically, as xenophobic movements and anti-black sentiment rose throughout the country. Mounting nativist and aggressive anti-immigrant sentiment led to the passage of twenty-four different acts restricting immigration over this period. The final act, the 1924 National Origins Immigration Law, was an explicit attempt to buttress the Anglo heritage and Anglo lineage of the American people. The 1924 act dramatically curtailed the flow of immigrants to the United States, and the debates that surrounded it reaffirmed an ideology of racial difference in American society (Smedley 1993).

By the end of World War I, population diversity was generally understood to be a significant threat to the nation. Discussions throughout the interwar years warned against the dangers of a "mongrel" society. In this context, it is not surprising that diverse immigration was thought to represent a direct threat to the "American nation" and the "American spirit." As Senator Williams remarked in the 1914 *Congressional Record*, racial homogeneity was critical to American identity: "If that does not exist, there can not be homogeneousness of race; there can not be homogeneousness of purpose; there can not be homogeneousness of ideals; and there can not be a common patriotism."[4] In 1920, Congressman Box and others feared for the "de-Americanization" of the United States and the division of allegiances through the development of a "hyphenated population."[5] In the post–World War I context, hyphenation signaled a lack of allegiance. To consider oneself Irish American or German American was to commit "moral treason." As naive as it might seem, it was not until after World War I that legislators fully realized the extent to which immigrant populations were actually quite distinct and not necessarily fully

"Americanized." Mere habitation in the United States would not automatically assimilate diverse peoples. Nation building and the maintenance of national boundaries would have to be a "deliberate formative process, not an . . . accidental arrangement."[6] As a result, Americanization became a valued goal and a task for educators, religious leaders, and politicians.

While the first immigration period (1869–1924) is often described as an era of regulation and restriction, the second period (1965–1993) is often characterized as an era of policy liberalization (Bernard 1997). The second period begins with a dramatic shift in immigration policy: the erosion of the old national quota system, which concluded the first period. Imagery that depicted immigration as a threat to America can be analyzed directly in the political debates over immigration.[7] A healthy economy, coupled with the shifting national attitudes reinforced by civil rights, put immigration reform at the top of many political agendas. The 1965 U.S. Immigration Act sought to eliminate any hint of racial prejudice in policy by creating a new standard for admission. In contrast to his predecessors, Congressman Cellar's 1965 speech in Congress exemplifies this view: "You judge a man by his worth and not by his birth. We honor the uniqueness of a man, the boundaries of his mind and his soul, not the geographical boundaries of his place of birth."[8] To be sure, there was not complete agreement on the abolition of racial and ethnic immigration and naturalization exclusions:

> There is no question of "superior" or "inferior" races . . . [but] certain groups not only do not fuse easily, but consistently endeavor to keep alive their racial distinctions when they settle among us. They perpetuate they hyphen which is but another way of saying that they seek to create foreign blocs in our midst.[9]

Concerns also emerged that the United States was acting out of some misperceived sense of international norms. A well-publicized survey—noting that as of the 1960s neither Japan nor Switzerland allowed any immigration, Britain even limited access by its own colonists, Israel had a Jews-only policy, Liberia had a no-whites statute, and Australia had a no-blacks act—concluded that the United States misjudged the global liberalization of immigration controls and misperceived a loosening of borders.[10] Senator McClellan, noting that discrimination "is a natural compulsion of the human kind," reminded the Senate that discriminating tastes in food and clothing were considered admirable traits.[11] He implied that attempts to rid policy of any hint of discrimination were utopian. The significance of the act lay not in whether race was eradicated from policy but in the fact that explicit race could no longer be defended as a reason for or against admission. It is this historic moment of opening, if not welcoming, that marks the beginning of the second period.

The 1965 Immigration Act was followed in this period by some forty-seven other, largely minor changes in immigration legislation. Other significant reforms were seen only in the 1986 and 1990 acts. Indeed, the 1990 act has been nicknamed the "Diversity Act." Despite what appeared to be mounting popular concerns surrounding immigration, both acts constituted further liberalization of immigration policy. It seemed to some observers that migration to the United States had never been easier (Martin 1994; Reimers 1998). By the end of this second period, annual immigration averaged more than 850,000 per year. Despite a flourishing economy in the 1990s, there is some scattered evidence of mounting anti-immigrant sentiment in both public and policy debate. The 1996 Welfare Act limited for the first time social provisions to some immigrant populations. English-only referenda appeared in many state-level elections. While not directly tackling the issue of population flows, these initiatives suggest that the United States may well become an increasingly hostile environment for immigrants once again.

Thus, in each of the two historical moments of mass migration, the United States has embraced very different policies. In the first era, we see swift measures both to limit surges in immigration and to winnow the increasing diversification of immigrant flows. In the second period, we see a policy orientation that would be more open to a wide array of immigrant groups. Indeed, this constitutes a moment where, at least rhetorically, diversity is celebrated. In one period, diversity is deemed problematic; in the other, diversity is deemed an asset. How population diversity and the diversification of immigrant flows impact ethnic and racial collective mobilization is at the heart of the analyses that follow. We have now set the stage for our last question: Have the dynamics of ethnic and racial mobilization changed over the past century in America? In the next section, we discuss our strategy for gathering and assessing the evidence on this question.

Source of Data on Race and Ethnic Conflict Events

Following an established tradition in event analysis, our research design uses daily microfilm accounts from the *New York Times* to create chronological histories of events as they unfold over time.[12] Our coding protocol tracks all instances of racial or ethnic collective action that occurred in any one of the seventy-six of the largest American urban areas in two periods: 1869–1924 and 1965–1993 (see table 3.1 for a list of cities included).

We define racial or ethnic collective action as nonroutine, collective, public acts—both violent and nonviolent—that involve claims on behalf of a larger racial or ethnic collective. Our complete data set includes a diverse array of such acts, including both protests (e.g., boycotts, rallies, and marches) and conflicts (e.g., lynchings, riots, and firebombings). For theoretical reasons, we limit our statistical analyses to the rate of racial and/or ethnic conflict. We define *conflict* as the public expression of racially or ethnically based grievances against a specified ethnic or racial target. We gather information on a conflict event only if prejudices are carried out as public and collective displays of anger. This means that our coding rules require evidence of some threat of harm or damage to people, buildings, or property but not necessarily evidence of serious physical harm. Only a few events include fatalities. For an event to be included, the action must have targeted another (specific) racial/ethnic group or groups. Lynchings, mob attacks, group violence, and firebombings are examples of collective conflict.

Events are collected in a two-stage process. First, we identify "candidate events" from the *New York Times Index*. In this stage, we search the index using a broad set of key words that indicate contention, mob attack, violence, and race/ethnic categories of participants. In the second stage, we read individual daily newspaper accounts of each candidate event. Approximately 50 percent of all candidate events meet the criteria of being collective, public, and ethnic or racial in nature.

Our coding rules help make clear a distinction between racial/ethnic events and other forms of group conflict. For instance, we code information

Table 3.1.   Changing Regional Patterns of Racial and Ethnic Collective Conflict

Region	Period 1 (1869–1924)	Period 2 (1965–1993)
Northeast	102 events/49%	354 events/59%
South	34 /16%	73/13%
West	37/18%	34/6%
Midwest	36/17%	136/22%

from daily newspaper reports of labor disputes as ethnic or racial events only if there was evidence that these events had a major racial or ethnic dimension to them. Thus, strikes in which white workers yelled racist slogans and attacked African American strikebreakers physically would be counted as an anti–African American event. However, for example, strikes that did not report evidence of direct white–African American confrontation would not be counted as primarily an ethnic/racial conflict, even if the workers were described as white, Italian, or Irish (however, such strikes would be included in a measure of labor unrest).

As with any research strategy, our use of the *New York Times* to gather information on the timing of events is subject to some degree of measurement error (but see McCarthy et al. 1996; Oliver and Maney 2000; Oliver and Myers 1999). It is important to emphasize that we are not claiming to have captured the full universe of phenomena involving different racial and ethnic groups (although they are undoubtedly consequential for the formation and maintenance of these boundaries). Trials, editorials, cartoons, dairies, novels, plays, and other forms of public discourse all shape notions of racial boundaries (see Jacobson 1998). Nonetheless, we focus exclusively on collective action as dramatic, public, and traceable evidence of the consolidation, expression, and validation of group membership. Thus, we deliberately exclude interpersonal disputes, murder, or crimes, such as muggings, rapes, and other violence, where victims and perpetrators are from different racial and ethnic groups. They are important events in their own right, but we do not regard them as *collective* conflicts.

Although newspapers have been used increasingly as the main source of information on the timing of collective action, this strategy has been criticized. For instance, some observers have been skeptical that the *New York Times* would publish sufficient information on events that take place in regions far from New York, such as San Francisco, Detroit, or Dallas. This issue might be especially problematic in the early period of American history before the instantaneous transmission of news stories became common. Others have reasonably suspected that newspapers reflect various sources of bias that influence the nature of our data in a variety of ways, including political bias or bias toward more dramatic or violent events. One source of bias in representation remains fairly undisputed. This is the finding that events are far more likely to be reported when they occur in large urban areas. Thus, in seeking to curb as many sources of bias as we can, we have restricted our data to events that happen in urban settings. In this way, we minimize one well-known source of systematic bias in newspaper data.

For our purposes, many problems related to reporter or editorial bias are not relevant. This is because our analysis does not specifically characterize rhetoric or descriptive words used in newspaper reports, as would more traditional content analysis. We do not code editorials or speeches. Instead, our research focuses specifically on the timing of an event and thus relies on a researcher's ability to identify the group or groups involved in a public and collective attack. However, there is new evidence that a national newspaper, such as the *New York Times,* captures dramatic events, such as ethnic attacks and race riots, relatively well when compared to local accounts (McCarthy et al. 1996; Myers 1997; Olzak et al. 1996).

We developed coding rules that are informed by research on this problem. Recently, an enormous amount of scholarly research has examined local and national newspaper accounts for evidence that one or more of these sources contain various forms of "selection bias." Such forms might include effects of proximity, size, violence, and political bias. The results of these efforts are fairly straightforward. Events that have more participants are more likely to be reported in the *New York Times* than in local papers. Events in local papers are also likely to have more specific details, including neighborhood names or the ages and names of participants. However, analyses of race riots and ethnic attacks that have compared various local papers to the *New York Times* find that a collective conflict event among ethnic groups is often reported in similar fashion in both accounts (see McCarthy et al. 1996).

On the other hand, it does not seem reasonable to assume that newspaper reports contain a full accounting of everyday individual attacks on members of race and ethnic groups. Admittedly, these events are consequential and harmful, and they make up the majority of what has been labeled "bias crimes" in recent years (Green et al. 1998). However, primary sources of data on hate crimes have been limited largely to police or FBI records, which undoubtedly have their own sources of bias, political and otherwise. Furthermore, the data collection procedures, reporting bias, and definitions of what constitutes a hate crime vary over cities (indeed, the FBI data set combines data from a subset of U.S. cities, participating with the FBI project on a volunteer basis). These limitations would make a national comparison of hate crimes across cities difficult, if not impossible. Thus, while we believe that studying bias crimes is extremely useful, there are no comprehensive sources of data on bias crimes that would fit our purposes here.

Definition of the Dependent Variable

Our analyses use information on the timing of ethnic and racial conflicts in large American cities in two discrete periods of peak immigration. We have collected data on protest and conflict for all race or ethnic groups in both periods. For theoretical reasons, we highlight conflict against nonwhites throughout our analysis. The dependent variable is the rate, calculated using the duration between instances of conflict against nonwhite groups. In order to reflect common definitions of American minority groups, we include all events that suggest that African Americans, Asian Americans, or Latinos were targets. We analyze piecewise exponential models of the hazard rate in two periods: 1869–1924 and 1965–1993. (For explanations of event-history techniques, see Blossfeld and Rohwer 1995; Tuma and Hannan 1984.)

Urban America as the Unit of Analysis

Our study focuses on the largest seventy-six urban settings. We focus on urban settings for four reasons. First, ethnic and racial collective action requires the presence of some level of ethnic and racial diversity as well as some minimum population size (Tilly 1978). Second, because we rely on the *New York Times* as a continuous source of information on events, we require observations on a set of locations that receive at least some media attention over this period. This decision was based on evidence that newspaper coverage declines with a city's population size, density, and distance from the event (Barranco and Wisler 1999; McCarthy et al. 1996; Myers 2001; Myers and Caniglia 2000; Oliver and Myers 1999). Furthermore, rural areas are sorely underrepresented in news reports, and their inclusion as observational units might introduce bias. Third, city-level analyses require observations on discrete locations where information on occupational segregation, population composition, literacy, and so on can be traced back to 1865 and then forward in time. Fourth, because most immigrants have traditionally entered the United States through major urban centers, we can best capture the impact of immigration by examining urban settings (Cafferty et al. 1983).

Thus, by intention, we have chosen locations that were not necessarily settings of historical interest characterized by racial unrest or immigrant hostility. Rather, our sample is based on our knowledge that newspaper accounts are most likely to be unbiased in urban settings with large population sizes. In other words, we have avoided choosing a sample on the basis of some level of the dependent variable (as many case study accounts have done). Our concern is less to identify "hotbeds" of racial or ethnic conflict than to understand how racial boundaries emerge, change, and become contentious over time and space. Thus, places where racial boundaries are not the source of tension are as interesting to us as those where they are.

We recognize, however, that our emphasis on cities that were large at the turn of the twentieth century has certain limitations. This is, of course, particularly true of the South, where urban development has lagged significantly behind other regions. In particular, rural racial violence has an important history, which is a crucial part of any comprehensive understanding of U.S. race relations (Soule 1992; Tolnay and Beck 1995).

Modeling Technique

We employ a standard event-history modeling technique to estimate the effects of our two key variables, immigration and ethnic diversity, on a rate of conflict against nonwhites.[13] The dependent variable is the rate of collective conflict, defined as the duration between conflict events. In commonsense terms, this means that a year in which many events occur has a high rate of conflict. Conversely, the fact that many days have passed without any conflict events indicates a relatively low rate of conflict. Our task is to see whether immigration and ethnic diversity coincide with high rates of conflict when other measures are included in the model. These measures include economic fluctuation, wages, and other indicators suggested in prior research on collective violence. This technique allows us to estimate the effects of independent variables, net of other variables in the model. In other words, we hypothesize that immigration and diversity are systematically associated with the pace of attacks on nonwhites even when other possible influences are taken into account in the same model.

Immigration and Ethnic Diversity

Immigration statistics (including the composition and percentage annual change in immigration) and the timing of immigration laws are drawn from *Historical Statistics of the United States: Colonial Times to 1970* (U.S. Bureau of the Census 1975) and the annual volumes of the *Immigration Statistical Yearbook*. We also include the annual number of incoming immigrants who listed their occupations as laborers or unskilled workers. In this way, we hope to test arguments about the effects of immigration flows and split labor markets.

In each model, we also employ a measure of immigrant diversity where the immigrant population is divided according to country of origin. Our measure of diversity is the probability that randomly paired individuals in the population, k, will be different on a specified characteristic. A high level of this index indicates that immigrants were ethnically more heterogeneous, while a low level indicates relative homogeneity in the country of origin. Data to calculate this index are drawn from *Historical Statistics of the United States: Colonial Times* to *1970* and the annual volumes of the *Immigration Statistical Yearbook*.[14] Our argument rests on evidence that will show whether immigration and ethnic diversity are systematically related to periods of peak conflict directed against the nonwhite population in urban America.

Results

In a series of descriptive tables and figures,[15] we demonstrate changes in the timing and location of racial and ethnic unrest across more than a century. Moreover, we illustrate how the form and participants of collective action also change. Finally, we present the effects of our two key variables, immigration and ethnic diversity, on the rate of ethnic conflict against nonwhites.

Figures 3.1 and 3.2 compare the trends in immigration and conflict in each of our two periods. They provide a breakdown of all racial and ethnic collective conflict and immigration flow by year. The figures demonstrate the irregular flow of immigrants to the United States and the two important moments of mass migration. They also highlight variation in racial or ethnic conflict over this entire period.

The early period (see fig. 3.1), has three peaks of extensive conflict: in the early 1880s, in 1905, and then again in 1913. Each of these historical periods was a time of intense public and governmental debate over immigration and immigration policy. These peak periods were dominated by anti-Chinese and anti-black conflicts, respectively. In the later period (see fig. 3.2), ethnic conflict shows similar peaks and valleys. However, in the second period, the major trend shows that there was a gradual decline in conflict at the same time that immigration increased over the observed twenty-eight-year period.

Taken together, these figures tell an interesting historical story. They suggest that the temporal relationship between immigration and racial conflict is not straightforward. In the first wave of mass migration at the turn of the century, increases in immigrant flows parallel increases in racial and ethnic collective conflict. And yet, in the more recent era, we see a marked increase in immigration associated with a marked decline in conflict.

For some clues to understanding these patterns, we now turn to the identifiable characteristics of our data on ethnic events. Table 3.1 identifies the region of all the 209 collective events occurring in seventy-six large American cities between 1869 and 1924 and some 597 collective conflicts occurring in the same set of cities between 1965 and 1993. This table allows a comparison of regional and temporal patterns of events involving any race or ethnic group, including conflicts among minority groups. First, there are big differences in the scale of racial and ethnic collective mobilization between these two periods, with the second period experiencing twice as many conflicts as the first period (despite the fact that the first period is almost twice as long in years). It should not be surprising, given our data source and given its population size, that the Northeast (and, in particular, New York) was the most common site of collective action.[16] In the first period, almost half all events occurred in

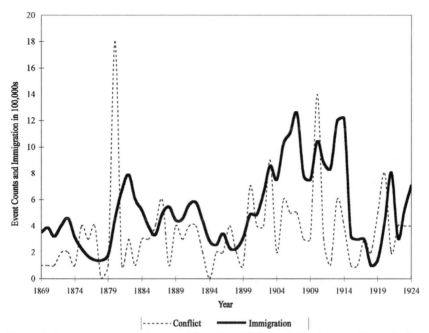

Figure 3.1. Immigration Flows and Racial and Ethnic Collective Conflict in Major American Cities, 1869–1924.

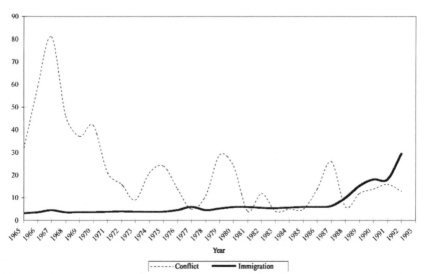

Figure 3.2. Immigration Flows and Racial and Ethnic Collective Conflict in Major American Cities, 1965–1993.

major cities of the Northeast, including Boston, Philadelphia, New York, and Washington, D.C. In the second period, almost 60 percent of all conflicts occurred within this same region. In the early period, between 1869 and 1924, we see an almost equal distribution of conflict across the other regions: the South with 16 percent, the West with 18 percent, and the Midwest with 17 percent. In the second period, however, we see a key set of regional shifts. The percentage of conflict increases in the Midwest (from 17 to 22 percent), but it drops off sharply in the West (from 18 to 6 percent of all conflicts). We see how the location of all conflicts shifted away from the West and toward both the Midwest and the Northeast. The Northeast, however, remained a key region for mobilization in both periods.

Table 3.2 identifies a subset of conflicts that involved those groups most likely to participate in racial and ethnic collective mobilization. We focus on four groups: blacks, Asians, Latinos, and Jews. Table 3.2 excludes those categories of events that involved white ethnic groups (in interethnic conflicts involving two or more groups) and/or events in which the majority white groups were targets of conflict. These residual categories of events were 11 percent of the total number of conflicts in 1869–1924, and they were 4.5 percent of the conflicts in 1965–1993. In other words, these events involved specific interethnic conflicts (e.g., Irish vs. Italian conflicts), or they involved attacks on the white majority group by some other aggrieved population.

In each period, the greatest majority of events (67 and 78 percent, respectively) involved persons of African American descent. Thus, while more than two-thirds of all collective conflicts involved blacks in the early period, more than three-fourths of all collective conflicts involved blacks in this latter era. We see a continuation of earlier findings here that

Table 3.2. Types of Ethnic and Racial Collective Conflict, 1869–1924 and 1965–1993

	Period 1 (1869–1924)	Period 2 (1965–1993)
Events involving blacks	139 events/67%	463 events/78%
Events involving Asians	45/21%	6/1%
Events involving Latinos	0/0%	43/7%
Events involving Jews	2/1%	58/9.7%
Total events with these minority groups	186/89%	570/95.5%
Events involving any race/ethnic group	209/100%	597/100%

suggests that despite the increasing diversity of immigration flows, blacks are increasingly likely to be targets of conflict.

The most dramatic change is in the number of events involving the Asian population. While events involving Asian, often anti-Chinese in orientation, constituted some 21 percent of all events in the early period, such events accounted for less than 1 percent in the latter period. This finding is striking given that Asian immigrants benefited most from the 1965 Immigration Act and the abolition of national origin quotas. Throughout this later period, there is considerable immigration from Asia, and yet there seems to be much less opposition to such immigration than a century earlier. We know, however, that this does not mean that Asians are free from ethnic hostilities since there has been evidence of substantial property damage of Asian establishments (e.g., in the Los Angeles riot of 1992), as well as other forms of anti-Asian hostility (Bergesen and Herman 1998). One way to interpret the relative decline in anti-Asian collective violence is to frame it in the context of immigrant adaptation and upward mobility. That is, Loewen's (1988) research on the Chinese in Mississippi suggests that hostilities against the Chinese in the South have largely disappeared as Chinese assimilated to the white caste boundary. If this argument can be generalized, we might expect to see a continuing decline in collective expressions of anti-Asian sentiment.

In contrast to events with Asian targets, there have been other changes in the groups involved in conflict. The proportion of collective events involving Jews increases in the latter period, rising from 1 percent to almost 10 percent. Furthermore, there is an increase in the number of events involving Latinos. However, these anti-Latino events still account for little of the total collective action, that is, around 7 percent of all collective conflicts. Finally, we see that the number of events involving one or more of these groups (Asians, blacks, Latinos, or Jews) increases distinctly in the second period. Between 1965 and 1993, 95.5 percent of all collective conflicts involve one of these minority populations. That is, we see far more conflicts involving one of these groups in the second period as compared to the first period.

In table 3.3, we examine various characteristics of racial and ethnic conflict across these two periods, including the size of events, the level of violence, and the degree of organization. While both the size and the organization of events are quite similar in the two periods, we see that col-

Table 3.3 Characteristics of Collective Conflict, 1869–1924 and 1965–1993

	Period 1 Collective Conflict	Period 2 Collective Conflict
Percent of events with more than 50 participants	63	59
Percent of violent events (weapons, physical harm, instigated by participants)	54	97
Percent of events with organizations present at event	24	21

lective conflicts in the latter period are much more violent. Over the past hundred years, the availability of weapons and the escalation of conflict may have contributed to this rise in violence. Indeed, 97 percent of all such conflicts in the 1965–1993 era involve some degree of violence as compared with only 54 percent in the earlier period.

Table 3.3 also addresses claims that ethnic conflict may mobilize more participants and that these participants may be more likely to be involved in specific ethnic or racial organizations (such as named ethnic movements or hate groups). Neither of these conventional assumptions finds support in this table.

The competition theory arguments outlined here suggest that the size and diversity of immigration would produce peaks in ethnic conflict, particularly conflict directed against nonwhites. How does our competition argument fare? As expected, table 3.4 shows that periods of peak ethnic immigration around the turn of the twentieth century produced waves of conflict against nonwhites in urban America. However, for the second period, there is no systematic effect of the annual change in immigration. Indeed, the coefficient for the effect of immigration is negative for the 1965–1993 period, but it is not statistically significant. How should we interpret these results?

One obvious explanation is that conflict involving nonwhites reflects different patterns in the two historical periods. Evidently, both immigration and its diversity affected ethnic tensions around the turn of the century. In contrast, in the latter period, ethnic diversity had this same effect on racial conflict. This suggests that while immigration and ethnic diversity increased the salience of a white/nonwhite boundary during the first period, only diversity has an enduring effect on this pattern in the second period.

We explore a more specific version of our immigration-conflict hypothesis in table 3.5. Following the literature on split labor markets, we

Table 3.4. Impact of Immigration and Diversity on Rate of Conflict against Nonwhites in Two Periods: 1869–1924 and 1965–1993

	First Period 1869–1924		Second Period 1965–1993	
Annual change in immigration (t-1) (percent multiplied by 100)	0.072**	(0.042)	0.001	(0.002)
Annual index of ethnic diversity	0.87**	(0.45)	0.66***	(.040)

*p<.05; **p<.01; ***p.001 (one-tailed tests for directional hypotheses—see text)
Note: Estimates are from Piecewise Exponential Models. Full models include annual measures of wages of laborers, economic fluctuation, timing of Immigration Acts, lagged number of conflicts against non-whites, and size of unskilled immigration flow.

Table 3.5. Impact of Unskilled Immigrants and Diversity on Rate of Conflict Against Nonwhites in Two Periods: 1869–1924 and 1965–1993

	First Period 1869-1924		Second Period 1965-1993	
Annual number of unskilled immigrants (in 100,000s)	8.57***	(3.01)	−0.030***	(0.010)
Annual index of ethnic diversity	1.24***	(0.60)	1.24***	(0.45)

*p<.05; **p<.01; ***p.001 (one-tailed tests for directional hypotheses—see text)
Note: Estimates are from Piecewise Exponential Models. Full models include annual measures of wages of laborers, economic fluctuation, timing of Immigration Acts, and lagged number of conflicts against non-whites, and the annual percentage change in immigration.

present another specification of this immigration effect. Table 3.5 specifies the effect of the annual variation in one specific group of immigrants: unskilled immigrants. Recall that earlier we hypothesized that unskilled labor might affect competition levels within the low-skilled niche. Does this effect of immigration hold up under scrutiny in both periods?

The split labor market argument finds support only in the early period: An increase in unskilled immigrants sharply increases the rate of conflicts against nonwhites. For the second period, the picture changes. In the second and more recent period, the effect of unskilled labor is actually negative and significant. This result suggests that immigration of unskilled workers actually reduces conflict. How can this be the case? To understand this result, we remind readers that while immigration policies during the 1965–1993 period were quite open, they sharply restricted the numbers of incoming immigrants who were unskilled. Thus, these effects represent only a very small proportion of all immigrants during this period. In addition, we suspect that immigration had a different relationship with business cycles in the latter period when compared to the first period. Taken together, the results that appear in tables 3.4 and 3.5 imply that immigration had sharply divergent effects in the two periods.

Recall that the cornerstone of our competition argument concerned the impact of ethnic diversity. We argued that during periods in which many diverse groups made up the flow of immigrants, a process of competition reinforced the consolidation of ethnic boundaries along race lines. We suggested that if this argument were true, ethnic diversity would be positively associated with periods experiencing a high number of attacks on nonwhites. In response to rising competition, native-born and immigrant whites mobilized against blacks and other nonwhites. The result would be that a racial caste line became increasingly entrenched. We further argued that this relationship might also explain the rising xenophobia and antiblack conflict that continues to this day in the United States. By this argument, we expected to see periods of high diversity associated with peak periods of conflict involving nonwhites.

As can be seen in both tables, ethnic diversity has a strikingly similar and positive effect on the rate of conflict against nonwhites, and this holds up across both historical periods. Taken together, the effect of ethnic diversity has a strong, consistent, and statistically significant effect on the rate of conflict that holds up under both periods and under a number of different model specifications. Thus, our ethnic diversity argument holds up under a variety of assumptions and conditions, lending credibility to our competition argument that the composition of immigration flows matters.

Discussion

This chapter began with a central question presented by American history: What is the relationship between immigration and racial and ethnic unrest? We found that it is not immigration per se but rather the ethnic diversity of immigration flows that raised rates of conflict around the turn of the twentieth and twenty-first centuries in America. Furthermore, we see evidence for a process of racial consolidation that is systematically related to rising ethnic diversity in America. Our results suggest that the enduring nature of racial animosity can be at least partly explained in terms of a racial consolidation process that began in the early twentieth century and continues to this day.

To this end, we compared patterns of racial and ethnic collective conflict in the United States during two key waves of mass immigration: 1869–1924 and 1965–1993. Building on competitive perspectives of ethnic relations, we have offered an account of the dynamics of collective conflict that emphasizes the historic institutionalization of the white/nonwhite boundary in American history. The results suggest that factors that raise the overall level of competition among increasingly diverse groups result in a rising salience of one particular boundary: that between whites and nonwhites. While this observation is not new, we find corroborating evidence for the idea that the sheer diversity of immigrants created the possibility for an enlarged definition of white ethnicity. On one side, there was a growing urban population of whites who were foreign born and who quickly learned that they would benefit to the extent that they emphasized the set of ethnic markers that assured them membership in a higher-status community. We speculated that membership inside this boundary was reinforced by participation in collective attacks on nonwhites. If ethnic boundaries are a function of normative activities sanctioned by both insider and outsider groups, then we suspect that these collective attacks on outsider groups help sharpen the boundary distinctions.

We suggested the possibility that a causal link exists between ethnic diversity and racial duality. Previous research has emphasized only the effects of immigration flows, but we argued that the diversity of immigrants also raised the salience of the white/nonwhite boundary at the turn of the century. Our results justify this new argument because our models take both immigration and diversity (and other measures) into account at the same time. That is, when all factors are considered, ethnic diversity shows the strongest and most consistent effects across a hundred years of American history.

Why would *ethnic* diversity encourage *racial* conflict? Our answer suggests that immigration raises rates of racial violence because that competition increases the salience of both race and ethnic boundaries. During periods in which highly diverse groups arrived in the United States, race and ethnic boundaries become more salient to all forms of interaction. Questions (and political debates) about who is and who is not "American" become more numerous and more contentious. We have recounted some of the more colorful language of the congressional debates. Often these debates spilled over into the street, as mobs attacked those who were perceived as "others" and thus perhaps "not deserving of citizenship." As a result, we find that ethnic diversity encouraged a resurgence of race and ethnic identity in both periods of peak immigration to the United States.

In cases that have been well documented by historians and sociologists, economic advantages and class mobility proved to be a strong incentive for many immigrant groups to take on new identities (Bodnar et al. 1982). At the turn of the twentieth century, the advantages of white identity were substantial, and they remain so today. Many poor immigrants who entered the United States at the turn of the century had few skills, little education, and even less money. As noted previously, it was not a forgone conclusion that these various groups would integrate easily, becoming a larger, white melting pot of immigrant America. Only by active identification, competition, and mobilization along the advantaged side of the white/nonwhite boundary would immigrants secure a foothold in American society during this period. Seen from the current vantage point, the reason for these choices seems obvious. On one side, it was a growing urban population of white foreign born who emphasized the set of ethnic markers that assured them higher status, employment, and access to other rewards. On the other side, it was a historically outcast population that was burdened with a legacy of slavery and forced migration.

Are we destined to live with racial conflict in America? We wonder whether DuBois (1969) was correct in claiming that "the problem of the twentieth century is the problem of the color-line—the relation of the darker to the lighter races of men in Asia and Africa, in America and the islands of the sea." Put differently, our research tried to find some answers to questions about why race seems to be such an enduring feature of our contemporary American society. In this chapter, we tested several arguments that suggest that the social mechanisms maintaining this boundary are fundamentally related to the ebb and flow of immigration and its composition.

We speculate here that collective attacks on nonwhite "others" served to reinforce the racial boundary (over the ethnic one) even further. Once consolidated, this boundary created an indelible fault line, fostering an enduring social logic and organizational form for twentieth-century ethnic and racial collective action. Thus, despite the "changing face" of recent immigration, patterns of racial discrimination, epithets, and stereotypes that were established decades before are still potent. Even as the nature of immigration changes in the contemporary era—as immigrants with different racial and ethnic backgrounds, better educational qualifications, higher occupational aspirations, and ready-made social and economic network ties migrate—institutionalized patterns of race relations remain in place. Thus, as we continue to experience immigration flows that appear unprecedented and diverse, we might reasonably expect the white/nonwhite boundary to remain a source of considerable conflict in urban America.[17]

And while the color line that DuBois so articulately lamented may well have characterized much of the twentieth century, what our research also illustrates is that neither the biracial caste system nor the violence that we have come to associate with it is inevitable. Racial and ethnic conflicts certainly do appear ubiquitous. But the fact that racial boundaries are social constructs is often ignored in discussions that lament the intractability of racial or ethnic hatred. As the history of white ethnic immigrants in the United States suggests, race and ethnic boundaries are less related to the so-called physical features than they are to dimensions of status, power, and hierarchy. If ethnic boundaries, such as the white "Caucasian" identity, can expand to include a wide variety of new nationalities as we have argued, then ethnic boundaries are more fluid than we have realized. This means that those cultural attributes that become associated with a given race/ethnic boundary can change. Indeed, there is mounting evidence that even this white/nonwhite boundary may be gradually eroding. Multiculturalism may be undermining the rigidity of this white/nonwhite caste line (Gans 1999; Hollinger 1994). Gans speculates that a new black/nonblack distinction has emerged in which the category "nonblack" is shared by most immigrants (except those from the Caribbean or Africa). In addition, recent research on immigrant adaptation, intermarriage, and mobility prompts us to reevaluate previous melting pot and queuing theories about the nature of ethnic categories (Alba and Nee 1997; Foner et al. 2000; Min 1999; Perlmann and Waldinger 1997; Waldinger 1996). If this is the case, then ethnic mobilization and violence based on the color line is not an inevitable feature of our society.

Conclusion and Suggestions for Future Research

We conclude by considering the generalizability of our findings. Are immigration and racial conflict related—as we find they are in moments of peak migration in the United States—elsewhere? Are these processes relevant to other settings and other time periods? Can ethnic problems in Kosovo, Rwanda, or Northern Ireland be attributed to similar shifts in population composition and competition? Did similar processes of racial consolidation occur in other settings as immigrants settled in such countries as South Africa or India? We believe that there are many advantages to investigating these questions using comparative data. Studies of ethnicity in a comparative context can identify the structural components that are shared across a number of settings and time periods. Another benefit of a comparative approach is that the assumption that ethnic conflict is a constant can be held up to scrutiny as well. In a comparative design, questions about the variation in the pace of conflict can be directly examined.

Only future research can adequately address the previously raised questions. However, we think that our results have several implications for the study of ethnic relations in other settings and historical periods. Our general argument is flexible in that it can be tested using longitudinal data on immigration flows and ethnic diversity. Moreover, our method of collecting data on ethnic conflict can be easily transplanted to other settings and can be used to study other forms of ethnic conflict.

The timing seems ripe for serious and systematic analyses of ethnic conflict across many settings. Indeed, the anti-foreigner attacks in northern and eastern Europe, the pogroms against refugees, and the ethnic cleansing attacks that occurred during the 1990s seem to be rising at an alarming rate. While the issue of ethnic conflict is a global concern, there has been relatively little systematic comparison of the sources of ethnic conflict. This is all the more surprising given the explosion in international migration and immigration flows, creating diasporas, irredentist groups, and separatist movements in many settings. In 1993, the annual *State of the World's Population* (United Nations 1993: 6) warned that "the scale and diversity of today's migration are beyond any previous experience. Responses to the questions they raise will help to determine the course of the 21st century." Thus, the question that remains unanswered is the extent to which changes in immigration and citizenship policy might impact this century-long pattern. How might proposals for changes in immigration law either reinforce or dilute what appears to be a fairly indelible boundary? This question is likely to haunt U.S. policymakers for some time.

Notes

1. We offer a very specific definition and operationalization of racial collective conflict. We define *racial collective conflict* as public attacks on persons identified by the majority (white) population by some set of ethnic markers. These markers include skin pigmentation, nationality, linguistic distinctions, and other cultural features (Barth 1969; Cornell and Hartmann 1998). In particular, we concentrate on the emergence and persistence of conflict directed at European, Asian, and Latino immigrants and African Americans by majority whites. Examples of conflicts include riots, vandalism, lynchings, and other forms of racial or ethnic attack. We do not include interpersonal disputes, such as muggings or murders.

2. See, for example, Cortner (1988), Hollandsworth (2001), Horne (1995), Porter (1984), Rudwick (1964), Senechal (1990), White (1943), and Wyllie (1954).

3. In contrast, Omi and Winant (1986) argue that racial formation emerged during the 1960s in the United States.

4. Senator Williams, *Congressional Record*, 52, daily ed. (December 13, 1914): 806.

5. Congressman Box, *Congressional Record*, 60, no. 1, daily ed. (December 9, 1920): 173–174.

6. Frances Kellor, cited in Higham (1988), 234.

7. Space limitations do not permit an adequate review of this topic. For an expanded treatment and evidence from archival sources, see Suzanne Shanahan, "The Taming of Difference: A Comparative History of Identity" (Ph.D. diss., Stanford University, 1997).

8. Congressman Celler, *Congressional Record*, 111, no. 16, daily ed. (1965): 21579.

9. Reprinted from a *New York Times* article published March 1, 1924, cited in the *Congressional Record*, 111, no. 18, daily ed. (1965): 24552.

10. United States, Harris Survey, cited in the *Congressional Record*, 111, no. 18, daily ed. (1965): 24447.

11. Senator McClellan, cited in the *Congressional Record*, 111, no. 18, daily ed. (1965): 24554.

12. For examples, see Kriesi et al. (1995), McAdam (1982), Tarrow (1989), and Tilly (1978).

13. We have employed a linear piecewise exponential model to attain our results. For explanations of event-history techniques, see Tuma and Hannan (1984) and Blossfeld and Rohwer (1995). For an example of using linear piecewise exponential models, see Olzak et al. (1994).

14. This index of immigration diversity is specified by an index, A_w, calculated following Lieberson (1969), summed over n, which is defined as the number of k ethnic groups in the population:

$$A_w = 1 - \sum_{k=1}^{k} n_k^2$$

15. Note that while there appear to be clear differences in the type and amount of racial collective action in each period, both population growth and changes in newspaper coverage may account for some of this variation. That is, larger urban populations may create more opportunities for more people to engage in collective action. Furthermore, the growth in the sheer number of collective events may be attributed to shifts in newspaper reporting due to a general societal increase in sensitivity toward racial and ethnic violence.

16. Did the location of the *New York Times* bias our findings in any way? One way to answer that question is to compare results in samples that include and exclude New York City and New Jersey urban areas to see whether immigration and diversity had the same effect in cities outside the metropolitan area. Our analysis of non–New York events showed no differences with respect to our key explanatory process of immigration and ethnic diversity.

17. For three recent arguments that see the possibility of a new racial configuration in U.S. society, see Alba and Nee (1997), Gans (1999), and Hollinger (1995).

References

Alba, Richard D. 1985. *Italian Americans: Into the Twilight of Ethnicity.* New York: Prentice Hall.

———. 1990. *Ethnic Identity: The Transformation of White America.* New Haven, CT: Yale University Press.

Alba, Richard D., and Victor Nee. 1997. "Rethinking Assimilation Theory for a New Era of Immigration." *International Migration Review* 31: 826–974.

Allen, Theodore. 1994. *Invention of the White Race.* New York: Verso.

Barranco, José, and Dominique Wisler. 1999. "Validity and Systematicity of Newspaper Data in Event Analysis." *European Sociological Review* 15: 301–322.

Barth, Fredrik. 1969. *Ethnic Groups and Boundaries.* New York: Little, Brown.

Bennett, David H. 1988. *The Party of Fear: From Nativist Movements to the New Right in American History.* Chapel Hill: University of North Carolina Press.

Bergesen, Albert, and Max Herman. 1998. "Immigration, Race, and Riot: The 1992 Los Angeles Uprising." *American Sociological Review* 63: 39–54.

Bernard, William S. 1997. "Immigration: History of U.S. Policy." In *The Immigration Reader*, edited by David Jacobson. New York: Blackwell.

Blalock, Hubert M., Jr. 1967. *Toward a Theory of Minority-Group Relations*. New York: John Wiley & Sons.

Blossfeld, Hanspeter, and Goertz Rohwer. 1995. *Techniques of Event History Modeling*. Mahwah, NJ: Lawrence Erlbaum Associates.

Bodnar, John. 1985. *The Transplanted: A History of Immigrants in Urban America*. Bloomington: University of Indiana Press.

Bodnar, John, Roger Simon, and Michael P. Weber. 1982. *Lives of Their Own: Blacks, Italians and Poles in Pittsburgh, 1900–1960*. Urbana: University of Illinois Press.

Bonacich, Edna. 1972. "A Theory of Ethnic Antagonism: The Split Labor Market." *American Sociological Review* 37: 547–559.

Boswell, Terry. 1986. "A Split Labor Market Analysis of Discrimination against Chinese Immigrants, 1850–1882." *American Sociological Review* 51: 352–371.

Cafferty, Pastora San Juan, Barry R. Chiswick, Andrew M. Greeley, and Teresa Sullivan. 1983. *The Dilemma of American Immigration: Beyond the Golden Door*. New Brunswick, NJ: Transaction Books.

Cornell, Steven, and Douglas Hartmann. 1998. *Ethnicity and Race: Making Identities in a Changing World*. Thousand Oaks, CA: Pine Forge Press.

Cortner, Richard C. 1988. *A Mob Intent on Death: The NAACP and the Arkansas Riot*. Middletown, CT: Wesleyan University Press.

Cose, Edward. 1992. *A Nation of Strangers*. New York: William Morrow.

DuBois, W. E. B. 1969. *The Souls of Black Folk*. New York: Signet.

Farley, Reynolds, and William Allen. 1987. *The Color Line in America*. New York: Russell Sage Foundation.

Foner, Nancy, Ruben G. Rumbaut, and Steven J. Gold, eds. 2000. *Immigration Research for a New Century*. New York: Russell Sage Foundation.

Foner, Philip S. 1974. *Organized Labor and the Black Worker*. New York: Praeger.

Fong, Eric, and William T. Markham. 1991. "Immigration, Ethnicity and Conflict: The California Chinese, 1849–1882." *Sociological Inquiry* 61: 471–490.

Fredrickson, George M. 1988. *The Arrogance of Race: Historical Perspectives on Slavery, Racism, and Social Inequality*. Middletown, CT: Wesleyan University Press.

Gans, Herbert J. 1999. "The Possibility of a New Racial Hierarchy in the Twenty-First Century United States." In *The Cultural Territories of Race: Black and White Boundaries*, edited by Miechelle Lamont. Chicago: University of Chicago Press.

Green, Donald P., Dara Z. Strolovitch, and Janelle S. Wong. 1998. "Defended Neighborhoods, Integration and Racially Motivated Crime." *American Journal of Sociology* 104: 372–403.

Hannan, Michael T. 1979. "The Dynamics of Ethnic Boundaries." In *National Development and the World System*, edited by John W. Meyer and Michael T. Hannan. Chicago: University of Chicago Press.

Hannan, Michael T., and John Freeman. 1988. "The Ecology of Organizational Mortality: American Labor Unions, 1836–1985. *American Journal of Sociology* 94: 25–52.

Higham, John. 1988. *Strangers in the Land: Patterns of American Nativism: 1860–1925.* 2nd ed. New Brunswick, NJ: Rutgers University Press.

Hollandsworth, James G. 2001. *An Absolute Massacre: The New Orleans Race Riot of July 30, 1866.* Baton Rouge: Louisiana State University Press.

Hollinger, David A. 1995. *Postethnic America.* New York: Basic Books.

Horne, Gerald. 1995. *Fire This Time: The Watts Uprising and the 1960's.* Charlottesville: University Press of Virginia.

Ignatiev, Noel. 1995. *How the Irish Became White.* New York: Routledge.

Jacobson, Matthew Frye. 1998. *Whiteness of a Different Color: European Immigrants and the Alchemy of Race.* Cambridge, MA: Harvard University Press.

Jenkins, J. Craig. 1983. "Resource Mobilization Theory and the Study of Social Movements." *Annual Review of Sociology* 9: 527–553.

Jordan, Winthrop D. 1968. *White over Black.* New York: W. W. Norton.

Kriesi, Hanspeter, Ruud Koopmans, Jan Willem Duyvendak, and Marco Guigni, eds. 1995. *New Social Movements in Western Europe: A Comparative Analysis.* Minneapolis: University of Minnesota Press.

LeMay, Michael C. 1987. *From Open Door to Dutch Door: An Analysis of U.S. Immigration Policy since 1820.* New York: Praeger.

Lieberson, Stanley. 1969. "Measuring Population Diversity." *American Sociological Review* 34: 850-862.

———. 1980. *A Piece of the Pie: Blacks and White Immigrants since 1881* Berkeley and Los Angeles: University of California Press.

Loewen, James W. 1988. *The Mississippi Chinese: Between Black and White.* Prospect Heights, IL: Waveland Press.

Martin, Phillip L. 1994. "The United States: Benign Neglect toward Immigration." In Wayne A. Cornelius, Philip L. Martin, and James F. Hollifield, eds., *Controlling Immigration: A Global Perspective.* Stanford, CA: Stanford University Press.

Marx, Anthony W. 1998. *Making Race and Nation.* New York: Cambridge University Press.

McAdam, Doug. 1982. *Political Process and the Development of Black Insurgency.* Chicago: University of Chicago Press.

McCarthy, John D., Clark McPhail, and Jackie Smith. 1996. "Images of Protest: Estimating Selection Bias in Media Coverage of Washington Demonstrations 1982 and 1991." *American Sociological Review* 61: 478–499.

Min, Pyong Gap. 1999. "A Comparison of Post-1965 and Turn-of-the Century Immigrants in Intergenerational Mobility and Cultural Transmission." *Journal of American Ethnic History* 18: 65–94.

Mink, Gwendolyn. 1986. *Old Labor and New Immigrants in American Political Development.* Ithaca, NY: Cornell University Press.

Model, Suzanne. 1988. "Italian and Jewish Intergenerational Mobility in 1910 New York." *Social Science History* 12: 31–48.

———. 1993. "The Economic Progress of Europeans and East Asian Americans." *Annual Review of Sociology* 14: 363–380.

Myers, Daniel. 1997. "Racial Rioting in the 1960s: An Event History Analysis of Local Conditions." *American Sociological Review* 62: 94–112.

———. 2001. " City Conditions and Riot Susceptibility Reconsidered." Paper presented at the annual meeting of the American Sociological Association, Anaheim, CA, August 18–21.

Myers, Daniel, and Beth Schafer Caniglia. 2000. "Selection Bias in National Newspaper Coverage of Civil Disorders, 1968–1969." Paper presented at the annual meeting of the American Sociological Association, Washington, DC, August 12–16.

Oliver, Pamela E., and Gregory Maney. 2000. "Political Processes and Local Newspaper Coverage of Protest Events: From Selection Bias to Triadic Interactions." *American Journal of Sociology* 106: 463–505.

Oliver, Pamela E., and Daniel J. Myers. 1999. "How Events Enter the Public Sphere: Conflict, Location, and Sponsorship in Local Newspaper Coverage of Public Events." *American Journal of Sociology* 105: 38–87.

Olzak, Susan. 1989. "The Changing Job Queue: Cases of Shifts in Ethnic Job Segregation in American Cities, 1870–1880." *Social Forces* 63: 996–1009.

———. 1992. *The Dynamics of Ethnic Competition and Conflict.* Stanford, CA: Stanford University Press.

Olzak, Susan, Suzanne Shanahan, and Elizabeth H. McEneaney. 1996. "Poverty Segregation, and Race Riots, 1960–1993." *American Sociological Review* 61: 590–613.

Olzak, Susan, Suzanne Shanahan, and Elizabeth West. 1994. "Antibusing Activity in Contemporary America." *American Journal of Sociology* 100: 196–241.

Omi, Michael, and Howard Winant. 1986. *Racial Formation in the United States.* New York: Routledge.

Perlmann, Joel, and Roger Waldinger. 1997. "Second Generation Decline? Children of Immigrants, Past and Present—A Reconsideration." *International Migration Review* 32: 893–922.

Porter, Bruce D. 1984. *The Miami Riot of 1980: Crossing the Bounds.* Lexington, MA: Lexington Books.

Reimers, David M. 1998. *Unwelcome Strangers : American Identity and the Turn against Immigration.* New York: Columbia University Press.

Roediger, David. 1991. *The Wages of Whiteness.* London: Verso.

Rudwick, Elliot M. *Race Riot at East St. Louis, July 2, 1917.* Carbondale: Southern Illinois University Press.

Saxton, Alexander. 1990. *Rise and Fall of the White Republic.* New York: Verso.

Senechal, Roberta. 1990. *The Sociogenesis of a Race Riot.* Urbana: University of Illinois Press.

Smedley, Audrey. 1993. *Race in North America: Origin and Evolution of a Worldview.* San Francisco: Westview Press.

Soule, Sarah. 1992. "Populism and Black Lynching in Georgia, 1890–1900." *Social Forces* 71: 431–449.

Sugrue, Thomas. 1996. *The Origins of the Urban Crisis.* Princeton, NJ: Princeton University Press.

Takaki, Ronald. 1989. *Strangers from a Different Shore.* New York: Penguin Books.

Tilly, Charles. 1978. *From Mobilization to Revolution.* New York: Random House.

Tolnay, Stewart, and E. M. Beck. 1995. *A Festival of Violence.* Urbana: University of Illinois Press.

Tuma, Nancy Brandon, and Michael T. Hannan. 1984. *Social Dynamics, Models and Methods.* New York: Academic Press.

United Nations. 1993. *State of the World's Population.* New York: United Nations.

U.S. Bureau of the Census. 1975. *Historical Statistics of the United States: Colonial Times to 1970.* Washington, DC: U.S. Government Printing Office.

Waldinger, Roger. 1996. *Still the Promised City? African-Americans and New Immigrants in Postindustrial New York.* Cambridge, MA: Harvard University Press.

White, Walter Francis. 1943. *What Caused the Detroit Riot: An Analysis.* New York: National Association for the Advancement of Colored People.

Wilson, William J. 1978. *The Declining Significance of Race.* Chicago: University of Chicago Press.

Woodward, C. Vann. 1964. *The Strange Career of Jim Crow.* Chapel Hill: University of North Carolina Press.

Wyllie, John. 1954. *Riot.* New York: London, Secker and Warburg.

CHAPTER FOUR

CONTEMPORARY IMMIGRANTS' ADVANTAGES FOR INTERGENERATIONAL CULTURAL TRANSMISSION
Pyong Gap Min

I n order to compare the adaptations of descendants of contemporary and turn-of-the-twentieth-century immigrants systematically, we need to examine the differences in 1) patterns of ethnicity, 2) patterns of social mobility, and 3) the relationship between ethnicity and social mobility. Recent theoretical discussions of adaptation patterns of the new second generation have focused on comparing the two waves of immigrants in intergenerational mobility and the importance of ethnicity for school performance and social mobility (Gans 1992; Gibson 1988; Portes 1996; Portes and Zhou 1993; Zhou and Bankston 1998). Researchers have neglected to compare the two waves of immigrants in ethnic retention itself.

This does not mean that no scholar has paid attention to the issue of contemporary immigrants' cultural transmission to their descendants. Several scholars have suggested that the descendants of contemporary immigrants are likely to generally follow those of turn-of-the-century immigrants in losing their cultural traditions over generations (Alba 1999; Alba and Nee 1997; Barkan 1995; Gans 1997, 1999).[1] Only Douglas Massey, to my knowledge, has indicated that contemporary immigrants will be more successful in transmitting their language and cultural traditions than the earlier white immigrant groups (Massey 1995). I agree with Massey that post-1965 immigrants have several advantages over turn-of-the-century immigrants in transmitting their cultural traditions. This chapter examines the structural factors that give post-1965 immigrants advantages over the earlier immigrants in transmitting their language and culture.[2]

Contemporary Immigrants' Higher Levels of Residential Concentration and Segregation

Contemporary immigrants have advantages for transmitting their cultural traditions over the turn-of-the-century immigrants partly because of their higher levels of population concentration and residential segregation. Table 4.1 shows the differences in settlement patterns between the earlier and contemporary immigrants based on the 1910 and 1990 census reports. While New York State and the New York metropolitan area were the only premier immigrant state and city in the 1880–1930 era, California and Los Angeles have attracted more immigrants than New York State and the city in the post-1965 era (see also Farley 1996: 169). This is not surprising, given that Los Angeles and other California cities are major destinations of many Latino and Asian immigrants. In 1990, 34 percent of Latinos were concentrated in California and 21 percent in the Los Angeles metropolitan area, while 39 percent of Asian and Pacific Islander Americans resided in the state and 18 percent in the city.

Table 4.1. Major Foreign-Born States and Cities in 1910 and 1990

Major States	Number (in 1,000s)	% of Total Foreign Born	Major Cities	Number (in 1,000s)	% of Total Foreign Born
1910					
New York	2,748	20.3	New York	1,944	14.4
Pennsylvania	1,442	10.7	Chicago	783	5.8
Illinois	1,205	8.9	Philadelphia	385	2.8
Massachusetts	1,059	7.8	Boston	243	1.8
Ohio	598	4.4	Cleveland	196	1.5
Michigan	597	4.4	San Francisco	142	1.1
Total	7,649	56.6	Total	3,693	27.4
U.S. total	13,516	100.0	U.S. total	13,516	100.0
1990					
California	6,459	32.7	Los Angeles	3,945	19.9
New York	2,852	14.4	New York	3,554	18.0
Florida	1,663	8.4	San Francisco	1,251	6.3
Texas	1,523	7.7	Miami	1,073	5.4
New Jersey	967	4.9	Chicago	910	4.6
Illinois	952	4.8	Washington	484	2.4
Total	14,416	72.9	Total	11,217	56.7
U.S. total	19,767	100.0	U.S. total	19,767	100.0

Source: U.S. Bureau of the Census (1913): tables 14 and 210; 1993c–1993d: table 148).

Although the New York metropolitan area is slightly behind of Los Angeles in attracting contemporary immigrants, it still remains as the major entry point of new immigrants, accepting far more immigrants than any other major immigrant city with the exception of Los Angeles. New York has received diverse immigrant populations, representing all four major immigrant groups—Latino, Caribbean, Asian, and white. Chinese, Indian, Korean, Dominican, Cuban, Colombian, Jamaican, Haitian, Guyanian, Jewish, Polish, and Irish immigrants are highly concentrated in the city (New York City Department of City Planning 1992: 29; 1996: 14). The concentration of the majority of Cuban immigrants in the Miami area and many other Latino and Caribbean immigrant populations there have established Florida as the third-largest immigrant state. Mexican immigrants comprise almost one-fourth of the immigrants admitted to the United States over the past thirty years (Massey 1995: 647), and Texas is the second-largest state of destination for Mexican immigrants, following California. The concentration of Mexican immigrants in Texas (29 percent) and the settlement of many Asian immigrants in Houston and Dallas[3] have made Texas the fourth-largest state of immigrant concentration.

A more important piece of information from table 4.1 for the purpose of this chapter is not the difference in the major destination states and cities between two waves of immigrants, but the differential levels of immigrants' concentration in particular states and cities. In 1910, approximately 57 percent of the immigrant population resided in six major immigrant states and 27 percent in six major immigrant cities. By contrast, in 1990, nearly three-fourths of the immigrant population was concentrated in the six major immigrant states, and the majority of immigrants lived in six major immigrant cities. Whereas in 1990 four cities had 5 percent or more of the immigrant population, in 1910 only New York and Chicago had such a large proportion of immigrants.

Contemporary immigrants' higher level of residential concentration generally suggests that they have advantages over the earlier immigrant groups for maintaining their language and culture. Yet we need to compare two immigration periods in residential concentration by the country of origin because members of each national origin group usually share the same language and culture. When examining settlement patterns by the country of origin, we find the differential levels of residential concentration between two waves of immigrants even greater. Contemporary Latino and Caribbean immigrant groups show extremely high levels of concentration in one or a few cities. For example, 70 percent of Guyanese, more than 60 percent of Dominicans, 50 percent of Ecuadorians, and 45 percent of Jamaicans who immigrated to the United States between 1972 and 1994 chose New York City as their destinations (New York City Department of City Planning 1996). The 1990 census shows that each of the three largest Latino groups is highly concentrated in a metropolitan area: 56 percent of Cubans in the Miami–Fort Lauderdale area, 47 percent of Puerto Ricans in the New York–New Jersey–Connecticut area, and 28 percent of Mexicans in Los Angeles–Anaheim–Riverside area (U.S. Bureau of the Census 1993b: tables 253 and 268).

However, with the exception of Jews in New York, the major immigrant groups at the turn of the century did not have the levels of residential concentration in one or a few areas comparable to contemporary immigrant groups. Italian, Russian, Irish, and Hungarian immigrants composed major non-Protestant immigrant groups at the turn of the century, and all had the largest population concentration in New York City. But their New York City concentration rates in 1910 were, respectively, 30 percent for Russians (mostly Jews), 26 percent for Italians, 19 percent for Irish, and 16 percent for Hungarians (U.S. Bureau of the Census 1913: tables 14 and 210).

Latino immigrants, who comprise the largest panethnic group in many cities, share a common language. Consequently, they have a huge advantage over both the earlier white immigrant groups and other contemporary immigrant groups in transmitting their language to their children. Already in 1990, Latinos comprised 24 percent of the population in New York City and 40 percent of the population in the city of Los Angeles, the two largest central cities in the United States, while they comprise the majority of the population in three other major central cities: El Paso (69 percent), Miami (63 percent), and San Antonio (56 percent) (U.S. Bureau of the Census 1993b: table 276). They comprise a significant proportion of the population in many other major cities, including Houston, Dallas, San Diego, and Chicago. Latinos in these cities have access to several Spanish-language television and radio channels. In these and other smaller cities with a large Latino population, Spanish is often used as a language for business transactions. By virtue of a large Latino population, Spanish has been adopted as the most important foreign language in American public schools for several decades. Thus, descendants of Latino immigrants can learn the Spanish language more easily than other immigrant groups.

I have shown in the preceding discussion using census aggregate data that contemporary immigrant groups are more highly concentrated in a few or several cities than the earlier white immigrant groups. Contemporary immigrants' higher level of concentration suggests that they may be residentially more segregated than white immigrants at the turn of the twentieth century. But we need empirical data, preferably census PUMS (Public Use Micro Sample) data, to make a stronger case for this. Fortunately, in chapter 6 of this volume, Andrew Beveridge presents the results of 1910 and 1990 PUMS data analyses to compare the turn-of-the-century and contemporary immigrant groups in New York City in segregation patterns. As shown in his chapter, while in 1910 two or more major immigrant groups lived more or less together in each of the five major immigrant areas, in 1990 each of the several major immigrant groups established its own enclave in a particular area in the New York–New Jersey metropolitan area.[4] This suggests that contemporary, Third World immigrant groups in New York are residentially more segregated than white immigrant groups at the turn of the century. In fact, Beveridge's analyses of the measures of segregation indices reveal that most contemporary immigrant groups are more highly segregated from both the general population and other immigrant groups than most of the earlier white immigrant groups were.

Given that because of housing and other forms of racial discrimination, blacks and other minority groups are more highly segregated, often involuntarily, than white ethnic groups, contemporary, nonwhite immigrant groups in New York City being residentially more segregated than the earlier white immigrant groups is not surprising at all. Moreover, the multicultural policy of the U.S. government, a topic to be discussed later in this chapter, is likely to encourage many contemporary immigrant groups to establish their own immigrant enclaves with native-language commercial signs. For the same two reasons, contemporary immigrant groups in other cities, overwhelmingly nonwhite, must be more segregated than the white immigrant groups at the turn of the century that were heavily concentrated in New York and other East Coast cities. Mexicans comprising nearly 40 percent of the population in the city of Los Angeles and Cubans making up the majority of Miami (central city) suggest that these two groups are likely to be highly segregated at least in those cities. Contemporary immigrants' higher levels of concentration in a few or several cities and higher residential segregation have multifaceted effects on their adjustments in the United States. One major effect is that they have advantages over the earlier white immigrant groups in transmitting their cultural traditions over generations.

Contemporary immigrants include a significant proportion of professional and entrepreneurial immigrants who have brought with them large amounts of money (Portes and Rumbaut 1996: 18–22; Rumbaut 1995). Many of these professional and entrepreneurial immigrants have directly settled in a white suburban neighborhood without living in an enclave. Many others have remigrated to a suburban area after their initial settlement in an immigrant enclave. Thus, post-1965 immigrants, especially Asian immigrants, live in suburban white neighborhoods in high proportion, higher than the earlier white immigrants at the turn of the twentieth century (Logan et al. 1996; Min 1995).

Some may point out that contemporary immigrants and their children settled in suburban white neighborhoods will acculturate to white society, losing their ethnic culture quickly. But I like to argue that professional and entrepreneurial immigrant families settled in suburban white neighborhoods do not have disadvantages for maintaining their ethnic culture. My argument is based on the following two factors. First, by virtue of highly developed ethnic media, contemporary immigrant families settled in suburban areas are well integrated into the immigrant community. For example, as illustrated in the next section, Korean immigrant families in Long Island and Bergen County (New Jersey) suburban areas, as well as those in New York (central city), have access to Korean-language television and radio programs as well as Korean-language dailies. While ethnic television programs and ethnic dailies offer news and information about the Korean community as well as about Korea on a daily basis, ethnic radio programs provide it on an hourly basis. In addition to access to these ethnic media, most Korean immigrants in New York suburban areas commute to a Korean church located several miles from their neighborhood. Thus, Korean immigrants in suburban white neighborhoods are inseparably tied to Korean ethnic networks.

Second, contemporary entrepreneurial and professional immigrant families in suburban white neighborhoods do not have disadvantage compared to working-class immigrant families, largely settled in immigrant enclaves, for teaching their children the ethnic language and culture because of their financial resources. As is discussed at the end of the last section of this chapter, many Korean professional immigrants in New York, settled mostly in suburban white neighborhoods, can afford to send their children to Korea during summer for ethnic education.

Contemporary Immigrants' Greater Proximity to and Transnational Ties with Their Home Countries

Latino and Caribbean immigrants have an additional advantage over the earlier white immigrants in transmitting their language and culture to their children partly because of their settlement in the cities close to their home countries. The earlier European immigrants usually chose New York and other East Coast cities as their destinations. Even these "Atlantic bridges," not to mention the cities in other parts of the United States, were geographically so far away from Europe that the immigrants had little linkage to their home countries.

By contrast, the post-1965 Latino and Caribbean immigrants are generally settled in the destinations physically close to their home countries. Mexican immigrants, who comprise approximately one-fourth of total post-1965 immigrants, are heavily concentrated in the border states, such as California, Texas, and Arizona. The Mexicans settled in the former Mexican territory can visit their home city within a matter of a few hours. Most Cuban immigrants are settled in Miami, a city only ninety miles away from Havana. For political reasons, Cubans in Miami currently do not maintain strong sociocultural ties with their home country. Yet the situation may change drastically when U.S.–Cuban political relations improve in the future. Other Latino and Caribbean immigrants maintain stronger ties with their home countries than both the earlier white immigrant groups and even contemporary Asian immigrant groups because of the physical proximity between Latin America and the Caribbean islands on the one hand and such American cities as New York, Miami, and Los Angeles on the other (Chaney 1987).

As noted previously, contemporary Latino and Caribbean immigrants maintain stronger sociocultural ties with their home countries partly because of their closer physical proximity to their homelands. However, the major factor that contributes to contemporary immigrants' multiple linkages to their homelands is not their physical proximity to their homelands, but the transnational ties made possible by technological advances in communication, transportation, and the mass media (Basch et al. 1992; Foner 1997; Glick-Schiller et al. 1994; Laguerre 1998; Levitt 1998, 2001; Min 1998; Morawska 2001). The turn-of-the-century immigrants, too, did maintain transnational ties with their home countries (Bourne 1920; Foner 1997; Joseph 1967; Morawska 2001; Wyman 1993). They usually sent letters to their relatives and friends in their homelands. Many immigrants at that time were male sojourners who left behind their spouses and children at home. They sent remittances to their family members regularly. Some of the immigrants even visited their home countries to see their relatives and friends, buy land, and/or bring their spouses (Wyman 1993).

However, by virtue of advanced technologies, contemporary immigrants maintain the high level of transnational ties with their home countries unimaginable to the earlier immigrants. The only means of communication between immigrants and their relatives in the home country in Europe at the turn of the century was to send letters, which took several weeks for delivery. By contrast, contemporary immigrants can communicate with their relatives and friends in the home country almost every day, using long-distance telephone calls, fax messages, and e-mail. The affordability of long-distance calls, in particular, has revolutionary effects on contemporary immigrants' communication patterns with their relatives left behind in their homeland. A 1996 survey in New York City revealed that about one-third of Korean immigrants talked to their relatives in Korea at least once a week, while half communicated by phone once or twice a month (Min 1998: 112).

The entry of the steamship into the immigrant trade since the mid-nineteenth century led to a drastic reduction in the length of passage from Europe to America. Yet the transatlantic voyage at the turn of the century still took approximately two weeks (Kraut 1982: 49). Because of great expenses, time, and the threats of accidents and epidemics involved in the voyage, only a small minority of immigrants visited their home countries to take care of important things, such as bringing their marital partners, inviting their relatives for permanent residence in the United States, or buying land.

By contrast, international air travel connecting contemporary immigrants' American destinations to their home cities in the Third World is far less expensive, far more convenient, and much faster than the turn-of-the-century transatlantic voyages. Most Latino and Caribbean immigrants in New York can fly to their home cities within four to six hours, while Asian immigrants in Los Angeles need to spend only seven to thirteen hours to visit their home cities in Asia. As a result, contemporary immigrants exchange visits with their relatives and friends at home regularly—to celebrate their parent's birthday, to participate in their brother's wedding, or to enjoy their vacation. In fact, some immigrants move back and forth between American destinations to Third World cities, while others maintain commuter marriages with wives and children remaining in American cities and their husbands working in Third World cities (Lessinger 1995: 88–91; Levitt 2001; Min 1998: 113–118; Wong 1998: chap. 6).

Finally, as noted with regard to the Korean community in New York (Min 2001), great improvements in media technologies during the past two decades have given contemporary immigrants access to active ethnic media—ethnic dailies and weeklies and ethnic radio and television programs. The earlier immigrants did establish a number of ethnic newspapers. Yet, as they did not have communication channels with their home countries on a daily basis, the ethnic media could not provide the earlier immigrants with day-to-day news from their homelands. By contrast, the ethnic media today tie immigrants with their homelands by supplying them with daily news from their home. Ethnic television programs also offer contemporary immigrants with ethnic movies and television programs on videotapes made in their home countries. For example, the Korean community in New York has three Korean-language dailies, all of which, as branches of major dailies in Korea, duplicate articles published in their headquarters in Seoul. There are also two Korean television stations and a Korean radio station in the Korean community in New York that air Korean-language programs twenty-four hours a day. Korean immigrants in New York as well as in other major Korean communities depend mainly on the Korean-language ethnic media for news, information, and leisure activities (Min 1998: 21–22). Their heavy dependence on the ethnic media, in turn, has strengthened their ties with the ethnic community and the home country. By virtue of contemporary technological advances, other immigrant groups have developed the similarly active ethnic media, which, in turn, tie immigrants with the homeland and the origin community at multiple levels (Laguerre 1998: chap. 6; Lessinger 1995: 67–70).

To sum up the foregoing discussion, technological improvements in international travel, telecommunications, and the media industry help contemporary immigrants maintain the active and continuous contacts with the homeland and community of origin, overcoming the barriers deriving from the physical boundary. Because of the active and sustained involvement of immigrants in the home country, several source countries of U.S. immigrants have taken measures during recent years to strengthen their overseas residents' cultural, social, and political ties to the home country. Mexico, the Dominican Republic, Columbia, Peru, and Haiti have recently passed a law that recognizes their American residents' dual citizenship.

The current literature on "transnational ties" and "diasporic citizenship" emphasizes the advantages of the first-generation immigrants in maintaining their ethnic culture but does not comment on the effects on the second generation. Yet the multiple linkages between host and home countries and between destination and origin communities help not only immigrants but also their children maintain their ethnic subculture and ethnic identity. Second-generation children can learn their ethnic language formally through the language instructions provided by the ethnic television stations, as most ethnic stations offer such instructions. Moreover, as international air travel is popularized, immigrant parents send their children to their home countries during the summer vacation to help them learn the ethnic language and culture. A 1989 survey showed that 80 percent of American-born Korean high school students in New York had visited Korea at least once and that 20 percent had visited Korea twice or more (Hong and Min 1999).

Because international travel has been more and more popularized since the late 1980s, a survey, if conducted now, would show second-generation Korean high school students making more frequent visits to their parents' homeland. Because of the physical proximity, Caribbean and Latino second-generation children seem to visit their parental home countries more frequently than their Korean and Asian American counterparts. In addition, popularization of music and videotapes helps second-generation children watch ethnic-language movies and learn ethnic pop songs (Lessinger 1995: 117), even if they may not be fluent in their mother tongues.

Segmented assimilation theory says that the second-generation adults who are fluent in their native language and culture can make successful economic adjustments in an immigrant enclave (Portes and Zhou 1993; Portes and Rumbaut 1996; Zhou 1997). However, the second generation who are fluently bilingual and/or bicultural can find even more satisfactory jobs in the transnational context. For example, some second-generation Korean Americans find their jobs in Korea as English teachers in high school or college. Other 1.5- and second-generation Koreans find employment in Korean companies in Seoul because of their advantages in English. Still other younger-generation Korean Americans who are employed in American companies are sent to the company branches located in Seoul. In addition, a number of 1.5- and second-generation Koreans find employment in branches of Korean corporations located in American cities.

Probably a tiny faction of 1.5- and second-generation Korean Americans work in Korea or in branches of Korean companies located in the United States. However, as the economy is likely to be more and more globalized in the twenty-first century, an increasing number of the children of immigrants are likely to find employment in this transnational context. The opportunity for employment for professional and managerial occupations in the transnational context, in turn, will encourage the children of immigrants to maintain their language and culture. Moreover, their actual employment in the transnational setting will further facilitate their learning of the parental language and culture.

Multicultural Policy since the Early 1970s

Multicultural policy is another factor that gives contemporary immigrant groups advantages over the earlier white immigrant groups in transmitting their language and culture to their children. The dominant social policy in the United States up to the 1960s had been Anglo conformity, according to which immigrants and members of minority groups should replace their language with English and their cultural patterns with those of

British origin (Gordon 1964: 88–89). The Anglo conformity policy or ideology was most influentially expressed in the Americanization movement that tried to force immigrants and their children to get rid of their cultural traditions and to accept American culture as soon as possible. The Americanization movement reached its peak during World War I after a large number of immigrants from eastern and southern European countries had arrived. At that time, many new immigrants were almost forced to change their names into American by immigration officials. A squad of women were sent out on home visits to immigrants, telling them to create a more "American household by preparing 'non-ethnic' foods, modifying their grooming and personal hygiene habits, and advocating the use of English in the home" (Jaret 1996: 402). The English language was associated with being "American" and "patriotic," and bilinguals were interpreted as a sign of being disloyal to the United States (Molesky 1988: 51-52). In this context, one major function of public schools was considered to "Americanize" immigrant children and children of immigrants by teaching them English and inculcating them with American values.

However, since the early 1970s, all levels of government—the federal government in particular—and local school districts have changed policies toward minority members and immigrants from "Anglo conformity" to cultural pluralism (Goldberg 1994). The changes in policies were partly responses to various minority movements—the civil rights movement, the black cultural nationalist movement, the Chicano movement, the Third World students' movement, and the women's movement—and partly responses to the influx of new immigrants from Third World countries. Affirmative action programs, the Ethnic Heritage Studies Act of 1973, the Bilingual Education Act of 1974, a series of amendments of the Voting Rights Act of 1965 since 1975, and the comprehensive race and ancestry questions in the 1980 and 1990 censuses are among the government programs reflecting multicultural policy (Barkan 1995: 58).

Probably the most noteworthy event in the U.S. government's multicultural policy in the early 1970s was the *Lau v. Nichols* Supreme Court decision. In 1974, the Supreme Court declared that the students with limited English proficiency be given special remedial aid to facilitate their learning of English. Armed with the landmark Supreme Court decision, the Office of Civil Rights of the Department of Health, Education, and Welfare established a series of guidelines in 1975 to require all school districts to provide bilingual education programs for "language minority children" (Chavez 1986: chap. 1). As a result, school districts in large cities have usually provided bilingual education for immigrant children with a language barrier, although the passage of the Proposition 287 in 1998 led to the abolition of bilingual education in California. In addition to bilingual programs, public schools have changed their curricula by including more courses related to minority groups' language, history, and culture. They have also tried to promote cultural diversity through such extracurricular activities as ethnic festivals and symposiums on minority groups to foster ethnic pride.

Colleges and universities, too, have done a great deal to increase ethnic diversity in curricular and extracurricular activities. As a result of the influx of nonwhite immigrants and minority groups' improvement in education, colleges and universities have become racially and ethnically far more diverse than before in the student body. Employment through affirmative action programs and the establishment of ethnic, area, and women's studies programs have also increased the number and proportion of minority and women faculty members. Under pressure from minority and women students and faculty members, many colleges and universities have revised the white male–oriented curriculum by including contributions made by people of color and women in traditional liberal arts courses and adding numerous courses pertaining to the experiences of minority groups and women. The establishment of ethnic and women's studies programs on many campuses in particular has resulted in a significant revision of the traditional curriculum (Hu-Dehart 1995).

There have been some conservative reactions to multiculturalism. In reaction to the rapid increase in the non-English-speaking immigrant population, more than a dozen states, including California and Florida, have passed a law that recognizes English as the standard language. In 1998, California passed a referendum that aimed to abolish bilingual education. Conservative intellectuals have attacked multicultural education in higher educational institutions (Bloom 1987; D'Souza 1991). Despite these reactionary movements and measures, both governments and schools are currently strongly committed to the multicultural policy. For example, in New York City, local government officials, social workers, and teachers try actively to promote festivals and events to foster ethnic pride and glorify the city's multiethnic character (Foner 1997). Both governments and schools are likely to strengthen, rather than weaken, the multicultural policy in the future, particularly because of the continuous increase in the nonwhite population and student body.

Because of this multicultural policy, the children of contemporary immigrants have huge advantages for retaining their ethnic culture over those of the earlier immigrants at the turn of the century. Multicultural education in particular has positive effects on the second generation's retention of their language and culture. Not only Latino but also many other minority high school students can now take their ethnic language as a foreign language, as many city school districts have adopted the languages of the major immigrant groups as foreign languages. Chinese, Korean, Russian, and Spanish have been included in the SAT II as foreign languages, which has encouraged the second-generation children of these ancestries to learn their mother tongue.

Various courses offered through area and ethnic studies programs in colleges and universities have helped many 1.5- and second-generation students learn their ethnic language, culture, and history. Moreover, the establishment of ethnic and area studies programs has led to the creation of many academic jobs for members of minority groups. Asian Americans are underrepresented in humanities and social sciences, while they are overrepresented in natural science and business fields. However, a large number of Asian Americans have recently found academic positions in social sciences and humanities mainly through ethnic and area studies programs. The increase in the number of teaching and research positions open in area and ethnic studies, in turn, has encouraged many 1.5- and second-generation students to learn their language and culture.

Permanence of Migration Flows and Growing Ethnic Diversity

Since new immigrants always replenish the ethnic community with the culture of their homeland, the continuity of immigration is essential to maintaining ethnic cultural traditions. One of the major reasons why the turn-of-the-century immigrant groups have almost completely lost their ethnic cultural traditions is that their immigration almost came to an end around the early 1930s and did not revive for a long period of time.

The current immigration flows are not likely to come to an end or even decline sharply in the foreseeable future. The liberalization of the immigration law in 1965 is partly responsible for the mass migration of immigrants from Third World countries in the post-1965 era. But the U.S. government's military, political, and economic linkages with many Latin American, Asian, and Caribbean countries, along with other structural factors, are mainly responsible for the current flow of migration to the United States (Laguerre 1998; Massey 1995). Considering the even more dominant role of the United States in the post–Cold War world order, the current immigration law is not likely to be drastically revised in the foreseeable future to substantially reduce the current level of immigration. Further, many researchers have warned that the U.S. government cannot stem the tide of the current immigration flow through policies once social networks between immigrants' American destination cities and their home cities have been established (Massey 1990, 1995; Portes and Rumbaut 1996: 272–284; Waldinger 1996).

As a result of the influx of immigrants from Third World countries over the past thirty years and their high residential concentration, non-Hispanic whites have already become a numerical minority in nearly half of the one hundred largest metropolitan cities, including New York, Los Angeles, San Francisco, and Miami. American cities have grown far more multiracial and multiethnic than they were thirty years ago. As long as the current patterns of immigration flow remain unchanged, Latino and Asian populations will continue to increase with a concomitant decline in the proportion of the white population. According to population projections, the non-Hispanic white population will be reduced to 53 percent by 2050, while the Latino, black, and Asian American populations will grow to 25, 14, and 8 percent, respectively (U.S. Bureau of the Census 1996: 19). The continuous immigration flows from Third World countries and the consequent increase in minority populations will lead minority and new immigrant groups to have a stronger cultural impact on American society in the future than now. This change in the direction of more ethnic and cultural diversity will help the descendants of immigrants maintain their language and culture.

Color-Based Prejudice and Reactive Ethnicity

As the turn-of-the-century mass migration flows almost came to an end in the early 1930s and the children of European immigrants became detached from their homelands, structural factors associated with their adjustments in the United States became major sources of their ethnicity

(Yancy et al. 1976). The previous discussion, however, suggests that primordial ties—homeland and ethnic culture—will be far more important sources of ethnicity for the descendants of contemporary immigrants than for those of the earlier white immigrant groups.

In addition to stronger primordial ties, the children of contemporary immigrants may have stronger structural sources of ethnicity than the "old second generation" because they are likely to encounter prejudice and discrimination because of their skin color (Gans 1992; Portes and Zhou 1993). Because of their differences in language, religion, and "races," the southern and eastern European immigrants, too, initially encountered prejudice and discrimination by Protestant Americans. But over generations, these "inassimilable races" have melted into white American society. One of the reasons why the third- and fourth-generation white ethnics have lost their cultural traditions almost completely is that as whites they have been accepted as full American citizens. However, the descendants of contemporary Third World immigrants are not likely to be accepted as full American citizens, no matter how many generations they live in this country. When they experience racial prejudice and discrimination, as a defense mechanism they may try to selectively assimilate to American culture while holding on to their positive cultural traditions (see Gibson 1988).

To avoid being labeled as *black* by white students, the children of Caribbean black immigrants emphasize their ethnic culture (Waters 1994). The third- and fourth-generation Caribbean blacks may ultimately assimilate to African Americans. Yet because of their experiences with prejudice and discrimination, they will maintain strong ethnic identity. The descendants of Asian immigrants generally do well in school performance and social mobility, better than white Americans.[5] Yet they, too, encounter a moderate level of rejection by white Americans as indicated by such remarks as "What country are you from?" and "Go back to your country" (Min and Kim 1999). For third- and fourth-generation white Americans, ethnicity is a matter of option to meet their yearning for community (Waters 1990). But later-generation Asian Americans do not have the same option. Based on her personal interviews with third- and fourth-generation Chinese and Japanese Americans, Tuan (1999: 123) concludes that "being ethnic remains a societal expectation for them despite how far removed they are from their immigrant roots or how much they differ from their foreign-born."

Bilingual and Bicultural Orientations

I have thus far examined several factors that give the children of contemporary immigrants advantages for preserving their cultural traditions over those of the earlier immigrants. However, by emphasizing their advantages for retaining their language and culture, I do not intend to suggest that the children of contemporary immigrants have disadvantages for acculturation. In fact, the children of contemporary immigrants are under greater pressure to assimilate to American culture than those of the turn-of-the century immigrants for two major reasons.

First, the media, American peers, and schools currently have stronger effects on the behaviors and attitudes of children than at the turn of the century. As a result, immigrant parents have less control over their children than before. Contemporary immigrant parents may be less effective for preventing their children from being culturally Americanized than the immigrant parents one hundred years ago, particularly because, as shown in chapter 7, a much larger proportion of contemporary immigrant mothers work full time outside the home than those before.

Second, the children of today's immigrants have a greater pressure to assimilate to American culture than their counterparts a century ago partly because of the global influence of American popular culture today (Gans 1997: 877; Hollinger 1995: 153). Because of the presence of American servicemen, multinational corporations, and/or media in their home countries, most contemporary immigrants from Third World countries, including immigrant children, became familiar with American mass culture prior to migration.

My argument that the children of contemporary immigrants have advantages over those of the earlier immigrants for both retaining their ethnic culture and acculturating to American society may sound contradictory to many readers. But it is not contradictory because retention of ethnic culture and acculturation are not always mutually exclusive. Classical assimilationists proposed a zero-sum model of acculturation, according to which, immigrants' acculturation involves a gradual replacement of their ethnic culture with American culture. As indicated elsewhere (Min 1999), although the zero-sum model may be useful as a description of the Anglo conformity policy or ideology up to the 1960s, it is not helpful to understanding the experiences of contemporary immigrants and their children.[6] Contemporary immigrants can achieve a high level of acculturation while maintaining their ethnic culture almost perfectly, whereas their Americanized children can achieve a high level of ethnic attachment. A large proportion of the descendants of post-1965 immigrants—much larger than those of the turn-of-the century immigrants—are likely to remain fluently bilingual and strongly bicultural because of the previously described factors.

A more systematic survey study of ethnic attachment among the descendants of post-1965 immigrants is needed to test the validity of the previously discussed bilingual, bicultural hypothesis. However, both quantitative and qualitative data available at present seem to be in support of the hypothesis. Lopez (1996, 2000) analyzed the PUMS of the 1989 Current Population Survey to examine intergenerational language maintenance and shift among Latino and Asian populations in Los Angeles. According to his analysis, 53 percent of twenty-five- to forty-four-year-old second-generation Hispanics spoke English "very well" but used their ethnic language at home, in comparison to 19 percent of their Asian American counterparts. It also showed that 47 percent of third- and later-generation Latino adults (natives of natives) and 11 percent of their Asian American counterparts were fluent in English but used their ethnic language at home.

The Latino and Asian American adults who can speak English very well, but use their ethnic language at home can be considered fluent bilinguals. As expected, Latinos show a much higher rate of intergenerational transmission of their ethnic language than Asian Americans. But even third-generation Asian Americans include a higher proportion of bilinguals (11 percent) than expected from the studies of the descendants of the 1880–1930 wave of immigrants. According to these studies, "by the third generation, knowledge of an ethnic language beyond a few words and phrases is often lost" (Alba 1990: 11; see also Lieberson et al. 1975). Waters (1990) personally interviewed sixty third- and fourth-generation Catholic ethnics for her study of ethnic identity. She reported that only four (7 percent) of her sixty informants were able to speak their native language fluently. The earlier Japanese immigrants came to the United States between 1885 and 1924, roughly during the European mass migration period. A major survey study of Japanese Americans conducted in the early

1960s revealed that only 2 percent of the third-generation respondents reported that they spoke Japanese fluently (Woodrum 1981).

The Latino and Asian American respondents (twenty-five to forty-four years old) included in the 1989 Current Population Survey were born and grew up before the mass influx of post-1965 Latino and Asian immigrants. Thus, they did not benefit from the structural factors facilitating the retention of their ethnic language discussed in this chapter. Accordingly, the descendants of post-1965 Latino and Asian immigrants are likely to retain their ethnic language more successfully than the sample of the 1989 Current Population Survey: the descendants of the pre-1965 Latino and Asian immigrant cohorts.

Recent studies of the children of post-1965 immigrants suggest that fluent bilingualism is highly correlated with the professional family background (Portes and Rumbaut 1996: 223–225). The children who have grown up in an immigrant enclave may be fluent in their ethnic language but may not be fluent in English. Yet professional families in a suburban white middle-class neighborhood have resources to make their children fluent bilinguals. Many Korean professional and high-income business families in a white middle-class neighborhood in New York enroll their children in a Saturday ethnic language school and regularly send them to Korea for a Korean cultural program during the summer vacation. Some of them send their college-graduated children to college in Korea for a long-term ethnic education. Personal narratives by 1.5- and second-generation young Asian American professionals reveal that many, including those married to white partners, have strong bicultural and binational orientations, although all grew up in predominantly white middle- and upper-middle-class neighborhoods and graduated from prestigious universities (Min and Kim 1999).

Conclusion

The white immigrant groups at the turn of the twentieth century lost their cultural traditions quickly in a generation, while it took them three or four generations to catch up with Protestant ethnic groups in socioeconomic status. However, post-1965 immigrant groups will be more successful than the turn-of-the-century European immigrant groups in preserving their language and culture over generations. There are several structural factors that give contemporary immigrant groups advantages over the earlier immigrant groups for transmitting their cultural traditions to their children.

First, contemporary immigrant groups have advantages in transmitting their cultural traditions to their children because they are more highly concentrated in a few cities and more highly segregated in each city than the earlier white immigrant groups. Latino groups in particular have a huge advantage over other contemporary immigrant groups in transmitting their language because they use the same language. The continuous influx of Mexican and other Latino immigrants to Los Angeles, Miami, New York, and other Latino centers is likely to make the cities bilingual if not multilingual.

Second, contemporary immigrants have advantages in intergenerational cultural transmission over the earlier white immigrant groups because they have much stronger ties to their home countries. They have stronger ties to their homelands partly because of their physical proximity and partly because of their transnational ties to them. Because of their physical proximity, Latino and Caribbean immigrants have advantages over Asian immigrants in maintaining their ties with their home countries. Yet technological improvements in air travel, communications, and the media industry help even Asian immigrants overcome the geographical distance in maintaining contacts with their home countries on a daily basis. Transnational ties between immigrants' host and home societies help the immigrants' offspring maintain their cultural, social, and psychological ties with their parents' home countries.

Third, the descendants of contemporary immigrants have advantages in retaining their ethnic culture partly because of the multicultural policy and trend, in sharp contrast with the rigid Anglo conformity policy and ideology in the earlier period. The massive influx of immigrants from Third World countries has contributed to ethnic and racial diversity in many American cities. In positive responses to the diversification of the population in American society and various minority groups' movements, federal and local governments have adopted the multicultural policy since the early 1970s. An emphasis on multicultural education has changed not only the formerly Eurocentric curriculum, but also methods of instruction and extracurricular activities. The strong multicultural trend in American society in general and multicultural education in particular helps the children of post-1965 immigrants maintain their cultural traditions.

Finally, the uninterrupted, continuous migration flows from the major Third World countries will help the descendants of post-1965 immigrants preserve their cultural traditions. One of the major reasons why the earlier white ethnics lost their language and culture was that their migration flows came to an end in the early 1930s. Although everything comes to an end, the contemporary mass migration is unlikely to end or be reduced substantially in the foreseeable future.

As the earlier white ethnics lost their cultural traditions and ties with their homelands, structural conditions associated with their residential and occupational concentrations in American cities became the important sources of their ethnicity. However, primordial ties will continue to be important sources of ethnicity for the descendants of post-1965 immigrants because of their retention of ethnic heritage and ties with the homelands. As minority racial groups, the descendants of contemporary immigrants are not likely to be accepted as full American citizens no matter how well they do socioeconomically. Therefore, they will have strong structural sources of ethnicity as well—stronger sources than the descendants of the earlier white immigrants. This suggests that the descendants of contemporary immigrants will maintain stronger ethnic identity over generations than the earlier white immigrant groups.

Notes

This chapter is an expansion of one of the two main themes of my article "A Comparison of Contemporary and Turn-of-the-Century Immigrants in Intergenerational Mobility and Cultural Transmission," included in a special issue of the *Journal of American Ethnic History* (vol. 18, spring 1999) that compared the classical and contemporary mass migration periods. I thank Ms. Linda Morris at the U.S. Census Bureau for checking the 1910 historical census and faxing me copies of several tables.

1. The major point these scholars have made is that despite a great emphasis on pluralism during recent years, assimilation theory, associated with Robert Park and Milton Gordon, is still useful in understanding the adaptation patterns of contemporary immigrants and their descendants as well as those of turn-of-the-century immigrant groups. But they have also suggested that the children of contemporary

immigrants are likely to be acculturated into American society in a similar manner that the children of the earlier white immigrant groups were acculturated.

2. By "contemporary immigrants' cultural transmission over generations," I do not mean to suggest that the descendants of contemporary immigrants inherit ethnic culture without revising them. In the social construction perspective, ethnic culture actively interacts with the host society to create ethnicity. Thus, ethnic culture is not "given," "fixed," "inherited," or "vertically transmitted." Rather, ethnic cultural traditions consist of selective ethnic cultural components, revisions of inherited cultural traditions, and inventions of new traditions. Nevertheless, we can measure the extent to which the second and later generations have retained ethnic cultural traditions such as language, customs, rituals, and food, as Alba (1990) and Waters (1990) did.

3. Texas was the fourth-largest Asian state with more than 132,000 Asian Americans in 1990. Approximately 72 percent of Asian Americans in Texas resided in Houston and Dallas. See U.S. Bureau of the Census (1993d: tables 266 and 276).

4. Beveridge's data analysis in chapter 6 shows that Western Queens was the only area of immigrant concentration in New York in 1990, similar to the major immigrant areas in the city in 1910, where several different immigrant groups lived together.

5. According to the *1990 Census of Population* (U.S. Bureau of the Census 1993a: table 4; 1993c: table 45), 36 percent of native-born Asian Americans completed four years of college in comparison to 22 percent of white Americans, and 34 percent of them held professional or managerial occupations compared to 27 percent of white Americans.

6. For example, on the basis of data collected in Los Angeles, Hurh and Kim (1984: 219–222) demonstrated that Korean immigrants achieved cultural and social assimilation in proportion to their length of residence in the United States but that their strong ethnic attachment was largely unaffected by their assimilation rates. See also Portes and Rumbaut (1996: 219–222).

References

Alba, Richard. 1990. *Ethnic Identity: Transformation of White America.* New Haven, CT: Yale University Press.

———. 1999. "Immigration and the American Realities of Assimilation and Multiculturalism." *Sociological Forum* 14: 3–25.

Alba, Richard, and Victor Nee. 1997. "Rethinking Assimilation Theory for a New Era of Immigration." *International Migration Review* 31: 826–874.

Barkan, Elliot. 1995. "Race, Religion, and Nationality in American Society: A Model of Ethnicity—From Contact to Assimilation." *Journal of American Ethnic History* 14: 38–101.

Basch, Linda, Nina Glick-Schiller, and Christina Szanton-Blanc, eds. 1992. *Nations Unbounded: Transnational Projects, Postcolonial Predicaments, and Deterritorialized Nations.* New York: Gordon and Beach Science.

Bloom, Allan. 1987. *The Closing of the American Mind.* New York: Simon & Schuster.

Bourne, Randolph. 1920. *History of a Literary Radical and Other Essays.* New York: B. W. Huebsch.

Chaney, Elsa. 1987. "The Context of Caribbean Migration." In *Caribbean Life in New York City,* edited by Constance Sutton and Elsa Chaney. Staten Island, NY: Center for Migration Studies.

Chavez, Linda. 1986. *Out of the Barrio: Toward a New Politics of Hispanic Assimilation.* New York: Basic Books.

D'Souza, Dinesh. 1991. *Illiberal Education: The Politics of Race and Sex on Campus.* New York: The Free Press.

Farley, Reynolds. 1996. *The New American Reality: Who We Are, How We Got Here, Where We Are Going.* New York: Russell Sage Foundation.

Foner, Nancy. 1997. "What's New about Transnationalism? New York Immigrants Today and the Turn of the Century." *Diaspora* 6: 355–375.

Gans, Herbert. 1992. "Second-Generation Decline: Scenarios of the Economic and Ethnic Futures of the Post-1965 Immigrants." *Ethnic and Racial Studies* 15: 173–192.

———. 1997. "Toward a Reconciliation of 'Assimilation' and 'Pluralism': Interplay of Acculturation and Ethnic Retention." *International Migration Review* 31: 875–892.

———. 1999. "The Possibility of a New Racial Hierarchy in the Twentieth-First-Century United States." In *The Cultural Territories of Race: Black and White Boundaries,* edited by Michele Lamont. Chicago: University of Chicago Press.

Gibson, Margaret. 1988. *Accommodation without Assimilation: Sikh Immigrants in an American High School.* Ithaca, NY: Cornell University Press.

Glick-Schiller, Nina, Linda Basch, and Christina Szanton-Blanc. 1994. *Toward a Transnational Perspective on Migration: Race, Class, Ethnicity, and Nationalism Reconsidered.* New York: New York Academy of Science.

Goldberg, David Theo. 1994. *Multiculturalism: A Critical Reader.* New York: Blackwell Publishers.

Gordon, Milton. 1964. *Assimilation in American Life: The Role of Race, Religion, and National Origin.* New York: Oxford University Press.

Hollinger, David A. 1995. *Postethnic America: Beyond Multiculturalism.* New York: Basic Books.

Hong, Joanne, and Pyong Gap Min. 1999. "Ethnic Attachment among Second-Generation Korean Adolescents." *Amerasia Journal* 25 (1): 165–180.

Hu-Dehart, Evelyn. 1995. "P.C. and the Politics of Multiculturalism in Higher Education." In *Race,* edited by Steven Gregory and Roger Sanjek. New Brunswick, NJ: Rutgers University Press.

Hurh, Won Moo, and Kwang Chung Kim. 1984. *Korean Immigrants in North America: A Structural Analysis of Ethnic Confinement and Adhesive Adaptation.* Madison, NJ: Fairleigh Dickinson University Press.

Jaret, Charles. 1996. *Contemporary Racial and Ethnic Relations.* New York: HarperCollins College Publishers.

Joseph, Samuel. 1967. *Jewish Immigration to the United States: From 1881–1910.* New York: AMS Press.

Kraut, Allan. 1982. *The Huddled Masses: The Immigration in American Society, 1880–1921.* Arlington Heights, IL: Harlan Davidson.

Laguerre, Michel. 1998. *Diasporic Citizenship: Haitian Americans in Transnational America.* New York: St. Martin's Press.

Lessinger, Johanna. 1995. *From the Ganges to the Hudson: Indian Immigrants in New York City.* Boston: Allyn and Bacon.

Levitt, Peggy. 1998. "Social Remittances: Migration Driven Local-Level Forms of Cultural Diffusion." *International Migration Review* 32: 926–948.

———. 2001. *The Transnational Villagers.* Berkeley and Los Angeles: University of California Press.

Lieberson, Stanley, Guy Dalto, and Mary Ellen Johnston. 1975. "The Course of Mother Tongue Diversity in Nations." *American Journal of Sociology* 81: 34–61.

Logan, John, Richard Alba, and Shu-Yin Leung. 1996. "Minority Access to White Suburbs: A Multiregion Comparison." *Social Forces* 74: 851–881.

Lopez, David. 1996. "Language Diversity and Assimilation." In *Ethnic Los Angeles,* edited by Roger Waldinger and Mehdi Bozorgmehr. New York: Russell Sage Foundation.

———. 2000. "Social and Linguistic Aspects of Assimilation Today." In *The Handbook of International Migration,* edited by Charles Hirschman, Philip Kasinitz, and Josh DeWind. New York: Russell Sage Foundation.

Massey, Douglas. 1990. "Social Structure, Household Strategies, and the Cumulative Causation of Migration." *Population Index* 56: 3–26.

———. 1995. "The New Immigration and Ethnicity in the United States." *Population and Development Review* 21: 631–652.

Min, Pyong Gap. 1995. "An Overview of Asian Americans." In *Asian Americans: Contemporary Trends and Issues.* Thousand Oaks, CA: Sage Publications.

————. 1998. *Changes and Conflicts: Korean Immigrant Families in New York.* Boston: Allyn and Bacon.

————. 1999. "Ethnicity: Concepts, Theories, and Trends." In *Struggle for Ethnic Identity: Narratives by Asian American Professionals,* edited by Pyong Gap Min and Rose Kim. Walnut Creek, CA: AltaMira Press.

————. 2001. "Koreans in New York: An Institutionally Complete Community." In *New Immigrants in New York,* edited by Nancy Foner. New York: Columbia University Press.

Min, Pyong Gap, and Rose Kim, eds. 1999. *Struggle for Ethnic Identity: Narratives by Asian American Professionals.* Walnut Creek, CA: AltaMira Press.

Molesky, Jean. 1988. "Understanding the American Linguistic Mosaic: A Historical Overview of Language Maintenance and Language Shift." In *Language Diversity: Problem or Resource,* edited by Sandra Lee McKay and Sau-ling Cynthia Wong. Boston: Heinle and Heinle.

Morawska, Ewa. 2001. "The New-Old Transmigrants, Their Transnational Lives, and Ethnization: A Comparison of 19th/20th- and 20th/21st Century Situations." In *Immigrants, Civic Culture, and Models of Political Incorporation,* edited by Gary Gerstle and John Mollenkoph. New York: Russell Sage Foundation.

New York City Department of City Planning. 1992. *The Newest New Yorkers: An Analysis of Immigration into New York City during the 1980s.* New York: New York City Department of City Planning.

————. 1996. *Newest New Yorkers, 1990–1994.* New York: New York City Department of City Planning.

Portes, Alejandro. 1996. *The New Second Generation.* New York: Russell Sage Foundation.

Portes, Alenjandro, and Ruben Rumbaut. 1996. *Immigrant America: A Portrait.* 2nd ed. Berkeley and Los Angeles: University of California Press.

Portes, Alenjandro, and Min Zhou. 1993. "The New Second Generation: Segmented Assimilation and Its Variants among Post-1965 Immigrant Youth." *Annals of the American Academy of Political and Social Science* 530 (November): 74–98.

Rumbaut, Ruben. 1995. "Origins and Destinies: Immigration, Race, and Ethnicity in Contemporary America." In *Origins and Destinies: Immigration, Race, and Ethnicity in America,* edited by Silvia Pedraza and Ruben Rumbaut. Belmont, CA: Wadsworth.

Tuan, Mia. 1999. "Neither Real Americans nor Real Asians? Multigeneration Asian Ethnics Navigating the Terrain of Authenticity." *Qualitative Sociology* 22: 105–125.

U.S. Bureau of the Census. 1913. *Thirteenth Census of the United States Taken in the Year of 1910.* Washington, DC: U.S. Government Printing Office.

———. 1993a. *1990 Census of Population, Asian and Pacific Islanders in the United States* (CP-3-5). Washington, DC: U.S. Government Printing Office.

———. 1993b. *1990 Census of Population, General Population Characteristics, United States* (1990 CP-1-1). Washington, DC: U.S. Government Printing Office.

———. 1993c. *1990 Census of Population, Social and Economic Characteristics, Metropolitan Areas, Section 2* (1990 CP-2-2). Washington, DC: U.S. Government Printing Office.

———. 1993d. *1990 Census of Population, Social and Economic Characteristics, United States* (1990 CP-2-1). Washington, DC: U.S. Government Printing Office.

———. 1996. *Statistical Abstracts of the United States, 1996.* Washington, DC: U.S. Government Printing Office.

Waldinger, Roger. 1996. "Ethnicity and Opportunity in Plural Society." In *Ethnic Los Angeles,* edited by Roger Waldinger and Mehdi Bozorgmehr. New York: Russell Sage Foundation.

Waters, Mary. 1990. *Ethnic Options: Choosing Identities in America.* Berkeley and Los Angeles: University of California Press.

———. 1994. "Ethnic and Racial Identities of Second-Generation Black Immigrants in New York." *International Migration Review* 28: 795–820.

Wong, Bernard. 1998. *Ethnicity and Entrepreneurship: The New Chinese Immigrants in the San Francisco Bay Area.* Boston: Allyn and Bacon.

Woodrum, Eric. 1981. "An Assessment of Japanese American Assimilation, Pluralism, and Subordination." *American Journal of Sociology* 87: 157–169.

Wyman, Mark. 1993. *Round-Trip America: The Immigrants Return to Europe, 1880–1930.* Ithaca, NY: Cornell University Press.

Yancy, William, Eugene Ericksen, and Richard Juliani. 1976. "Emergent Ethnicity: A Review and Reformulation." *American Sociological Review* 76: 391–403.

Zhou, Min. 1997. "Growing Up American: The Challenge Confronting Immigrant Children and Children of Immigrants." *Annual Review of Sociology* 23: 63–95.

Zhou, Min, and Carl Bankston III. 1998. *Growing Up American: How Vietnamese Children Adapt to Life in the United States.* New York: Russell Sage Foundation.

CHAPTER FIVE

NATURALIZATION AND U.S. CITIZENSHIP IN TWO PERIODS OF MASS MIGRATION (1890–1930 AND 1965–2000)

Dorothee Schneider

The naturalization of immigrants has been an important facet of American constitutional and immigration history ever since the early days of the republic. The history of naturalization spans over two centuries and must always be seen in the context of the development of American citizenship rights in general. Yet a comparative analysis of naturalization in the two most recent periods of mass migration can illustrate some of the most salient aspects of this history. In both periods of mass migration, naturalization laws reflect the fact that the nation tried to welcome millions of immigrants from many parts of the world and make them part of the fabric of the American citizenry. But the federal government also had to negotiate a central dilemma of American national consciousness through the use of naturalization laws. On the one hand, it was an important part of American national identity to show that citizenship for immigrants was accessible and easy. On the other hand, large-scale naturalizations of diverse immigrant groups also raised fears about the quality of new citizens and the nature of their commitment to the nation. Both periods are therefore characterized by attempts to increase the number of new citizens and the urge to control the naturalization process in the name of creating better citizens.

This chapter focuses on this and related themes that permeate naturalization laws and practices during two periods of mass migration. It outlines how the importance of naturalization gradually increased as the full social and political rights of American citizenship expanded and covered an ever-growing part of the American population before and during the first period of mass migration. This expansion continued during the second period. In tandem with this process of an increasing expansion of citizenship rights came the expansion of federal control over the awarding of naturalization. During the first period, the federal government assumed a gatekeeper function: It excluded immigrants considered unfit to become citizens in the future and gave preferential treatment to certain groups of immigrants through education for citizenship. The second period is characterized by a strong continuing federal presence in the administration of naturalization but a weakening of the gatekeeper functions of the naturalization laws and practices. Today, immigration restrictions, rather than informal and formal restrictions on naturalization, are the primary controls in shaping the new citizenry of the nation.

Another theme that is examined throughout both periods is the relationship between the U.S. government's role and the immigrant communities in regard to naturalization. Throughout the past one hundred years, federal laws have intended policy effects that the immigrants resisted or reinterpreted so that naturalization patterns were often more than a direct reflection of federal intentions. For example, in both periods immigrants have taken advantage of the inducements to naturalize selectively and have sometimes avoided connecting naturalization with increased cultural assimilation. The importance of naturalization has also continued to differ greatly for various immigrant communities that have shown a great variation in naturalization rates.

While the continuities in naturalization law and practice are considerable through the two periods, there are also significant differences in some themes. For one, local control over naturalization, so important in the late nineteenth century, had vanished by the 1960s. In addition, the deeply racial and gendered character of naturalization law has largely disappeared in the past decades. The past thirty years have also seen a fundamental shift in the importance of American citizenship in general. As social citizenship rights have become separated from political citizenship, so, too, has the value of naturalization shifted decisively. A discussion of naturalization and U.S. citizenship in two periods of mass migration will therefore be an examination of the continuities as well as the contrasts between the two periods.

Because research on the history of naturalization is not well established as a field within U.S. social history, much of the following account relies on aggregate statistics and institutional and legal sources for the topic. Such sources answer some of the fundamental questions about the history of citizenship well. But other issues, such as what motivated individuals to become citizens and what impact cultural differences had on naturalization rates, will have to remain largely unanswered at this time. This chapter therefore points to the continuing need to reexamine an important topic within the context of immigration and the social history of the United States.

Constitutional Inclusion and Exclusion during the Nineteenth Century

From the early days of the American republic, the United States was conceived as a nation where immigrants were welcome and expected to become full-fledged citizens of the new nation. Therefore, the Naturalization Law of 1790, which regulated access to American citizenship for the first time, had two basic requirements of foreigners who wanted to become U.S. citizens: They had to be "free white persons," and they had to prove two years of continuous residence in the United States. The access to federal citizenship was administered by "courts of record," that is, federal and some designated state and municipal courts. The federal government did not administer naturalizations and kept no records on completed naturalizations. States added to this bare minimum of regulations by imposing additional requirements. After Congress made some changes in 1795 and 1798, the Naturalization Act of 1802 fixed the fundamentals of the naturalization process, most of which are still in place today: a waiting period of five years of residency, a "declaration of intention" that prospective citizens had to file two years prior to their naturalization, an oath of allegiance containing a renunciation of all former allegiances and aristocratic titles, and two citizen witnesses attesting to one's moral character (Hyneman 1994: 67–86; Kettner 1978: 214–218, 228–236; Le May and Barkan 1999: 11–18).[1] The straightforward and simple naturalization process for federal citizenship stood in sharp contrast to the restricted access to naturalization in European countries, the original home for the vast majority of nineteenth-century immigrants (Bauböck 1994: 71–121, Brubaker 1992: 33–34, 77–84, Kettner 1978: 127). But the simplicity of the process that made foreigners into American citizens also disguised the limited citizenship rights that accompanied naturalization (Kettner 1978: 219). The contours of political citizenship, as linked to naturalization, only gradually emerged between the passage of the Bill of Rights and the Fifteenth Amendment. As the rights of political citizenship became more clearly defined and more comprehensive during the nineteenth century, the struggle over who would be eligible to exercise these rights to their fullest degree became central to American political life (Smith 1997).

In the attempt to define the meaning and boundaries of political citizenship during the nineteenth century, the position of immigrants served to highlight the relationship between race and citizenship law in important ways. Naturalization laws explicitly covered only white immigrants early in the nineteenth century, but this changed with passage of the Fourteenth Amendment, which rendered people of African descent eligible for naturalization. Other attempts to redraw the boundaries of race and citizenship included the treaty of Guadalupe Hidalgo, which included the former citizens of Mexico into the territory of the United States as full-fledged U.S. citizens in 1848. Though this meant that Mexicans were classified as "white," southwestern states curtailed property and other citizen rights of the former Mexicans in various laws (Gutierrez 1995: 17–18; Smith 1997: 229). Chinese immigrants, on the other hand, were declared racially unsuited for American citizenship in a series of court decisions from 1878 on. The right to U.S. citizenship of U.S.-born Chinese Americans was not affirmed until the 1898 *Wong Kim Ark v. United States* decision (Le May and Barkan 1999: 82–84; Salyer 1995: 13–17). The attempt to exclude Irish immigrants of the famine years from naturalization for "racial reasons" failed in the 1840s and 1850s (Franklin 1906: 191–218). Because race was such a defining aspect of citizenship in the United States, racial classification also became a fundamental factor in the admission of immigrants to residency and naturalization in the United States. Other characteristics, such as gender and political and cultural background, would also emerge as important factors in immigrant admission and naturalization. But the parameters of race in connection to citizenship were well established long before the federal government began to administer and regulate the naturalization of immigrants around the turn of the twentieth century.

Administrative Practice and Social Reality of Naturalization during the First Period of Mass Migration

As the nature of American citizenship changed and more inhabitants of the United States became eligible for full citizenship rights, the stakes for naturalization also began to rise. But the federal government had few means to control access to naturalizations in an administrative manner. Although the naturalization of aliens was regulated by federal laws, the administration of naturalization procedures was mostly in the hands of local and state courts during the nineteenth century. The access to federal citizenship and the procedures one needed to follow to gain it could therefore vary considerably from place to place and reflected the circumstances of local politics. Depending on the local social and political status of the immigrant in his or her particular community, the naturalization process could be unproblematic for those with well-connected facilitators in such matters. But the procedures could pose complex and nearly insurmountable hurdles for those without such help. Urban political machines, usually dominated by the Democratic Party, were quick to exploit the peculiarities of the system to their advantage, as they, not the federal government or an independent judiciary, controlled access to citizenship (Myers 1917: 128–129, 154–156, 209, 217). Only immigrants who were likely to be of benefit to a large political party as future voters could get help in naturalization—and thus to be naturalized in disproportionate numbers. Irish men and other immigrants who were considered likely Democratic voters were recruited by ward bosses who supplied the necessary papers and witnesses and coached immigrants through citizenship examinations (Myers 1917: 155–156; *New York Tribune,* July 20, October 22, October 30, 1880; October 23, 1891).[2] By the late nineteenth century, the naturalization hearings were often conducted by sympathetic judges, themselves appointees of the political machine, who transformed hundreds of petitioners into newly minted Americans in a single day (*New York Times,* October 24, 1866; September 11, 1871; *New York Tribune,* November 28, 1878; October 2, 3, 4, and 28, 1894; July 31, 1905). Immigrants who were unlikely to vote for the political party in charge were naturalized in much smaller numbers, though the opposition parties, the

Republicans or various labor groups, tried to furnish an alternative apparatus for their likely clients. Ethnic voters who tried to become naturalized without help were often challenged by the courts as to the veracity of their information, their knowledge of English, or the qualifications of their witnesses (*New York Tribune*, October 24, 1891; October 18, 1892; August 5, 1895; May 21, 1903; December 5, 1904).

The system of naturalization based on what Buenker (1988) called "organic networks" had a number of different consequences. For one, it tended to exclude more recent immigrant groups from naturalization in disproportionate numbers, unless they enlisted the help of "old-timers" as facilitators. Gavit's (1992) study of urban naturalization records in 1913–1914 shows that 6.7 percent of naturalization petitioners were from Ireland, even though foreign Irishmen made up only 3.8 percent of all city dwellers four years earlier. Russian Jews were also overrepresented in Gavit's sample of naturalization petitioners, possibly because they received the help of German Jewish aid associations in this regard. Italian and Greek immigrants, on the other hand, were only half as numerous as should have been expected from their numbers in urban areas. Together they made up 14 percent of all petitioners even though they were almost a quarter of all urban dwellers four years earlier (Gavit 1922: 229).[3] In part, this may have been due to the high percentage of Italian and Greek immigrants who returned to Europe after a few years in the United States. But Italians also lacked the protection and support of urban political machines. In those places where they had organized systems facilitating naturalization, they were exposed to criminal investigations for citizenship fraud (*New York Tribune*, June 10, 1903; April 6, August 11 and 13, 1904; President's Commission on Naturalization, 1905: 76–78). At least in major urban centers, the low naturalization rates of some groups were more a result of a lack of political and institutional support systems than of any inherent cultural or political bias on the part of immigrants.

Neither the uneven access to citizenship nor the principle of local control prompted calls for reform in the late nineteenth century. Instead, the instrumentalization of citizenship for machine voting and the corruption surrounding it became the focus of reforms. The fear that new voters were not ready for the duties of American citizenship had always accompanied the debate about naturalization. But it was not until the early twentieth century that lasting reform on the federal level was attempted to amend the perceived problems. The first of a number of recurring cycles of change designed to reassert federal control over naturalization and a rationalized, centralized system of administration occurred between the 1890s and 1907. It began with investigations of naturalization fraud on the local level, conducted mostly by newspapers, but also by municipal reform politicians. The investigations led to the arrest of corrupt officials and the removal of judges in some cities, but for the most part they targeted immigrant facilitators and naturalization petitioners (*Chicago Record Herald*, August 18, 1904; *New York Tribune*, October 30, 1895; February 2 and March 30, 1896; December 20, 1903; April 5 and August 13, 1904; January 11 and February 11, 1906). Beginning in 1895, New York and some other cities also tried to fix the systemic problems in naturalization procedures by enacting laws that restricted voting to those who had become naturalized at least six or three months prior to an election. Such laws, which were passed on the municipal level, thus weakened the direct connection between naturalization and suffrage in local and national elections (*New York Tribune*, February 1 and 9, May 8, July 11, and August 7, 1895).[4]

In the early twentieth century, the federal government became involved in the attempt to reform naturalization partly as a response to municipal reformers and partly in response to the calls for immigration restriction.[5] In 1904, Theodore Roosevelt appointed the President's Commission on Naturalization, which collected opinions from members of the court system and immigration experts on ways to reform and rationalize naturalization under federal auspices. Many of the comments the commission received focused on eliminating corruption in the court system and strengthening federal oversight in naturalization procedures. These recommendations ultimately led to the Naturalization Act of 1906, the first law to comprehensively regulate naturalization since 1802 (President's Commission on Naturalization 1905).[6] Its main purpose was to establish federal control over the naturalization process. The law unified naturalization procedures and fees nationwide and put them under the supervision of the newly founded Division of Naturalization under the auspices of the (renamed) Federal Bureau of Immigration and Naturalization, part of the Department of Commerce and Labor.

From then on, field examiners of the Division of Naturalization, located in the major centers of immigration, checked the petitions of citizenship candidates before recommending them for court approval. The central office in Washington issued policy recommendations and decisions in cases where the existing naturalization law was unclear. The law also authorized the commissioner of naturalization to gather statistical information on all naturalizations (*New York Tribune*, July 3, 1906; Smith 1926: 7–10).[7] These reforms not only heightened vigilance toward corrupt local practices and irregularities, but also led to a decline in the number of applicants for citizenship since many petitioners were rejected by the examiners before their petitions reached the courts (see figure 5.1). The law itself raised the hurdle for naturalization for individual immigrants in another respect. It required all applicants to show their familiarity with the English language in addition to the required knowledge of the Constitution, although how this examination was to be conducted was left open (Smith 1997: 447; U.S. Bureau of Immigration and Naturalization 1908).[8]

For the most part, it was the administrative controls put in place by the 1906 law that increased the role of federal authorities as gatekeepers to U.S. citizenship. Naturalization reform, while focusing on rationalizing

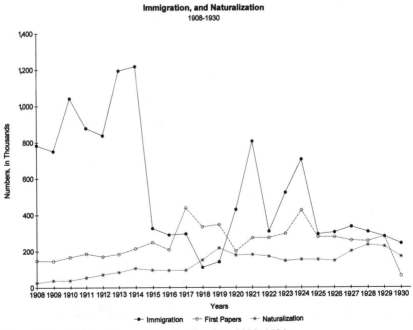

Figure 5.1. Immigration and Naturalization, 1908–1930

and centralizing the administration of citizenship, clearly had an exclusionary effect on some immigrant groups. The naturalization petition cost ($5.00) and a lack of knowledge of English were the most often cited reasons for not naturalizing among immigrants in subsequent years. The strict record-keeping requirements by the federal bureau also made it difficult for many immigrants to furnish all the necessary information about the date of original arrival and past residences (*The Interpreter* 1928b: 3–7, 1929: 35–37, 156–159; U.S. Department of Labor 1926: 16).[9]

The statistical data gathered by the Division of Naturalization beginning in 1907 allows us to corroborate this information by comparing the number of people declaring their intention to naturalize (a relatively easy procedure) with those who applied for citizenship with its more complex requirements.[10] Until the 1920s, the number of those who filed a "declaration of intention" (first papers) was three or four times the number of those who were awarded citizenship. Completed naturalizations were very low in the early years of the law, numbering almost 26,000 in 1907–1908 nationwide and below 40,000 in the two following years (U.S. Bureau of Immigration and Naturalization 1908, 1909, 1910). This contrasts with up to 15,000 naturalizations in one New York court alone during 1888 and 1892 (*New York Tribune*, August 7, 1895).

Gradually, naturalizations began to increase, climbing to 105,493 in 1913–1914 and again to more than twice that number by 1919. These figures, however, bear little relationship to the very large number of immigrants entering the country during 1900–1914. According to the census of 1920, the majority of foreign-born residents were not naturalized U.S. citizens. It was not until the census of 1930 that the majority of the foreign born had become naturalized (U.S. Bureau of the Census 1949: 32).

The assertion of the federal government's role as a gatekeeper to citizenship was complemented by a growing federal role in the restriction of immigration and residency of immigrants between 1903 and 1924. Those deemed unsuitable for immigration or residency (people belonging to the so-called excludable classes) were often also barred from naturalization. The connection was most obvious in the case of East Asian immigrants who were barred from entering the United States if they were Chinese or admitted only under very limited conditions if they were Japanese. Both groups were barred from naturalization. In other cases, the two sets of laws did not mesh as well. The racial exclusions to immigration were not applied to men and women from India or to Armenians and Syrians. But immigrants from these countries often found themselves excluded from naturalization as "Asiatics," a charge they fought in the courts, where they tried to prove their whiteness with varying success (Smith 1997: 447–448; Ueda 1980; Vecoli 1987: 76–78). Citizens of the Philippines, on the other hand, were excluded from U.S. citizenship unless they had served in the U.S. Navy. Puerto Ricans, though not excludable from living in the United States since they were not foreigners, were not granted citizenship until 1917 (Le May and Barkan 1999: 112, 295; Smith 1997: 429–430).

Other immigrant groups were caught in two nets: immigration restriction and limited access to naturalization. Federal law excluded from residency those deemed "likely to become a public charge" and those suspected of immoral conduct, as well as anarchists and polygamists, and rendered them deportable within three years of entry. While only a small proportion of immigrants overall were excluded by these provisions, the scrutiny of immigration officials tended to focus on certain groups: single women, working-class Mexicans, suspected radicals from eastern Europe, and Muslims from Turkey. They had a somewhat more difficult time to enter the country and were less likely to apply for citizenship later.[11] The federal gatekeepers could thus use immigration indirectly to discourage naturalization of certain immigrant groups.

But the Federal role was not limited to denying immigrants access to residency and citizenship. Parts of naturalization law also tried to shape the citizenry in active ways. Thus, the admission of women and men as immigrants and citizens was calibrated to build a nation of citizen families headed by men. For example, women's close connection to kin in the United States was a crucial element in judging their admissibility (U.S. Immigration and Naturalization Service, Records of the INS 51451/329, 51598, 51698/7, 51777/265, and 52503/13, 55235/188). The absence of family and kin, on the other hand, rendered women immigrants suspect in the eyes of the authorities. Naturalization law formalized this discrepancy. Both single men and single women could apply for naturalization. However, between 1855 and 1921, married women automatically assumed the nationality of their husbands under the American law and could not petition for naturalization in their own right. According to a 1907 law, American-born women who married non-U.S. citizens lost their American citizenship and could not regain it unless their husbands became naturalized.[12] Conversely, between 1855 and 1921, American citizenship was automatic for foreign women on marriage to a U.S. citizen or their husband's naturalization. No "test" of English, knowledge of the Constitution, or testimony of good conduct needed to be furnished for these women (Bredbenner 1998: 50–54).[13] Indeed, the Bureau of Naturalization, which did not count women in its naturalization statistics, assumed that for every successful petition at least three additional certificates of naturalization would be issued, namely, those for the wife and the minor children of the petitioner.[14]

The Cable Act of 1922 separated the citizenship of married women from that of their husbands and made most of them subject to the same rules and qualifications as men. Even though some gender differences would persist, the act was a fundamental step in rendering American naturalization and immigration law gender neutral. The result of the law was at first an apparent drop in the number of women who became naturalized citizens. During fiscal year 1922–1923, the first year during which women became naturalized independently, statistics published (for the first time) on women's naturalizations showed that about 11 percent of all petitions were filed by women. The number climbed gradually throughout the 1920s and 1930s, and by 1941 the majority of certificates of naturalization were issued to women.[15]

As early as the turn of the twentieth century, long before women immigrants had to seek naturalization in their own right, reformers had become concerned that immigrants who completed the naturalization process successfully were far from being equipped to fully understand their obligations and rights as citizens. Screening immigrants for reasons to exclude them from naturalization did not make good citizens out of those who passed the test. Progressive reformers therefore began a push to add instruction in American citizenship to prepare for naturalization in order, as they imagined it, to secure continuity in the character of American democracy (Abbott 1917: 247–266; *Chicago Record Herald,* October 2, 1905; Herrmann 1994: 30–60; *Immigrant in America Review* 1915: 75–76; *New York Tribune,* August 11, 1904). World War I put "Americanization," as it was soon called, at center stage in the home-front effort to unite the nation. For the first time, the campaign involved the federal government in the effort to make Americans out of immigrants. Amid the heightened nationalist fervor, a wide-ranging partnership of reformers, patriotic groups, and businesses, as well as municipal, state, and federal authorities, took up the campaign for Americanization and institutionalized it in countless lectures, classes, and evening schools (Hartman 1948: 164–187; Herrmann 1994: 73–178).

It was an integral part of this campaign that naturalization was linked closely to the cultural and social Americanization of immigrants. By 1916, the power of the federal government was harnessed to serve in this campaign of assimilation in a number of ways. During World War I, the Bureau of Naturalization helped initiate a large network of citizenship programs run by nongovernmental agencies (staffed mostly by volunteers) in public schools, clubs, and civic organizations. The bureau wrote up and printed materials and kept tabs on the materials taught in countless citizenship classes with the goal of increasing the number of well-informed naturalized citizen voters (Herrmann 1994: 154–170; U.S. Bureau of Immigration and Naturalization 1917–1921). Some municipalities, states, and employers coupled the exhortations to Americanize with more substantial pressure: Employers linked job promotions or even the jobs themselves to the acquisition of citizenship. Some made the attendance of citizenship classes obligatory for their immigrant employees. Congress mandated that the newly established income tax was twice as high for "nonresident aliens" (though the particular meaning of this phrase was left unclear). Some states forbade instruction in foreign languages in public schools or even the speaking of German in public. Though naturalization itself could not be mandated by states or the federal government (except for government employees), noncitizens were vulnerable to loss of job opportunity, political disenfranchisement, and exclusion, especially during World War I and the subsequent Red Scare of 1919–1920 (Bierstadt 1922: 42–49, 95–100; Herrmann 1994: 258–264; Higham 1955: 247–250).[16]

The close connection between Americanization and government coercion had a powerful negative effect on immigrant communities. Coercive methods and the pressure to deny one's cultural heritage were criticized in the immigrant press and by immigrant aid organizations. Immigrants themselves offered their own passive resistance by refusing to enroll in Americanization programs on a sustained basis. This backlash from the groups the Americanizers sought to serve made progressive reformers reconsider their use of political and legal powers to further their goal of increasing and improving American citizenship among immigrants (Bierstadt 1922: 93–136; Hartman 1948: 253–266; Higham 1955: 261–263).

Overall, the impact of the Americanization campaign on the rate of naturalization had been modest by the end of the war. Despite the steeply climbing number of "declarations of intention" between 1914 and 1917, the actual number of petitions for naturalization did not show a discernible increase: The figure for 1917 was barely higher than in 1914 and dipped in the intervening period. Completed naturalizations actually declined during the war years and rose only in 1918, reaching their apex in the following year.

The only naturalization program that could be called a success was military naturalization. Introduced by a special congressional law in 1918, it allowed members of the armed forces to naturalize without filing a declaration of intention first and with a minimum of formality (in most cases, no citizenship or English examination took place). In all, more than 288,000 men took advantage of this law until 1924. The program was based on the notion that draftees were already fulfilling the most fundamental of citizenship duties and therefore should not be barred from citizenship because they lacked other, lesser qualifications (Gavit 1922: 255–294; Roberts 1920: 119–120; U.S. Bureau of Immigration and Naturalization 1924).[17] But the procedure also did exactly the opposite of what Americanizers intended: It emphasized the quid pro quo character of naturalization. In exchange for a soldier's willingness to give his life, he received U.S. citizenship.

Forced by congressional budget cuts to scale back their efforts after 1919, the Americanizers continued, on a more modest level, educational programs in English-language literacy and American history in order to help immigrants become American citizens. These classes had better-trained teachers and more appropriate textbooks to work with than during the earlier years. Immigrants appreciated these offerings, especially if fellow ethnics taught them. Citizenship classes could serve as conduits for further education in night schools, or they would simply provide a socially approved institutional setting for the more isolated immigrants (especially women) when they wanted to venture out in public.[18]

Given the intensive Americanization efforts, some people may be surprised that, after a high of more than 217,000 in 1919, naturalizations fell in the following years. However, the fall was caused mainly by a drop-off in military naturalizations. After 1923, the numbers climbed again, reaching more than 228,000 in 1928, and then leveled off again thereafter. Between 1921 and 1931, the largest groups of the newly naturalized were Italians, Poles, and eastern European Jews. With the exception of eastern European Jews, these were precisely the groups that had been most numerous among immigrants during the previous decades and that had often delayed their naturalization the longest. Together with other southern and eastern Europeans (especially Greeks and Czechs), they made up more than 50 percent of newly naturalized citizens in the 1920s (U.S. Bureau of Immigration and Naturalization 1930).

Three factors seem to have motivated men and women from southern and eastern Europe to become U.S. citizens during the 1920s. The first and foremost was the passage of quota laws in 1921 and 1924. Both the 1921 and the 1924 immigration acts subjected all immigrants to a system of immigration controls based on race, nationality, and family ties. Prospective immigrants from eastern and southern Europe were assigned low annual immigration quotas, whereas those from western and northern Europe benefited under this system with high quotas. But the law gave preference within the quotas to wives and minor children of U.S. citizens. Thus, longtime resident aliens from southern and eastern Europe could more easily negotiate the quota hurdle and bring their families to the United States if they acquired citizenship (Foreign Language Information Service 1926; Kansas 1953).[19]

A second factor to impel a larger percentage of immigrants to become naturalized was the fact that American citizenship began to hold out the promise of more than just basic legal and political rights in the 1920s. As the social and regulatory functions of the state increased, notions of social citizenship grew as well. The 1920s witnessed the large-scale growth of public secondary and higher education, for example, and also saw the modest growth of government-supported social services. In some states, such as Illinois, women could receive mothers' pensions only if they were citizens. Immigrant women, usually less motivated to become U.S. citizens for the voting rights than men, found it important to render themselves eligible for social benefits that could keep their families afloat during hard times. In this context, many women welcomed Americanization programs because they facilitated naturalization for the less educated or less well connected (Breckinridge 1932: 101, 106, 111; Gordon 1994; Skocpol 1992: 424–479).

The end of the first period of mass migration was marked by the implementation of the first comprehensive immigration restrictions in the nation's history. But when it came to naturalizations, no comprehensive change took place. The basic principles governing the making of new citizens embodied in the early laws of the nineteenth century were still in place. What had changed were administrative procedures that governed naturalizations. By and large, a more centralized and bureaucratized naturalization process tried to rationalize the making of citizens. A more fundamental change, which would shape naturalization policy during the second period of mass migration, had only just begun: the elimination of racial and gender barriers to becoming an American citizen.

Naturalization in the Interim Period

Even though the decades from the passage of the quota laws to their elimination in 1965 separate the two periods of mass migration, important developments regarding naturalization took place during this intermediate period. In a trend that began with the passage of the 1922 Cable Act, naturalization law became more gender and race neutral during this period of much-diminished immigration and naturalization. In effect, this meant that the right to become an American citizen was extended to larger segments of the immigrant population at the same time that full citizenship rights in general (especially regarding social citizenship) gradually covered a larger part of the American people. Thus, while the 1930s, 1940s, and 1950s can be regarded as an interim period in which immigration declined and naturalization numbers remained low during most years, these decades also mark a turning point in the history of citizenship and naturalization rights in general.

Immigration declined quickly after the enactment of the first quota laws in 1921. It remained at an all-time low throughout the 1930s because of the State Department's reluctance to issue immigration visas—even in countries whose quotas were ample (such as Britain and Germany). Naturalization figures also dropped. The legal advantages of citizenship for helping relatives immigrate diminished in the 1930s and 1940s. Few American consuls would give immigrant visas even to those with family ties and within quota limits. The first steep decline in naturalizations between 1929 and 1931 was probably due to a sudden rise in application fees mandated by Congress in 1929. But applications for citizenship rose only gradually until the outbreak of World War II, reaching a sudden all-time high during the period 1943–1944. A number of factors seem to have been responsible for this drop and the subsequent rise.[20] During the Depression years, the cohort eligible for naturalization shrank, as many older immigrants died or remigrated to Europe and few replaced them in the United States. Of those who remained, many may have taken out citizenship papers in order to qualify for Works Progress Administration (WPA) jobs or other New Deal programs open only to U.S. citizens. Others were requested to become American citizens by their private-sector employers. World War II and the years immediately preceding it brought a turnaround as new immigrants (many of them refugees from the Nazis) as well as the remaining old-timers sought U.S. citizenship in unprecedented numbers. Naturalizations reached an all-time high of more than 450,000 in 1944 as enemy aliens sought to shed this label and become U.S. citizens. The largest groups to naturalize during the early 1940s were Italians, immigrants from the British Empire, and Germans, but Czechs were also numerous, reflecting the proportions in the first era of mass migration (Le May and Barkan 1999: 196, 220–231). As a result of the relatively high naturalization but low immigration rates in the 1930s and early 1940s, the percentage of nonnaturalized immigrants in the United States dropped to an all-time low. Only 21.3 percent of immigrants living in the United States in 1950 were not naturalized, according to statistics from the U.S. Bureau of the Census (Gibson and Lennon 1999).

The postwar period was characterized by an increasing number of persons admitted as refugees from Europe rather than as immigrants. Most of these refugees, let in under special provisions or congressional acts, were either displaced as a result of World War II or had fled the advance of communist governments in eastern Europe. Despite the anticommunist beliefs of many of these newcomers, they were not quick to become naturalized. With the exception of 1956, post–World War II naturalization figures remained low, with fewer than 150,000 naturalizations per year. The most important change in naturalization law and practice during this interim period, which would have long-term structural effects, was the gradual elimination of racial limitations on naturalizations. In

1943, Congress repealed the Chinese Exclusion Act, and the president subsequently authorized a minimal yearly quota of 105 under which Chinese immigrants could be admitted. The repeal of the act rendered Chinese eligible for naturalization (Le May and Barkan 1999: 196–197). The statistical effects of this on the naturalization figures for the small Chinese American community were minimal at first: Just under 500 Chinese were naturalized in 1943 and more than 700 in 1944 and 1945, but the principle of racial exclusion had been greatly weakened. The 1952 McCarran–Walter Act banned all racially based prohibitions against the naturalization of immigrants, rendering Japanese and Koreans eligible for naturalization for the first time. Thousands of Japanese immigrants, most of them elderly, took advantage of this right to naturalize in the first two years of the law (Le May and Barkan 1999: 218–225). The law also contained a provision formalizing the English-language requirement for applicants for citizenship and abolished the declaration of intent as a required first step for naturalization.

Naturalization Policy and Practice after the End of the Nationality Quotas

The second era of mass migration began with the abolition of nationality quotas in 1965 and is still under way. It is most obviously characterized by the large absolute numbers of immigrants who have arrived in the United States from a very diverse array of countries and cultures. Today, U.S. immigration law contains no racial or ethnic preferences and excludes no nationality groups. But as in the earlier period of mass migration, immigration continues to be regulated by an array of laws limiting admission. Trends and developments in naturalization policy and its administration since 1965 fall into two periods. The first era followed the passage of the 1965 law and ended with significant legislative changes designed to remedy problems left unregulated by the immigration law. During the second period, from about 1982 on, the full effect of both the 1965 law and the legislation of the early and mid-1980s became obvious in patterns of immigration and naturalization (see figure 5.2).

The immigration law of 1965 fundamentally changed the composition and size of immigrant cohorts over the next decades. The new law gave immigrants with exceptional professional qualifications and those

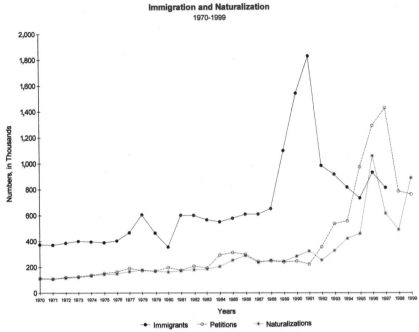

Immigration and Naturalization
1970-1999

Figure 5.2. Immigration and Naturalization, 1970–1999

with close family members who were U.S. citizens the highest priority in the allotment of visas. At first, the system favored immigrants from traditional countries of emigration in Europe and Canada since those were the people with close family ties to U.S. citizens. Thus, the largest groups of new immigrants remained Europeans and Canadians (combined) until 1968. Therefore, until 1977, the plurality of citizenship applications also came from European immigrants.[21] But with the gradual increase in immigration from outside Europe after 1965, the composition of naturalization petitioners slowly began to change. Accompanying this change was a gradual but steady increase in the number of naturalizations beginning in 1972—a change from the stagnant and very low numbers of the 1960s (U.S. Immigration and Naturalization Service 1996). The connection between a rise in naturalizations and an increasing proportion of immigrants from non-European countries was demonstrated by a 1979 statistical report of the Immigration and Naturalization Service that tracked the naturalization status of a statistical sample of those who had entered the country as immigrants in 1972. The researchers found that immigrants from non-European countries, especially those from East and Southeast Asia, filed naturalization applications much sooner than European immigrants. More than 80 percent of Koreans and 73 percent of Chinese who were still in the United States eight years later had become naturalized. The percentages were not much lower for Filipinos and Asian Indians (both more than 67 percent). Among Mexicans, only 5 percent had become naturalized after eight years of residence. Among Canadians, only 3.4 percent had. Almost 20 percent of European immigrants had become citizens in the same time period (Barkan 1983; U.S. Interagency Task Force on Immigration Policy 1979). A rough comparison of 1964–1974 immigrant cohorts from a dozen nations with the 1973–1982 cohorts of naturalizations yielded a similar range of percentages (North 1986: 42).

No comprehensive explanations were offered regarding the different naturalization rates of people from different countries, although the low naturalization rates of Latino immigrants did attract the attention of policymakers and researchers in the 1980s. Much of the research covering the 1970s and early 1980s focused on obstacles to naturalization such as bureaucratic hurdles, social isolation, and lack of resources on the part of immigrants. As in the older studies of Breckinridge (1932) and Gavit (1922), scholars of the past two decades have linked naturalization rates to socioeconomic and cultural factors of integration, such as home ownership, number of children born in the United States, and citizenship status of spouse. The cultural specificity of these factors for Mexicans (in contrast to, for example, Chinese) was not analyzed but only implied (Yang 1994). Research on naturalization conducted for much of the 1970s and 1980s also paralleled the efforts of social scientists during the first period of mass migration in that very few studied the meaning of naturalization and the uses of U.S. citizenship for discrete immigrant communities (Chen 1992; DeSipio1987; Kasinitz 1992). In some cases, political mobilization (usually around local issues) occurred in tandem with naturalization, but the connection was not always clear. Some immigrant groups, such as Filipinos and Koreans, became naturalized in high numbers without becoming politically active and visible. Other immigrant groups, such as Latinos, were politically visible even though a relatively large proportion of activists may not have been naturalized (Jones-Correa 1998).

American citizenship was seen as useful and important by those immigrants who became naturalized at high rates for reasons other than the right to vote. As the wait for immigrant visas in general lengthened in the 1980s and 1990s, the importance of U.S. citizenship grew for close relatives of those applying for visas under family reunification preferences. East Asian and Caribbean immigrant groups, who had a very high rate of continuous immigration under family reunification provisions, therefore also had high naturalization rates from the 1960s on. For others, such as Mexicans, formal family reunification was not as urgent a concern and did not serve to raise naturalization rates significantly (Barkan 1983; Yang 1994).

The aggregate numbers of the U.S. Bureau of the Census show that during the 1970s and 1980s, the overall rate of naturalization failed to keep up with the more rapidly rising rate of immigration. While the number of foreign-born residents of the United States increased by 35 percent in the 1970s and another 34 percent in the 1980s, the percentage of naturalized citizens among the U.S. population declined in these decades. By 1990, only 40.5 percent of all foreign-born residents were naturalized, the lowest percentage ever recorded by the census (Gibson and Lennon 1999). At the same time, the rapid diversification of immigrants as a whole beginning in the mid-1960s gradually made naturalized citizens into a very heterogeneous group as well. The five largest immigrant groups to naturalize made up only about 50 percent of all naturalizations in the 1970s, whereas fifty years earlier, the five largest groups had provided more than 65 percent of all new citizens. By the 1990s, the diversity of the newly naturalized as a group had increased so that the five largest countries of origin made up only about 40 percent of the total.

Immigration and Naturalization Policies in the 1980s and 1990s

Few observers paid much attention to the changing makeup of new citizens before the mid-1980s. Instead, politicians and policymakers sought to remedy problems perceived as more urgent in the late 1970s and early 1980s: refugee admissions and illegal immigration. The Refugee Act of 1980 was the first comprehensive legislation to create a unified procedure for refugee admission separate from regular immigration and outside the existing preference system. Passed originally in response to the continued need to deal with the refugee flow from Southeast Asia and the Soviet

Union, the act allowed just over one million refugees to become permanent residents in the 1980s and another million between 1990 and 1998 (Reimers 1985: 153–199; U.S. Immigration and Naturalization Service 1997; U.S. Select Commission on Immigration and Refugee Policy 1980). These high numbers began to have an impact on naturalizations by the 1980s, as refugees generally have shown a higher propensity to naturalize than other immigrants.

Illegal immigration, in many ways a more complicated political issue than refugee admission, became the second focus of the debate on immigration and naturalization. By the mid-1980s, the flow of undocumented workers had reached new heights. The U.S. Immigration and Naturalization Service (1996) recorded almost 1.6 million "voluntary departures" of illegal aliens caught by the agency in 1986 alone. The 1986 Immigration Reform and Control Act (IRCA) attempted to overhaul the admission process for workers, change the role of employers in the system, and strengthen the law enforcement role of the Immigration and Naturalization Service. The act promised penalties for those who employed illegal aliens, imposed stricter border controls, and allowed for easier deportations of illegal border crossers. Most important for purposes of naturalization, it provided an amnesty for illegal immigrants who could prove that they had resided in the United States continuously since 1982. Amnestied immigrants would be eligible for naturalization beginning in 1992 (Le May and Barkan 1999: 282–288).

Naturalization figures in the 1980s and 1990s reflect the effects of both the refugee admissions and IRCA closely. From 1982 to 1986, almost 1.3 million immigrants applied to the Immigration and Naturalization Service to become U.S. citizens. This represented a more than 60 percent increase over the previous five years. A closer look at these figures hints that the sudden rise was influenced by the large percentage of refugees from Southeast Asia and Cuba who had come in the late 1970s and early 1980s. Indeed, Asians made up almost 50 percent of the new citizen cohort on the average, immigrants from the Americas about one-third. The impact of IRCA on naturalizations was even more dramatic. When the first group of amnestied immigrants became eligible to apply for naturalization in 1992, petitions for U.S. citizenship suddenly shot up by almost 50 percent, to 342,269. The unprecedented figure of 1992 was eclipsed in subsequent years; by 1998, it had reached more than 1.4

million petitions, exceeding any previous records. The sudden rise in naturalization petitions clogged up the machinery of making citizens despite a 1990 effort at procedural reform (Aleinikoff 1993: 953–955; DeSipio and de la Garza 1998: 75–78).[22] Therefore, the number of completed naturalizations climbed much more slowly than the number of petitions for citizenship. By the end of fiscal year 1998, the backlog of pending naturalization cases had swelled to almost 1.9 million, and waiting periods of two years had now become routine. Since then, the number of naturalization applicants has declined significantly, and by August 2000 it had returned to the levels experienced in the early 1990s (U.S. Immigration and Naturalization Service 1997: 142).[23]

Researchers and political observers have come to the conclusion that the developments in the 1990s were caused by a combination of factors. The increase in citizenship applications overall has commonly been understood to be a result of the large number of new immigrants in the past two decades. Especially aliens who came in the 1970s or 1980s were legalized under IRCA provisions and became eligible for naturalization in the early or mid-1990s.

In order to uncover what specific factors influenced the naturalization rates of different groups of immigrants, since 1990 the Immigration and Naturalization Service has conducted two record-linked studies of the immigrants who came in 1977 and 1982, respectively.[24] DeSipio and de la Garza did a smaller analysis of immigrant cohorts and naturalization trends in the 1980s and 1990s, focusing specifically on Latino immigrants (DeSipio and de la Garza 1998: 81–85). In addition, Yang (1994: 449–473) did a broader study using a sample from the Public Use Microdata Sample (PUMS) data. All these studies have shown that the length of time until naturalization varies according to country of origin, visa category at time of arrival, and age at time of arrival, confirming the earlier analyses of Portes and others. Regardless of economic and educational background, refugee status or status as an amnestied illegal alien under IRCA provisions also increased the likelihood of naturalization. Those whose status as parolees and asylees gave them limited opportunity to qualify for permanent residence showed, unsurprisingly, less propensity to become naturalized. The distribution of nationality groups also shows a shift in the past decade and a half with a larger percentage of new citizens coming from the Americas (especially Mexico) than ever before. Mexicans are still underrepresented among new citizens, compared to their number among new legal immigrants, but they have been the largest nationality group to become naturalized since 1993.

The growing eagerness of Mexicans to take on U.S. citizenship has been attributed to the political mobilization that occurred mainly in southern California in response to a growing anti-immigrant and anti-affirmative action movements that culminated in a California ballot initiative known as Proposition 187 (Reimers 1998: 31–33, 100–101, 133–135). This vocal, though largely regional, movement had among its goals a more drastic enforcement of border controls, the elimination of bilingual education and bilingualism in public life, and the screening of all users of public institutions (hospitals, schools, and so on) for immigrant status. The movement was endorsed by some mainstream political candidates during electoral campaigns, especially in California and Arizona, and during the presidential race of 1992 and the elections of 1994, giving it widespread publicity (Le May and Barkan 1999: 296–301; Perea 1997:61–161). Within a few years, however, it had become obvious that the new restrictionist movement had helped foster a large-scale counter-movement of Latino and other immigrant communities that focused on large-scale naturalization and voter registration among new Latino immigrants. By 1996, the growth of the Latino electorate in southern California had helped defeat some notable proponents of immigrant restriction. The potential power of Latino voters and the return of economic prosperity silenced other politicians whose otherwise conservative attitudes would have made them likely allies for a new restrictionist movement.

The mobilization of immigrants as U.S. citizens and voters has always been regarded with ambivalence by many politicians in Congress. Such large-scale movements can change the political balance of power not just regionally; they can also change the character of political parties and constituencies in fundamental ways. In the mid- and late 1990s, the possibility for such a change and the danger it would bring were of particular concern to conservative politicians, especially to Republicans. At the same time, conservatives were also expressing growing anxiety over what was widely seen as the diminishing importance of political citizenship and the rising importance of social citizenship rights. The debate over the latter issues took place mostly in the context of welfare reform, but important components of it also touched on the rights of immigrants and resident aliens.

Since the 1960s, the growing network of social support programs in the United States has also meant an expansion of rights and entitlements for noncitizen resident aliens. Almost all the rights (and some of the duties) traditionally assumed to be part of American citizenship had become available to resident aliens by the early 1980s. Participation in Social Security, supplemental Social Security, Aid to Families with Dependent Children (AFDC; welfare), Medicare and Medicaid programs, as well as expanding protections from deportations were part of this catalog. With the importance of social rights eclipsing the right to vote for many residents, there was little incentive for many immigrants to become naturalized citizens in the 1970s and 1980s, at least if they did not feel the need to gain political empowerment as voters (Schuck 1984; Yang 1994: 451–454).

Congress and the executive branch were of two minds over these developments. On the one hand, the expansion of social rights and entitlements for all residents was part of the legacy of the 1960s civil rights movements and Great Society programs, which in turn were part of the bedrock of national consciousness. On the other hand, the naturalization of a large percentage of immigrants also continued to be seen as one of the underpinnings of American immigration policy. The lack of interest in becoming naturalized was considered detrimental to the legitimacy of traditional American immigration policy and representative government in general (U.S. Commission on Immigration Reform 1994). The congressional majority reacted to these issues with a "carrot and stick" set of policies. On the one hand, it increased the incentive to become a U.S. citizen through a set of policies that diminished the social rights of noncitizen residents. In 1996, Congress passed the Personal Responsibility and Work Opportunity Act and the Illegal Immigration Reform and Immigrant Responsibility Act, both of which were designed to exclude noncitizens from an array of "welfare" programs, such as supplemental Social Security income (Schneider 2000).

This set of punitive laws (as far as noncitizens were concerned) was somewhat counterbalanced by the Clinton administration's large-scale publicity and administrative project in 1995, called Citizenship 2000, which sought to facilitate the naturalization of newcomers, especially beneficiaries of the 1986 IRCA amnesty. But this program, with its implication of increased access to naturalization and citizenship for hundreds of thousands of working-class Latinos, also alarmed conservatives in Congress who wanted the Immigration and Naturalization Service's gatekeeper function in naturalization strengthened. They accused the agency of naturalizing thousands of unqualified aliens as part of the program by using sloppy procedures and insufficient background checks. The accusations focused on southern California, where in 1996 longtime Republican Congressman Robert Dornan had been narrowly defeated by a Democrat of Latino descent after a heavy naturalization and voter registration program directed at Latino voters. The vociferous debate about voting fraud, which was reminiscent of similar accusations after elections of late nineteenth-century urban Democrats in immigrant districts, resulted in the abandonment of Citizenship 2000. Instead, Congress passed a law mandating more stringent background checks of naturalization petitioners. This law further contributed to the already enormous backlog of naturalization applications but did not slow down the rate of petitions (Congressional Research Service 1998).

Immigrants' desire to take out American citizenship in the past two decades should not be seen solely as a result of domestic U.S. politics. The changing importance of citizenship and the shape of nationality laws in the immigrant's country of origin are also a factor. Unlike during the first period of migration, when only a minority engaged in regular remigration back and forth to the country of origin, late twentieth-century immigrants to the United States are increasingly seen as migrants engaged in a continual cycle of migration between their homes with multiple loyalties and social citizenships. As a result, many nations—the United States among them—have shown an increasing tolerance toward persons with dual citizenship. This development, part of the phenomenon commonly referred to as transnationalism, had its origins in the liberal citizenship policies of formerly British colonies in the Caribbean, such as Jamaica and Trinidad and Tobago, which, as independent nations, encouraged their overseas citizens to retain their citizenship and participate in the political life of the homeland (Basch et al. 1994; Foner 1997; Kearney 1995; Portes et al. 1999). Since the mid-1990s, some larger countries of emigration to the United States (such as Mexico and the Dominican Republic) also changed their laws permitting dual citizenship for emigrants. Meanwhile, the United States has continued its silent toleration of naturalized citizens who maintain their old citizenship. Transnational citizens with multiple political identities form a small part of the immigration cohort in the United States so far. But, unlike in the early twentieth century, immigrants with more than one national citizenship are likely to increase in the United States. This factor will have impact on the American political scene as well. Citizenship and national allegiance have assumed multiple meanings by the twenty-first century, a reality insufficiently absorbed by U.S. policymakers.

Conclusion

Naturalization policies are always a reflection of a nation's identity and its relationship to its citizens and to its noncitizen immigrants. During the past century and a half, naturalization policies and practices in the United States defined the country's identity to an important degree. They have also undergone some fundamental changes with three areas of change particularly important: 1) Over the two periods of mass migration, U.S. citizenship has become increasingly accessible to a wider range of immigrants; 2) the citizenship rights one acquires as a U.S. citizen have become less distinct from those of resident aliens in the same period; and 3) immigrants' use of naturalization and U.S. citizenship has also changed over the past 150 years.

Under the Constitution, naturalization law has always been a federal prerogative, and therefore the federal government has always regulated access to U.S. citizenship for immigrants. But the federal government traditionally used this power only to a limited degree. Since 1802, all adult white immigrants could qualify for citizenship after five years of residence and proof of good character. Nonwhite immigrants were barred from naturalization prior to the Fourteenth Amendment. The Naturalization Act of 1870 implicitly denied Asian immigrants the right to become naturalized U.S. citizens. Laws passed in 1855 and 1906 also limited the right of women to gain or retain U.S. citizenship on their own in this period. But except for these racial and gender exclusions, substantial as they were, much of the regulatory power of the federal government remained unused during the first period of mass migration. For most of that time, naturalization procedures remained without federal supervision and subject to much local corruption and irregularity for most immigrants. The Naturalization Act of 1906 centralized the process of naturalization and made it uniform for the entire country, reasserting federal control at least administratively. For immigrants who sought to become citizens, both the localized and the centralized systems of naturalization had their own pitfalls. The earlier, decentralized system of local control favored those immigrant groups with strong local political ties, shutting out those whose political views were not represented in the established local power structure. Under a more centralized and less politicized naturalization system, preferential treatment for some was no longer the rule, but this did not ease access for the previously excluded. Thus, naturalization rates dropped after 1906. Overall, immigrants who had lived in the United States for a long time also had a high naturalization rate during the first period of mass migration. Efforts by the federal government to boost naturalization rates during World War I and thereafter and also to exert some ideological control over the process through Americanization programs had a very limited impact.

During the second period of mass migration, the federal government made very little use of the naturalization laws' potential power to limit access to U.S. citizenship. Race and gender restrictions were abolished in the interim period between 1922 and 1952. By the beginning of the second period of mass migration, U.S. citizenship was accessible to anyone who fulfilled the basic residency, English-language, and good-conduct requirements that had been in force since 1906. Meeting these requirements was not too difficult for most immigrants during the second period of mass migration, especially after having negotiated the increasingly steep hurdles of the immigration law. By the time of the second period, the federal government had retreated from regulating the shape of the U.S. citizenry via naturalization law. Instead, it increasingly focused on fine-tuning the influx of immigrants (and future citizens) with a multitude of restrictive immigration provisions.

Improved access to naturalization during the second period of mass migration did not result in higher naturalization rates during much of this period. The reason for the continuing low numbers during the 1960s and 1970s lay in the changing importance of U.S. citizenship for immigrants. During the first period of mass migration, citizenship rights expanded for natives and naturalized citizens alike: A growing percentage of the adult population gained the franchise, enjoyed equal protection under law, and gained social rights as well. As these rights expanded during the first period, the line between aliens and citizens became more significant. The most extensive catalog of rights was reserved for (white) U.S. citizens; resident aliens had to make with a somewhat reduced list. Not only was U.S. citizenship closely tied to federal and state voting rights, but U.S. citizenship was required in many states to buy land and sometimes to gain or retain certain jobs or professional licenses. This catalog of citizenship rights became more extensive during the 1920s and 1930s as a growing array of, for example, social programs, mothers' pensions, Social Security, and public works jobs became available to U.S. citizens but not to nonnaturalized immigrants.

The difference in rights that separated U.S. citizens from immigrants was no longer as dominant during the second period of mass migration. A growing number of social programs during the 1960s and 1970s were open to U.S. citizens as well as to permanent resident aliens. In addition, courts had determined that many basic social rights, such as the right to public schooling and the right to emergency health care or food support, were independent of one's residency status altogether. The 1996 attempt to turn back the clock and once again restrict access to social services and support programs to U.S citizens and exclude aliens (especially undocumented immigrants) was by and large not successful, though it did motivate a large number of immigrants to seek citizenship.

Immigrants themselves have always reacted flexibly and pragmatically to the changes in citizenship rights and laws during the two periods of mass migration. During the first period, only those immigrant groups able to negotiate the increasingly bureaucratic naturalization process became U.S. citizens in large proportion. For them, the motivating factor was the increase in political influence and the access to economic opportunity that citizenship could bring to longtime residents. Less established immigrant groups were often unable to master the process, and therefore they were underrepresented among naturalized U.S. citizens during the first period of mass migration. During the interim years, a growing proportion of the foreign born became naturalized citizens, as immigration declined and old-time immigrants reacted to increasing advantages of U.S. citizenship during the Depression and World War II.

During the second period of mass migration, immigrants perceived a different set of advantages to naturalization compared to the earlier years. With access to immigration visas increasingly restricted to those with superior professional qualifications and close family members of U.S. citizens, recent immigrants have often sought U.S. citizenship as a way to help their close kin advance in the waiting line for an immigrant visa. The groups who most systematically used naturalization as a way of furthering immigration of kin were immigrants from formerly underrepresented countries in East and South Asia. They in turn contributed to a rapid rise in the number of immigrant admissions from these parts of the world as well. Political refugees, who came in great numbers during the 1970s and early 1980s, also tended to become U.S. citizens rapidly since their commitment to staying in the United States was especially strong. Refugees from Southeast Asia, Russia, and Cuba thus contributed to a growing number of naturalizations in the 1980s. Immigrants from Mexico and Central America, on the other hand, did not systematically advance family migration through these channels, and their naturalization remained disproportionately low during much of the second period of mass migration. Following a wave of legalization of formerly undocumented immigrants in the wake of the 1986 IRCA, only the most recent years have seen a surge in naturalizations and naturalization applications from Mexican and other Latin American immigrants as well. Thus, family migration strategy and political allegiance were important indicators responsible for naturalization rates in the second period of mass migration rather than the general level of cultural and economic assimilation that comes with length of residency—a decisive factor during the first period.

The late twentieth century is also distinct in that changing patterns of migration and the increasing openness of nations toward dual citizenship made U.S. citizenship a choice for those uncertain of their loyalties or future residence. Citizenship in this matrix is no longer equivalent to citizenship rights in one nation, nor is it the expression of political loyalties to one nation alone. American lawmakers have not confronted the complex consequences of such a trend toward multiple citizenship among Americans in the late twentieth century. It remains to be seen how the character of U.S. citizenship will change during the ongoing second period of mass migration as it has sometimes become the by-product of a life that is increasingly lived within the borders of many different countries. But for most of those immigrants who seek U.S. citizenship, their range of attitudes and motivations to seek U.S. citizenship reflects a pragmatic view of the costs and benefits of naturalization that has existed for more than one hundred years. The promise of a job, the hope for political influence, or the desire to bring family members into the United States has always outweighed the more transcendent motivations, such as patriotism or love of democratic freedoms for immigrants. This does not reflect a weak allegiance to the United States by its citizens or a general lack of patriotism, as some politicians seem anxious to note. Rather it shows a diverse tradition of thinking and acting in regard to citizenship in a multifaceted society.

Notes

1. Only during the period 1799–1801 was the law changed to include a fifteen-year waiting period. This Federalist reaction to a fear of radical aliens from Ireland and France—part of the Alien and Sedition Acts—was never revived during the nineteenth century, even though the Know-Nothing movement pressed for a similarly lengthened probationary period for immigrants before they could become citizens (Franklin 1906: 110–111; Strauss 1901).

2. Much of the rich literature on political machines and ethnic voters comments on the connection between immigrants and political machines, but few authors mention naturalization (Buenker 1988; Higham 1955: 98). Some urban areas introduced citizenship as a requirement to hold municipal jobs in the early twentieth century, which also prompted many recent immigrants to become naturalized (*Immigrant in America Review* 1915).

3. Though Gavit noted the discrepancy, he did not analyze its causes. Length of residence was his only determinant.

4. The *New York Tribune* ran a series of articles on naturalization frauds almost every week between early August and early October 1894; see also *New York Tribune,* December 8, 1897; August 19, 1900; and October 23, 1904.

5. The first important immigration law passed since the 1892 Geary Act, the law of 1903 widened the scope of excluded classes and strengthened deportation laws. Anarchists and those who had committed a crime of moral turpitude were now judged deportable (Le May and Barkan 1999: 90–93; Ueda 1980).

6. Some recommendations also went further, suggesting the elimination of what were considered to be incentives for cheapening citizenship: low naturalization fees, the requirement to become a citizen before taking a job as a street cleaner, and so on.

7. The field examiners were originally paid by the Department of Justice and under its nominal supervision. This unwieldy structure proved to be impossible to

maintain, and in 1909 the field examiners were put under the direct control of the commissioner of naturalization alone, and the budget of the Division of Naturalization was enlarged accordingly. For the activities and the broadening scope of the commissioner's work, see also *Annual Report of the Commissioner of Naturalization* (U.S. Bureau of Immigration and Naturalization 1908–1932). From 1931 to 1941, the *Report* was published only in much abbreviated form as part of the *Annual Report of the Secretary of Labor.* Thereafter, the Immigration and Naturalization Service published its own *Annual Reports* again. Since 1978, the most comprehensive data can be found in the *Statistical Yearbook of the INS.*

8. The law also made naturalization more difficult to obtain and retain because it specified that a declaration of intent (the "first papers") was valid for only seven years.

9. See also *The Interpreter* (1929).

10. *The Annual Report of the Commissioner of Naturalization* collected data on the number of declarations filed, petitions filed, and certificates issued beginning with the second quarter of 1907.

11. The most comprehensive information on such borderline cases can be gleaned from the Records of the Immigration and Naturalization Service (National Archives, Washington, DC), Record Group 85, Entry 9, especially files 52737/499, 52903/43, 54261, and 55739/930.

12. Women who married foreigners were not the only people to have trouble retaining their citizenship. With the Expatriation Act of 1907, a long-standing expatriation policy of the State Department (upheld by courts in the United States until the 1960s) also became official: If naturalized Americans left the United States to reside abroad for extended periods of time, the State Department could revoke their citizenship unilaterally (Bredbenner 1998: 58–79; Vecoli 1987: 94–96).

13. On women and naturalization in general, see also Gavit's (1922: 296–334) description and comments.

14. The naturalization petition and the naturalization certificate listed the names of the wife and minor children of the petitioner/citizen; this served as proof of citizenship for them. For a sample form, see Moley (1918).

15. As Bredbenner (1998), Cott (1998), and Kerber (1999) have pointed out, the conservative principles embodied in the acts of 1855 and 1907 had always stood in contradiction to other equally cherished ideas about what it meant to become an American citizen, for example, individual responsibility and individual rights. Therefore, the Cable Act of 1922 also relied on a traditional interpretation of citizenship, albeit a different one from the one invoked by the previous laws. The Cable Act's reforms remained incomplete for some women because

American women who married foreigners ineligible for U.S. citizenship (e.g., Asians) continued to lose their citizenship and were unable to regain it until a new law remedied the situation in 1931; see also Le May and Barkan (1999: 69–70, 173) and U.S. Bureau of the Census (1949: 38).

16. Nonnaturalized immigrants who were active in socialist and communist and anarchist groups were particularly vulnerable to government harassment during these years. More than 2,600 aliens were judged to be deportable by the end of 1919 for political reasons alone. In that year, 249 Russian immigrants were deported (Claghorn 1923: 335–461; Clark 1931).

17. Aliens who had served in the Army or the Navy until the end of World War I could be naturalized without having filed a declaration of intent between 1818 and 1924 (Le May and Barkan 1999: 117–118; U.S. Department of Labor 1926).

18. The history of the Americanization and citizenship instruction movement in the inter-war years has not been sufficiently researched. The most useful and mostly unknown material is found in Records of U.S. Immigration and Naturalization Service, Record Group 85, Entry 30 "Education and Americanization," 1914–1936; Entry 33, "Citizenship Education Programs," 1935–1954; and Entry 34, "Citizenship Training Texts" (all in the National Archives, Washington, DC).

19. Some judges refused to naturalize immigrants whose families resided abroad, citing insufficient evidence that these men would continue to live in the United States. This represented a Catch-22 situation for some men whose families were unable to join them under the strict quota laws for noncitizens and their families (*The Interpreter* 1924, 1928b).

20. Fees for filing a declaration of intent and for naturalization were raised from $1.00 to $4.00 and from $5.00 to $10.00, respectively, discouraging applicants in 1929.

21. About half of all immigrants during 1950s came from Europe, 15 percent were Canadians, and 8 percent were Asians. The rest were from South America and the Caribbean; during the 1960s, a third of all immigrants came from Europe, 13 percent were Canadians, and 15 percent were Asians. These figures do not include refugees and displaced persons, the vast majority of whom were also from Europe at that time (U.S. Immigration and Naturalization Service 1977: 125).

22. The 1990 Immigration Act reorganized naturalization procedures by removing them from the judicial system and putting them in the hands of the Immigration and Naturalization Service. Naturalization thus became an administrative rather than a judicial procedure, although prospective citizens retained the

right to ask for judicial review if their naturalization petition was denied. As in the 1906 reforms, the new process was supposed to make naturalization more uniform and more accessible. As it turned out, however, the Immigration and Naturalization Service was insufficiently equipped to handle the additional administrative and quasi-judicial burdens.

23. The most recent numbers on naturalizations can be found on the Web site of the Immigration and Naturalization Service: <www.usdoj.ins.gov>.

24. The most recent decline may have been at least partly due to the much higher fees charged for such applications since January 1999.

References

Abbott, Grace. 1917. *The Immigrant and the Community*. Chicago: University of Chicago Press.

Aleinikoff, T. Alexander, and David A. Martin. 1993. *Immigration, Process and Policy*. 2nd ed. St. Paul, MN: West Publishers.

Barkan, Elliott. 1983. "Whom Shall We Integrate: A Comparative Analysis of the Immigration and Naturalization Trends of Asians before and after the 1965 Immigration Act (1951–1978)." *Journal of American Ethnic History* 2: 29–57.

Basch, Linda, Nina Schiller, and Cristina Szanton. 1994. *Nations Unbound: Transnational Projects, Postcolonial Predicaments and Deterritorialized Nation States*. Basel: Gordon and Breach.

Bauböck, Rainer. 1994. *Transnational Citizenship: Membership and Rights in International Migration*. Aldershot, Hants, England: Rowman & Littlefield.

Bierstadt, Edward H. 1922. *Aspects of Americanization*. Cincinnati: Stewart Kidd Co.

Breckinridge, Sophonsiba. 1932. *Marriage and the Civic Rights of Women*. Chicago: University of Chicago Press.

Bredbenner, Candice L. 1998. *A Nationality of Her Own: Women, Marriage and the Law of Citizenship*. Berkeley and Los Angeles: University of California Press.

Brubaker, Rogers. 1992. *Citizenship and Nationhood in France and Germany*. Cambridge, MA: Harvard University Press.

Buenker, John D. 1988. "Sovereign Individuals and Organic Networks: Political Cultures in Conflict during the Progressive Era." *American Quarterly* 40: 187–204.

Chen, Hsiang-Shui. 1992. *Chinatown No More: Taiwan Immigrants in Contemporary New York*. Ithaca, NY: Cornell University Press.

Chicago Record Herald. August 18, 1904; October 2, 1905.

Claghorn, Kate Holaday. 1923. *The Immigrant's Day in Court.* New York: Harper Brothers.

Clark, Jane Perry. 1931. *The Deportation of Aliens.* New York: Columbia University Press.

Congressional Research Service. 1998. "Naturalization: Trends, Issues, and Legislation." 98–190 EPW. Washington, DC: U.S. Government Printing Office.

Cott, Nancy. 1998. "Marriage and Women's Citizenship in the United States, 1830–1934." *American Historical Review* 105: 1440–1471.

DeSipio, Louis. 1987. "Social Science Literature and the Naturalization Process." *International Migration Review* 21: 390–405.

DeSipio, Louis, and Rodolfo de la Garza. 1998. *Making Americans, Re-Making America.* Boulder, CO: Westview Press.

Foner, Nancy. 1997. "What's New about Transnationalism? New York's Immigrants Today and at the Turn of the Century." *Diaspora* 6 (3): 355–375.

Foreign Language Information Service. 1926. *How to Become a Citizen of the United States.* New York: Foreign Language Information Service.

Franklin, Frank G. 1906. *The Legislative History of Naturalization in the United States, from the Revolutionary War to 1861.* Chicago: University of Chicago Press.

Gavit, John P. 1922. *Americans by Choice.* New York: Harper Brothers.

Gibson, Campbell, and Emily Lennon. 1999. "Historical Census Statistics on the Foreign-Born Population of the United States: 1850–1990." U.S. Bureau of the Census Population Division Working Paper No. 29. Washington, DC: U.S. Government Printing Office.

Gordon, Linda. 1994. *Pitied but Not Entitled: Single Mothers and the History of Welfare, 1890–1935.* New York: The Free Press.

Gutierrez, David. 1995. *Walls and Mirrors: Mexican Americans, Mexican Immigrants and the Politics of Ethnicity.* Berkeley and Los Angeles: University of California Press.

Hartman, John. 1948. *The Movement to Americanize the Immigrant.* New York: Columbia University Press.

Herrmann, Dietrich. 1994. *Be an American: Amerikanisierungsbewegung und Theorien zur Einwandererintegration.* Frankfurt: Campus Verlag.

Higham, John. 1955. *Strangers in the Land: Patterns of American Nativism, 1860–1925.* New Brunswick, NJ: Rutgers University Press.

Hyneman, Charles. 1994. *The American Founding Experience: Political Continuity and Republican Government.* Urbana: University of Illinois Press.

Immigrant in America Review. 1915. Vol. 1, no. 1: 3–5.

The Interpreter. 1924. Vol. 3, no. 6: 3–5.

————. 1928a. Vol. 8, no. 4: 3–6.

————. 1928b. Vol. 8, no. 10: 3–6.

————. 1929. Vol. 9, no. 3: 35–37, 156–159.

Jones-Correa, Michael. 1998. *Between Two Nations: The Political Predicament of Latinos in New York City.* Ithaca, NY: Cornell University Press.

Kansas, Sidney. 1953. *Immigration and Nationality Act.* New York: Immigration Publications.

Kasinitz, Philip. 1992. *Caribbean New York: Black Immigrants and the Politics of Race.* Ithaca, NY: Cornell University Press.

Kearney, Michael. 1995. "The Local and the Global: The Anthropology of Globalization and Transnationalism." *Annual Review of Anthropology* 4: 547–545.

Kerber, Linda. 1999. *No Constitutional Right to Be Ladies: Women and the Obligations of Citizenship.* New York: Hill & Wang.

Kettner, James. 1978. *The Development of American Citizenship, 1608–1870.* Chapel Hill: University of North Carolina Press.

Le May, Michael, and Eliott Barkan. 1999. *U.S. Immigration and Naturalization Laws and Issues.* Westport, CT: Greenwood Press.

Moley, Raymond. 1918. *Lessons on American Citizenship.* Cleveland: Cleveland Board of Education.

Myers, Gustavus. 1917. *The History of Tammany Hall.* New York: B. Franklin Co.

New York Times. October 24, 1866; September 11, 1871.

New York Tribune. November 28, 1878; July 20, October 22, October 30, 1880; October 23 and 24, 1891; October 18, 1892; October 2, 3, 4, and 28, 1894; Feb. 1 and 9, May 8, July 11, August 5 and 7, and October 30, 1895; February 2 and March 30, 1896; December 8, 1897; August 19, 1900; May 21, June 10, and December 20, 1903; April 5 and 6, August 11 and 13, October 23, and December 5, 1904; July 31, 1905; January 11, February 11, and July 3, 1906.

North, David S. 1986. *The Long Gray Welcome: A Study of the American Naturalization Program.* Washington, DC: NALEA Fund.

Perea, Juan F. 1997. *Immigrants Out: The New Nativism and the Anti-Immigrant Impulse in the United States.* New York: New York University Press.

Portes, Alejandro, Luis E. Guarnizo, and Patricia Landolt. 1999. "Transnational Communities: Pitfalls and Promises of an Emergent Research Field." *Ethnic and Racial Studies* 22 (2): 217–237.

President's Commission on Naturalization. 1905. *Report of the President's Commission on Naturalization,* 59th Cong., 1st sess., House Doc. 46. Washington, DC: U.S. Government Printing Office.

Reimers, David. 1985. *Still the Golden Door: The Third World Comes to America.* New York: Columbia University Press.

———. 1998. *Unwelcome Strangers: American Identity and the Turn against Immigration*. New York: Columbia University Press.

Roberts, Peter. 1920. *The Problem of Americanization*. New York: Harper Brothers.

Salyer, Lucy. 1995. *Laws Harsh as Tigers: Chinese Immigrants and the Shaping of Modern Immigration Law*. Chapel Hill: University of North Carolina Press.

Schneider, Dorothee. 2000. "Symbolic Citizenship, Nationalism and the Distant State: The United States Congress in the 1996 Debate on Immigration Reform." *Citizenship Studies* 4: 255–273.

Schuck, Peter. 1984. "The Transformation of Immigration Law." *Columbia Law Review* 85: 1–90.

Skocpol, Theda. 1992. *Protecting Soldiers and Mothers: Political Origins of Social Policy in the United States*. Cambridge, MA: Harvard University Press.

Smith, Darrell Hevenor. 1926. *The Bureau of Naturalization: Its History, Activities and Organization*. Baltimore: The Johns Hopkins University Press.

Smith, Rogers. 1997. *Civic Ideals: Conflicting Visions of Citizenship in U.S. History*. New Haven, CT: Yale University Press.

Strauss, Oscar. 1901. "The United States Doctrine of Citizenship and Expatriation." *Proceedings of the American Social Science Association* (1901): 1–20.

Ueda, Reed. 1980. "Naturalization and Citizenship." In *Harvard Encyclopedia of American Ethnic Groups*, edited by Stephan Thernstrom. Cambridge, MA: Harvard University Press.

U.S. Bureau of the Census. 1949. *Historical Statistics of the United States, 1789–1945*. Washington, DC: U.S. Government Printing Office.

U.S. Bureau of Immigration and Naturalization. 1908–1932. *Annual Report of the Commissioner of Naturalization*. Washington, DC: U.S. Government Printing Office.

U.S. Commission on Immigration Reform. 1994. *U.S. Immigration Policy: Restoring Credibility*. Washington, DC: U.S. Government Printing Office.

U.S. Department of Labor, Bureau of Naturalization. 1926. *Historical Sketch of Naturalization in the United States*. Washington, DC: U.S. Government Printing Office.

U.S. Immigration and Naturalization Service. Records of the Immigration and Naturalization Service, Record Group 85, Entries 9, 26. Washington, DC: National Archives.

———. 1977. *Annual Report*. Washington, DC: U.S. Government Printing Office.

———. 1995–1998. *Statistical Yearbook of the INS*. Washington, DC: U.S. Government Printing Office.

U.S. Interagency Task Force on Immigration Policy. 1979. "Staff Report of the Select Commission on Immigration and Refugee Policy." Washington, DC. Typescript.

U.S. Select Commission on Immigration and Refugee Policy. 1980. "Staff Report." Washington, DC. Typescript.

Vecoli, Rudolph. 1987. "Immigration, Naturalization and the Constitution." *Studi Emigrazione* 24: 75–101.

Yang, Philip Q. 1994. "Explaining Immigrant Naturalization." *International Migration Review* 28: 449–473.

CHAPTER SIX

IMMIGRANT RESIDENCE AND IMMIGRANT NEIGHBORHOODS IN NEW YORK, 1910 AND 1990

Andrew A. Beveridge

I n 1910, more than two of every five people living in New York City were born outside the United States. The wave of immigration beginning after 1880 and reaching a peak in the decade before 1910 transformed New York City and other places that became home to many immigrants, such as Chicago and Philadelphia. Ellis Island served as a major entry point for immigrants into the United States around the turn of the twentieth century. Some estimate that as many as two out of five Americans can trace their ancestry to someone who disembarked at Ellis Island. Indeed, in 1910, New York City contained about one-sixth of all the foreign born in the United States. Many of the immigrants coming during this period were from central and southern Europe. Embarking on the trip to the New World from Russia, Italy, Austria, and the area that was and would be Poland, these groups were different linguistically and culturally from the immigrants who had settled in the United States during the earlier periods.

Once again, New York City itself has reached similar heights as in 1910 with respect to the new wave of immigrants, who began arriving shortly after the immigration laws were changed in the mid-1960s.[1] New York City's population in 1999 was more than 40 percent foreign born. New York City again has become one of the primary points of disembarkation for the immigrants. Indeed, in 1990, almost one-fifth of all the U.S. foreign born lived in the New York metropolitan area. It is true, of course, that New York is no longer the only immigrant destination. The Los Angeles metropolitan area has more immigrants than the New York metropolitan area. As of 1990, the figures were 3.9 million for Los Angeles versus 3.6 million for New York. Almost half of the immigrants of Los Angeles are from nearby Mexico, while no one group dominates in New York. In Los Angeles, large numbers are from some of the other Latin American countries, and immigrants from Asia are also in evidence. By contrast, New York has immigrants from Asia, the Caribbean, Mexico and Latin America, and Europe. No other major city or metropolitan area has anything like the immigrant diversity of New York City.

Many popular commentators have compared the new wave of immigration to the New York metropolitan area to that at the turn of the century. Newscasts and newspapers once again are showing pictures of the Lower East Side and the Ellis Island arrival hall from around the turn of the century. The initial residential patterns of immigrants are very important since they define in part the relationship between each immigrant group and the host society as well as the relationships among various immigrant groups. This chapter examines the settlement patterns of immigrants in New York City in 1910 and compares them with those of immigrants in New York City today. For this comparison, newly available materials from the 1910 census, along with similar materials from the 1990 census, were used. Recently organized data, which presents the early census tract tabulations for New York City in 1910, made this analysis possible.[2] The U.S. Bureau of the Census compiled this data for New York City and for the seven other cities in the United States that had populations of 500,000 or more in 1910. It is possible that only the New York City data survived.[3] For the 1990 data, computerized maps and data provided by the Bureau of the Census were used.[4] In short, materials that are broadly comparable in 1910 and 1990 were used to analyze the settlement patterns of the emigrants in the two periods. Thus, this chapter represents the first rigorous look at the similarities and differences in New York immigrant settlement patterns for the two major waves of immigration.

This chapter consists of three interrelated sections. The first section examines and compares the diversity of immigrant groups in 1910 and 1990. The second section delineates patterns of immigrant residential settlement with a focus on the following two questions: (1) To what extent are the new immigrants to New York following the patterns of residential settlement that occurred at the turn of the century, and (2) did the immigrants in 1910 settle in areas that were easy to define and characterize with respect to specific immigrant groups? The third section addresses the extent to which immigrant groups are segregated from the population at large and other immigrant groups. From this comparison, it will be possible to assess something about the similarities and differences of the early experience of immigrants to the New York area in 1910 and 1990.[5]

New York and Its Immigrant Waves Compared

The census tabulations for 1910 provide information on some forty-four countries of origin, and it should be noted that the census explicitly tabulated "white" foreign born from most European countries. Of nearly two million immigrants to New York City in 1910, three immigrant groups—Russians, Italians, and Germans—accounted for well over half of all foreign born. When the Irish and Austrians are added, the figure is nearly four-fifths. One-sixth of all immigrants to the United States lived in New York City in 1910, even though the city accounted for only about 5 percent of the total U.S. population. The foreign-born residents comprised 40 percent of the population in New York City in 1910. It was the center of immigration in 1910, and the groups found in New York more heavily reflected the newer immigrant groups. The other major groups are delineated in table 6.1.

Among the Russian, Austrian, Romanian, and other European immigrants to New York City were many Jews who had escaped persecution, discrimination, and economic dislocation in eastern and central Europe.[6] Using a sample of 1910 census records and analyzing first language as well as origin, Watkins (1994) estimated that almost one-third of the immigrants in New York City in 1910 were Jewish.[7] More than two-thirds of this group had entered the United States since 1900 and accounted for about one-third of all Jewish immigrants in the United States. As we will see, they settled in specific areas in the city, especially in the Lower East Side.

Italians made up the other large immigrant group to New York City in 1910. Many had come from rural areas of southern Italy and ended up doing various types of unskilled or physical labor. Some of the push factors that accounted for the immigration include a series of natural disasters in Italy in the first decade of the twentieth century.[8] As with the Jewish immigrants, almost two-thirds of Italian immigrants had entered the

United States since 1900. Those in New York City accounted for one-quarter of all Italian immigrants in the United States.[9]

In 1910, there were also large numbers of English, Irish, and German immigrants. About one-quarter of the English and one-sixth of the Germans and Irish living in New York City in 1910 had entered since 1900. For the latter two groups, almost two-thirds had entered before 1890. Thus, in 1910, these groups were the "older" immigrants, when compared with the Italians and the Jews from central and eastern Europe. Table 6.1 presents the number and percentage of the eleven top immigrant groups in New York City in 1910, which together account for more than 93 percent of all immigrants. New York City in 1910 was a heavily immigrant city, with a large number of Jews and Italians and significant representation from the Irish, German, and English origins, who had immigrated largely before 1890.

The current wave of immigration to New York is vastly different. Where the three largest immigrant groups accounted for more than half of all immigrants in 1910, it takes fourteen groups to reach that level in 1990. Where five groups accounted for four-fifths of all immigrants in

Table 6.1. Foreign Born in New York City, 1910 and 1990, and Metropolitan Area, 1990

	New York City	
Total population	4,766,883	
Total foreign born	1,946,108	40.8%
Russia	484,183	24.9%
Italy	340,768	17.5%
Germany	278,114	14.3%
Ireland	252,664	13.0%
Austria	190,237	9.8%
England	78,135	4.0%
Hungary	76,625	3.9%
Sweden	34,951	1.8%
Romania	33,583	1.7%
Scotland	23,115	1.2%
Norway	22,279	1.1%
All others[1]	131,454	6.8%

[1]The other origins supplied the following number of immigrants in 1910: Norway, 22,279; Canada (English), 21,773; Other, 18,656; France, 18,265; Switzerland, 10,452; Greece, 8,038; Denmark, 7,989; Finland, 7,408; Turkey (Asia), 6,159; Holland, 4,190; West Indies, 4,190; Turkey (Europe), 3,694; Spain, 3,323; Canada (French), 2,844; Belgium, 2,258; South America, 1,864; Cuba, 1,791; Wales, 1,778; Canada (Other), 1,455; Newfoundland, 860; Africa, 700; Australia, 658; Balkans, 544; Portugal, 422; Mexico, 404; Atlantic Islands, 359; At Sea, 348; Other Europe, 231; India, 227; Other Asia, 189; Pacific Islands, 138; Luxembourg, 95; Unknown, 91; China, 37; and Japan, 24.

	New York City		Suburbs		Total	
Total population	7,322,564		11,444,348		18,766,912	
Total foreign born	2,082,932	28.4%	1,521,024	13.3%	3,603,955	19.2%
Dominican Republic	225,017	10.8%	50,068	3.3%	275,085	7.6%
Italy	98,868	4.7%	134,432	8.8%	233,300	6.5%
Jamaica	116,128	5.6%	49,712	3.3%	165,840	4.6%
China	114,099	5.5%	25,688	1.7%	139,787	3.9%
Colombia	65,731	3.2%	57,945	3.8%	123,676	3.4%
Poland	61,265	2.9%	54,955	3.6%	116,220	3.2%
Cuba	41,039	2.0%	72,785	4.8%	113,824	3.2%
India	40,419	1.9%	69,922	4.6%	110,341	3.1%
Germany	38,259	1.8%	71,926	4.7%	110,185	3.1%
Russia	80,815	3.9%	27,518	1.8%	108,333	3.0%
Haiti	71,892	3.5%	32,926	2.2%	104,818	2.9%
Ecuador	60,451	2.9%	30,928	2.0%	91,379	2.5%
Korea	56,949	2.7%	34,024	2.2%	90,973	2.5%
Guyana	76,150	3.7%	13,913	0.9%	90,063	2.5%
England	28,740	1.4%	57,597	3.8%	86,337	2.4%
Philippines	36,463	1.8%	46,570	3.1%	83,033	2.3%
Trinidad and Tobago	56,478	2.7%	11,673	0.8%	68,151	1.9%
Ireland	31,252	1.5%	33,137	2.2%	64,389	1.8%
Mexico	32,689	1.6%	22,239	1.5%	54,928	1.5%
Greece	31,894	1.5%	22,967	1.5%	54,861	1.5%
Portugal	3,234	0.2%	50,805	3.3%	54,039	1.5%
El Salvador	18,453	0.9%	31,911	2.1%	50,364	1.4%
All others[2]	696,646	33.4%	517,383	34.0%	1,214,029	33.7%

[2]The other origins supplied the following in 1990: (New York City, Suburb) Other Caribbean, 38,540, 10,266; Peru, 19,818, 28,091; Canada, 13,818, 27,415; Japan, 12,837, 26,418; Yugoslavia, 21,926, 15,168; Taiwan, 18,983, 17,594; Hong Kong, 27,317, 7,467; Israel, 19,876, 11,068; Hungary, 14,631, 16,278; Panama, 25,278, 4,168; Barbados, 24,671, 4,010; Honduras, 17,890, 9,429; Other Asia, 17,624, 9,144; Romania, 17,585, 8,204; Argentina, 12,082, 12,772; Guatemala, 12,888, 11,744; Pakistan, 14,911, 9,101; Brazil, 8,832, 14,911; France, 11,609, 11,592; Austria, 12,072, 10,343; Egypt, 10,304, 12,041; Czechoslovakia, 11,825, 10,494; Other Africa, 12,822, 9,076; Spain, 8,438, 12,641; Iran, 7,372, 10,990; Vietnam, 9,492, 6,570; Turkey, 7,355, 8,403; Grenada, 11,784, 1,337; Chile, 5,034, 7,783; Costa Rica, 5,745, 5,957; Nicaragua, 7,348, 3,707; Balkans, 3,587, 6,407; Netherlands, 2,275, 7,618; Uruguay, 2,284, 999; Burma, 2,321, 592; Finland, 967, 1,874; Iraq, 1,317, 1,360; Bahamas, 1,778, 691; Ethiopia, 1,453, 742; Kenya, 451, 1,743; Other North America, 766, 1,190; Laos, 315, 1,456; Other Central America, 909, 289; Senegal, 1,056, 123; Saudi Arabia, 604, 354; New Zealand, 279, 620; Cape Verde Islands, 167, 650; Other Oceania, 300, 168; Fiji, 35, 83; Western Samoa, 29, 16; Tonga, 10, 13; Not Reported, 130,882, 64,263.

New York City, to get to the same level in 1990 one would need to include thirty-seven different groups. Beyond this, the source of immigrants is very different. In 1990, the Bureau of the Census tabulated some one hundred countries of origin. Table 6.1 presents data for those countries that supplied at least 50,000 immigrants to the New York City metropolitan area as of 1990. Strikingly, they include at least one immigrant group, Germans, who were present in the mid-nineteenth century, and several other groups that were very large in the early twentieth-century wave, especially Italians, Poles, and Russians. In addition, there are the new immigrant groups: Dominicans, Jamaicans, Chinese, Colombians, Cubans, Indians, and Haitians. The immigrant streams in New York City are very diverse and are in no way dominated by people from one or a few groups, as is the case in some other metropolitan areas.[10]

The largest source of immigrants to the New York City metropolitan area is the Dominican Republic. In 1990 in the New York metropolitan area, there were about 275,000 Dominican immigrants, accounting for about 80 percent of all Dominicans in the United States and about 8 percent of all immigrants in the metropolitan area. Most live in New York City, and by 1999, according to data from a census survey, there were almost 400,000 foreign-born Dominicans in New York City and an additional 100,000 people who were of Dominican ancestry.[11] The initial immigration of Dominicans in the 1960s and 1970s included many people from urban areas with reasonable levels of skills. However, the poor economic situation of the Dominican Republic in the 1980s unleashed a large wave of immigration that continued through the 1990s. For those Dominican immigrants in New York City in 1990, about half had entered during the previous decade. The Dominicans, as we will see in this chapter, are heavily concentrated in one area in Manhattan. Furthermore, economically they lag behind many other immigrant groups, even those from Central and South America. Because of the proximity of the Dominican Republic, there is much travel back and forth to the home area. Time-Warner Cable, a cable television system serving Manhattan and Queens, just added a Dominican service. Many Dominican immigrants recently kept a close watch on the presidential elections in the Republic, and some even flew home to vote.[12]

Other groups among the top twenty-two immigrant groups coming from the Caribbean basin include Jamaicans, the third-largest immigrant group; Haitians; and Trinidad and Tobagoans. More than 50 percent of these three groups who are in the United States settled in the New York City area. About 45 percent of Jamaican immigrants to the United States came to New York during the 1990s, in comparison to about 40 percent of the Trinidadians and almost 60 percent of the Haitians. The English-speaking Caribbean immigrants have moved to various black neighborhoods in New York. As is well known, U.S. Secretary of State Colin Powell is of Jamaican descent, and his family lived in the Bronx in New York City. The Jamaicans and other English-speaking West Indians moved mainly for economic reasons, but many who have come since 1965 are not as highly educated as those who came before. More recent West Indian immigrants tend to settle in Brooklyn.[13]

Many Haitians fled Haiti in the late 1980s and early 1990s because of repression at home. Indeed, the issue of whether to grant Haitians refugee status during that period was very controversial. Haitians began arriving after François Duvalier took power in 1957. Dissident politicians first came, followed by middle-class professionals and finally by tradespeople. In the late 1970s and early 1980s, the Haitian boat people arrived in southern Florida. Speaking a Creole variant of French, the Haitians are concentrated in black neighborhoods.[14] Immigrants from the Caribbean basin flow mainly to New York. Many are black West Indians; others are somewhat dark, as are many Dominicans. However, many of the Cubans who have migrated to the New York area are white. Most of them in the New York area in 1990 had entered the United States before 1980; 45 percent entered during the 1960s and about 17 percent in the 1970s. The New York area has about one-sixth of the Cuban immigrants in the United States. Mostly, these immigrants had fled the Castro regime. Obviously, their immigration experience is quite different than others from the Caribbean basin.

Aside from the Dominicans, New York also has a large number of Ecuadorians and Colombians. For both groups, more than half of all immigrants in the United States in 1990 were in New York. For the Colombians in the United States in 1990, half had arrived since 1980; for Ecuadorians, slightly more than one-third arrived in the past decade. Recent data indicates that Mexicans in New York have grown very rapidly and may now be larger than the Colombian and Ecuadorian immigrant groups.

New York has also become home to many people from a variety of Asian countries. The largest of these groups is from the Chinese mainland. More than 25 percent of all Chinese immigrants from the mainland to the United States made the New York area their home in 1990. Aside from the mainland Chinese, the census distinguished those from Taiwan and Hong Kong. About half of all three groups arrived during the 1980s. Thus, New York's Chinese group is split by origin. It is also split with respect to class and education. While some Chinese serve as immigrant labor in the restaurants and sweatshops of Chinatown, Flushing, and other areas throughout the metropolitan area, others have become wealthy entrepreneurs. The Chinese, along with other Asian immigrant groups, have contributed to the renaissance of downtown Flushing in Queens.[15]

South Asians—Indians, Pakistanis, and Bangladeshis—are now among the fastest-growing immigrant groups in New York City. In 1990, about 25 percent of those in the United States were in the New York metropolitan area. Recent data from a census survey indicate that these groups have grown very rapidly. Large Asian groups include the highly entrepreneurial Koreans, the highly professional Filipinos, and Southeast Asians as well as the Japanese. Though many of these groups are in the top twenty-two in New York, for most groups only 7 percent of the total group is in New York.

Unlike any other destination, New York City also has a significant number of European immigrants. These include Italians, Poles, Germans, and the citizens of the former Soviet Union, which were included among the twenty-two largest groups in 1990. New York City had the largest concentration for each of these groups. In 1990, New York had about 40 percent of all Italian immigrants in the United States, 29 percent of the Poles, 12 percent of the Germans, and 35 percent of those from the former Soviet Union. A majority of the Italians arrived in the United States before 1960 and only a small proportion after 1980. For the Poles, larger numbers arrived before 1960 but only one-third after 1980. Germans followed a similar pattern as the Poles. For those from the former Soviet Union, the figures are greater before 1960 and after 1980. Since 1990, the Russian population in New York has increased almost twofold, while immigrant populations from other European countries have declined. Most of those who recently came from the former Soviet Union are of Jewish heritage and have waited a long time to leave the Soviet Union. These immigrants have been resettled by welfare agencies with federal funding. However, because of the breakup of the former Soviet Union and changes in refugee status, this new wave of immigration from the former Soviet Union has diminished somewhat, although family-sponsored immigration from the successor states is still ongoing.[16]

Immigrant Residence and Immigrant Neighborhoods

The residential patterns and neighborhoods of early immigrants have been of intense interest for years. Did immigrants form their own easily identifiable quarters? Did they co-reside with some groups but not with others? What sort of housing and neighborhoods did immigrants live in? Did they inhabit tenements or "flophouses" that others would find uninhabitable? Did they displace earlier groups in the pattern of "invasion and succession" made famous by the early Chicago school sociologists? Did they live close to their work, or was there public transportation to take them from home to work?

Scholars have addressed all these questions in one way or another with respect to the wave of immigration at the turn of the twentieth century. One of the best empirical accounts of the situation of the first wave of immigrants was based on a sample of 1910 census records. Residential analysis was forced to rely on very complex manipulation of data and could not give present neighborhood analysis for specific cities.[17] Work by Duncan (1957) and Lieberson (1962) used large-scale ward-level tabulations to chart the levels of residential segregation of various immigrant groups in various cities.[18] Such work is not comparable to analyses that use census tracts, which were defined mainly in the second half of the twentieth century. They do, however, give some inkling of residential patterns. By using the newly available census tract tabulations from 1910, explicit comparisons will be made between residential patterns in the two periods.

In 1910, immigrants were not only moving to New York City, but also adding significantly to the population. One can see this by comparing figure 6.1 (which presents a map of New York City in 1910) with figure 6.2 (which presents a similar map for the metropolitan area in 1990). The map insets provide information on population density. As we will see in this chapter, immigrants in 1990 were also moving to New York, but rather than adding to the population, they were replacing it. In 1910, only portions of New York City were settled. These included Manhattan, especially the Lower East Side, Northwest Brooklyn, and Southeast Bronx. Queens, Staten Island, the rest of the Bronx, and the rest of Brooklyn were sparsely populated, and most of the subway lines remained to be constructed. Figure 6.1 also shows the foreign-born population very heavily concentrated in Manhattan, particularly in the Lower East Side, and

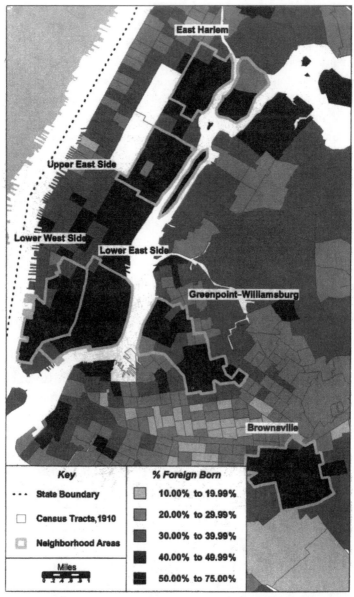

Figure 6.1. New York City Foreign Born, 1910. Source: Census data and boundaries compiled and map created by Andrew A. Beveridge.

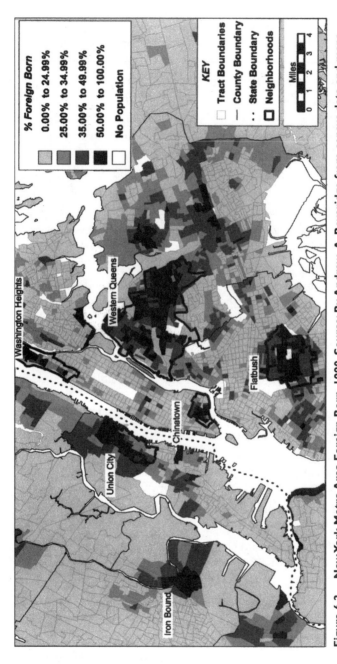

Figure 6.2. New York Metro Area Foreign Born, 1990. Source: By Andrew A. Beveridge from census data and maps.

highlights five other areas or neighborhoods with especially high concentrations of immigrant population, which are examined more carefully here.

By 1990, all of New York City was developed, and the metropolitan area included the city, suburbs, and other urban centers as well as some lightly populated areas. In 1910, Manhattan had about 2.3 million people, and one-third lived south of 18th Street in areas that included the Lower East Side. Today, Manhattan's population is 1.4 million, almost one million less than it was in 1910. Though every borough had a large fraction of foreign born, almost half of Manhattan's population was foreign born in 1910. In the Lower East Side area, about two-thirds of the 600,000 people were foreign born. Manhattan then was almost a "foreign" borough, and the Lower East Side was a "foreign" enclave. After the advent of the subways in the 1920s and 1930s, more than 600,000 housing units were built throughout New York City to accommodate the immigrants.

The pattern of very high density immigrant settlement was also true for the settled parts of Brooklyn and the Bronx. Most of the 1.6 million residents in Brooklyn lived quite near to Manhattan. Today, Brooklyn has about 2.3 million, but the whole borough is heavily settled. In 1910, the settlement, where it existed, was much denser. The same pattern holds for the settled part of the Bronx. All these patterns are evident by comparing figure 6.1 with figure 6.2. Queens and Staten Island were largely unsettled in 1910. Today, Queens (along with Brooklyn and Manhattan) is a heavily immigrant borough. The borough of Queens exceeded two million in population for the first time in 1999. In 1910, it had 280,000 residents. Staten Island still seems like a suburb today with a population of about 390,000. In 1910, only 85,000 people lived there.

This massive change in urban structure, much of it spurred by the wave of immigrants and their children at the turn of the twentieth century, means that the setting of immigration in late twentieth and early twenty-first-century immigration is much different than it was around 1910. In the New York City metropolitan area that comprised about 18.8 million people, there were 3.5 million immigrants in 1990. Only a small number of people lived in the same area outside New York City's borders in 1910. All the areas of high immigrant concentration were in Manhattan and Brooklyn in 1910. In 1990, they were spread through three boroughs of New York City, and two areas were in New Jersey. In 1910, most of the areas were not completely dominated by one group. In 1990, five of the six neighborhoods were easy to characterize. The neighborhoods are highlighted in figures 6.1 and 6.2. In each of these areas, there are sections where more than 50 percent of the residents were immigrants. The areas were chosen to illustrate immigrant settlement patterns found in 1910 and 1990 and do not make definitive statements about the boundaries or placement of specific neighborhoods.

For ease of reference, the name associated with each area was used, though in many cases the area shown on the map is substantially larger. In 1910, they included the following: the Lower East Side, the Lower West Side, the Upper East Side, East Harlem, Greenpoint–Williamsburg, and Brownsville. Each of these areas can be located on the map in figure 6.1.[19] Four of them are in Manhattan, and two are in Brooklyn. The area farthest from the center of population is Brownsville, which was accessible by elevated railway. All the other areas were accessible either by streetcar or by bridge.

As figure 6.2 shows, the immigrants are much more spatially dispersed in 1990 than they were in 1910. Yet there are definite areas of high immigrant settlement, and six of them are identified on the map in figure 6.2. These six areas include the following: Washington Heights, Chinatown, Flatbush Plus, Western Queens, Union City, New Jersey, and the Ironbound section of Newark, New Jersey.[20] Two of these neighborhoods are in Manhattan, one in Brooklyn, one in Queens, and two in New Jersey. Today, immigrants are moving into areas that are already heavily populated and are replacing the population that lived there. For instance, the area called Chinatown actually includes much of what was called the Lower East Side in 1910. Indeed, Chinatown has encroached on "Little Italy," for very few Italians now live there.

Distributions of foreign origin in the areas of high immigrant concentration in 1910 and 1990 are presented in tables 6.2 and 6.3, respectively. In 1910, almost half of all immigrants to New York City made one of these areas home, while in 1990 it is not even one-quarter. In 1910 and 1990, about half the people living in these neighborhoods were from abroad. In 1910, these areas were home to people from countries that had recently become large sources of immigrants to New York, including Russia, Italy, Austria, and Hungary, as well as to people from Ireland and Germany, who had participated in earlier waves.

Table 6.2. Distributions of Immigrants in Areas of High Immigrant Settlement, 1910

	Greenpoint–Williamsburg		Brownsville		Lower East Side		Lower West Side		Upper East Side		East Harlem		Total Six Neighborhoods	
Total population	356,852		143,690		601,995		181,672		186,485		278,791		1,749,485	
Total foreign born	152,977	42.9%	80,596	56.1%	401,485	66.7%	85,565	47.1%	87335	46.8%	149,689	53.7%	957,647	54.7%
Russia	60,796	39.7%	58,891	73.1%	191,501	47.7%	2,130	2.5%	5,832	6.7%	53,673	35.9%	372,823	38.9%
Italy	27,959	18.3%	6,617	8.2%	49,806	12.4%	52,989	61.9%	6,699	7.7%	45,284	30.3%	189,354	19.8%
Austria	15,911	10.4%	7,261	9.0%	86,539	21.6%	1,860	2.2%	18,489	21.2%	10,633	7.1%	140,693	14.7%
Germany	18,176	11.9%	1,739	2.2%	13,969	3.5%	4,969	5.8%	16,628	19.0%	9,862	6.6%	65,343	6.8%
Ireland	11,763	7.7%	784	1.0%	7,224	1.8%	12,903	15.1%	17,115	19.6%	9,966	6.7%	59,755	6.2%
Hungary	4,465	2.9%	700	0.9%	23,004	5.7%	1,086	1.3%	11,305	12.9%	6,693	4.5%	47,253	4.9%
Romania	3,758	2.5%	1,919	2.4%	17,152	4.3%	157	0.2%	415	0.5%	3,459	2.3%	26,860	2.8%
England	4,169	2.7%	1,524	1.9%	3,758	0.9%	2,271	2.7%	2,707	3.1%	3,380	2.3%	17,809	1.9%
Sweden	789	0.5%	170	0.2%	376	0.1%	556	0.6%	2,006	2.3%	832	0.6%	4,729	0.5%
All others	5,191	3.4%	991	1.2%	8,156	2.0%	6,644	7.8%	6,139	7.0%	5,907	3.9%	33,028	3.4%
		100.0%		100.0%		100.0%		100.0%		100.0%		100.0%		100.0%

Table 6.3. Distributions of Immigrants in Areas of High Immigrant Settlement, 1990

	Flatbush Plus		Western Queens		Washington Heights		Chinatown Plus		Union City		Iron Bound		Total Six Neighborhoods	
Total population	317,479		595,215		280,038		118,402		111,412		29,464		1,452,010	
Total foreign born	158,618	49.96%	305,641	51.35%	125,355	44.76%	54,304	45.86%	60,295	54.12%	18,418	62.51%	722,631	49.77%
Dominican Republic	2,512	1.58%	22,238	7.28%	74,696	59.59%	4,498	8.28%	5,530	9.17%	62	0.34%	109,536	15.16%
China	2,145	1.35%	16,104	5.27%	1,162	0.93%	31,167	57.39%	69	0.11%	114	0.62%	50,761	7.02%
Not reported	10,748	6.78%	15,833	5.18%	7,403	5.91%	5,039	9.28%	3,248	5.39%	951	5.16%	43,222	5.98%
Cuba	561	0.35%	8,547	2.80%	8,705	6.94%	400	0.74%	23,455	38.90%	1,249	6.78%	42,917	5.94%
Colombia	671	0.42%	31,366	10.26%	1,824	1.46%	210	0.39%	5,699	9.45%	160	0.87%	39,930	5.53%
Haiti	30,236	19.06%	2,013	0.66%	1,128	0.90%	163	0.30%	29	0.05%	0	0.00%	33,569	4.65%
Jamaica	28,697	18.09%	1,970	0.64%	1,903	1.52%	54	0.10%	7	0.01%	0	0.00%	32,631	4.52%
Ecuador	534	0.34%	17,584	5.75%	4,168	3.32%	203	0.37%	4,299	7.13%	555	3.01%	27,343	3.78%
Guyana	16,410	10.35%	3,960	1.30%	254	0.20%	86	0.16%	31	0.05%	6	0.03%	20,747	2.87%
Trinidad and Tobago	18,381	11.59%	1,427	0.47%	677	0.54%	135	0.25%	72	0.12%	6	0.03%	20,698	2.86%

(Continued)

Table 6.3. Distributions of Immigrants in Areas of High Immigrant Settlement, 1990 (Continued)

	Flatbush Plus		Western Queens		Washington Heights		Chinatown Plus		Union City		Iron Bound		Total Six Neighborhoods	
Korea	526	0.33%	18,872	6.17%	659	0.53%	74	0.14%	348	0.58%	22	0.12%	20,501	2.84%
India	310	0.20%	11,986	3.92%	422	0.34%	155	0.29%	785	1.30%	18	0.10%	13,676	1.89%
Greece	52	0.03%	12,261	4.01%	928	0.74%	70	0.13%	93	0.15%	17	0.09%	13,421	1.86%
Italy	309	0.19%	10,210	3.34%	201	0.16%	544	1.00%	1,865	3.09%	136	0.74%	13,265	1.84%
Russia	1,407	0.89%	9,721	3.18%	1,323	1.06%	419	0.77%	96	0.16%	0	0.00%	12,966	1.79%
Other Caribbean	7,902	4.98%	1,708	0.56%	1,073	0.86%	161	0.30%	541	0.90%	0	0.00%	11,385	1.58%
Portugal	137	0.09%	289	0.09%	16	0.01%	28	0.05%	88	0.15%	10,473	56.86%	11,031	1.53%
Philippines	476	0.30%	9,095	2.98%	647	0.52%	254	0.47%	218	0.36%	167	0.91%	10,857	1.50%
Peru	284	0.18%	7,803	2.55%	779	0.62%	75	0.14%	1,316	2.18%	72	0.39%	10,329	1.43%
Mexico	830	0.52%	6,606	2.16%	856	0.68%	134	0.25%	1,159	1.92%	34	0.18%	9,619	1.33%
Hong Kong	253	0.16%	4,318	1.41%	111	0.09%	4,682	8.62%	17	0.03%	7	0.04%	9,388	1.30%
Barbados	8,301	5.23%	331	0.11%	161	0.13%	0	0.00%	0	0.00%	0	0.00%	8,793	1.22%
Panama	7,040	4.44%	464	0.15%	692	0.55%	129	0.24%	85	0.14%	0	0.00%	8,410	1.16%
Other countries	19,896	12.54%	90,935	29.75%	15,567	12.42%	5,624	10.36%	11,245	18.65%	4,369	23.72%	147,636	20.43%

The most important area in 1910 was the Lower East Side. According to the newly available census tabulations, just over 600,000 people lived in the area marked as the Lower East Side in 1910, and some two-thirds were foreign born. Although the Lower East Side as defined here consisted of a large fraction of Jewish immigrants, the immigrant residents did hail from a variety of nations. Furthermore, the Italians were the third-largest group in the Lower East Side and represented a large presence. Packed together in tenements and slums, more than 40 percent of all the immigrants in the six neighborhoods were in the Lower East Side. The neighborhood became synonymous with "big-city slum." Jacob Riis, the photographer and journalist, focused on the Lower East Side and other tenement areas. The following is a description of the tenement situation:

> Tenement houses were designed for twenty families, but these buildings often housed as many as one hundred residents, as well as their boarders. Upwards of 200 licensed "flophouses" with nearly eighteen thousand bunks lined the Bowery and Oliver, Chatham, and Mulberry streets. Many people lived in basements subject to tidal seepage.... Apartments with two rooms had no closets: tenants hung their clothing from nails that they tacked into recesses in the walls six inches deep. Bedrooms had no space for washbasins or bureaus and kitchens were rarely large enough for people to sit around the four sides of a table.... Cleanliness was of essential importance: only one third of the tenements had running water, and in some blocks it was lacking altogether.

These conditions were those found at the turn of the century in the Lower East Side and in other areas of recent immigrant settlement. Reform efforts began, and some improvements were made. However, until the advent of the subways and the movement of people to the outer boroughs, some of these conditions continued. In the 1920s, many of these buildings were boarded up as the Lower East Side lost about 250,000 in population.[21]

Despite the substandard housing and the crowding, many cultural and other institutions developed on the Lower East Side. It was the site of Yiddish theater as well as an area for unionism and radical politics. Also distinct on the map in figure 6.1 is an area dubbed the Lower West Side. Its composition was much more Italian than the nearby the Lower East Side. Residents from here walked to factories along the Hudson River, while there also were many factories in the Lower East Side. The living conditions were quite similar to those on the Lower East Side, but here the cultural and other institutions were largely Italian.

The Upper East Side was very different from both the Lower East Side and the Lower West Side. It was much more a location for northern European immigrants than either area, although it also included some of the other immigrant groups. The area includes Yorkville, which until very recently had a large set of German restaurants and shops. Another part of the Upper East Side had a large number of Irish shops. Most residents lived in "brownstones." The area developed when the elevated railroad was extended up Third Avenue. When the railroad was razed in 1916, the area became much more "upscale." Unlike the Lower East Side, the immigrants to the Upper East Side were much less likely to be Jewish. The area defined as East Harlem, which is somewhat farther north in Manhattan, had about 150,000 immigrants in 1910. It developed with the extension of the elevated railroad. Tenements were constructed, and the immigrant residents broadly reflected the origins of immigrants in all of New York City in 1910.

All four Manhattan immigrant areas had some presence of Russians, Austrians, Italians, Hungarians, Romanians, Germans, and Irish. However, the Russians congregated much more in the Lower East Side and East Harlem, while the Italians dominated in the Lower West Side. The Irish were concentrated in the Lower West Side and the Upper East Side. The largest concentration of Austrians, Hungarians, and Germans was also to be found in the Upper East Side.

The two Brooklyn neighborhoods had very different compositions. Greenpoint–Williamsburg, across the East River from the Lower East Side, was an area of great diversity; the residents included Russians, Italians, Germans, Austrians, and Irish. The area began to develop as an immigrant area when the Williamsburg Bridge was opened in 1903. By 1917, it was the most densely populated area in the entire city. Jews from a variety of countries, Russian Orthodox Catholics, and Italians all had various cultural institutions in the area. Indeed, the annual Italian festival of the dancing of the *Giglio* is still a major event to this day.[22] The Brownsville neighborhood is the only neighborhood where one immigrant group completely dominated. In 1887, a Jewish entrepreneur purchased land, built tenements, and enticed to the area several Jewish garment makers from the Lower East Side. The opening of an elevated line in 1889 spurred its growth. The area was largely a Jewish slum, with sweatshops and pushcarts and no sewers or paved streets. The area had 81,000 immigrants in 1910.[23] Almost three-quarters of these were from Russia, and most worked in the nearby factories.

The immigrants in New York City in 1910 were highly concentrated in the Lower East Side as well as a few other areas in New York City, and only a few groups made up the vast bulk of immigrants in 1910. All large immigrant groups were from Europe. It is indisputable that in 1910, Russian Jews and Italians, along with Jews from other countries, settled in a much more concentrated way than the other older immigrant groups, such as the Irish and Germans. The concentration in Manhattan, especially in Lower Manhattan, was phenomenal. About 750,000 people, more than half of Manhattan's present population, lived below 18th Street. About 500,000 of them were immigrants, and most were recent immigrants. They had come to New York from Italy, Russia, and Austria. They lived near, some would say on top of, one another, and many also worked nearby.

The pattern in 1990 is starkly different. Immigrants have replaced other residents in many neighborhoods, and instead of "immigrant" housing stock, the immigrants lived in older high-rise and multifamily units. This process takes times, as people need to move out and more immigrants need to move in before an area gets a particular "character." It is also the case that certain shopping or commercial areas can develop such a "character" before nearby residential areas since people may travel to shop for specific national or ethnic goods and experiences. The same is also true today for cultural institutions. Since public transportation exists and many people have access to automobiles, residential, employment, and commercial patterns do not overlap as much as they did at the turn of the twentieth century. In short, immigrant neighborhoods or immigrant enclaves are not as important for the maintenance of immigrant ties as they were then.

Despite this fact, the areas of high immigrant settlement in 1990, except for Western Queens, have unique characteristics. The proportions of immigrants from various countries are displayed in table 6.3. The variation among these neighborhoods is especially remarkable. In 1990, 54,000 immigrants lived in Chinatown, a Chinese immigrant enclave. Washington Heights is a Dominican enclave, though the Dominicans can now be found in many

ANDREW A. BEVERIDGE

other parts of New York City as well. The area designated as "Flatbush Plus" includes Flatbush and areas adjacent to it. No single immigrant group dominates in Flatbush Plus, but the largest immigrant groups are from the West Indies, including Haiti, and together they make up about three-quarters of the population in the area. Not surprisingly, it is the site of the annual West Indian parade and festival in New York.

Of the six immigrant neighborhoods, Western Queens is by far the most diverse. It has become one of the areas of intense immigration. It developed in the 1930s and 1940s with immigrants from Germany, Ireland, Italy, and Greece. Now it is often the first stop for immigrants from many different countries. It is the area through which the Number 7 IRT subway runs, which has been named a "National Trail" and has been dubbed the "International Express." [24]

Both areas in New Jersey present very different patterns. The small section in Newark called "Ironbound" has about 18,418 immigrants, almost three-fifths from Portugal. The name "Ironbound" comes from the fact that the area is completely defined by several railroad lines. Many Portuguese arrived during the collapse of Portugal's African colonies in the early 1960s and the eventual overthrow of the dictator Antonio de Oliveira Salazar in 1968. This group is much more akin to the white European groups that came to the United States seeking refuge at the turn of the century than the newer immigrants coming in today. Recently, to service the Portuguese-speaking Catholics in this area, the local bishop traveled to Portugal to recruit priests for some of the parishes. Including the city and the surrounding suburbs, the area designated as "Union City" contains about 60,000 immigrants. This area has a large proportion of Cuban immigrants as well as several groups of other Latin American immigrants. It includes about one-fifth of the Cuban Americans in the New York City metropolitan area and has become predominantly settled by white Cubans and other Latin American immigrants.

In 1910, New York's immigrants did have many things in common: coming to Ellis Island, settling in the Lower East Side or other areas of intense immigrant concentration, living close to immigrants not only from the same origin but also from different origins, and being packed into substandard housing and working for very low wages in sweatshops and warehouses. In the contemporary migration period, things are very different. Except for Western Queens, each immigrant area in 1990 could be easily

218

identified with one immigrant group or (in the case of Flatbush Plus) a set of groups that were racially distinct. Chinese are in Chinatown, Dominicans are in Washington Heights, black West Indians are in Flatbush Plus, Portuguese are in Iron Bound, and Cubans are in Union City. Simply put, the pattern of immigrant settlement in 1990, except in Western Queens, could be seen as "from many groups, many enclaves." The idea of one common immigrant experience, even in myth, is unlikely to take hold on the basis of the settlement patterns in 1990. Though the analogy is quickly drawn in the popular press, there is nothing equivalent to the Lower East Side in the early twenty-first century. Instead of being concentrated, the immigrant groups are found in several different areas of the city.

Segregation among Immigrant Groups, 1910 and 1990

It is possible to rigorously assess the extent to which various groups are settling widely dispersed in the whole population and among other immigrant groups. To do this requires the computation of a measure of segregation. The most commonly used segregation index is *dissimilarity,* which measures how unevenly dispersed a group is with respect to the whole population or other groups. This measure and others developed out of a long line of work on segregation in the United States.[25] Others have applied such measures to analyses of immigrant settlement patterns, but this is the first attempt to do so in a comprehensive way for New York City for 1910 and 1990.[26]

How segregated were major immigrant groups in 1910 and 1990? Table 6.4 summarizes the results for the major groups in both years using the dissimilarity index. This index reports the proportion of a group that needs to be "spread out" to make the group completely evenly distributed in the population by geographical unit, the census tract here. As is immediately apparent, the immigrants in 1990 are more segregated than they were in 1910. The four most segregated groups in 1910—Russians, Italians, Austrians, and Hungarians—have index values between 0.50 and 0.60. This means that about half the members of each group would need to be spread out to make them completely even in the population. Irish, Germans, and English all have index values less than 0.40. These groups would not be considered segregated in any great degree, but they were the "older" immigrant groups in 1910. In 1990, except for Italians and Germans, all major groups—Haitians, Dominicans, Jamaicans, Chinese, Russians, Colombians, Cubans, Indians, and Poles—had index values on the order of 0.60 or higher. Race, it seems, plays a definite part in this pattern since Haitians, Jamaicans, and even Dominicans tend to have darker complexions than members of other groups. Nonetheless, the major finding, which is mirrored by the discussion of specific neighborhoods, is that except for members of the now older groups—Italians and Germans—segregation of immigrants in 1990 is much higher than it was in 1910.

Beyond segregation from the population at large, it is important to know the extent to which the various groups in 1910 and 1990 settled together or settled apart. To examine this rigorously, the dissimilarity index was used again, but this time the reference groups were other foreign-born groups. The results of this analysis for 1910 and for 1990 are presented in table 6.5. Remember that for dissimilarity, a measure of 0.0 means that two groups are distributed completely evenly. An index value of 1.0 says that the groups are completely segregated residentially. Empirically, a value around 0.3 or 0.4 demonstrates that the pattern of segregation is quite limited.

Applying this index to the six largest groups for 1910 presents the following patterns. Russians (and many of them are Russian Jews) are segregated from four out of the other five groups: Germans, Italians, Irish, and

Table 6.4. Segregation (Dissimilarity) Indexes for Major Groups in New York City, 1910, and New York City Metropolitan Area, 1990 (Reference Group All Others in Population)

Dissimilarity, 1910		Dissimilarity, 1990	
Russia	0.60	Haiti	0.78
Italy	0.58	Dominican Republic	0.73
Austria	0.50	Jamaica	0.70
Hungary	0.50	China	0.68
Ireland	0.37	Russia	0.66
Germany	0.29	Colombia	0.64
England	0.24	Cuba	0.62
		India	0.59
All foreign born	0.26	Poland	0.56
Other foreign born	0.28	Italy	0.47
		Germany	0.40
		All foreign born	0.37
		Other foreign born	0.34

Table 6.5. Segregation (Exposure) Indexes for Major Groups in New York City, 1910, and New York City Metropolitan Area, 1990 (Reference Group All Others in Population and All Immigrants)

Isolation from All, 1910		Isolation from All, 1990	
Russia	0.31	Dominican Republic	0.15
Italy	0.27	China	0.12
Austria	0.14	Cuba	0.08
Ireland	0.10	Russia	0.08
Germany	0.09	Haiti	0.07
Hungary	0.05	Jamaica	0.07
England	0.02	Colombia	0.04
		Italy	0.04
All foreign born	0.46	Poland	0.04
Other foreign born	0.08	India	0.03
		Germany	0.01
		All foreign born	0.30
		Other foreign born	0.18

Foreign-Born Exposure, 1910		Foreign-Born Exposure, 1990	
England	1.00	Germany	0.90
Hungary	0.90	Colombia	0.89
Austria	0.76	India	0.87
Ireland	0.73	Poland	0.85
Germany	0.72	Cuba	0.83
Italy	0.50	Russia	0.81
Russia	0.49	Haiti	0.81
		Italy	0.78
All foreign born	0.54	Jamaica	0.77
Other foreign born	0.79	China	0.77
		Dominican Republic	0.64
		All foreign born	0.70
		Other foreign born	0.40

English. The lowest index value among them is 0.66. Russians are only moderately segregated from Austrians with an index value of 0.39. Austria in 1910 included much of Poland and portions of the old Austro-Hungarian Empire. Like the Russians, many of the Austrians were Jewish, explaining the moderate segregation between the two groups in 1910. Patterns for the other groups are quite straightforward. Germans, English, and Irish do not seem to be highly segregated from one another, while Italians are highly segregated in 1910 from most other groups.

The patterns in 1990 involve many more groups. Here, segregation indices for eleven groups are presented. When the segregation indices of the Dominicans from other major groups are computed, the levels of segregation are quite high throughout. It is true that segregation between Dominicans and other Hispanic groups is slightly lower than that between Dominicans and Asian, European, or West Indian groups. The average with the Hispanic groups is 0.66, while the levels with respect to West Indians, Asians, and Europeans of various origins vary between about 0.80 and 0.91. This would support the notion that the Dominicans are well apart from all other groups and even more apart from Asians, West Indians, and Europeans.

The two other large Hispanic groups—Colombians and Cubans—are segregated at relatively high levels from other groups, including other Hispanic groups. But the Indians are the least segregated from Colombians than from any other group examined, while Cubans are the least segregated from Germans. Both groups are largely segregated from all other groups.

When the West Indians are considered, it is obvious that the various West Indian groups are segregated from one another only at moderate levels, about 0.54, but heavily segregated from Dominicans, as seen previously, and from the Asian and European groups. West Indians, including Jamaicans and Haitians, are much more segregated from various Asian and European groups at the level of 0.85 or higher. This level approaches almost complete separation. When the various Asian groups are considered together, except for China and Hong Kong, the levels of segregation are quite high. The levels of segregation tend to be about 0.70 or even higher. This means that Asians are not settling near one another or at least within the same census tracts. The index values between some Asian groups and the European groups are about as high as within the various Asian groups. When the four European groups are considered, German immigrants are only moderately segregated from Italians and Poles. The Italians are segregated from the Russians and the Poles, but the Poles are not very segregated from the Russians. All four white groups are very segregated from Dominicans and West Indians and moderately segregated from the various Asian groups. This reflects the tendency of many Asian immigrants to remigrate to white neighborhoods.

The segregation indices examined buttress the basic findings about New York immigrants in 1910 and 1990. In 1910, they were much less diverse and much less segregated. At the same time, groups with large proportions of Jewish immigrants settled more together, as did the German,

English, and Irish immigrants. Separate and apart from both, the other immigrants were the Italians.

In 1990, immigrants are much more diverse and much more segregated. Race has a big effect on the pattern of settlement for black and white immigrants but not for Asians. The various West Indian groups are only moderately segregated from one another, while Germans are not highly segregated from Italians and Polish. As has been seen, the West Indians together dominate the area designated as Flatbush Plus. In the same way, the Dominicans seem to be mostly apart from other groups, and they are dominant in Washington Heights. There is limited evidence of less segregation with respect to other Hispanic immigrant groups. When the Asian groups are considered, there are very high levels of segregation among the various East Asian, South Asian, and Southeast Asian groups. As of 1990, the Russian immigrants were highly segregated from all groups and only slightly less segregated from other European immigrants except for Poles. A large proportion of immigrants from Russia and the other states of the former Soviet Union at the beginning of the twenty-first century are recent refugees, many of Jewish heritage. They are new immigrants, albeit European and white.

Conclusion

New York City in 1910 is very different from the New York metropolitan area of today. In 1910, only a small portion of it was settled, but where immigrants were settling, it was densely packed. Immigrants lived and worked in cramped and impoverished conditions. Today, immigrants are settling throughout the metropolitan area, though more concentrated in New York City. The immigrants coming to New York now are very different from the 1910 immigrants. In 1910, most immigrants originated from several European countries. The present wave of immigrants is from the Caribbean, Mexico, Central and South America, Asia, and even Europe. Now more immigrants settle in enclaves compared to 1910. When explicit measures of segregation are applied, it is obvious that immigrants now are much more segregated than those at the turn of the century.

What is the significance of the patterns of immigration residential settlement in the New York area? It can be said that there was some commonality to the immigrant experience in New York around 1910. Most immigrants came to New York City and lived in extremely harsh conditions on the Lower East Side or in other immigrant neighborhoods. They were packed into substandard housing and worked for many hours in sweatshops. Their cultural and social activities, as well as their jobs and shopping areas, were very near their place of residence. But they likely shared the area with immigrants from other countries, whether from Italy, Orthodox Russia, Austria, Jewish Austria or Russia, or elsewhere. Because of their packed living conditions, they could not escape contact with immigrants of other origins. Because of this pattern, it is not surprising that the idea of a common immigrant experience has gained credence in the United States. The museum at Ellis Island is one of the most visited tourist attractions in the United States. Children of immigrants from a wide variety of countries, all in Europe, have made historical experience part of their tradition.

Examining the patterns in 1990, one might expect a very different outcome. Immigrants are coming from many more countries for many more reasons. They are settling in a very segregated pattern. Where there are large enough numbers, an enclave is likely to develop. At this point, there is little evidence, except for the West Indians, of mixed-group settlement. Indeed, the various Asian groups and the various Hispanic groups are almost as segregated among their own racial or linguistic groups as they are from groups of other races or other languages. The Bureau of the Census, following government mandates, imposes racial and Hispanic identity in the United States. Each respondent applies it on the basis of these guidelines. From the data presented here—except for the West Indians, who share the stigmatized black race—little mixed-group settlement is occurring among the new immigrants.

The patterns presented here will only be heightened by the immigration that has continued unabated to the New York area since 1990. Preliminary estimates from the 1999 New York City Housing and Vacancy Survey (U.S. Bureau of the Census 1999a) find that several immigrant groups discussed here have grown very rapidly. They include people from the former Soviet Union, 229,000 (up 184 percent); the Philippines (up 35 percent); Mexico, 133,000 (up 278 percent); Pakistan and Bangladesh, 82,000 (up 246 percent); India, 64,000 (up 48 percent); and the Dominican Republic, 387,000 (up 69 percent). Growth also occurred in other Asian, Central and South American, Caribbean, and even African groups, while Puerto Rican, European, and "born in the United States" groups fell.[27]

Today, the immigrant from the Dominican Republic does not go to Ellis Island and move to a flophouse and work in a sweatshop in the Lower East Side. Rather, he or she flies to Kennedy Airport and goes to live with or near relatives in Washington Heights in an older apartment building. Many find work for low wages in the service sector. The pattern is repeated for each and every group. The Chinese, if from the mainland, may work in a garment factory or a restaurant and live in a furnished room in Chinatown or Flushing. Other entrepreneurs may come from Taiwan, set up businesses, and live in the New Jersey, Long Island, or Westchester suburbs. The West Indian, whether from Haiti, Jamaica, Trinidad or elsewhere, may move to Flatbush. New immigrants from Portugal or Cuba (and there are only a few) will settle near those groups, perhaps in Ironbound or Union City. Only in Western Queens is there a mixture of many different groups.

Surely, immigrants to New York today have a very different experience than did immigrants at the turn of the twentieth century. For each foreign group, the experience will be specific to the given group. Beyond this, many more groups from many more countries characterize this wave of migration. Furthermore, beyond simply the cultural and class differences, many immigrants are racially distinct and fall into one of the racial classifications of the United States. West Indians are black; Asians are Asian; Russians, Italians, Poles, and Germans are white; and some Dominicans and some others from Latin America might classify themselves as "other." Such distinctions also affect residential patterns and immigrant experience.

It is much too early to speculate on the eventual outcome to New York and the United States of this wave of immigration. But the residential patterns and neighborhoods in New York today, when compared to those from the early twentieth century, make it obvious that the outcome may be very different. To understand this new wave of immigration, one must not assume that it will follow the pattern of the immigrants from a century ago.

Notes

I wish to acknowledge the work of Susan Weber, Iris Schweitzer, Michiyo Yamashiki, Handan Hizmetli, and Justin Stoger in deciphering the 1910 data from microfilm records, entering it into a computer, and editing it. Kenneth "Nick"

Trippel helped devise and implement the method to computerize the maps. James Schumm also assisted. The Newspaper Division of the *New York Times* provided funds for the data and map editing. Terry Schwadron's faith and forbearance are gratefully acknowledged. The continued involvement and assistance of Dylan McClain at the *New York Times* was vital. I am grateful to Pyong Gap Min and Susan Weber for comments on an earlier draft of this chapter. The conclusions of the author are his alone. The analyses presented in the paper are drawn from four sources of data: (1) the census tabulations by tract carried out in 1910 and 1990 that present country of origin for the foreign born by census tract, (2) analyses of the 1910 and 1990 Public Use Microdata Samples (PUMS) data of the original census records, (3) the 1910 census data derived from the IPUMS project at the University of Minnesota, and (4) analyses based on the 1999 New York City Housing and Vacancy Survey carried out by the U.S. Bureau of the Census.

1. See Lambert (2000).

2. The "census tract movement" began in New York City and was spurred by Walter Laidlaw. In 1906, he suggested that the city be divided into units according to population for the 1910 census. For the most populous neighborhoods, such as most of Manhattan and portions of Brooklyn and the Bronx, a measure of approximately forty acres was used, with each tract averaging about eight city blocks. The rest of the city was divided into larger areas. There were two volumes of transcribed items prepared by the Bureau of the Census in 1910. They included an array of data relating to the social situation of residents, including much detail about age, sex, race, education, foreign-born status, and the like. All in all, over 500 data items existed for each of 704 populated tracts in 1910. Population data from the New York state census in 1915 was tabulated on the basis of the 1910 tracts, and later block population data from the 1905 New York state census were recompiled on the basis of the 1910 geography. The census data from 1910 were computerized, as were the maps that depicted the location of the census tracts. Census tracts at present are small, defined areas within cities and suburbs that have populations between 2,000 and 4,000. See Bowser et al. (1979).

3. Luckily, the New York City data was preserved and microfilmed. At this writing, data from the other cities has not been unearthed. Those cities include Boston, Philadelphia, Baltimore, Pittsburgh, Cleveland, Chicago, and St. Louis.

4. The TIGER/Line files were created from the Bureau of the Census's TIGER (Topologically Integrated Geographic Encoding and Referencing) database of selected geographic and cartographic information. They contain a street map with all levels of political and census boundaries for the entire United States. See U.S. Bureau of the Census (1999b).

5. Throughout this chapter, New York City of 1910 was compared with the New York consolidated metropolitan area of 1995. This was done because, as of 1910, little of the metropolitan area was developed and much of New York City remained to be developed. However, by 1990, New York City was part of a large metropolis. See Beveridge and Weber (in press).

6. Accounts of the Jewish immigrant experience in America abound. See Kraut (1982), and Gold and Phillips (1996). A seminal work related to New York is Kessner (1977).

7. This analysis is drawn from Watkins (1994: 372, table B.1).

8. For an account of the Italian American experience in the United States and factors that fostered immigration from Italy, see Kessner (1977) and Nelli (1983).

9. Analyses of year of entry of members of various groups and the proportions living in New York of all those in the United States are taken from analyses performed using 1910 and 1990 PUMS data of the Bureau of the Census.

10. The reported place of birth is used rather than the administrative category "immigrant" as tabulated by the Immigration and Naturalization Service (INS). While the census tabulations will include some individuals who have lived in the United States for a long period of time, they include all individuals who live in the United States at a given time as reported to the Bureau of the Census. They include students, undocumented aliens, those on work visas, and so on. The INS counts only people who have the documentation to live permanently in the United States, so-called green-card holders. As such, the INS will miss those from new streams of immigrants unless they have been granted refugee status and can easily receive green cards. The INS does not track foreign-born residents, as they move from place to place and have only recently reported the ZIP code of residence when the green card was issued. The Bureau of the Census has always collected year of entry for the foreign-born residents; however, it has not tabulated it by group. Here, both tabulated data and PUMS data are used to take into account the recency of immigration for specific groups.

11. From an analysis of data from the 1999 Housing and Vacancy Survey conducted by the Bureau of the Census for the New York City's Department of Housing Preservation and Development.

12. The major source of more qualitative information about Dominicans comes from Grasmuck and Pessar (1991). This study was somewhat updated by 1990 census figures in Grasmuck and Pessar (1996: 280–292). Recent data is from the author's analysis of the 1999 New York City Housing and Vacancy Survey data, which is collected by the Bureau of the Census every three years. See Lambert (2000).

13. See Kasinitz (1992) and Waters (2000). Some discussion of the Jamaican community can be found in Nossiter (1995).

14. See Sontag (1994).

15. Among other recent accounts of Chinese immigration are Kwong (1996).

16. Many of the former Soviet Union immigrants have moved to particular neighborhoods in Brooklyn. See Lewine (1999).

17. See White et al. (1994).

18. See Duncan (1957) and Lieberson (1962).

19. The Lower East Side is roughly bounded by 18th Street on the north and the Bowery on the west, running to the tip of Manhattan. The Lower West Side, directly west of the Lower East Side, runs from 18th Street to the tip of Manhattan. The Upper East Side is the area that extends from about 59th to 84th Street from Central Park to the East River. East Harlem extends from about 94th to 126th Street between Fifth Avenue and the East River. Greenpoint–Williamsburg, an area of northern Brooklyn just across the river from the Lower East Side and accessible by the Williamsburg and Brooklyn Bridges, is the area defined by Flushing Avenue and the East River. Brownsville, an area accessible by one of the early subway lines, is just southeast of what is now the Cemetery of the Evergreens and Highland Park. Atlantic, Miller, Hegeman, and Remsen bound it.

20. Washington Heights, for our purposes, is the area bounded by 125th Street on the south and St. Nicholas on the east, extending to the northern tip of Manhattan. This area does include some of what is usually considered part of Harlem, but it is an area of intense immigration. Chinatown extends from the East River to Broadway, between Fulton and Houston. This area includes some of both the Lower East Side and the Lower West Side, as defined in the discussion of immigrants in 1910. Flatbush Plus extends roughly from Coney Island Avenue to Ralph and Ditmars, between Avenue 1 and Lefferts Boulevard. Western Queens incorporates several neighborhoods, including Jackson Heights, Elmhurst, Long Island City, Steinway, Hunter's Point, Woodside, and Sunny Side. Such areas as Corona and Astoria are also in the area. The names for specific neighborhoods are never fixed. Union City includes Union City, New Jersey, and its environs. Ironbound is a section of Newark, New Jersey.

21. From Schwarts (1995). See also Jackson (1976).

22. Based on Berck (1995). It includes reports on the festival of the *Giglio* by students who are present residents of the area.

23. Based on Rawson (1995).

24. See Harlow (1995).

25. This measure is discussed in Massey and Denton (1988). It is the main measure of segregation and has been used for years to assess the segregation of African Americans. One of the classic analyses is Taeuber and Taeuber (1969).

26. See White et al. (1962). See also Lieberson (1962).

27. See Lambert (2000). This is based on an analysis of the 1999 New York City Housing and Vacancy Survey (U.S. Bureau of the Census 1999a).

References

Berck, Judith. 1995. "Williamsburgh." In *The Encyclopedia of New York City,* edited by Kenneth T. Jackson. New Haven, CT: Yale University Press.

Beveridge, Andrew A., and Susan Weber. In press. "Shifting Patterns of Spatial Inequality: Race and Class in the Developing New York and Los Angeles Metropolises: 1940 to 2000." In *New York and Los Angeles in the 21st Century,* edited by David Halle. Chicago: University of Chicago Press.

Bowser, Benjamin P., Evelyn S. Mann, and Martin Oling. 1979. *Census Data with Maps for Small Areas of New York City, 1910 to 1960: A Guide to the Microfilm.* Ithaca, NY: Cornell University Libraries.

Duncan, Otis Dudley. 1957. *The Negro Population of Chicago: A Study of Residential Succession.* Chicago: University of Chicago Press.

Gold, Steven J., and Bruce Phillips. 1996. "Mobility and Continuity among Eastern European Jews." In *Origins and Destination: Immigration, Race and Ethnicity in America,* edited by Silvia Pedraza and Ruben G. Rumbaut. Belmont, CA: Wadsworth.

Grasmuck, Sherri, and Patricia R. Pessar. 1991. *Between Two Islands: Dominican International Migration.* Berkeley and Los Angeles: University of California Press.

———. 1996. "Dominicans in the United States: First and Second-Generation Settlement." In *Origins and Destination: Immigration, Race and Ethnicity in America,* edited by Silvia Pedraza and Ruben G. Rumbaut. Belmont, CA: Wadsworth.

Harlow, Ilana. 1995. *The International Express.* Queens Council on the Arts, Woodhaven, NY. Brochure.

Jackson, Anthony. 1976. *A History of Low Cost Housing in Manhattan.* Cambridge, MA: MIT Press.

Kasinitz, Phil. 1992. *Caribbean New York: Black Immigrants and the Politics of Race.* Ithaca, NY: Cornell University Press.

Kessner, Thomas. 1977. *The Golden Door: Italian and Jewish Immigrant Mobility in New York City, 1880–1915.* New York: Oxford University Press.

Kraut, Alan M. 1982. *The Huddled Masses: The Immigrant in American Society, 1880–1921.* Wheeling, IL: Harlan Davidson.

Kwong, Peter. 1996. *The New Chinatown.* New York: Hill & Wang.

Lambert, Bruce. 2000. "40 Percent in New York Born Abroad." *New York Times*, July 24, B1.

Lewine, Edward. 1999. "From Brighton Beach to America." *New York Times*, March 14, A14.

Lieberson, Stanley. 1962. *Ethnic Patterns in American Cities*. Glencoe, IL: The Free Press.

Massey, Douglas S., and Nancy Denton. 1988. "The Dimensions of Residential Segregation." *Social Forces* 67: 281–315.

Nelli, Humbert. 1983. *From Immigrants to Ethnics: The Italian Americans*. New York: Oxford University Press.

Nossiter, Adam. 1995. "A Jamaican Way Station in the Bronx: Community of Striving Immigrants Fosters Middle-Class Values." *New York Times*, October 25, B1.

Rawson, Elizabeth Reich. 1995. "Brownsville." In *The Encyclopedia of New York City*, edited by Kenneth T. Jackson. New Haven, CT: Yale University Press.

Schwarts, Joel. 1995. "Tenements." In *The Encyclopedia of New York City*, edited by Kenneth T. Jackson. New Haven, CT: Yale University Press.

Sontag, Deborah. 1994. "Haitian Migrants Settle in, Looking Back." *New York Times*, June 3, A1.

Taeuber, Karl E., and Alma F. Taeuber. 1969. *Negroes in Cities: Residential Segregation and Neighborhood Change*. Chicago: Aldine.

Waters, Mary. 2000. *Black Identities: West Indian Immigrant Dreams and American Realities*. Cambridge, MA: Harvard University Press.

Watkins, Susan Cott, ed. 1994. *After Ellis Island: Newcomers and Natives in the 1910 Census*. New York: Russell Sage Foundation.

U.S. Bureau of the Census. 1999a. *New York City Housing and Vacancy Survey: 1999*. Washington, DC: U.S. Bureau of the Census. Machine-readable file.

———. 1999b. *1999 TIGER/Line Files Technical Documentation*. Washington, DC: U.S. Department of Commerce, Bureau of the Census, Geography Division.

White, Michael J., Robert F. Dymowski, and Shilan Wang. 1994. "Ethnic Neighbors and Ethnic Myths." In *After Ellis Island: Newcomers and Natives in the 1910 Census*, edited by Susan Cott Watkins. New York: Russell Sage Foundation.

CHAPTER SEVEN

IMMIGRANT WOMEN AND WORK IN NEW YORK CITY, THEN AND NOW

Nancy Foner

T oday's immigrant women enter a society that has undergone remarkable changes since the last great immigrant influx early in
the twentieth century. Perhaps most dramatic, is the virtual revolution in women's involvement in the labor force. Whereas in 1900 only
20 percent of the nation's women were in the paid labor force, by 1995 the
figure had reached nearly 60 percent. There is a difference in who works,
too. At the turn of the twentieth century, the vast majority of women
workers were young and single. It was generally assumed that work outside the home was temporary for a young girl; when she married, she
would move back into the domestic domain. Indeed, in 1900, only 6 percent of the nation's married women were in the labor force.

Today, working daughters have given way to working mothers.[1]
Women now enter the labor force later—and they stay. Whether they
work for economic need, to maintain or raise their family's living standards, or for personal satisfaction, the fact is that, by 1990, almost three-
quarters of married women in the United States with children under
eighteen worked in the paid labor force, many doing so full time and year-
round.

How have these broad changes in women's participation in the American labor force affected the experiences of immigrant women today as
compared to the past? An analysis of immigrant women and work that
compares past and present is useful for a number of reasons. We have
come a long way from the days when scholars lamented that women were
ignored in migration studies, yet the growing literature on contemporary

immigrant women in the United States often proceeds without much awareness of the experiences of, or the literature on, migrant women of earlier eras. Historian Donna Gabaccia's important and wide-ranging book, *From the Other Side* (1984) provides an overview of immigrant women's experiences past and present, but she emphasizes the continuities that characterize women of both the nineteenth-century and the present-day migrations (see also Gabaccia 1992). Here, the stress is on the differences, particularly those shaped by the contrasting structure of work opportunities—and cultural norms and attitudes to women's work—that greeted immigrant women on arrival. As Bendix (1964: 17) has noted in another context, a comparison of this sort increases "the 'visibility' of one structure" by contrasting it with another. Comparing a time when few married immigrant women worked for wages to a period when most do brings into sharper focus the relationship between migrant women's work and their overall status—and helps us understand the conditions that lead women to experience gains as well as losses when they come here.

This analysis is part of a larger comparative project on immigrants in New York today and at the beginning of the twentieth century, the two peak periods in the city's immigration history (Foner 2000). Between 1880 and 1920, more than one million immigrants arrived and settled in New York City so that, by 1910, fully 41 percent of all New Yorkers were foreign born. In this earlier period, the focus is on eastern European Jews and Italians—the vast bulk of the new arrivals at the time who defined what was then thought of as the "new immigration." Today, no two groups predominate this way, and New York's immigrants now include sizable numbers from a variety of Asian, West Indian, and Latin American nations and European countries as well. For this reason, the discussion of the present draws on material on a larger number of groups. Since the late 1960s, immigrants have been streaming into New York City at what was, in the 1990s, a rate of more than 100,000 a year. All together, by 1998, according to Current Population Survey estimates, some 2.8 million New Yorkers were foreign born, representing more than one-third of the city's population.

A comparison of migrant women in the two eras reveals some striking differences. Wage work has empowered immigrant wives and mothers in late twentieth-century New York in ways that were not possible for Jewish and Italian married women of an earlier era, who rarely worked outside the home. Yet despite this contrast, gender inequalities are still very much with us, and despite improvements in their status as women in New York, migration has not emancipated the latest arrivals. As feminist scholars have emphasized, migration often leads to losses as well as gains for women.[2] The analysis of contemporary migrant women shows that "traditional" patriarchal codes and practices may continue to have an impact, and women—immigrants as well as the native born—still experience special burdens and disabilities as members of the "second sex." Indeed, immigrant mothers' continued responsibilities for child care and domestic tasks add new complications for them today, when they are more likely to work outside as well as inside the home.

Jewish and Italian Women Then

From the beginning, in the move itself, Jewish and Italian women typically followed men—husbands, fiancés, and fathers—who led the way. Women were a minority, too. The Italian migration was, more than anything else, a movement of single men coming to make money and go home. In most years of the peak migration between 1880 and 1910, about 80 percent of Italian immigrants to the United States were male.[3] The Jewish movement was mainly a family affair, but even then men predominated; women made up 43 percent of the migration stream to the United States between 1899 and 1910.[4]

What work did women do in the Old World? In eastern Europe, Jewish women had a central role in economic life. Patriarchy ran deep in Jewish communities—women were excluded from seats of power and positions in the religious sphere—but they were expected to, and did, make important economic contributions to their households. Indeed, the hardworking scholar's wife who supported a highly respected man who devoted himself to full-time religious study "acted as a legitimating symbol of the female breadwinner for the masses of east European Jews. If the scholar's wife worked, then why not the merchant's, the trader's, the watchmaker's, or the tailor's? And that was the pattern" (Glenn 1990: 12). Women's work, throughout the world of eastern European Jews, was considered necessary and respectable. "The frequency of married women's work was high enough and had sufficient cultural support to make it something of a norm" (Glenn 1990: 14).

Large numbers of Jewish wives worked in business or trade, sometimes helping in a store formally run by their husbands or keeping a store or stall on their own where they sold food, staples, or household wares. Some women were peddlers who stood in the marketplace or went from house to house selling food they had prepared at home or manufactured goods that were bought in small lots in cities (Baum et al. 1976: 68). Jewish wives became tough bargainers who developed knowledge of the marketplace and a certain worldliness about the society outside their own communities. In the market, women had a better command of local languages spoken by the peasants than did the more learned men, and many developed a reputation for being outspoken and aggressive (Ewen 1985: 39–40).

The Jewish community itself provided some jobs for women, for example, rolling and baking matzos at Passover. By the end of the nineteenth century, with the development of factory production in Russia and the movement of many Jews to cities, increasing numbers of unmarried Jewish women were drawn to artisans' shops and small factories, making matches, cigarettes, and other goods. When they married, Jewish women rarely took factory jobs that demanded long hours away from home, but many were involved in various kinds of home-based production. The sewing machine created new opportunities for doing outwork, and thousands of Jewish married and single female home workers made dresses or did other kinds of needlework for contractors who then distributed the garments to stores.

In the Sicilian and southern Italian villages that most Italian immigrant women left behind, married women supervised household chores, organized the making of clothes and food preparation, and managed the family budget. Often, they tended animals and tilled the garden, producing food for family consumption and for sale at local market. While artisans' wives, who helped out in the shop, worked in the privacy of their homes, peasant women's work took them outside the house as they hauled water, sat together at open streams laundering clothes, or did their chores in the street or courtyard alongside neighbors. Wives in poor families often had no choice but to help in the fields as day laborers during harvest periods, picking fruits and nuts, husking almonds, and threshing wheat (Cohen 1992: 15–36; Gabaccia 1984: chap. 3).

These patterns of work underwent significant change in New York. Although it may be too strong to say along with one historian (Friedman-Kasaba 1996: 184) that immigration disempowered women who came as wives and mothers and intensified their subordination, for many Jewish and Italian women, the journey to New York led to new constraints, and they were forced to lead more sheltered lives than they had in the Old World.

Hardly any Jewish or Italian wives went out to work for wages. The 1905 census recorded only 1 percent of immigrant Russian Jewish households in New York City with wives working outside the home; for Italians the figure, at 6 percent, was not much higher (Kessner and Caroli 1978).[5] Marriage, typically around the age of twenty to twenty-two, spelled the end of wage work for the vast majority of Italian and Jewish immigrant women. Eventually, some returned to the paid workforce for a stretch in the 1930s and 1940s when their children were grown, but immigrant women who came to New York as married adults often never worked outside the home at all.

Most Italian and Russian Jewish wives and mothers earned money by working at home. In the early years of the immigration, in the 1880s and 1890s, many Jewish women did piecework at home in the needle trades, but by the early twentieth century, the numbers had fallen sharply. By this time, taking care of boarders, virtually indistinguishable from other domestic duties, had become a more attractive alternative—and the main way Jewish wives contributed to the family income. According to the Immigration Commission's 1911 report, as many as 56 percent of New York Russian Jewish families had boarders living with them (Glenn 1990: 74). Many immigrant wives helped their husbands in "mom and pop" stores, and some ran shops of their own. Minding the store was considered an extension of a woman's proper role as her husband's helpmate; often the family lived above or in back of the store so that wives could run back and forth between shop counter and kitchen.

Although many Italian wives added to the family income by taking in boarders, this was a less frequent practice than among Jews. Home work was more common. By the first decade of the twentieth century, most industrial home workers in New York City were Italian. Working in the kitchen or a bedroom, Italian women finished garments or made artificial flowers while raising their children and caring for the house. Women were aware that factory jobs paid better, but the demands of caring for young children and household duties, as well as the widely accepted notion that women should leave the workplace after marriage, usually kept them at home.[6]

In one view, immigrant women's "retirement" to the domestic arena was a blessing (Tentler 1979: 176–179). By taking in boarders and doing piecework at home, they contributed much-needed money to the family income at the same time as they reared children and performed time-consuming domestic duties. Cleaning, cooking, and doing the laundry were labor-intensive chores for poor immigrant women who could not afford mechanical conveniences or hired help. The weekly laundry, for example, meant a laborious process of soaking, scrubbing, wringing, rinsing, and drying and ironing clothes. Although women did a tremendous amount of daily housework, they defined their own rhythms.

Unlike the factory, where bosses were in control, women exercised real authority and set the pace in their own households. Apart from nurturing and disciplining children, women managed the family budget. Husbands and sons usually gave them the larger part of their wages each week; most daughters handed over their entire paycheck. The role of housewife and mother, moreover, if done well, carried with it respectability and approval of family and neighbors.

Yet women's housebound existence had a downside as well. By and large, married women's lives were more circumscribed in New York. Immigrant mothers did, of course, socialize with friends and neighbors and went out to shop. The Jewish housewife, as the family member most responsible for decisions about household purchases, presided over a process of acquisition of consumption items (see Heinze 1990). But whereas in eastern Europe, Jewish wives were often the worldly ones, in America their housebound existence made it more difficult to learn the new language and customs. Their husbands picked up English in the workplace; their daughters learned American ways in factory work groups. Many Jewish mothers, however, remained fluent only in Yiddish and felt uncomfortable in new situations outside the Jewish community (Baum et al. 1976: 214). They had to depend on their children to learn American customs or, as a few managed to do, attend night school to learn English.[7] Italian women working at home were also more insulated than other family members from the world outside. While Andrea Bocci's father frequented a Prince Street saloon every night, her mother never went out: "If one of her friends would be sick, she would go and help them out, but otherwise she would stay at home" (Peiss 1986: 25).

Most household chores, as well as industrial home work, were done within the walls of their tenement apartments. Those from small towns and villages, used to doing chores such as laundry in the company of other women, now faced the more lonely and difficult task of washing clothing by themselves inside cramped tenement apartments (Breckinridge 1994: 104–105; Glenn 1990: 71). Because they now lived a more "inside" life, the move from Sicily to Elizabeth Street "limited immigrant women's opportunities to interact with others," and these limitations were a source of dissatisfaction with their new environment (Gabaccia 1984: 99).

Even as modern plumbing freed women from some of the more rigorous chores they had known in the Old World, the more rigorous standards of cleanliness and new household acquisitions complicated housework. In small eastern European towns and villages, women went to the nearest stream or lake once a month to wash clothes; now the laundry was a weekly task. Mattresses in eastern Europe were generally made of straw; in cold weather, feather bedding was common. In America, beds came with mattresses that required sheets and blankets; these needed washing and airing on a regular basis (Ewen 1985: 149).

For the Jewish women who had been charged with providing a major portion of the family livelihood in eastern Europe, migration reduced their economic role. In New York, immigrant wives' income-earning activities rarely represented the major contribution to the family economy. Industrial home work or taking in boarders was not as lucrative as work outside the home, and wives were seen as helping out their husbands in family businesses. Married women's earnings in America were now eclipsed by the wages of working daughters in the industrial labor force who emerged as the main female breadwinners in the Jewish family (Glenn 1990: 89).

Immigrant Women Now

Much has changed for the latest arrivals. Women immigrants now outnumber men in virtually all the major groups in New York, and more women come on their own rather than follow in men's footsteps.[8] Today's immigrant women also include a much higher proportion with professional and middle-class backgrounds.[9] Above all, the world they live in gives women opportunities and benefits unheard of a century ago—and this is particularly evident in the sphere of work.

Today, adult immigrant women are the main female contributors to the family income, while their teenage daughters are generally in school. With the expansion of high schools and colleges over the course of the twentieth century and the raising of the school-leaving age, women (and men) start working later than they used to (Goldin 1994). Today's immigrant daughters are often eighteen or older when they enter the labor market full time compared to age fourteen or fifteen a century ago. Marriage no longer spells a retreat from paid employment outside the home. Industrial home work, while not entirely a thing of the past, is much rarer than in the era of Italian and Jewish immigrants. Now it is socially accepted, even expected, throughout American society that wives and mothers will go out to work.

As of the 1990 census, 60 percent of New York City's working-age foreign-born women (compared to 66 percent of the city's working-age women generally) were in the labor force. At the high end, Filipino women, who often came to work in health care jobs, have a labor force participation rate of more than 85 percent; West Indian women are not far behind, with labor-force participation rates in the 70- to 80-percent range. Dominican women are near the bottom, with 52 percent in the workforce. Given the wide variety of groups today and the diversity of immigrant backgrounds, immigrant women occupy an equally wide range of jobs, from nurses, secretaries, and health technicians to domestics and factory workers (see Foner 1998).

These new patterns have important consequences. Now that most immigrant women work outside the home, they are able to obtain a kind of independence and power that was beyond the reach of Jewish and Italian wives and mothers a century ago. And that was often beyond their own reach before migration. How much improvement women experience when they migrate depends to a large degree on their role in production and their social status in the home country as well as on their economic role in New York. What is important here is that migration, for the majority of female newcomers today, has led to gains because they earn a regular wage for the first time, earn a higher wage than in the country of origin, or make a larger contribution to the family economy than previously.[10]

In cases where women did not earn an income or earned only a small supplementary income prior to migration, the gains that come with a shift to regular wage work in New York are especially striking. The much-cited case of Dominican women fits this pattern. They left a society where, in 1990, only 15 percent of women were in the labor force (Grasmuck and Grosfoguel 1997: 353). Now that so many Dominican immigrant women work for wages—often for the first time—and contribute a larger share of the family income, they have more authority in the household and greater self-esteem. They use their wages, anthropologist Patricia Pessar (1995: 44) observes, "to assert their right to greater autonomy and equality within the household" (see also Pessar 1984, 1987, 1996).

In New York, Dominican women begin to expect to be copartners in "heading" the household, a clear change from more patriarchal arrangements in the Dominican Republic. Whereas men used to control the household budget, now husbands, wives, and working children usually pool their income in a common fund for shared household expenses. Indeed, Pessar reports that Dominican women are eager to postpone or avoid returning to the Dominican Republic, where social pressures and an unfavorable job market would probably mean their retirement from work and a loss of newfound gains.

Of course, many immigrant women, including some Dominicans, had regular salaries before emigration. Even these women often feel a new kind of independence in New York because jobs in this country pay more than most could ever earn at home and increase women's contribution to the family economy. This is the experience for many Jamaican women, who come from a society where almost 70 percent of women engage in paid work (Grasmuck and Grosfoguel 1997: 355). Many Jamaican women I interviewed who had held white-collar jobs before emigration said they had more financial control and more say in family affairs in New York, where their incomes are so much larger (see Foner 1986).

The sense of empowerment that comes from earning a wage—or a higher wage—and having greater control over what they earn comes out in studies of many different groups. Paid work for Chinese garment workers, according to one report, not only contributes to their families' economic well-being but also has "created a sense of confidence and self-fulfillment which they may never have experienced in traditional Chinese society." "I do not have to ask my husband for money," one woman said. "I make my own" (Zhou and Nordquist 1994: 201). For many Salvadoran women, the ability to earn wages and decide how they should be used is something new. As one woman explained,

> Here [in the United States] women work just like the men. I like it a lot because managing my own money I feel independent. I don't have to ask

my husband for money but in El Salvador, yes, I would have to. Over there women live dependent on their husbands. You have to walk behind him. (Mahler 1996)

Or listen to a Trinidadian woman of East Indian descent: "Now that I have a job I am independent. I stand up here as a man" (Burgess and Gray 1981: 104).

The female-first migration pattern involving adult married women that is common in some groups reinforces the effects of wage earning on women's independence. Many women who have lived and worked in New York without their husbands become more assertive; one Dominican woman noted that she had changed "after so many years of being on my own, being my own boss" (Pessar 1995: 60). One study suggests that Asian men who move to the United States as their wives' dependents often have to subordinate their careers, at least initially, to those of their wives since the women have already established themselves in this country (Espiritu 1997: 70).

Work outside the home in New York brings about another change that women appreciate. Many men now help out more *inside* the home than before they moved to New York. Of course, this is not inevitable. Cultural values in different groups, as well as the availability of female relatives to lend a hand, influence the kind of household help men provide. Korean men, staunch supporters of patriarchal family values and norms, generally still expect their wives to serve them; these men resist performing household chores, such as cooking, dish washing, and doing the laundry. Such resistance is more effective when the wife's mother or mother-in-law lives in the household, a not infrequent occurrence in Korean immigrant families. Yet much to their consternation, Korean men in New York with working wives often find themselves helping out with household work more than they did in Korea—and wives often make more demands on them to increase their share (Min 1998; Park 1997; see also Lim 1997 on Korean women in Texas).

Research on Latin American and Caribbean groups shows that when wives are involved in productive work outside the home, the organization of labor within it changes. We are not talking about a drastic change in the household division of labor or the emergence of truly egalitarian arrangements. Indeed, Latin American and Caribbean women strongly identify as wives and mothers, and they like being in charge of the domestic domain. What they want—and what they often get—is more help from men than they were accustomed to back home. Men oblige mainly because they have little choice.

West Indian men, for example, recognize that there is no alternative to pitching in when their wives work and children (particularly daughters) are not old enough to lend a hand. Working women simply cannot shoulder all the domestic responsibilities expected of them, and they do not have relatives available to help as they did back home. Even if close kin live nearby, they are usually busy with work and their own household chores. Wives' wages are a necessary addition to the family income, and West Indians cannot afford to hire household help in New York (see Foner 1986). A middle-class Trinidadian woman said,

> In order to have a family life here, he [her husband] realizes he has to participate not only in the housework but in the childrearing too. It's no longer the type of thing where he comes home and the maid is there, having prepared the dinner. . . . Here . . . [he] has to pick up the children, or take them to the babysitter, or come home and begin the dinner. (Burgess and Gray 1981: 102)

Indeed, West Indian couples with young children often arrange their shifts so that the husband can look after the children while the wife works.

While the exigencies of immigrant life—women working outside the home, a lack of available relatives to assist, and an inability to hire help—are mainly responsible for men's greater participation in household tasks, American cultural beliefs and values have an influence, too (see Foner 1997). Many Dominicans whom Grasmuck and Pessar (1991: 152) spoke to claimed that they self-consciously patterned their more egalitarian relations on what they believed to be the dominant American model. They saw this change as both modern and a sign of progress. Whatever men think, immigrant women may feel that they can make more demands on their husbands in this country, where the dominant norms and values back up their claims for men to help out.

In addition to the independence, power, and autonomy that wages bring, there are the intrinsic satisfactions of work itself. Women in professional and managerial positions gain prestige from their positions and often have authority over others on the job (see Foner 1994 on immigrant nurses). Those in lower-level occupations often get a sense of satisfaction from doing their job well and from the new skills they have learned in New York.[11] And there is the sociability involved. In factories, hospitals, and offices, women make friends and build up a storehouse of experiences that enrich their lives and conversations. Indeed, when women are out of work, they often complain of boredom and isolation. "Sometimes," said a Chinese garment worker, "I get frustrated if I am confined at home and don't see my coworkers" (Zhou 1992: 178). Dominican women who are laid off say that they miss not only the income but also the socializing with workmates and the bustle of the streets and subways (Pessar 1995: 45). Indeed, friendships formed on the job may extend outside the bounds of the workplace as women visit and phone each other or go to parties and on shopping jaunts with coworkers (Foner 1994).

There is, however, a negative side to women's increased participation in the paid labor force. Wage work brings burdens as well as benefits to immigrant women and may create new sets of demands and pressures both on the job and at home. Moreover, despite changes in women's status in New York, premigration gender role patterns and ideologies do not fade away; they continue to affect the lives of migrant women, often in ways that constrain and limit them. Cultural ideas about gender and spousal relations held at the point of origin, observes Hondagneu-Sotelo (1999: 569), influence the outcome of the changing balance of economic resources in the United States.

Going out to work, as immigrant women commonly explain, is not an option but a necessity for their family's welfare. And it typically brings a host of difficulties. On the job, women's wages are still generally lower than men's. In addition, women are limited in their choice of work because of gender divisions in the labor market—often confined to menial, low-prestige, and poorly paying jobs. Working in the ethnic economy does not help most women, either. Recent studies of Chinese, Dominican, and Colombian women in New York who work in businesses owned by their compatriots show that they earn low wages and have minimal benefits and few opportunities for advancement (Gilbertson 1995; Zhou and Logan 1989). Sociologist Greta Gilbertson (1995) argues that some of the success of immigrant small-business owners and workers in the ethnic enclave is due to the marginal position of immigrant women. The many Korean women who work in family businesses are, essentially, unpaid family workers without an independent source of income. Although many are working outside the home for the first time, they are typically thought of as "helpers" to their husbands; the husband not only legally owns the enterprise but also usually controls the money, hires and fires employees, and represents the business in Korean business associations (Min 1998: 45–46).

For many immigrant women, working conditions are extremely difficult. Apart from the low wages and long hours, most garment workers have to keep up a furious pace in cramped conditions in noisy, often unsafe sweatshops; domestic workers often have to deal with humiliating and demeaning treatment from employers. Some women with full-time jobs have more than one position to make ends meet. I know many West Indian women, for example, who care for an elderly person on the weekend to supplement what they earn from a five-day child-care job.

Added to this, of course, are the demands of child care and burdens of household work. Going outside to earn means that child rearing is more complicated than at the turn of the twentieth century, when married women typically worked at home. Only very affluent immigrants can afford to hire maids or housekeepers, and female relatives, if present in New York, are often busy at work themselves. Occasionally, women can juggle shifts with their husbands so that one parent is always around; sometimes an elderly mother or mother-in-law is on hand to help out. Many working women pay to leave their children with baby-sitters or, less often, in day-care centers. Child-care constraints are clearly a factor limiting women to low-paid jobs with flexible schedules; they may prevent women from working full time or, in some cases, at all. Sometimes, women leave their young children behind with relatives in the home country so that they can manage work more easily, a common pattern among West Indian live-in household workers (see Colen 1989; Soto 1987).

Immigrant women in all social classes have the major responsibilities for household chores as well as child rearing so that a grueling day at work is often followed or preceded by hours of cooking, cleaning, and washing. "I'm always working," is how Mrs. Darius, a Haitian nursing home aide with eight children put it. Although her husband, a mechanic, does not help much around the house, Mrs. Darius gets assistance from her mother, who lives with her. Still, there is a lot to do. "I have to work 24 hours.

When I go home, I take a nap, then get up again; sometimes I get up at two in the morning, iron for the children, and go back to sleep" (Foner 1994: 107).

Korean working wives, according to sociologist Pyong Gap Min (1998), suffer from overwork and stress due to the heavy demands on their time. After doing their work outside the home, they put in, on average, an additional twenty-five hours a week on housework, compared to seven hours done by their husbands. Altogether, working wives spend seventy-six hours a week on the job and housework—twelve more hours than men do. Although professional husbands help out more around the house than other Korean men, their wives still do the lion's share.

Or take the case of Antonia Duarte, a Dominican mother of three children who put in a seventeen-hour day. At 5:00 A.M., she was up making breakfast and lunch for the family. She woke her three children at 6:00; got them dressed, fed, and ready for school; and then took them to the house of a friend who cared for the four-year-old and oversaw the older children's departure to and return from school. By 7:15, Antonia was on the subway heading for the lamp factory where she worked from 8:00 A.M. to 4:30 P.M. five days a week. She collected her children a little after 5:00 and began preparing the evening meal when she got home. She did not ask her two oldest children to help—the oldest is a twelve-year-old girl—because "I'd rather they begin their homework right away, before they get too tired." Her husband demanded a traditional meal of rice, beans, plantains, and meat that could take as long as two hours to prepare. She and the children ate together at 7:00, but her husband often did not get back from socializing with his friends until later. He expected Antonia to reheat the food and serve it on his arrival. By the time she finished her child care and other domestic responsibilities, it was 11:30 or 12:00. Like other Dominican women, she explained that if she did not manage the children and household with a high level of competence, her husband would threaten to prohibit her from working (Pessar 1982).

Women in groups where strong "traditional" patriarchal codes continue to exert an influence may experience other difficulties. In some better-off Dominican families, wives are pressured by husbands to stay out of the work force altogether as a way to symbolize their household's respectability and elevated economic status (Pessar 1995: 41–44). It is still a point of pride for a Latin American man to say that his wife does not work; part of making it into the middle class is seeing to it that the women in the household remain at home (Jones-Correa 1998: 171). In many groups, working women who are now the family's main wage earners may feel a special need to tread carefully in relations with their husbands so as to preserve the appearance of male dominance. Indeed, one study shows professional Korean women making conscious attempts to keep their traditional lower status and to raise the position of their husbands by reducing their incomes. A nurse explained,

> My basic salary exceeds his. If I do overtime, my income will be too much—compared to his—and so, when overtime work falls on me, I just try so hard to find other nurses to cover my overtime assignments. . . . By reducing my income, I think, my husband can keep his ego and male superiority. (Kim 1996: 170)

Finally, there is the fact that women's increased financial authority and independence can lead to greater discord with their spouses. Conflicts often develop when men resent and try to resist women's new demands on them; in some cases, the stresses ultimately lead to marital breakups. There are special difficulties when men are unemployed or unsuccessful at work and become dependent on women's wage-earning abilities, yet still insist on maintaining the prequisites of male privilege in the household (see Margolis 1998; Min 1998; Pessar 1995). In extreme cases, the reversal of gender roles can lead to serious physical abuse for women at the hands of their spouses (Lessinger 1996; Mahler 1996). Indeed, in some instances, increased isolation from relatives in the immigrant situation creates conditions for greater abuse by husbands, who are freer of the informal controls that operated in their home communities (for a discussion of marital abuse in the South Asian community, see Abraham 2000).

Conclusion: Immigrant Women in the Two Eras

Comparing immigrant women today and at the turn of the twentieth century makes clear that women's involvement in the world of work is critical to understanding why moving to New York has been liberating in many ways for so many contemporary immigrants—and why, at least for immigrant mothers and wives, it was more limiting in the past. Jewish and

Italian women came to New York at a time when there was a social stigma attached to the wife who worked for wages outside the home; the mother's wage was considered a "final defense against destitution," to be undertaken only on account of severe economic or family emergency (Tentler 1979: 139–142; Weiner 1985: 84–85). Often, Jewish and Italian immigrant wives found themselves more cloistered in their homes than in the Old World. The work they did to earn money—taking in boarders and industrial home work—did not lead to reallocating household tasks among other household members. Because virtually all their income-producing activities were done in the home, these activities ended up preserving and intensifying the gender division of housework and child care (see Lamphere 1987). The main female wage earners in the family, immigrant daughters, handed over their pay to their mothers, who, as managers of daily financial affairs, used it for running the household.

Now that female wage earners are typically wives and mothers, they have more leverage in the household than working younger daughters once had. Indeed, adult women's employment has begun to transform their family relationships more so than in the earlier generation. Because an immigrant working mother today is often absent from the home for forty to forty-five hours a week or sometimes longer, someone must fill her place—or at least help out. Often, it is her husband. Women's labor force participation, in other words, frequently increases husbands' participation in household work and leads to changes in the balance of power in immigrant families.

As the main female wage earners in the family, today's immigrant mothers contribute a larger share of the household income than they did a hundred years ago. Their regular access to wages—and to higher wages—in the United States often gives them greater autonomy and power than they had before migration. Working outside the home also broadens their social horizons and enhances their sense of independence. "A woman needs to work," said one Cuban sales worker. "She feels better and more in control of herself. She doesn't have to ask her husband for money. It seems to me that if a woman has a job, she is given more respect by her husband and her children" (Prieto 1992: 190). Many contemporary immigrant women would heartily agree. For a good number, the opportunities to work—and earn more money—represent a major gain that has come with the move to New York.

If immigrant wives and mothers have come a long way in the past hundred years, it is clear that they are not fully emancipated. Not only do they suffer from gender inequalities that are a feature of American society generally, but important vestiges of premigration gender ideologies and role patterns may place additional constraints on them. Wage labor, as one scholarly observer puts it, both oppresses and liberates immigrant women (Espiritu 1997: 117; see also Brettell and Simon 1986). Many work in low-status, dead-end positions that pay less than men's jobs. Immigrant working wives in all social classes experience a heavy double burden since the household division of labor remains far from equal. If husbands help out with domestic burdens, they may do so only grudgingly, if at all, and it is women more than men who make work choices to accommodate and reflect family and child care needs. While many, perhaps most, immigrant women feel that the advantages of wage work outweigh the drawbacks, others would, if they could afford it, prefer to remain at home. As a Korean woman who worked as a manicurist in a nail salon fifty-four hours a week said, "If my husband makes enough money for the family, why should I take this burden?" (Min 1998: 38).

A comparison of women in the two eras should not, in short, blind us to the barriers and difficulties immigrant women still face. Improvements in women's status today go hand in hand with the persistence of male privilege. At the same time, the comparison is a powerful reminder that "the New York we have lost," to paraphrase Laslett (1965), was hardly a utopia for women and that working outside the home, for all its problems, has brought significant benefits to migrant women today.

Notes

1. Among the factors that explain this shift are the growth of the clerical and sales sectors and the rising demand for white-collar office workers, declining fertility rates and the proliferation of labor-saving devices in the household that made mothers more available for work outside the home, and the expansion of high school education and the raising of the school-leaving age, which kept teenage girls out of the labor market. See Goldin (1994), Kessler-Harris (1982), Lamphere (1987), and Weiner (1985). On the contemporary period, see Spain and Bianchi (1996).

2. See, for example, Espiritu (1997), Morokvasic (1984), and Pessar (1999).

3. The percentage of women in the Italian immigration increased over time, from 21.2 percent in 1881–1890 to 22.9 percent between 1901 and 1910 and 30.6 percent between 1911 and 1920. See Tomasi (1975: 22).

4. Although Jewish men usually made the journey first, later sending for working-age children and then arranging for wives and younger family members to follow, occasionally Jewish daughters came first. Once a network of relatives was established in New York, according to Glenn (1990: 48), many Jewish families were willing and found it practicable to send one or more children, including working-age daughters, in advance ahead of the rest of the immediate family.

5. The argument has been made that, for Italians in particular, these figures are probably too low. A 1913 study of Italian women in Lower Manhattan found that in more than half (279) of the 515 families where the mother lived at home, she contributed to the family income; as many as a third of the income-earning mothers did factory work. See Odencrantz (1919: 20). More Italian than Jewish married women worked in factories outside the home or in formal employment because their husbands generally earned less. See Cohen (1992) and Friedman-Kasaba (1996).

6. On patterns of industrial home work among Italian women, see Cohen (1992), Friedman-Kasaba (1996), and Van Kleeck (1913).

7. The great bulk of first-generation Jewish women attending evening school in New York City were single working women or women preparing themselves for the job market. Married immigrant women may have been overwhelmed by the pressures of home work, household tasks, and family life. Many would have felt uncomfortable in alien surroundings or had to remain home with their children since Jewish men were reluctant to become baby-sitters. See Baum et al. (1976: 128–129).

8. In the early 1990s, there were ninety-two male immigrants for every one hundred female immigrants entering New York City, down from ninety-eight males per one hundred females in the 1980s (Lobo et al. 1996: 19–20). Among the reasons for the predominance of females are U.S. immigration law, which favors the admission of spouses and children to reunite families and has made it relatively easy for certain kinds of workers, such as nurses, to get immigrant visas (see Donato 1992; Houston et al. 1984).

9. In the 1980s, a fifth of the working-age immigrant women intending to live in New York City who reported an occupation to the Immigration and Naturalization Service were in professional/technical and administrative/managerial positions; in the early 1990s, the share in these categories went up to 36 percent (Lobo et al. 1996).

10. The focus here is on gains that contemporary immigrant women reap from working outside the home, but migration has improved their status as women in

other ways that are particular to the current era. See Foner (1998) for a discussion of the impact of liberalized legislation about divorce, greatly expanded government social welfare programs, improvements in household technology, and increased freedom for wives and mothers outside the home.

11. See Foner (1994, 1986) on the satisfactions that immigrant nursing home aides and home care attendants receive from caring for the elderly.

References

Abraham, Margaret. 2000. *Speaking the Unspeakable: Marital Violence among South Asian Immigrants in the United States.* New Brunswick, NJ: Rutgers University Press.

Baum, Charlotte, Paula Hyman, and Sonya Michel. 1976. *Jewish Women in America.* New York: Dial Press.

Bendix, Reinhard. 1964. *Nation-Building and Citizenship.* New York: John Wiley & Sons.

Breckinridge, Sophonisba. 1994 [1921]. "The Duties of the Housewife Remain Manifold and Various." In *Immigrant Women,* 2nd ed., edited by Maxine Seller. Albany: State University of New York Press.

Brettell, Caroline, and Rita Simon. 1986. "Immigrant Women: An Introduction." In *International Migration: The Female Experience,* edited by Rita Simon and Caroline Brettell. Totowa, NJ: Rowman & Allenheld.

Burgess, Judith, and Meryl Gray. 1981. "Migration and Sex Roles: A Comparison of Black and Indian Trinidadians in New York City." In *Female Immigrants to the United States: Caribbean, Latin American, and African Experiences,* edited by Delores Mortimer and Roy Bryce-Laporte. Washington, DC: Research Institute on Immigration and Ethnic Studies.

Cohen, Miriam. 1992. *Workshop to Office: Two Generations of Italian Women in New York City, 1900–1950.* Ithaca, NY: Cornell University Press.

Colen, Shellee. 1989. "Just a Little Respect: West Indian Domestic Workers in New York City." In *Muchachas No More: Household Workers in Latin America and the Caribbean,* edited by Elsa Chaney and Mary Garcia Castro. Philadelphia: Temple University Press.

Donato, Katharine. 1992. "Understanding U.S. Immigration: Why Some Countries Send Women and Others Send Men." In *Seeking Common Ground: Multidisciplinary Studies of Immigrant Women in the United States,* edited by Donna Gabaccia. Westport, CT: Praeger.

Espiritu, Yen Le. 1997. *Asian American Women and Men.* Thousand Oaks, CA: Sage Publications.

Ewen, Elizabeth. 1985. *Immigrant Women in the Land of Dollars: Life and Culture on the Lower East Side, 1890–1925.* New York: Monthly Review Press.

Foner, Nancy. 1986. "Sex Roles and Sensibilities: Jamaican Women in New York and London." In *International Migration: The Female Experience,* edited by Rita Simon and Caroline Brettell. Totowa, NJ: Rowman & Allenheld.

———. 1994. *The Caregiving Dilemma: Work in an American Nursing Home.* Berkeley and Los Angeles: University of California Press.

———. 1997. "The Immigrant Family: Cultural Legacies and Cultural Changes." *International Migration Review* 31: 961–974.

———. 1998. "Benefits and Burdens: Immigrant Women and Work in New York City." *Gender Issues* 16: 5–24.

———. 2000. *From Ellis Island to JFK: New York's Two Great Waves of Immigration.* New Haven, CT, and New York: Yale University Press and the Russell Sage Foundation.

Friedman-Kasaba, Kathie. 1996. *Memories of Migration: Gender, Ethnicity, and Work in the Lives of Jewish and Italian Women in New York, 1870–1924.* Albany: State University of New York Press.

Gabaccia, Donna. 1984. *From Sicily to Elizabeth Street.* Albany: State University of New York Press.

———, ed. 1992. *Seeking Common Ground: Multidisciplinary Studies of Immigrant Women in the United States.* Westport, CT: Greenwood Press.

———. 1994. *From the Other Side: Women, Gender, and Immigrant Life in the U.S., 1820–1990.* Bloomington: Indiana University Press.

Gilbertson, Greta. 1995. "Women's Labor and Enclave Employment: The Case of Dominican and Colombian Women in New York City." *International Migration Review* 19: 657–671.

Glenn, Susan. 1990. *Daughters of the Shtetl: Life and Labor in the Immigrant Generation.* Ithaca, NY: Cornell University Press.

Goldin, Claudia. 1994. "Labor Markets in the Twentieth Century." Working Paper Series on Historical Factors in Long Run Growth No. 58. Cambridge, MA: National Bureau of Economic Research.

Grasmuck, Sherri, and Ramon Grosfoguel. 1997. "Geopolitics, Economic Niches, and Gendered Social Capital among Recent Caribbean Immigrants in New York City." *Sociological Perspectives* 40: 339–364.

Grasmuck, Sherri, and Patricia Pessar. 1991. *Between Two Islands.* Berkeley and Los Angeles: University of California Press.

Heinze, Andrew R. 1990. *A Search for Abundance: Jewish Immigrants, Mass Consumption, and the Search for an American Identity.* New York: Columbia University Press.

Hondagneu-Sotelo, Pierrette. 1999. "Introduction: Gender and Contemporary U.S. Immigration." *American Behavioral Scientist* 42: 565–576.

Houston, Marion, Roger Kramer, and Joan Mackin Barrett. 1984. "Female Predominance of Immigration to the United States since 1930: A First Look." *International Migration Review* 18: 908–963.

Jones-Correa, Michael. 1998. *Between Two Nations: The Political Predicament of Latinos in New York.* Ithaca, NY: Cornell University Press.

Kessler-Harris, Alice. 1982. *Out to Work.* New York: Oxford University Press.

Kessner, Thomas, and Betty Boyd Caroli. 1978. "New Immigrant Women at Work: Italians and Jews in New York City, 1880–1905." *Journal of Ethnic Studies* 5: 19–31.

Kim, Ai Ra. 1996. *Women Struggling for a New Life: The Role of Religion in the Cultural Passage from Korea to America.* Albany: State University of New York Press.

Lamphere, Louise. 1987. *From Working Daughters to Working Mothers: Immigrant Women in a New England Industrial Community.* Ithaca, NY: Cornell University Press.

Laslett, Peter. 1965. *The World We Have Lost.* New York: Scribner's.

Lessinger, Johanna. 1996. *From the Ganges to the Hudson: Asian Indians in New York City.* Boston: Allyn and Bacon.

Lim, In-Sook. 1997. "Korean Immigrant Women's Challenge to Gender Inequality at Home." *Gender and Society* 11: 31–51.

Lobo, Peter Arun, Joseph Salvo, and Vicky Virgin. 1996. *The Newest New Yorkers, 1990–1994.* New York: Department of City Planning.

Mahler, Sarah. 1996. "Bringing Gender to a Transnational Focus: Theoretical and Empirical Ideas." Unpublished manuscript.

Margolis, Maxine. 1998. *An Invisible Minority: Brazilians in New York City.* Boston: Allyn and Bacon.

Min, Pyong Gap. 1998. *Changes and Conflicts: Korean Immigrant Families in New York.* Boston: Allyn and Bacon.

Morokvasic, Mirjana. 1984. "Birds of Passage Are Also Women." *International Migration Review* 18: 886–907.

Odencrantz, Louise. 1919. *Italian Women in Industry: A Study of Conditions in New York City.* New York: Russell Sage Foundation.

Park, Kyeyoung. 1997. *The Korean American Dream.* Ithaca, NY: Cornell University Press.

Peiss, Kathy. 1986. *Cheap Amusements: Working Women and Leisure in Turn-of-the-Century New York.* Philadelphia: Temple University Press.

Pessar, Patricia. 1982. "Kinship Relations of Production in the Migration Process: The Case of Dominican Emigration to the United States." Occasional Paper

No. 32. New York: Center for Latin American and Caribbean Studies, New York University.

———. 1984. "The Linkage between the Household and Workplace of Dominican Women in the United States." *International Migration Review* 18: 1188–1211.

———. 1987. "The Dominicans: Women in the Household and the Garment Industry." In *New Immigrants in New York,* edited by Nancy Foner. New York: Columbia University Press.

———. 1995. "On the Homefront and in the Workplace: Integrating Immigrant Women into Feminist Discourse." *Anthropological Quarterly* 68: 37–47.

———. 1996. *A Visa for a Dream: Dominicans in the United States.* Boston: Allyn and Bacon.

———. 1999. "The Role of Gender, Households, and Social Networks in the Migration Process: A Review and Appraisal." In *The Handbook of International Migration,* edited by Josh DeWind, Charles Hirschman, and Philip Kasinitz. New York: Russell Sage Foundation.

Prieto, Yolanda. 1992. "Cuban Women in New Jersey: Gender Relations and Change." In *Seeking Common Ground,* edited by Donna Gabaccia. Westport, CT: Praeger.

Soto, Isa Maria. 1987. "West Indian Child Fostering: Its Role in Migrant Exchanges." In *Caribbean Life in New York City,* edited by Constance Sutton and Elsa Chaney. New York: Center for Migration Studies.

Spain, Daphne, and Suzanne M. Bianchi. 1996. *Balancing Act: Motherhood, Marriage, and Employment among American Women.* New York: Russell Sage Foundation.

Tentler, Leslie Woodcock. 1979. *Wage-Earning Women.* New York: Oxford University Press.

Tomasi, Silvano. 1975. *Piety and Power.* New York: Center for Migration Studies.

Van Kleeck, Mary. 1913. *Artificial Flower Makers.* New York: Russell Sage Foundation.

Weiner, Lynn. 1985. *From Working Girl to Working Mother: The Female Labor Force in the United States, 1820–1980.* Chapel Hill: University of North Carolina Press.

Zhou, Min. 1992. *Chinatown: The Socioeconomic Potential of an Urban Enclave.* Philadelphia: Temple University Press.

Zhou, Min, and John Logan. 1989. "Returns on Human Capital in Ethnic Enclaves: New York City's Chinatown." *American Journal of Sociology* 86: 295–319.

Zhou, Min, and Regina Nordquist. 1994. "Work and Its Place in the Lives of Immigrant Women: Garment Workers in New York City's Chinatown." *Applied Behavioral Science Review* 2: 187–211.

CHAPTER EIGHT

FROM *THE JAZZ SINGER* TO *WHAT A COUNTRY!* A COMPARISON OF JEWISH MIGRATION TO THE UNITED STATES, 1880 TO 1930 AND 1965 TO 1998

Steven J. Gold

The twentieth century was a time of enormous change for the Jewish people. Momentous events included the Nazi Holocaust, the founding of the state of Israel, the relocation of the center of Jewish civilization from eastern Europe to the dual axes of North America and the Jewish state, and Jews' movement from marginal status to the cultural, economic, and political forefront of several Western countries. Despite these transformations, at both the dawn and the close of the century, Jewish migrants to the United States display notable similarities.

During both periods, Jewish immigrants (especially those from Russia) ranked among the major groups to enter the country and revealed similarities in their origins and characteristics, including comparatively high levels of occupational skill, significant rates of self-employment, urban concentration (especially in New York City), assistance from established coethnics, and infrequent return migration. At the same time, migrants entering during these two periods exhibited dramatic contrasts in their levels of education, bases of identity, and patterns of adjustment to and acceptance in the United States.

Membership in the Jewish population is defined in terms of religion and ethnicity, not nationality. Accordingly, government statistics, which rarely report religion, are of limited utility in identifying Jews. As a consequence, other sources are used for many estimates and descriptions of this population. In many cases, "Russian" nationality is used as a proxy for Jewishness since well over half of all immigrants from Russia to the United States have been Jews (Lieberson and Waters 1988; Simon 1997).

Because recent Jewish immigrants come from diverse origins and are themselves difficult to define, there is no single comprehensive source of data on them.[1] Accordingly, in evaluating contemporary migration, this chapter relies on various surveys and ethnographies, especially those concerning the two largest recent groups (Jews from the former Soviet Union and Israelis) who have settled in New York and Los Angeles.

Numbers, Origins, and Motives for Migration

From 1881 to 1928, 2,414,989 Jews entered the United States. During those same years, 112,611 Jews (5 percent) departed, yielding a net increase in population of 2,302,378 (*American Jewish Yearbook* 1929: 326–327). The overwhelming majority came from Russia and other areas of eastern Europe, including Romania and Austria–Hungary. Even those entering the United States from other locations (Germany, France, the United Kingdom, Canada, and Africa) were largely "transmigrants from Eastern Europe" (Rischin 1970: 270). Hailing from the "pale of settlement," they shared many commonalties in culture, religion, diet, and language (Yiddish, the German-based, Hebrew-scripted language of eastern European Jews). These similarities excepted, this group was also stratified by considerable differences in urban experience, political outlook, religiosity, work experience, cultural orientation, and time of arrival.

In addition to the great preponderance of eastern European Ashkenazi Jews, small numbers of Jews did arrive from other regions, including Sephardim (those tracing their origins to Spain and Portugal). Twelve thousand Sephardic Turkish Jews entered the United States between 1899 and 1914 (Rischin 1970: 270). According to Thomas Archdeacon's (n.d.) statistics, the 1.8 million "Hebrews" were the second-largest immigrant group to enter the United States from 1899 to 1924, their numbers surpassed only by Italians.

While the growth of recent migration for many nationality groups can be traced to the enactment of new immigration laws in 1965, a large majority of recent Jewish migrants entered the United States as refugees and, as such, have been little affected by the 1965 law. In fact, during the years of immigration restriction (from 1924 to 1965), more than 350,000 Jews were able to enter the United States.[2]

In the past decade, Russian-origin Jews have continued to rank among the larger migrant nationalities entering the United States but as a smaller fraction of all immigrants than during the earlier period. In 1990, the former Soviet Union was the eighth-largest source country of immigration to the United States. From the late 1980s until the mid-1990s, mostly Jewish former Soviets, numbering about 30,000 annually, were the single largest refugee group to enter the United States (Fix and Passel 1994: 25; Hebrew Immigration Aid Society 1997; Office of Refugee Resettlement 1997: 5). Other countries and regions have also been important sources of Jewish migration, including Iran, Israel, North Africa, Latin America, and Canada.

While few if any Iranian or North African Jews trace their families to eastern Europe, a significant proportion of Israeli (about 60 percent), South African, and Latin American migrants share Russian origins with the vast majority of American-born Jews. From 1954 through 1995, HIAS (the Hebrew Immigration Aid Society) assisted 519,750 Jewish arrivals. The largest numbers of these were from the former Soviet Union (367,021), North Africa (61,430), other countries (80,496), and Iran (10,803). While the HIAS figure for Jews from the former Soviet Union is a fairly accurate enumeration of all entrants from that country, large numbers of Jewish migrants from other nations were not assisted by HIAS and hence do not appear in their counts. According to the 1990 U.S. census, approximately 200,000 Israelis (including some 90,000 Israeli-born persons)[3] reside in the United States. Israelis are not eligible for HIAS aid and so are excluded from that agency's tabulations. Similarly, while HIAS has assisted fewer than 11,000 Iranians, the 1997 Los Angeles Jewish Population Survey enumerated almost 17,000 Iranian Jews in that city alone (Hebrew Immigration Aid Society 1997; Herman 1998: 14).

The majority of Jews entering the United States during both periods came in search of refuge from prejudice and assault, as well as for economic opportunity. The "Great Immigration" of eastern European Jews from 1881 to 1924 was initiated by a series of anti-Semitic edicts, called the "May Laws," which concentrated Jews into "the pale of settlement" and further curtailed their already limited civil and economic rights. "These laws and the extensions of them left most Jews no choice but to emigrate" (Farber et al. 1988: 403). Similarly, post-1965 Soviet and eastern European émigrés left to escape daily anti-Semitism, discrimination in schooling and jobs, and right-wing activism, while Iranian, North African and other Middle Eastern Jews fled because they were harassed as official enemies of anti-Zionist regimes (Goldstein 1995: 46).

Locations of Settlement

Jewish migrants to the United States have traditionally settled in cities where coethnics are already established. During both earlier and current periods of migration, New York City has remained the hub of Jewish American life and concentration. As such, it has been the principal location of settlement for Jewish migrants. In the decade prior to World War I, New York was the major point of entry for Jews and approximately 70 percent of arrivals remained there (Goren 1970: 18). By 1995, about 48 percent of America's foreign-born Jews resided in the New York area (*American Jewish Yearbook* 1996; Herman 1998: 14).

Since the turn of the twentieth century, American Jews have moved in large numbers to Sunbelt locations, especially California and southern Florida. In 1927, the American Jewish population was 4,228,029. Of these, 54 percent, or 2,302,378, had entered the country between 1881 and 1927. The remainder included Jews present in the United States prior to 1881 and children born to established or recently arrived parents. In 1880, at the start of the major migration, the American Jewish population was about 240,000 (*American Jewish Yearbook* 1929: 307–310; Glazer 1955: 7). By 1995, the American Jewish population had grown to 5.9 million. However, its foreign-born component had shrunk from greater than 50 percent in 1927 to 8.6 percent in 1990 (Herman 1998: 14).

The 1991 New York Jewish Population Study (New York Jewish Population Study 1993) determined that 83.3 percent of Jewish New Yorkers were born in the United States, making New York's fraction of foreign-born (16.7 percent) somewhat less than that of Los Angeles at 21 percent.[4] As of 1991, the largest groups of foreign-born Jews age 18 or older in New York were from the former Soviet Union (49,000), other eastern European countries (49,000), western Europe (40,000), Israel (22,000), Latin America (10,000), and Canada (5,000). However, there is some contention over these figures, especially with regard to Soviet Jews. For example, the New York Association for New Americans, the agency that resettles Soviet Jews in New York, claimed that the 1991 population was 130,000 (Horowitz 1993: 25).

According to the 1997 Los Angeles Jewish Population Survey, 21 percent of Jewish Angelenos are foreign born, and 45 percent are immigrants or the children of immigrants. Reflecting their recent derivation, only 12 percent of Los Angeles Jews had American-born grandparents. Major nationality groups include the former Soviet Union (24,526); Iran (16,782); Israel (14,170); other eastern European countries (12,483); western Europe (10,884); other Middle Eastern, North African, and Asian countries (7,010); Canada (6,615); Latin America (3,080); and other (12,744) (Herman 1998: 14). Chicago, the third-largest center of American Jewish population, resettled 19,134 Soviet Jews between 1974 and 1993. With the addition of secondary migrants,[5] the population was close to 24,000 by the end of 1993, making recent Soviet immigrants alone account for about 10 percent of Chicago's Jewish population (Gitelman 1996: 20).

Family Patterns

The family patterns of Jewish immigrants during both migration periods show significant continuity. Unlike many other migrant populations, most Jews (with the exception of recent arrivals from Western countries, such as Canada, France, England, and Israel) have been de facto or de jure refugees. Accordingly, they left not as individuals planning to work for a few years and return but as families seeking liberation. Social features of Jewish immigrants include intact families, permanent settlement (generally in economically dynamic urban settings), low rates of fertility, and women's involvement in economic life. These contributed to the group's economic mobility at both the start and the conclusion of the twentieth century.

Jewish immigrants who arrived in the United States early in the century were noted for their intact families. The large number of school-age children (those under fourteen) who accompanied them (about 25 percent of the group) gave Jews a head start over other contemporaneous immigrants whose numbers included few children (Joseph 1914: 180). Permanence of settlement and access to American schools also led Jews to learn

English much faster than other immigrant groups. As Goldscheider and Zuckerman (1984: 168) point out, "Within five years from immigration, two-thirds of Jewish industrial workers spoke English compared to 29 percent of all other immigrants."

No matter how important the family has been, American Jews have long had relatively few children. "Since the mid 1920s, fluctuations around replacement level fertility have characterized Jews marrying"(Goldscheider and Zuckerman 1984: 177). A study of contraceptive practices in the United States during the 1930s "indicates that a higher proportion of Jews used contraceptives, planned their pregnancies, used more efficient methods of birth control, and began the use of contraception earlier in marriage than Protestants and Catholics" (Chiswick 1988: 587). Along with their lower fertility, Jewish women were less likely to work outside the home when children were small. With women at home and fewer children, more parental time was devoted to each child, a pattern associated with upward mobility.

During the period of great migration of Jews from 1880 to 1930, because of poverty and the high cost of living, Jewish women and children were often active in generating income. They frequently worked in garment assembly, an occupation that involved a large proportion of the entire population. When children were small, women often engaged in home-based production, allowing them to both earn money and care for offspring. Immigrant women participated in labor unions, political movements, and fraternal associations and created Hebrew free-loan organizations: "The small pro-feminist investment banks that were set up around the country in the 1920s and 1930s as Jewish women's loan funds, lending money exclusively from women and to women for everything from dentists' bills to venture capital for entrepreneurs" (Weinberg 1988: 188; see also Schneider 1995: 99; Tenenbaum 1993).

As time passed, the women of upwardly mobile families often became housewives. In *World of Our Mothers*, Weinberg (1988) describes the lives of pre–World War II Jewish women as concerned with the domestic duties of child rearing and nurturing. She also noted that while Jewish women were limited in their expression of power in public life, they retained considerable influence at home "behind the facade of paternal authority." Immigrant women were also involved in the *Landsmanschaften* (hometown lodges) that were a basic component of the social and philanthropic life of immigrant Jews, but generally women were in subordinate and segregated roles. Not all accepted their secondary standing. Challenging the financial control of their husbands, the women's auxiliary of one Bronx-based group obtained a court order that required the organization to relinquish to women members the funds that they had contributed (Weinberg 1988: 188; Weisser 1989: 259, 268–269).

Despite gender conflicts within Jewish immigrant families, parents approached their children's future occupations with a degree of equality and encouraged the education of their daughters as well as their sons. By 1934, about half the women college students in New York City were Jewish, even though Jews accounted for less than a third of the city's population and most were recently arrived (*American Jewish Yearbook* 1929: 309; Weinberg 1988: 175).

Today's Jewish migrants exhibit several of the family patterns associated with earlier arrivals, including intact, two-parent families; high rates of marriage; and small numbers of children. However, the various nationality groups maintain several unique characteristics. Soviets are older and have the fewest children, high rates of women working outside the home, and multigenerational families. Israelis tend to be younger and have more children and lower rates of women's employment (Gold 1994c; Gold and Phillips 1996).

The significant number of elderly among the Soviet Jewish population yields a distinct pattern of adjustment. Unlike most immigrant and refugee groups who are characterized by a youthful population, Russian Jewish families include many elderly individuals. Refugee families experience problems because the elderly have difficulties learning English, finding employment, and making their way in the United States. At the same time, aged relatives assist with child care and build stable and interconnected communities as they interact in parks, agencies, and apartment buildings.

Like those arriving early in the century, most recent Jewish immigrants also enter as family migrants and maintain cooperative economic arrangements among their members. Iranian, Israeli, and Soviet Jewish women are very well educated and, if they work, often find well-paid professional jobs. This is especially the case among Soviet Jewish women. The two Middle Eastern groups—Israelis and Iranians—have lower rates of female labor force participation.[6]

Social Conditions

Housing conditions for Jewish immigrants early in the century in the Lower East Side of New York and the Jewish ghettos of Chicago and Philadelphia were abysmal. With nearly 700 persons per acre, the Lower East Side was more crowded than the worst slums of contemporary Bombay. Tenement fires were common. Because of the outhouses, cooking, and industrial activities, the polluted environment was described as "the eyesore of New York . . . the filthiest place in the Western continent"(Sowell 1981: 83). Alcoholism was rare, but Jewish immigrants suffered from other diseases associated with overcrowded urban settings, such as tuberculosis, venereal disease, mental health problems, and diabetes. Despite its low quality, housing was costly, and thousands of families were evicted because of their inability to pay the rent. Simon (1997: 31) cites 1930 data demonstrating that (mostly Jewish) Russians paid the highest monthly rents of seventeen European immigrant groups (Goren 1970: 147–148; James et al. 1907; Rischin 1970: 87–88; Wirth 1928).

Like other poor ethnic groups, Jewish communities were plagued by social pathologies and crime. Just after the turn of the century, authorities noted that within a heavily Jewish area of the Lower East Side consisting of one square mile, "there were approximately two hundred disorderly houses, three hundred and thirty-six gang 'hang-outs' and over two hundred pool hall-cum betting establishments; dance halls, a rendezvous of pimps and procurers were found every two and a half blocks, while gambling establishments blanketed the neighborhood" (Joselit 1983: 15, 24). As a result of the immigrants' criminality, in 1905, more than a third of the inmates of two New York correctional institutions were Jewish.

Finally, while many scholars attribute the unprecedented mobility of Jewish immigrants to their love of education, ample evidence suggests that their educational status was mediocre. Twenty-six percent of Jews who arrived during the first decade of the century were illiterate, including 40 percent of the women. Jews were better educated than southern Italians, Lithuanians, and Poles (whose illiteracy rates were 54, 49, and 35 percent, respectively) but well below western Europeans. Only 2.6 percent of the Irish and 0.7 percent of the Scots who arrived during the same decade could not read or write (Joseph 1914: 193–194).

In contrast, today's Jewish immigrants settle in established Jewish neighborhoods, which are often middle class. Within them, they find a variety of amenities and services provided by conationals, the American Jewish community, and the larger society. As refugees, most Russians and some Iranians are eligible for a variety of benefits. In fact, Markowitz (1993) reports that Soviet émigrés' American Jewish neighbors express more than a little jealousy at the opulent lifestyle displayed by these newcomers.

School-aged immigrant Jews generally have a strong educational background and do well in American schools. For example, in a 1991 comparison of the twelve largest immigrant groups attending New York City public schools, grades 3 to 12, who had been in the country three years or less, students from the former Soviet Union ranked first in reading scores, second in math, and fifth in English. Their reading and math scores were much higher than the average for all students, including the native born. In addition, their mean increase in score over the previous year was the highest of all groups in both reading and English and among the highest in math (New York City Public Schools 1991). A study of Israeli adults in New York also revealed educational progress. It indicates that while 28 percent had a bachelor's degree or greater in Israel, the proportion increased to 39 percent in the United States. Similarly, of respondents' spouses, the fraction with a college-level education increased from 28 percent in Israel to 45 percent in the United States (Rosenthal 1989: 67). Jewish immigrants' educational accomplishments make sense because many describe America's educational opportunities as a major reason for their immigration (Gold 1992, 1997; Markowitz 1993).

Experience of Discrimination

During the late nineteenth and early twentieth centuries, immigrant Jews faced many kinds of discrimination, ranging from street violence to institutional exclusion. Jews were often the targets of attacks from neighboring Irish, Italian, and Polish youth gangs, occasionally abetted by Irish police. For example, in 1902, a rabbi's Lower East Side funeral procession was attacked by Irish bystanders who were hostile to the burgeoning Jewish population that was overtaking their neighborhood. The police responded by vigorously beating, arresting, and fining the funeral marchers.

Allegedly, their commander ordered his men to "club their brains out" (Howe 1976: 129).

Eastern European Jews confronted extensive discrimination and prejudice in attacks by the media, in housing, and in employment. Such maltreatment can be attributed partly to nativist and anti-leftist sentiments—to which all immigrants were subject—as well as to specifically anti-Jewish campaigns. Jews also faced anti-Semitic diatribes, especially during economic downturns. While such bigotry is normally associated with marginal groups such as the Ku Klux Klan, some well-known anti-Semites were figures of national prominence, including the 1930s radio priest Father Charles Coughlin and automotive pioneer Henry Ford, who published Jew-baiting harangues during the 1920s in his newspaper *The Dearborn Independent* and promoted *The International Jew*. Other elite anti-Semites included author Henry James, who, in 1904, wrote that he was disgusted by the "swarming" Jews of New York's Lower East Side who reminded him of "small strange animals—snakes or worms." Senator Henry Cabot Lodge, Henry Adams, and several academics, such as sociologist E. A. Ross and Harvard psychologist William McDougall, were equally vitriolic. They asserted that Jews (and other southern and eastern Europeans) were racially distinct from the northern European, Protestant population of America and believed that their interbreeding with old American stock would yield national degeneration (Simon 1997: 19; see also Dinnerstein et al. 1990). By the late 1920s, their demands for immigration restriction had been fully implemented (Gabaccia 1994).

As the children of immigrant Jews sought to move from the ethnic ghetto to mainstream American life, their efforts were hampered by pervasive social discrimination. Some policies established in the 1880s remained in effect through the late 1960s. Jews were generally prohibited from joining social and athletic clubs as well as from living in exclusive neighborhoods. Growing anti-Semitism even impacted the elite of established Jews whose sons were barred admittance to social clubs that their fathers had helped to found (Rischin 1970: 262). After the 1920s, many private colleges and universities, especially those in the Northeast, established quotas to limit the number of Jewish students, regardless of their qualifications. For example, in the 1920s, Harvard University President Abbott Lawrence Lowell decried the college's "Jewish problem" and limited the fraction of Jews in attendance to 15 percent in order to "reduce anti-Semitism" and protect Harvard from the same fate among Gentiles as was suffered by "the summer hotel that is ruined by admitting Jews" (Takaki 1993: 306). A study made two decades later, in 1949, determined that "whatever way you adjust and reassemble the data, applications made by Jews to north eastern colleges are less often accepted than those of the Protestant or Catholic" (Ivy and Ross 1957: 136).

If admission to colleges and universities was difficult, getting accepted to graduate programs, especially in professional fields, was an even greater challenge. The proportion of Jews enrolled in law, engineering, medicine, architecture, dentistry, commerce, fine art, and social work all dropped substantially between 1935 and 1946—even though the pool of Jewish applicants for such opportunities continued to grow. From 1920 to 1940, the percentage of Jews in Columbia University's College of Physicians and Surgeons fell from 50 percent to less than 7 percent. Because of the combination of quotas and the large number of Jewish applicants, in 1940 non-Jews had a one in seven chance of admission to Cornell Medical School, while Jews had only one-tenth of that likelihood for admission, one in seventy (Dinnerstein 1981: 139; Glazer and Moynihan 1963: 156).

While Jews were well represented in certain industries, such as textiles, sales, entertainment, teaching, and the independent professions, they were systematically excluded from employment in elite firms and leading corporations. In the early 1950s, studies of the job markets in Los Angeles and Chicago found that between 17 and 20 percent of all job openings requested non-Jewish applicants, and the highest rates of exclusion were for white-collar and professional jobs, especially in law, insurance, and accounting (Waldman 1956: 211–214). In 1960, 8 percent of the country's college graduates were Jewish. However, they accounted for less than one-half of 1 percent of the executive personnel at the leading American industrial companies (Glazer and Moynihan 1963: 148).

In a dramatic contrast to the experience of earlier arrivals, recent Jewish immigrants have benefited from a radical reduction in American anti-Semitism that took place between the end of World War II and the late 1960s. Of this transformation, journalist J. J. Goldberg writes, "The astounding drop in American anti-Jewish prejudice . . . is probably the least studied aspect of Jewish political power in the modern era; yet it may be the most important. In the space of five years, America's image of the Jews changed from conspiratorial foreigners to good neighbors" (Goldberg

1996: 12). In mid-1944, long after the Nazis' persecution of the Jews was common knowledge, a poll found that 24 percent of Americans believed that Jews were "a menace to America," while another survey that same year determined that 46 percent of Americans wanted to stop the entry of Jews (Goldberg 1996: 116; Simon 1997: 21). Roper polls conducted between 1944 and 1946 found that almost 60 percent of Americans agreed with the statement "Jews have too much power in America" (Dinnerstein 1981: 135). However, by 1982, a Gallup poll found public evaluation of Jews to be the third highest of all groups (closely following the English and Irish), receiving more positive ratings than Germans, Italians, and Poles as well as several non-European groups (Barkan 1996: 195).

While earlier Jewish immigrants encountered many forms of discrimination and prejudice, recent Jewish immigrants find themselves among the upper echelon of all migrants largely because of their European origins, high levels of education, legal status, connections to established co-ethnics, and white skin. In fact, various Jewish immigrants observe that their social status is higher in the United States than it was in the country of origin. For example, émigrés from the former Soviet Union often lose their public Jewish identity since non-Jewish Americans see them simply as white foreigners and American Jews find them lacking in religious knowledge. One émigré commented, "Here I feel less a Jew than in Russia . . . I live calmly and nobody bothers me. . . . Nobody tells me I'm Jewish" (Ritterband 1997: 332; see also Gold 1995b; Markowitz 1988).

Economic Adaptation

Immigrant Jews of the turn of the century had only moderate educational credentials, suffered from discrimination, and lived in crowded urban ghettos. However, they were able to find jobs in a rapidly growing economy. The presence of families offered stability and resource-yielding networks. Patterns of chain migration—facilitated by Jews' extensive ties with relatives and former townsfolk—reduced the cost and effort involved in emigrating to and getting established in the United States. Their access to kin-based resources can be seen in that 62 percent of Jewish immigrants who arrived in the United States between 1908 and 1914 had their passage paid for by relatives. In contrast, among non-Jews, less than half that fraction (29 percent) received such aid (Kuznets 1975: 113).

Whether they hailed from small villages or large cities such as Warsaw, Jews were familiar with the patterns of urban life prior to migration (Steinberg 1989). By contrast, other nationality groups were rural in origin. Moreover, a large proportion of Jewish immigrants had worked in factories and other industrial settings prior to migration. While 67 percent of all Jewish immigrants had worked in skilled trades prior to their emigration, between 75 to 80 percent of all Polish, Slovakian, and Italian immigrants had previously been unskilled laborers.[7] In fact, while Jews accounted for only 12 percent of all immigrants to enter the United States in the first decade of the century, they constituted more than 29 percent of all skilled immigrants (Joseph 1914: 189–190).

The economic mobility of immigrant eastern European Jews in the first decades of the twentieth century was also fostered by the help provided them by the established German Jewish population. German Jews, who entered the United States in the 1840s and 1850s, were socially, economically, and politically much more westernized and secularized prior to their arrival than eastern European Jews. German Jews quickly became concentrated in business and retail trade and had made major progress in assimilating to middle-class American culture, politics, and language when the mass of eastern European Jews began to enter the country around 1880.

Out of sincere concern for their Jewish brethren and wary that the presence of these impecunious kinfolk—exotic in their dress, Orthodox in their religion, socialistic in their politics, and Yiddish speaking—might arouse anti-Semitism, the German Jewish community sought to aid and Americanize the newcomers. Resettlement programs, which were extensive yet sometimes heavy handed and condescending, ranged from economic help and job placement to Jewish reform schools for wayward youth.

German Jews also provided eastern European Jewish immigrants with access to employment since, by 1870, German Jews owned virtually the entire New York clothing industry, both retail and wholesale. About 50 percent of eastern European Jews had worked in this industry prior to migration. Since Jewish immigrant workers were already experienced in this type of work, employers prized them as they required little on-the-job training. Accordingly, Jews all but monopolized garment jobs, driving out natives and other immigrant groups until they abandoned them for more desirable positions. During the fifteen-year period from 1899 to 1914, the garment industry absorbed 400,000 workers. Immigrant Jews preferred to enter the garment industry because, as a heavily Jewish endeavor, it reduced the likelihood of contact with anti-Semites, allowed workers some ability to conform to their laws of religious observance, and offered a path for mobility based on coethnic cooperation and trust (Butler 1991; Goldscheider and Zuckerman 1984: 160; Kahan 1978; Kessner 1977; Lipset 1990).

Because much of the actual work of garment assembly was done in apartment-based sweatshops (a form of production introduced by immigrant Jews), the cost of setting up one's own enterprise was extremely low. Consequently, many employees were able to save up the small investment needed to become self-employed. At the same time, the location of businesses in and near residential tenements permitted owners to put their family members, relatives, and recently arrived friends to work. Moreover, because the garment industry was so heavily saturated by Jews, it was soon characterized by vertical integration and a multilevel system of ethnic-based cooperation that is now referred to as an "enclave economy". Bonds rooted in language, religion, and common region of origin brought together workers and employers with suppliers, manufacturers, subcontractors, and retailers. While wages were kept low, flexibility and stability were maximized. Moreover, as long as the garment industry continued to expand—from the manufacturing of clothes to the broader area of retail sales—and new arrivals came in from overseas, avenues for mobility were ensured. As Kahan (1978: 178) underscored, "With older cohorts moving from the home industry sector, from the sweatshop into the factories, into clerical positions, management and entrepreneurship, there existed a special dynamic pattern of economic adjustment for this group, the largest single occupational group in the Jewish immigration." While the garment industry was the most important source of employment, Jewish immigrants, many of whom possessed useful skills, were extensively involved in other industries that were developing in the early part of the century, including construction, manufacturing, cigar and cigarette making, shoemaking, and food preparation (Joseph 1914: 188; Kahan 1978: 245).

Another low-investment business occupation favored by immigrant Jews was pushcart peddling. Waldinger (1994: 15–16) highlighted that "of the roughly 5000 pushcart peddlers in Manhattan at the turn of the century, approximately 60 percent were Jews. In turn, peddlers bought their merchandise from Jewish wholesalers and retailers, providing jobs for many other Jews." Patterns of economic cooperation and trust associated with Jewish families and communities also provided valuable entrepreneurial resources, especially parents' support for their children's entrepreneurship. Finally, Jewish entrepreneurs were noted for their flexibility and willingness to accept low wages, develop new systems of production, and tolerate a lack of amenities (Goldscheider and Kobrin 1980; Sarachek 1980).

For some, this pattern paid off. In a relatively short time, many Jewish immigrants moved out of the bottom rung of the occupational ladder, the ethnically dominated occupations of home-based garment assembly and pushcarts, to the higher rung of retail trade, real estate, and other enterprises. "Indeed," stressed Kessner (1977: 65), "among the first generation immigrants it was not medicine, law or even their vaunted thirst for education that carried them forward. It was business." Finally, immigrant Jews in the early period were also very involved in union activities that provided an avenue to better wages, political incorporation, and communal organization (Gorelick 1982).

The social characteristics that distinguished Jews from other immigrants of the same era allowed them to make more money and live more stable lives. In turn, these advantages facilitated their children's educational achievements. Jewish children were able to remain in school longer and often attended college (Goldscheider and Zuckerman 1984: 168). For example, relatively few Jewish daughters were removed from school to perform domestic duties and were thus able to continue their education at higher rates than non-Jewish immigrant girls (Chiswick 1991; Weinberg 1988: 178).

The timing of the garment industry's rapid growth at the start of the century provided Jewish immigrants who brought the appropriate skills with a viable economic foothold in America. Then, changes in American society that included the vast expansion of the public and service sectors of the economy, coupled with the growth of public higher education, offered their educated offspring ample opportunities to gain white-collar jobs.

Most recent Jewish immigrants are highly educated and skilled and have access to coethnic networks and American Jewish communal services. Consequently, they tend to prosper. Like the native-born Jewish population, they are active in professions and entrepreneurship. According to the 1990 census, more than 50 percent of both Soviet- and Israel-born persons in New York and Los Angeles, ages twenty-four to sixty-five, had one or more years of college, and more than 30 percent of both nationality groups were college graduates. Thus, Jewish migrants are much better educated than the U.S. population at large, which has a 20 percent rate of college graduation. Reflecting their high levels of education, recent Jewish immigrants experience rapid economic mobility. According to the 1990 census, established,[8] employed Soviet- and Israel-born men residing in New York City and Los Angeles were making more than $32,000 annually in 1990. The average earnings for employed white men in the United States was just under $31,000. Established, employed Soviet- and Israel-born women residing in New York City and Los Angeles were making more than $21,000 annually in 1990. For purposes of comparison, the average earnings for employed white women in the United States was about $21,000 in 1990. As might be expected, recently arrived Jewish immigrants, especially refugees from the former Soviet Union, made much less in 1990 than those émigrés with longer tenure in the United States.[9]

While the average income of Jewish migrants suggests a generally successful merger into the American middle class, the economic adjustment of this population covers a wide range from poverty to significant wealth. For example, about 30 percent of Soviets who had been in the United States for a year or less in June 1991 were receiving cash assistance—an indicator of low income. In contrast, employed Israeli men in Los Angeles made almost $49,000 in 1989, a figure that exceeds the earnings of native-born white men in that city by almost $3,000.

According to the 1990 census, in both New York and Los Angeles, more than a third of Soviet immigrants are employed as managers, administrators, professionals, or technical specialists, while just under half of Israelis hold such jobs. About 25 percent of Israelis and 10 percent of Soviets in either city are employed in sales. Other important occupational categories are gender based: craft work (frequently in construction and jewelry) for men and clerical occupations for women.

One economic asset of recent Jewish immigrants over natives and other immigrant groups is the high number of women with professional and technical skills. Sixty-seven percent of Soviet Jewish women in the

United States were engineers, technicians, or other kinds of professionals prior to migration. In contrast, only 16.5 percent of American women work in these occupations (Simon 1985: 17). According to the 1990 census, 29 percent of Soviet émigré women in New York City and 21 percent of Soviet émigré women in Los Angeles County work as professionals, while the rate for Israeli women is 41 percent in New York and 33 percent in Los Angeles. In both cities, a smaller proportion of Jewish immigrant men are employed in these occupations. Among Israeli women, the high rate of professional employment reflects the large fraction who find jobs in Jewish communal occupations, notably as Hebrew teachers.

Data from the 1990 census suggest that a sizable fraction of recent Jewish immigrants are self-employed. This makes good theoretical sense since immigrants have greater rates of self-employment than the native born, and Jews, foreign and native born alike, are also characterized by high rates of self-employment (Fratoe 1984; Herman 1998). In New York, 15 percent of Soviets (21 percent of men and 8 percent of women) and 26 percent of Israelis (31 percent of men and 14 percent of women) were self-employed. In Los Angeles, rates of self-employment were even higher, with 24 percent of Soviets (31 percent of men and 13 percent of women) and 29 percent of Israelis (36 percent of men and 16 percent of women) self-employed.[10] When compared to census data descriptive of various migrant groups, the Los Angeles figure puts Soviet Jews among those with the very highest rates of self-employment. This is an impressive finding, considering that as refugees from a communist nation, Soviet Jews lack two of the most essential resources for entrepreneurship: business experience and investment capital.

High rates of self employment are maintained by extensive economic cooperation involving coethnic hiring, subcontracting, and ethnic economic specialization. In Los Angeles, Israelis are especially active in real estate, construction, jewelry and diamonds, retail sales, security, garments, engineering, and media industries (Gold 1994b). In New York, Freedman and Korazim (1986: 148) found similar patterns and determined that at least two-thirds of Israelis rely on ethnic ties and resources in their occupational lives. One illustration of Israelis' entrepreneurial orientation can be found in the form of the *Jewish/Israeli Yellow Pages of Los Angeles*. Originally started as an offshoot of the Hebrew newspaper *Hadashot LA*, the directory is more than 300 pages long and bilingual (in both Hebrew and

STEVEN G. GOLD

English) and advertises some 1,500 Israeli-owned businesses. The publisher estimated that there were close to 3,500 Israeli-owned businesses in Los Angeles in 1995 (Gold and Phillips 1996: 76).

While many Jewish migrants become self-employed, others enter white-collar and professional occupations. This pattern is consistent with that revealed by other highly skilled, educated, and English-speaking migrant groups, such as Indians and Filipinos. Finally, it should be noted that various professions, such as doctor, dentist, or engineer (ones that involve a significant proportion of Jewish immigrants), are often practiced independently and hence constitute both professional and self-employment. In sum, recent Jewish immigrants are much more highly skilled and professional than were turn-of-the-century arrivals. However, both cohorts reveal high rates of self-employment, extensive coethnic economic cooperation, and involvement in similar economic sectors, such as garments and retail sales.

Relations with the American Jewish Community

Early in the century, established German Jews provided their eastern European coethnics with organizations, activities, and jobs. At the same time, the eastern Europeans brought with them a strong tradition of communal organization and extensive involvement with social movements and political activism developed after their emancipation in eastern Europe. Jews transplanted, modified, and invented a diverse array of associations, clubs, *Landsmanschaften,* synagogues, and mutual benefit societies that made up the communal basis of Jewish American life. The groups they created provided religious and moral guidance, education, political socialization, economic aid, health care, burial services, musical training, dancing lessons, summer excursions—in sum, support, a social life, and entertainment. Despite their Jewish constituencies, many immigrant organizations maintained a secular orientation, fostering the inclusion of nominally religious and nonreligious Jews together with their Orthodox cousins (Schwartz 1988). All offered a myriad of services, bases for mutual aid, and a place for the social incorporation of new arrivals.

Like the earlier arrivals, recent Jewish immigrants have received assistance from established coethnics. Soviets and some Iranians have been the beneficiaries of extensive, high-quality official programs funded by the U.S. government in conjunction with the American Jewish community. While Israelis are not eligible for refugee status and its associated benefits, they have engaged in extensive cooperation with American Jewish communities where they live and often work. Moreover, because about one in three Israelis is married to an American Jew, this group is characterized by a multitude of personal connections with native coethnics.

At the same time, like turn-of-the century Jews, recent Jewish immigrants sometimes lock horns with the host community in disputes about the nature of group identity, religious involvement, and location of settlement. While conflicts between migrants and hosts have endured, sociologist Paul Ritterband (1997: 333) argues that current issues of contention are distinct from those of the past:

> The 1880–1914 Russian Jewish immigrants were offered a network of settlement houses and other institutions designed by the earlier wave of German Jewish immigrants as a means of Americanizing their all too traditional and exotic co-religionists. By contrast, the contemporary American Jewish community, itself composed largely of descendants of earlier waves of East European immigrants, has attempted to Judaize the immigrants.

In both periods, conflicts developed as hosts directed new arrivals toward patterns of adaptation that were not of their own choosing.

Despite their many similarities, Soviet Jews and Israelis have been treated in very different ways by American Jews, who often view Soviet Jews as modern-day counterparts of their own grandparents: Jews leaving the oppressive and anti-Semitic lands of eastern Europe for the freedom and opportunity of America. While a small fraction of the American community argued that Soviet Jews should settle in Israel rather than the United States, these objections failed to carry the day. Instead, the American Jewish community and the government provided the Soviets with prized refugee status and a generous package of services and benefits to help them build new lives. Compared with the refugee resettlement systems devoted to other ethnic and nationality groups, Soviet Jews' agencies are highly centralized and integrated, long established, well funded, and few in number. Because of their access to matching grants, they enjoy a level of government and private funding per refugee that is considerably greater than that allocated for most other groups (Eckles et al. 1982).

The resettlement experience of Israelis in the United States contrasts with that of Soviet Jews. This is because it is framed by the relationship between American Jews and the state of Israel. Most American Jews support and admire Israel. In varying degrees, they also endorse its founding ideology, Zionism, which calls for the creation and settlement of a Jewish homeland (Cohen 1991). Consequently, the very existence of an Israeli community in the United States is a topic of controversy. American Jews and Israelis alike often consider Israeli emigrants as violators of the Zionist philosophy and, as such, as a potential hazard to the Jewish state. Until recently, Israeli emigrants have been referred to as *Yordim*, a stigmatizing Hebrew term that describes those who "descend" from the "higher" place of Israel to the Diaspora, as opposed to immigrants, the *Olim*, who "ascend" from the Diaspora to Israel (Rosen 1993). Most literature on Israeli immigrants asserts that members of the group accept some elements of the *Yordim* stereotype and, as a result, remain marginal to both Israel and the American Jewish community. Reflecting on this conflict, Kass and Lipset (1982: 289) assert, "If Jews have been the proverbial marginal people, Israeli emigrants are the marginal Jews." As a consequence of this controversy, organized American Jewry has been more reluctant and less generous in its efforts to assist Israelis than has been the case with other groups of Jewish immigrants.

Contemporary Jewish immigrants are characterized by distinct cultural, linguistic, and national heritages. Accordingly, Soviet Jews, Israelis, Iranians, and other Jewish migrants often gravitate toward their own enclaves where they can interact in a familiar environment. Because these groups have high rates of self-employment, their neighborhoods feature numerous ethnically oriented shops, restaurants, and media industries that provide a venue for socializing and identity maintenance. While these subcommunities have geographic, cultural, religious, and economic links with those of American Jews, the conational preference often predominates. Further, such communities are themselves often stratified into subgroups on the basis of class, ideology, region of origin, occupation, religiosity, ethnicity,[11] tenure in the United States, and other factors (Gitelman 1978; Gold 1994a; Kelley and Friedlander 1993; Shokeid 1988; Uriely 1995).

Jewish immigrant enclaves have a strong attraction for their residents, who often commute long distances to and from work in order to live among coethnics. Within them, a fairly high level of institutional completeness exists. For example, in West Los Angeles or Brooklyn, an immigrant Jew can interact with neighbors; shop for food, clothes, appliances, or medication; see a doctor or dentist; attend religious services; read a newspaper; watch cable television; visit a local park to play dominoes; spend an evening in a nightclub; and interact with numerous acquaintances, all without speaking a word of English (Gold 1995b; Markowitz 1993; Orleck 1987).

Immigrant and American Jews maintain distinct attitudes and social habits that often reinforce the immigrants' desire to stay among their own. Immigrants generally think that Americans are superficial and lacking in passion and warmth. Making this point, Mila, a Russian immigrant I interviewed in 1994, contrasted an American wedding with a Russian one:

> Big things like weddings, anniversaries, parties are just done in a different way. A Russian wedding, I mean you go all out. You have the whole synagogue. You have the wedding in the chapel and then there's a huge reception. Huge meals and appetizers and an emcee and a band and flowers and balloons and God knows what else. It's like a big occasion. Where Americans, they're like, "well the wedding's at seven and we'll leave by nine and just have appetizers—cheese and crackers. (Gold 1995b: 114–115)

Immigrant Jews' shared dislike of American values and cultural patterns is a reason some turn away from American coreligionists. In the realm of political affiliation, American Jews tend to be Democrats; many immigrants are politically conservative and, when they become naturalized citizens, join the Republican Party (Lipset 1990; Noonan 1988: 31). As these examples show, the cultural, linguistic, and political differences between immigrant and American Jews are enduring and as such continue to shape the two groups' patterns of interaction. In the course of fieldwork in Los Angeles, my associates and I identified some twenty-seven Israeli organizations and countless informal networks, ranging from business associations to religious congregations to Hebrew schools and even a flying club (Gold 1994a; Sachal-Staier 1993). These allow Israelis to maintain various home-country practices and outlooks in California. While Soviets,

Iranians, and others have not created this multitude of organizations, they too have established many religious and ethnic organizations (Dallalfar 1994; Feher 1998). The durability of these values, neighborhoods, and social patterns suggests that at least some fraction of the migrant population favors coethnic and colinguistic interaction rather than a quick merger into the American or American Jewish landscape.

Reflecting something similar to the adaptation pattern of eastern European Jews one hundred years ago, today's immigrant Jews feel significant social distance from American coreligionists in terms of language, values, sociability, and life-shaping experiences. However, in reflecting on these differences with American Jews, most hope for improved relations with Americans. In the words of David, an Israeli community activist,

> These two communities need each other. And I'm not saying the Israelis should assimilate into the Jewish community and become Americans because they won't. Their children probably will, but they won't. And they can keep their uniqueness, but in total cooperation. I think that instead of having their divisive or divided Jewish community, we need to have one strong united community. Not to show the resentment of Americans to Israelis and for Israelis to see themselves as outsiders. I mean it will take time. This is not a process that will happen overnight, but it will happen. (Gold and Phillips 1996: 95)

Religiousness

Interestingly, some of the greatest differences between American Jews and Jewish migrants (during both periods of migration) are found in their patterns of religious and ethnic identification—apparent commonalties that would seem to bring these groups together. In the late nineteenth and early twentieth centuries, the established German American Jewish community believed that modernization was vital to keeping Judaism alive in America (Wirth 1928). By the 1920s, as part of an effort to win acceptance from the Protestant establishment, they had constructed synagogues on the major thoroughfares of American cities, alongside the edifices of Presbyterians, Methodists, and Baptists. And like those of their Christian neighbors, these houses of worship included stained-glass windows, organs, and Sunday worship—features not part of the Jewish tradition. Rabbis were even referred to as "ministers". In contrast, the eastern European immigrants of the time were accustomed to a more passionate and orthodox religion and often viewed the watered-down rituals of their coethnic hosts with disdain (Hertzberg 1989; Howe 1976).

In the late twentieth century, Jewish immigrants and American Jews continue to disagree over contrasting interpretations of Jewish identity. American Jews emphasize religious knowledge and ritual, while secular Israelis focus on nationality, Iranians feel most comfortable with their long-established Persian traditions, and Russians stress emblematic ethnicity shaped by their unique history in eastern Europe.

A major reason for these conflicts is that Reform and Conservative Judaism, Western denominations with which the vast majority of American Jews affiliate, are all but unknown in the major source countries of Jewish immigration. Rejecting American denominations, many Jewish migrants prefer to affiliate with Chabad, an ultraorthodox, Hassidic movement considered exotic by mainstream American Jews. While American Jews may see Chabad as a throwback, immigrants are drawn to its familiar ambience. Moreover, the sect has organized extensive immigrant-oriented programming that delivers social and religious services with conational, multilingual rabbis in a highly personal context. During fieldwork in Los Angeles, I frequently saw Iranian, Israeli, and Russian Jews display pictures of the Chabad movement's now deceased leader, Rebbe Menachem M. Schneerson, in their homes and businesses. Moreover, in interviews, Jewish immigrants were much more familiar with Chabad personnel than they were with American Jewish leaders. Many utilized Chabad's social services and attended its High Holiday observances.

Because of their differences with American Jews, Jewish immigrants face a dilemma as they plan for their children's Jewish education. If they do nothing, their children will lose touch with their Jewishness. However, if they enroll the youngsters in American Jewish institutions, they are confronted with another foreign notion of identity: American Judaism. As a consequence, immigrant parents must choose between having their children socialized in either of two unfamiliar cultural traditions—those of non-Jewish Americans and American Jews.

Nevertheless, as in the case of communal life, while they feel some distance from American Jews, they see amalgamation with coethnic hosts as both positive and inevitable (Feher 1998; Ritterband 1997). For example, one Israeli woman who claimed that she had little premigration

Jewish involvement now sends her preschool-aged child to the orthodox Chabad program in Los Angeles. Like this woman, several Jewish migrants who presented themselves as having been radically secular prior to migration claimed that they were more religious in the United States than they ever had been at home.

The trend toward growing religious involvement among Jewish immigrants has been documented in recent surveys of Jewish communal life. When comparing both Israeli and former Soviet Jewish immigrants' observance of religious customs—lighting candles on Shabbat and Chanukah, attending synagogue on the High Holy Days and Shabbat, and fasting on Yom Kippur—with their patterns of ritual observance prior to migration, these practices tend to increase. Based on his analysis of the New York Jewish Population Study of 1991, Ritterband (1997: 333) argues, "In many ways, the new immigrants, despite their lack of religious training and with few exceptions, score as high—or higher—on the religious, secular and affiliational dimensions of Jewishness as do other New York Jews" (see also Gold 1994c; Gold and Phillips 1996). In sum, while eastern European Jewish migrants early this century were more religious than the host community of German American Jews, the majority of today's Jewish migrants are less pious than many American Jews would like. Yet some evidence suggests that in adjusting to American life, migrants are becoming more observant.

Conclusion

Given the many changes experienced by both U.S. and world Jewry in the past one hundred years, it is remarkable that Russian Jews can be counted among the top ten immigrant groups entering the United States in both the first and the last decade of the century and the only European group near the top during both periods. While the ranking of Jewish immigrants, along with their concentration in New York City and some family and economic patterns, reveals surprising consistency throughout both eras, we also witness dramatic contrasts.

Early in the century, American Jews were overwhelmingly a foreign-born population, and new arrivals vastly outnumbered native-born coethnics. By the 1990s, most American Jews had been in the United States three or more generations, and only 8.6 percent of the group was born outside the country. For native-born Jews of the 1900s, the task of aiding the vast number of recently arrived coethnics was a major challenge. Today, it is just one of the group's many philanthropic endeavors. Turn-of-the-century Jewish immigrants were poor, lived in slums, and were subject to harsh discrimination. By contrast, contemporary Jewish immigrants generally enter the society's middle class and avoid maltreatment.

While the European component remains significant among today's Jewish migrants, it accounts for a smaller fraction than was the case early in the century. Just as the majority of all immigrants have Third World origins, so too do many new Jewish immigrants. Alongside the longtime residents and more recently settled Jewish yuppies in the older Jewish neighborhoods of major American cities, we now find increasing numbers of Israeli, Persian, Latin American, and Russian Jews. The presence of Jewish immigrants is what allows these neighborhoods to retain their Jewish complexion in a context of rapidly changing demographics. Recent arrivals purchase existing neighborhood businesses and create new ones. They rent apartments, buy homes, and attend neighborhood synagogues and public and day schools. As a case in point, in Los Angeles, directly across Robertson Boulevard from the Workman's Circle building (Workman's Circle is a secular/socialist organization that was influential among European Jewish immigrants early in the century), is the newly created Orthodox Gan Chabad program for Israelis, staffed by a Yemenite rabbi. In the garment center and jewelry district of New York and Los Angeles, Hebrew and Farsi conversations echo Yiddish ones of decades past, as workers relish their lunch of pita bread, shwarma, and Turkish coffee as much as previous generations enjoyed corned beef and knishes. Like the Russian Jews who early in the century sought to demonstrate their independence from uptown German Jews by creating a downtown Jewish hospital in New York City, Persian Jews in Los Angeles have worked to establish a new garment district over the protests of American Jewish property owners (Sahagun 1991: B-3). It is clear that new Jewish migrants often take over elements of American Jewish life. In so doing, they will maintain but also transform these institutions and change the nature of the American community. The experience of Jewish immigrants making a place for themselves in the United States can be viewed as the unfolding of another chapter in Jewish American history, distinct from but similar to the experience of earlier waves of Jewish immigrants to the United States.

Jews who arrived early in the century were concerned with economic survival and avoiding anti-Semitism. In contrast, the major issues confronting Jewish migrants today have more to do with cultural preservation. They (like their native-born Jewish hosts) have easy access to the institutions of the larger society. Consequently, assimilation and intermarriage into Christian, American society threatens to dilute their religious, ethnic, and national identity beyond recognition. Such risks are especially great for Russians, Israelis, and others who have limited Jewish knowledge and lack a tradition of retaining their identity in a society that is both open and non-Jewish. While the risks of assimilation are considerable, the presence of these new immigrants also infuses American Jewry with diversity, cultural richness, and vitality. By working together, natives and new immigrants hope to apply their many opportunities and traditions to building a joint community that can sustain both parties along with the larger society in the years to come.

Notes

The first major sound film, *The Jazz Singer* (1927), starring Al Jolson, is the story of the son of Jewish immigrants who is raised to sing in the synagogue but falls in love with American popular music and follows a career of performing in blackface. *What a Country!*, headlined by Soviet émigré comedian Yakov Smirnoff, was a 1980s television sitcom about a multiethnic group of immigrants in an English class.

I wish to thank Ken Waltzer, Lisa Gold, Pyong Gap Min, and Ronald Bayor for valuable comments on this chapter.

1. National origin data is unreliable because some Israelis and Russians are not Jewish. Moreover, since Jews are a peripatetic group, country of birth and country of last residence are not always the same. Finally, Jewishness itself is subject to multiple definitions, based on parenthood and religious beliefs. See Gold (1994c) and Gold and Phillips (1996).

2. Immigration restrictions during the 1920s through the 1940s did exclude thousands of European Jews seeking refuge from the Nazis (Breitman and Kraut 1987: 9; Goldberg 1996: 129; Goldscheider and Zuckerman 1984: 174).

3. Because it is a country of immigration, Israel's population includes a large number of persons born outside the Jewish state.

4. However, with over 10,000 Soviet refugees entering New York annually during most of the 1990s, it is possible that by 2001 the fraction of foreign born in New York met or even exceeded that in Los Angeles.

5. Secondary migrants are persons resettled in one location who then migrate to another.

6. According to the 1990 census, 60 percent of Israeli women and 58 percent of Iranian women (including non-Jews) were employed. (Bozorgmehr et al. 1996: 356). Sixty-three percent of all Soviet Jewish women in Los Angeles were employed in 1990, but excluding those in the United States three or fewer years, their labor force participation rate was higher at 71 percent. Similar results were found in New York (Gold 1994c: 19–20).

7. Unskilled migrants often increased their levels of skill during employment, thus reducing skill differentials between various groups (Bodnar et al. 1982).

8. This figure reflects Soviets who had been in the United States at least nine years.

9. All census data from the U.S. Bureau of the Census (1990).

10. Nationally, Israelis achieved the second-highest rate for self-employment among all nationality groups in the 1990 census. Only that of Koreans was higher (Yoon 1997: 201).

11. As a nation of immigrants, Israel is made up of diverse nationalities from eastern and western Europe, North Africa, and the Middle East. Social life there and among Israeli emigrants in the United States is often organized around these ethnic communities.

References

American Jewish Yearbook. 1929. Volume 31. Philadelphia: Jewish Publication Society of America.

———. 1996. New York: American Jewish Committee.

Archdeacon, Thomas. N.d. "Immigration, 1899–1924" <http://www.wisc.edu.history/404tja/batv3.html>.

Barkan, Elliott R. 1996. *And Still They Come: Immigrants and American Society: 1920 to the 1990s.* Wheeling, IL: Harland Davidson.

Bodnar, John, Roger Simon, and Michael P. Weber. 1982. *Lives of Their Own: Blacks, Italians and Poles in Pittsburgh, 1900–1960.* Urbana: University of Illinois Press.

Butler, John Sibly. 1991. *Entrepreneurship and Self-Help among Black Americans.* Albany: State University of New York Press.

Bozorgmehr, Mehdi, Claudia Der-Martirosian, and Georges Sabagh. 1996. "Middle Easterners: A New Kind of Immigrant." In *Ethnic Los Angeles*, edited by Roger Waldinger and Mehdi Bozorgmehr. New York: Russell Sage Foundation.

Breitman, Richard, and Alan Kraut. 1987. *American Refugee Policy and European Jewry 1933–1945.* Bloomington: Indiana University Press.

Chiswick, Barry R. 1988. "Differences in Education and Earnings across Racial and Ethnic Groups: Tastes, Discrimination, and Investments in Child Quality." *Quarterly Journal of Economics* 103: 571–597.

———. 1991. "Jewish Immigrant Skill and Occupational Attainment at the Turn of the Century." *Explorations in Economic History* 28: 64–80.

Cohen, Steven M. 1991. "Israel in the Jewish Identity of American Jews: A Study in Dualities and Contrasts." In *Jewish Identity in America,* edited by David M. Gordis and Yoav Ben-Horin. Los Angeles: Wilstein.

Dallalfar, Arlene. 1994. "Iranian Women as Immigrant Entrepreneurs." *Gender and Society* 8 (4): 541–561.

Dinnerstein, Leonard. 1981. "Anti-Semitism Exposed and Attacked, 1945–1950." *American Jewish History* 1: 134–149.

Dinnerstein, Leonard, Roger L. Nichols, and David M. Reimers. 1990. *Natives and Strangers: Blacks, Indians and Immigrants in America.* 2nd ed. New York: Oxford University Press.

Eckles, Timothy J., Lawrence J. Lewin, David S. North, and Dangole J. Spakevicius. 1982. "A Portrait in Diversity: Voluntary Agencies and the Office of Refugee Resettlement Matching Grant Program." Lewin and Associates. Mimeograph.

Elizur, Dov. 1980. "Israelis in the U.S." *American Jewish Yearbook* 80: 53–67.

Farber, Bernard, Charles H. Mindel, and Bernard Lazerwitz. 1988. "The Jewish American Family." In *Ethnic Families in America,* 3rd ed., edited by Charles H. Mindel, Robert Habenstein, and Roosevelt Wright Jr. New York: Elsevier.

Feher, Shoshanah. 1998. "From the Rivers of Babylon to the Valleys of Los Angeles: The Exodus and Adaptation of Iranian Jews." In *Gatherings in the Diaspora: Religious Communities and the New Immigration,* edited by R. Stephen Warner and Judith G. Wittner. Philadelphia: Temple University Press.

Fix, Michael, and Jeffery S. Passel. 1994. *Immigration and Immigrants: Setting the Record Straight.* Washington, DC: The Urban Institute.

Fratoe, Frank A. 1984. "Abstracts of the Sociological Literature on Minority Business Ownership (with Additional References)." Research Division, Office of Advocacy, Research and Information, Minority Business Development Agency, U.S. Department of Commerce, Washington, DC.

Freedman, Marcia, and Josef Korazim. 1986. "Israelis in the New York Area Labor Market." *Contemporary Jewry* 7: 141–153.

Gabaccia, Donna. 1994. *From the Other Side: Women, Gender and Immigrant Life in the U.S., 1820–1990.* Bloomington: Indiana University Press.

Gitelman, Zvi. 1978. "Soviet Immigrants and American Absorption Efforts: A Case Study in Detroit." *Journal of Jewish Communal Service* 55 (1): 77–82.

———. 1996. "Becoming American Jews: Resettlement and Acculturation of Soviet Jewish Immigrants in Chicago." Report prepared for the Jewish Federation of Metropolitan Chicago.

Glazer, Nathan. 1955. "The Social Characteristics of American Jews." *American Jewish Yearbook* 56: 3–42.

Glazer, Nathan, and Daniel Patrick Moynihan. 1963. *Beyond the Melting Pot.* Cambridge, MA: MIT Press.

Gold, Steven J. 1992. *Refugee Communities: A Comparative Field Study.* Newbury Park, CA: Sage Publications.

———. 1994a. "Israeli Immigrants in the U.S.: The Question of Community." *Qualitative Sociology* 17: 325–363.

———. 1994b. "Patterns of Economic Cooperation among Israeli Immigrants in Los Angeles." *International Migration Review* 28: 114–135.

———. 1994c. "Soviet Jews in the United States." *American Jewish Yearbook* 94: 3–57.

———. 1995a. *From The Workers' State to the Golden State: Jews from the Former Soviet Union in California.* Boston: Allyn and Bacon.

———. 1995b. "Gender and Social Capital among Israeli Immigrants in Los Angeles." *Diaspora* 4: 267–301.

———. 1997. "Transnationalism and Vocabularies of Motive in International Migration: The Case of Israelis in the U.S." *Sociological Perspectives* 40: 409–426.

Gold, Steven J., and Bruce A. Phillips. 1996. "Israelis in the United States." *American Jewish Yearbook*: 51–101.

Goldberg, J. J. 1996. *Jewish Power: Inside the American Jewish Establishment.* Reading, MA: Addison-Wesley.

Goldscheider, Calvin, and Frances E. Kobrin. 1980. "Ethnic Continuity and the Process of Self-Employment." *Ethnicity* 7: 256–278.

Goldscheider, Calvin, and Alan S. Zuckerman. 1984. *The Transformation of the Jews.* Chicago: University of Chicago Press.

Goldstein, Joseph. 1995. *Jewish History in Modern Times.* Brighton: Sussex Academic Press.

Gorelick, Sherry. 1982. *City College and the Jewish Poor.* New York: Schocken Books.

Goren, Arthur A. 1970. *New York Jews and the Quest for Community.* New York: Columbia University Press.

Hebrew Immigration Aid Society. 1997. "HIAS Facts and Figures: Migration Figures, 1945–1995" <http://www.hias.org.fact_fig/annual.htm>.

Herman, Pini. 1998. *Los Angeles Jewish Population Survey '97*. Los Angeles: Jewish Federation of Los Angeles.

Hertzberg, Arthur. 1989. *The Jews in America: Four Centuries of an Uneasy Encounter: A History*. New York: Simon & Schuster.

Horowitz Bethamie. 1993. *The 1991 New York Jewish Population Study*. New York: United Jewish Appeal—Federation of Jewish Philanthropies of New York.

Howe, Irving. 1976. *World of Our Fathers*. New York: Harcourt, Brace, Jovanovich.

Ivy, A. C., and Irwin Ross. 1957. "Discrimination in College Admissions." In *American Minorities*, edited by Milton L. Barron. New York: Knopf.

James, Edmund J., Oscar Flynn, J. R. Paulding, Mrs. Simon N. Patton, Walter Scott Andrews, Charles S. Bernheimer, Henrietta Szold, and other writers, eds. 1907. *The Immigrant Jew in America*. New York: B. F. Buck and Company.

Joselit, Jenna Weissman. 1983. *Our Gang: Jewish Crime and the New York Jewish Community, 1900–1940*. Bloomington: Indiana University Press.

Joseph, Samuel. 1914. *Jewish Immigration to the United States from 1881 to 1910*. New York: Arno Press and the New York Times.

Kahan, Arcadius. 1978. "Economic Opportunities and Some Pilgrims' Progress: Jewish Immigrants from Eastern Europe in the U.S., 1890–1914." *Journal of Economic History* 38: 235–251.

Kass, Drora, and Seymour Martin Lipset. 1982. "Jewish Immigration to the United States from 1967 to the Present: Israelis and Others." In *Understanding American Jewry*, edited by Marshall Sklare. New Brunswick, NJ: Transaction Books.

Kelley, Ron, and Jonathan Friedlander, eds. 1993. *Irangeles: Iranians in Los Angeles*. Berkeley and Los Angeles: University of California Press.

Kessner, Thomas. 1977. *The Golden Door: Italian and Jewish Immigrant Mobility in New York City 1880–1915*. New York: Oxford University Press.

Kuznets, Simon. 1975. "Immigration of Russian Jews to the United States: Background and Structure." *Perspectives in American History* 9: 35–124.

Lieberson, Stanley. 1981. *A Piece of the Pie*. Berkeley and Los Angeles: University of California Press.

Lieberson, Stanley, and Mary C. Waters. 1988. *From Many Strands: Ethnic and Racial Groups in Contemporary America*. New York: Russell Sage Foundation.

Lipset, Seymour Martin. 1990. "A Unique People in an Exceptional Country." In *American Pluralism and the Jewish Community*. New Brunswick, NJ: Transaction Books.

Markowitz, Fran. 1988. "Jewish in the USSR, Russian in the USA." In *Persistence and Flexibility: Anthropological Perspectives on the American Jewish Experience,* edited by Walter P. Zenner. Albany: State University of New York Press.

———. 1993. *A Community in Spite of Itself: Soviet Jewish Émigrés in New York.* Washington, DC: Smithsonian Institution Press.

New York City Public Schools. 1991. *Test Scores of Recent Immigrants and Other Students, New York City Public Schools, Grades 3–12.* New York: Office of Research, Evaluation, and Assessment, New York City Public Schools.

New York Jewish Population Study. 1993. *The 1991 New York Jewish Population Study.* New York: United Jewish Appeal—Federation of Jewish Philanthropies of New York.

Noonan, Leo. 1988. "Russians Go Republican." *The Jewish Journal,* November 18–24, 31.

Office of Refugee Resettlement. 1997. *Annual Report to Congress: Refugee Resettlement Program.* Washington, DC: Office of Refugee Resettlement.

Orleck, Annalise. 1987. "The Soviet Jews: Life in Brighton Beach, Brooklyn." In *New Immigrants in New York,* edited by Nancy Foner. New York: Columbia University Press.

Rischin, Moses. 1970 [1962]. *The Promised City.* Cambridge, MA: Harvard University Press.

Ritterband, Paul. 1997. "Jewish Identity among Russian Immigrants in the U.S." In *Russian Jews on Three Continents: Migration and Resettlement,* edited by Noah Lewin-Epstein, Yaacov Ro'I, and Paul Ritterband. London: Frank Cass.

Rosen, Sherry. 1993. "The Israeli Corner of the American Jewish Community." Issue Series No. 3. New York: Institute on American Jewish-Israeli Relations, American Jewish Committee.

Rosenthal, Mira. 1989. "Assimilation of Israeli Immigrants." Ph.D. diss., Fordham University.

Sachal-Staier, Michal. 1993. "Israelis in Los Angeles: Interrelations and Relations with the American Jewish Community." Master's thesis, University of Judaism, Los Angeles.

Sahagun, Louis. 1991. "New Use Ok'd for May Co. Building." *Los Angeles Times,* September 18, B3.

Sarachek, Bernard. 1980. "Jewish American Entrepreneurs." *Journal of Economic History* 40: 359–372.

Schneider, Susan Weidman. 1995. "Women, Money and Power." In *The National Commission on American Jewish Women, Voices for Change: Future Directions for American Jewish Women.* Waltham, MA: Cohen Center for Modern Jewish Studies, Brandeis University.

Schwartz, Anita. 1988. "The Secular Seder: Continuity and Change among Left-Wing Jews." In *Between Two Worlds: Ethnographic Essays on American Jewry,* edited by Jack Kugelmass. Ithaca, NY: Cornell University Press.

Shokeid, Moshe. 1988. *Children of Circumstances: Israeli Immigrants in New York.* Ithaca, NY: Cornell University Press.

Simon, Rita J. 1985. *New Lives: The Adjustment of Soviet Jewish Immigrants in the United States and Israel.* Lexington, MA: Lexington Books.

———. 1997. *In The Golden Land: A Century of Russian and Soviet Jewish Immigration in America.* Westport, CT: Praeger.

Sowell, Thomas P. 1981. *Ethnic America.* New York: Basic Books.

Steinberg, Stephen. 1989. *The Ethnic Myth.* 2nd ed. New York: Atheneum.

Takaki, Ronald. 1993. *A Different Mirror: A History of Multicultural America.* Boston: Little, Brown.

Tenenbaum, Shelly. 1993. *A Credit to Their Community.* Detroit: Wayne State University Press.

Uriely, Natan. 1995. "Patterns of Identification and Integration with Jewish Americans among Israeli Immigrants in Chicago: Variations across Status and Generation." *Contemporary Jewry* 16: 27–49.

U.S. Bureau of the Census. 1990. *Census of Population,* 5% Public Use Microsample.

Waldinger, Roger. 1994. "When the Melting Pot Boils Over: The Irish, Jews, Blacks and Koreans of New York." In *The Bubbling Cauldron: Race, Ethnicity, and the Urban Crisis,* edited by Michael Peter Smith and Joe Feagin. Minneapolis: University of Minnesota Press.

Waldman, Lois. 1956. "Employment Discrimination against Jews in the United States—1955." *Jewish Social Studies* 18: 208–216.

Weinberg, Sydney Stahl. 1988. *The World of Our Mothers.* Chapel Hill: University of North Carolina Press.

Weisser, Michael R. 1989. *A Brotherhood of Memory: Jewish Landsmanschaften.* Ithaca, NY: Cornell University Press.

Wirth, Louis. 1928. *The Ghetto.* Chicago: University of Chicago Press.

Yoon, In-Jin. 1997. *On My Own: Korean Businesses and Race Relations in America.* Chicago: University of Chicago Press.

CHAPTER NINE

A COMPARISON OF PRE- AND POST-1965 ASIAN IMMIGRANT BUSINESSES

Pyong Gap Min

efore World War II, Asian immigrants were visible in California, Hawaii, and other West Coast states. Approximately 698,000 Asians immigrated to the United States between 1850 and 1930 (Arnold et al. 1987). Compared to the total immigrant flows to the United States at that time, the number of prewar Asian immigrants, consisting mainly of Chinese and Japanese, is insignificant. However, the earlier Chinese and Japanese immigrants in the West Coast were so active in small business that their commercial activities have attracted a great deal of scholarly attention. At least three books that have been considered classics in the field of ethnic/immigrant entrepreneurship focus on Chinese and/or Japanese immigrants before World War II (Bonacich and Modell 1980; Light 1972; Loewen 1971).

The post-1965 era has witnessed the influx of Asian immigrants in unprecedented numbers who have originated from many Asian countries. They are concentrated not only in West Coast cities but also in such cities as New York, Washington, Chicago, Houston, and Atlanta. Among contemporary Asian immigrants, Koreans show the highest self-employment rate among all ethnic and immigrant groups, while Chinese, Taiwanese, Indian, and Pakistani groups have higher self-employment rates than the native-born white population (Fairlie and Meyer 1996; Light and Roach 1996; Min 1996; Yoon 1997). Contemporary Korean and Chinese immigrants' commercial activities have received even greater scholarly attention than the earlier Asian immigrants' commercial activities (Light 1980; Light and Bonacich 1988; Min 1988, 1990, 1996; Sanders and Nee 1987; Tseng 1995; Wong 1998; Yoon 1997; Zhou 1992; Zhou and Logan 1989).

285

Because of their disadvantages for employment in the general labor market, immigrants in the United States historically have had a greater tendency to run their own businesses than the native-born population (Light 1979; Light and Sanchez 1987; Min 1987). Because of their physical differences, Asian immigrants have encountered more discrimination than white immigrants. Asian immigrants' barriers in the general labor market partly explain their great tendency to start their own businesses in both the pre- and the post-1965 era. However, the two periods show significant differences in Asian immigrants' motives for starting their own businesses, major strategies of their business establishment and operation, and business-related intergroup conflicts. These differences are due to the differences in Asian immigrants' class background and opportunity structure in American society in the two periods. This chapter compares Chinese- and Japanese-owned businesses in the pre-1965 period with the Korean- and Chinese-owned businesses in the contemporary period, focusing on the major differences.

There are many empirical studies focusing on Korean immigrant entrepreneurship that provide data useful for discussion in this chapter. But there are few studies on Chinese or other Asian immigrant entrepreneurship that offer information relevant to this chapter. Accordingly, discussions of contemporary Asian immigrant businesses in this chapter are based largely on data derived from studies of Korean immigrant entrepreneurship, although studies on other Asian groups are cited here.

Discrimination versus Disadvantage

Chinese immigration to the United States began in 1848 with the start of the California gold rush. Chinese laborers, overwhelmingly young men, initially worked in mines, on railroads and farms, and in factories in California and other West Coast states. Although white owners welcomed Chinese immigrants as cheap labor sources, white laborers and independent farmers gradually felt competition with hardworking and subservient Chinese workers (Asbury 1933; Bonacich 1972; Saxton 1971). The bitter feeling against Chinese laborers on the part of white workers took the forms of attacks on Chinese and their properties, burning of Chinatowns, and riots. An anti-Chinese riot in Los Angeles in 1871 claimed nineteen innocent Chinese lives (Chan 1991: 49). Anti-Chinese sentiments also led to the enactment of discriminatory legislation initially at the municipal and state levels in the West Coast and ultimately in the U.S. Congress. The passage of the Chinese Exclusion Act in 1882 by Congress was the culmination of anti-Chinese sentiments spurred by lobbies by white workers.

One of the major reactions by Chinese immigrants to anti-Chinese sentiments and violence during the exclusion era was to change their occupations from employment in men's jobs to "women's jobs" to avoid competition with white male workers. While many Chinese workers got into domestic service in white families, many more sought self-employment in "women's jobs," especially in laundry and Chinese restaurants, two major Chinese businesses during the exclusion era. Thus, discrimination in the general labor market pushed Chinese immigrants into laundry, Chinese restaurants, and other types of businesses (grocery). As Takaki (1989: 92) puts it, "Ethnic antagonism in the mines, factories, and fields reinforced the movement of Chinese into self-employment—stores, restaurants, and especially laundries." To escape from rampant racial violence, many Chinese immigrants in the West Coast moved to other parts of the United States. These remigrant Chinese were even more highly concentrated in laundry and restaurant businesses than those in the West Coast, as Chinese immigrants in Chicago were often called "laundrymen" (Chan 1991: 33; Siu 1987).

In *Ethnic Enterprise in North America*, Light (1972) showed how Chinese and Japanese immigrants could develop high levels of ethnic business in the first half of the twentieth century by virtue of their use of rotating credit association, the practice brought with them from their home countries. Because of his cultural explanation, some structurally oriented social scientists may not bother to read the book closely. However, in the introductory chapter of the book, he also emphasized how racial antagonism pushed Chinese immigrants to concentrate in domestic service, laundry work, Chinese restaurants, and retail stores (Light 1972: 7):

> Whites took steps to exclude Chinese labor from employment and Chinese firms from the market. These pressures left resident Chinese with few opportunities for earning a livelihood.
> For employment, Chinese had principally to look to domestic service, laundry work, restaurants, and small retail stores catering principally to

other Chinese. Whites did not object to Chinese in domestic service. They raised no barrier to Chinese in the laundry trade, since this occupation was not one in which white males cared to engage. Chinese restaurants were also tolerated. Serving cheap, appetizing meals, they were able, in the frontier period, to win the patronage of the white working class.

Japanese immigration to the United States began around 1895, after Chinese were excluded from immigration to the mainland United States, when white-owned plantations in Hawaii needed cheap laborers. Later, more Japanese immigrants migrated to the mainland Pacific coast than to Hawaii. In addition, lured by higher wages in employment for railroad construction and farming, many Japanese laborers in Hawaii moved to California and other West Coast states. Japanese immigrants in the West Coast were spared overt racial violence that Chinese immigrants encountered about twenty-five years before. But they, too, were subjected to exclusion from the general labor market and immigration restrictions (Daniels 1962; Hing 1993). The Gentleman's Agreement of 1907–1908 terminated the migration of Japanese laborers to the United States, although it allowed the already imported Japanese bachelor immigrants to bring their spouses and children. The Asiatic Exclusion of 1924, which barred all Asian nationals from immigrating to the United States for about forty years, targeted mainly Japanese immigration.

Japanese laborers were imported to Hawaii and the mainland United States mainly as cheap labor sources in agriculture (plantations in Hawaii and farming in the West Coast).[1] However, they refused to work as cheap laborers under oppressive conditions by repeatedly organizing strikes for higher wages and better working conditions and by leasing and buying farmland. California and other West Coast states passed the Alien Land Laws in the early twentieth century mainly to prevent the Japanese from acquiring land (Chan 1991: 47).

The labor market discrimination that Japanese immigrants encountered pushed them to pursue self-employment in grocery stores, hotel/boardinghouses, restaurants, and other business lines (Kurokawa 1970; Light 1972: 9–10; McWilliams 1944). In the following paragraph, Light explains how Japanese immigrants' tendency to gain commercial self-employment was caused by their experiences with discrimination in job opportunity (Light 1972: 10):

> Squeezed off the land and deprived of nonmenial wage and salary employment opportunities, what were the Japanese to do for a living? Confronting this question, California Board of Control anticipated that "the Oriental, if crowded out of the agricultural field, will rapidly increase his commercial activities." Urban self-employment absorbed the energies of Japanese men who faced discriminatory barriers in agriculture and in the urban labor market. . . . Although a culturally derived preference for self-employment clearly supported this development, the Japanese interest in commercial self-employment was also a plain response to a discriminatory opportunity structure which precluded wage or salary employment at nonmenial level.

It was in the area of farming and sales of farm products that Japanese ethnic business developed most successfully, especially in California. The Alien Land Laws did reduce the Japanese ownership and lease of farmland but never stopped it. To circumvent the laws, many Japanese farmers leased land from white owners but made unwritten arrangements, while many others made arrangements with their children or friends who were citizens. Moreover, many Japanese immigrants who could not legally or financially buy farmland obtained land to farm through methods of contract or share (Takaki 1989: 188–189).[2] Thus, a large proportion of Japanese in California engaged in fruit and vegetable farming in the early twentieth century, producing the majority of some fruits and vegetables, such as strawberries, fresh snap beans, and fresh tomatoes. In 1918, 15,794 Japanese in California engaged in farming and, along with their wives and children, comprised 55 percent of the Japanese population (Ichioka 1988: 156).

As noted previously, the earlier Chinese and Japanese immigrants were concentrated in self-employment in small business mainly because white laborers did not allow them to compete in the general labor market. By contrast, contemporary Asian immigrants seek self-employment in small business mainly because of their inability to find jobs commensurate with their educational levels. Several studies have shown that Korean immigrants have chosen small business mainly because of their language barrier and other disadvantages for employment in the general labor market

(Kim 1981; Min 1984, 1988; Yoon 1997). For example, in a survey study of Korean immigrant entrepreneurs in Atlanta, I tried to determine why the respondents entered business using both closed- and open-ended questions. In their responses to closed-ended questions, 90 percent of the respondents cited their language barrier and other disadvantages for employment in the general labor market as the main reason for their entry into small business (Min 1984, 1988: 67). In the open-ended question of why they started their businesses, more respondents (45 percent) chose factors reflecting their labor market disadvantage as the main reason. The vast majority of the respondents had professional and white-collar occupations in Korea, but their initial jobs in the United States were largely low-level blue-collar and service-related jobs. They started small business as an alternative to low-level blue-collar jobs available in the United States, although their anticipation of economic mobility through business also played an important role in their decision to start their businesses.

On the basis of these findings, I made the following conclusion regarding the different motivations of the earlier and contemporary Asian immigrants (Min 1984: 350):

> The earlier Chinese and Japanese immigrants were ready to take any kind of manual work for survival, but native labor did not allow them to compete in the labor market. They turned to small business because employment in the general labor market was completely blocked by host discrimination. Recent Korean immigrants of white-collar background have a more sophisticated problem. Unhappy in jobs that involve manual work, they seek meaningful white-collar occupations. However, factors such as their language barrier and unfamiliarity with American customs, more than host discrimination, prevent them from holding the high-status, white-collar occupations for which they are trained.

Compared to their educational level, Korean immigrants appear to have a more severe language barrier than other Asian immigrant groups. Thus, Korean immigrants may best fit the disadvantage thesis. But an analysis of the 1980 U.S. census (Public Use Microsample) data reveals that the disadvantage thesis is applicable to other contemporary Asian immigrant groups. Dividing the sample into three groups—noncollege graduates, home-country college graduates, and U.S. college graduates—Kim et al. (1989) examined the probability of Chinese, Indian, and Korean immigrant workers engaging in self-employment. They have found that home-country college graduates are more apt to start a business than the other two groups. The authors concluded that college graduates with more class resources have more advantages for establishing their own businesses than noncollege graduates and that home-country college graduates have a greater probability to start a business than U.S. college graduates because of their language barrier and other labor market disadvantages. A study of Asian and Latino immigrants in New York and Los Angeles based on the 1980 U.S. census also reveals that the number of years of schooling in the United States is negatively related to self-employment (Sanders and Nee 1996). Gold (1989) also shows that many Chinese refugees from Vietnam started their own businesses as an alternative to underemployment.

Many middle-class Korean and other Asian immigrants' entry into small business is semi-involuntary in that their language barrier and other labor market disadvantages lead them to enter it. However, studies of Asian immigrant professional and large businesses have shown that labor market disadvantages are not as important as other factors in their decision to start their own businesses (Hosler 2000; Tseng 1995). For example, according to Hosler's study (2000), highly educated Japanese immigrants in New York have a severe language barrier because much of their education was gained in Japan. However, their language barrier is not a labor market disadvantage because the local branches of Japanese firms create many high-paying managerial and professional jobs. About one-third of Hosler's sample gave "wanted to make the best use of my skills" as their main reason for starting their own businesses. This suggests that "opening a business is the realization of their training and previous career, and not a situation adaptation" to their labor market disadvantages (Hosler 2000: 86).

A Middleman Minority Role

The concept of middleman minorities was introduced in the U.S. social science literature in the late 1960s and early 1970s (Blalock 1967: 79–84; Eitzen 1971; Loewen 1971; Rinder 1959). The central characteristic of middleman minorities emerging from the literature is playing an intermediary economic role that links dominant group producers and minority group customers.[3] Most middleman minority theorists have emphasized structural factors, especially a rigid status gap, in the host society as the major determinants of the middleman minority adjustment of a particular immigrant or minority group. They have cited the Jews in Europe, the Chinese in Southeast Asia, Indians in Africa, and the Parsis in India as typical examples of middleman minorities.

Middleman minorities typically existed in preindustrial societies, where social strata were more or less fixed and polarized and no significant middle class developed. The twentieth-century United States, with the middle class accounting for a significant or a majority of the population, was not a society favorable for the development of a middleman minority. However, Rinder (1959: 257) pointed out that "although strata boundaries are continuous and flexible in American society a status gap is apparent in the margin of white-Negro relations." In the early twentieth century, Jews in New York, Los Angeles, Chicago, and other cities dominated retail businesses in many black neighborhoods, playing a middleman minority role bridging white manufacturers/suppliers and poor black residents (Capeci 1985; Cohen 1970). Compared to the number of Jewish merchants, the number of Chinese merchants in black neighborhoods was insignificant. Yet the middleman role of the earlier Chinese immigrants in black neighborhoods, too, received scholarly attention.

For example, Loewen (1971) focused on the white–black status gap in explaining the concentration of Chinese immigrant families in the Mississippi Delta in the black-oriented grocery business. According to Loewen, there were some 1,200 Chinese in fourteen Mississippi Delta counties, more Chinese than in any other Southern state, excluding Texas, in 1960. He found that nearly all Chinese families in the Mississippi Delta were running grocery stores serving poor black customers and that almost all Chinese grocers were successful as petite bourgeoisie. In Loewen's view, the social structure of the Delta, which was characterized by a rigid segregation, a large racial status gap, and a sizable social distance between blacks and whites, was mainly responsible for the Chinese immigrants' concentration and success in black-oriented grocery retailing. Few whites in the Delta wanted to operate grocery stores exclusively for blacks because operating close to the caste line stigmatized the white businessman and lowered his standing in the white status system. Thus, "the white population in the Delta did not present a formidable adversary to the beginning Chinese merchant in his struggle for business" (Loewen 1971: 37).

Some Chinese immigrants in California as well engaged in grocery retail stores in black neighborhoods in the first half of the twentieth century. A Chinese grocery retail business in a black neighborhood before the civil rights era can be considered a typical middleman business because it bridges white suppliers and black customers, the two racially and socially stratified groups. Thus, other social scientists mentioned the status gap between whites and blacks to explain the Chinese grocery business in black neighborhoods in the prewar years (Shibutani and Kwan 1966: 191–197; Wong 1977).

Compared to a small number of Chinese immigrants running grocery stores in black neighborhoods in the pre-1965 period, an exceptionally large number of post-1965 Korean immigrants engage in grocery, liquor, produce, and other types of retail businesses in black neighborhoods in Los Angeles, New York, and other major cities (D. Kim 1999; Light and Bonacich 1988; Min 1988, 1996). The similar structural forces relating to the black–white racial stratification system that contributed to the prevalence of Jewish-owned businesses in black neighborhoods in the earlier period have helped Korean immigrants establish these retail stores in black neighborhoods. The high level of blacks' residential segregation in major cities has been persistent over the past several decades (Massey and Denton 1987). The poor economic conditions of residents in inner-city black neighborhoods have not been improved (Hacker 1992; Wilson 1987), although many blacks have achieved social mobility through education. Because of the residents' low spending capacity and high crime rates, large chain stores and independent white merchants are unwilling to invest in low-income black neighborhoods or are disinvesting from the areas. This situation has created the small business niches in black neighborhoods for Koreans and other immigrants (D. Kim 1999; Min 1988, 1996: 68–69). Thus, Korean merchants in black neighborhoods have been able to run businesses without encountering strong competition with chain stores or white store owners.

Historically, middleman merchants in different societies encountered boycotts, arson, and riots by customers (Bonacich and Modell 1980;

Eitzen 1971; Palmer 1957). They can be easy targets by minority customers because they often have the language barrier and lack political power. Similarly, Jewish merchants in black neighborhoods in the United States as middlemen suffered from boycotts and riots during three decades before the contemporary mass immigration wave started (Capeci 1985; Cohen 1970; Light 1972: 1–3).

As noted previously, Loewen (1971) wrote his book focusing on the middleman role of the Chinese grocers in the Mississippi Delta mainly to explain structural factors facilitating Chinese businesses rather than to explain Chinese–black conflicts. But he also devoted a few pages to discussing Chinese-owned stores singled out for attack by black rioters in the 1960s. He suggested that Chinese grocers became easy targets because of their lack of power and that the white police did not protect them. As he put it (1971: 175–176),

> A first consideration is that the Chinese stores are located directly in black areas. White-owned stores are mostly downtown, in the central business district. Rioters usually stay in their own neighborhood, where they know the turf and can remain more anonymous than if they venture outside. In addition, because whites, too, are still prejudiced against the Chinese, Chinese stores are perhaps a safe target than businesses owned by Caucasians. The Chinese cannot mobilize the police or other forces of repression against vandals as effectively as white merchants could. Chinese merchants in Greenville have complained publicly that little action has been taken by police there to aid them.

Loewen's book remains the only record that informs us of the victimization of the earlier Chinese grocery owners by black customers due to their middleman role.

Contemporary Korean merchants in black neighborhoods in New York, Los Angeles, and other major cities have encountered physical violence and other forms of rejection, including boycotts and riots. For example, Korean merchants in black neighborhoods in New York City encountered five long-term boycotts between 1981 and 1990 (Kim 2000; Min 1996). In the 1992 Los Angeles riots, approximately 2,300 Korean stores in South Central Los Angeles and Koreatown were looted and/or burned. Korean merchants suffered the property damages of $350 million, accounting for about 45 percent of the total property damages (Chang

1996; Kim and Kim 1999; Min 1996: 90). Korean-owned stores became targets of destruction and looting in the Los Angeles riots partly because a disproportionately large number of them were located in black neighborhoods in South Central Los Angeles, where the destruction was the most severe. However, evidence exists that African American rioters selectively targeted Korean-owned stores. Though Koreatown is about four miles away from South Central Los Angeles, rioters attacked 340 stores there. According to an investigation by the FBI, black gangs, who were responsible for planning the Los Angeles riots, deliberately chose to loot and burn Korean-owned stores (Min 1996: 90–91).

Historically, governments have failed to protect the rights of middleman merchants during periods of civil unrest, often taking a passive position (Blalock 1967: 84). This passive position was exemplified by the Los Angeles Police Department's failure to protect Korean merchants during the Los Angeles riots. During the 1990 Brooklyn boycott of a Korean produce store, New York City Mayor David Dinkins failed to enforce a court order to keep picketers fifty feet away from the entrance of the boycotted store (Min 1996: 78). It may be seen as another example of the government failing to protect the rights of middleman merchants.

While Loewen's book devoted only a few pages to discussing black customers' hostility against Chinese grocers in the pre-1965 period, several books and a dozen journal articles, as well as many newspaper and magazine articles, have covered "Korean–black conflicts" related to Korean immigrants' commercial activities in black neighborhoods (Ablemann and Lie 1995; Cheng and Espiritu 1989; Jo 1992; Kim 2000; K. Kim 1999; Light et al. 1994; Min 1990, 1995, 1996; Min and Kolodny 1994; Park 1996; Weitzer 1997; Yoon 1997). This suggests both the prevalence of Korean immigrants' commercial activities in low-income black neighborhoods and the intensity of the conflicts between Korean merchants and black customers/activists in the post-1965 period. The Chinese and Japanese immigrants in the pre-1965 period encountered rejection and violence by white workers when they were seeking employment in the general labor market. To avoid conflicts with white workers, they had to run small businesses. By contrast, contemporary Korean immigrants have had conflicts with blacks mainly because of their commercial activities in black neighborhoods.

Dependence on Ethnic Resources and Ethnic Solidarity

Ivan Light, a pioneer for research on immigrant and ethnic entrepreneurship, has emphasized what he called "ethnic resources for business establishment and operation" (Light 1972, 1980, 1984). Significantly, his insight about the importance of ethnic resources for the establishment and operation of immigrant/ethnic entrepreneurship derived originally from his study of Chinese and Japanese immigrants in the West Coast during the prewar years (Light 1972).

The earlier Chinese and Japanese immigrants, mostly of the heavily peasant background, came to the United States with no money. In fact, many of them arrived in the United States in debt, as recruiting or emigration companies paid their transportation costs. Given the lack of their class resources, an important issue is how the earlier Chinese and Japanese immigrants could accumulate capital to establish their businesses. Using various published materials, Light (1972: 23) showed that "the immigrants from southern China and Japan employed traditional rotating credit associations as their principal device for capitalizing small business." The rotating credit association is a close-knit association of people that lends money to each member on a rotating basis. It has been widely practiced in East Asian countries. Light (1972) argued that Chinese and Japanese immigrants were far more successful than African Americans in establishing small businesses, mainly because they brought with them the cultural tradition of the rotating credit association as a means to amass business capital.

An interesting question is to what extent contemporary East Asian immigrants depend on the rotating credit association for accumulating business capital. Many researchers have tried to answer this question using survey studies, especially involving samples of Korean immigrants, who have an exceptionally high self-employment rate (Kim and Hurh 1985; Light and Bonacich 1988: 247–259; Light et al. 1990; Min 1988: 80, 1996: 102; Yoon 1997: 147). With an exception of a study by Light et al. (1990), these studies show that few Korean immigrants depend on the rotating credit association as the major device for business capitalization. For example, my survey studies indicate that only four of the 159 Korean business owners in Atlanta and three of the eighty-six Korean business owners in New York City used money from rotating credit associations as their major source of business capital (Min 1988: 80; 1996: 102).

Instead, Korean immigrants of heavily middle-class background depend mainly on money brought from Korea and savings accumulated in the United States for business capitalization. For example, my 1992 survey of Korean merchants in New York City shows that savings from U.S. earnings accounted for an average of 47 percent of their business capital and that the money brought from Korea provided about 22 percent on average (Min 1996: 102). While friends and relatives are a readier source of loans for Korean immigrants than for American citizens, private loans are not an important source of their business capital. Their class resources are more important than their ethnic resources for business capitalization. Other East Asian immigrant entrepreneurs of higher class background are known to depend on class resources to a greater extent than Korean immigrants. For example, 57 percent of Taiwanese immigrant entrepreneur respondents in Los Angeles reported that start-up capital was accumulated mainly in the homeland (Tseng 1995). In a study of Japanese immigrant entrepreneurs in New York City (Hosler 2000: 95), savings made in the United States were found to compose the single largest part of start-up capital (68 percent), while no one employed the rotating credit association.

Ethnic resources are less important for contemporary Asian immigrant businesses than for prewar Asian immigrant businesses not only in terms of sources of business capital but also in terms of business operation. Researchers describe Chinese immigrant businesses in prewar years, represented by Chinese restaurants and laundry, as primarily family run, although they do not provide hard data on the average number of paid employees (Glenn 1983; Light 1972; Wong 1950). Glenn used the phrase "small producer family" to describe Chinese small business families between 1920 and 1943 (Glenn 1983). According to Glenn (1983: 40):

> The small-producer family had several distinctive characteristics. First was the lack of any clear demarcation between work and family life. Child care, domestic maintenance, and income-producing activities occurred simultaneously in time and in the same location. Second was the self-contained nature of the family as a production and consumption unit. All members contributed to family income and domestic maintenance, including the children.

Thus, not only both partners but also second-generation children usually worked in a Chinese immigrant business.

Japanese-operated farms needed more laborers than family members. But unpaid family labor was essential to their success in farming as well. A 1942 survey by the Los Angeles Agricultural Commission found that the average Japanese farm had four workers in addition to the operator and that about half the workers were supplied by family members (Bonacich and Modell 1980: 53). This suggests that a Japanese farm operator depended on his wife and an average of one child.

Studies of contemporary Asian immigrant businesses show that family ties strongly correlate with the probability of self-employment or business success (Min 1988; Sanders and Nee 1996; Wong 1998: 66–81). However, they also indicate that professional and nonprofessional businesses differ significantly in the extent to which they depend on unpaid family labor. Korean immigrant businesses, largely nonprofessional labor-intensive businesses (Min and Bozorgmehr 2000), are heavily dependent on unpaid family labor. A study of Korean immigrant entrepreneurs in Atlanta shows that for 62 percent of married-couple respondents, both spouses worked at the same business and that the husband–wife coordination was essential to their business success (Min 1988: 113–115). Furthermore, most of the respondents with adult children (22 percent of the respondents) were helped by their children with ten or more hours per week, usually after school or on weekends. By contrast, Asian immigrants who own professional and medium-size businesses depend on unpaid family labor much less. For example, in a survey of Japanese immigrant businesses in New York (Hosler 2000: 216), only 38 percent of the respondents reported that their spouses were involved in the same business.

The assumption that an Asian immigrant business, typically family operated, has no paid employees is no longer supported by data. Heavily labor-intensive, Korean immigrant businesses rely more on unpaid family labor than other Asian immigrant businesses. But they, too, usually have at least one paid employee. For example, a 1986 survey indicates that 72 percent of the Korean businesses in Los Angeles had one or more paid employees (Min 1989: 93). Not surprisingly, even a higher percentage of Japanese immigrant businesses (86 percent) have at least one paid employee (Hosler 2000: 126).

If Chinese and Japanese entrepreneurs in the prewar years needed to hire employees, they tended to hire coethnic employees, especially kin members and/or people of the same region through the mediation of surname and/or regional associations (Bonacich and Modell 1980: 48–55; Light 1972: chaps. 4 and 5). The relations between Chinese and Japanese immigrant business owners and their coethnic employees were characterized by paternalism. The paternalistic relations "imposed on the employer the duty of fair treatment for his employees in return for his employees' loyalty and submission" (Light 1972: 79). The owners preferred coethnic employees to nonethnic employees because the former are cheap and loyal. In return, the employees gained employment security and business training to start their own businesses. In the following paragraph, Bonacich and Modell (1980: 54–55) describe apprenticeship as an important aspect of labor paternalism in Japanese American firms:

> One important aspect of labor paternalism in Japanese American firms was that the community formed a kind of apprenticeship system. More recent immigrants would work in the business of their *kenjin*, or relatives, as a means of getting established. There they would learn the ropes of the particular business with a view of setting up their own small firms.

In paternalistic labor relations, customs and social obligations rather than the direction of the market were supposed to determine labor issues. Moreover, because the employees worked for coethnic firms partly or mainly to gain business training, they identified with the interests of business rather than with labor. Thus, the Chinese and Japanese employees working for coethnic businesses in prewar years did not use strikes or other class-based strategies to increase their wages and to improve their working conditions (Bonacich and Modell 1980; Light 1972; Miyamoto 1939; Modell 1977).

Overall, contemporary Asian immigrant entrepreneurs tend to depend on coethnic employees at a much lower level than the earlier Chinese and Japanese immigrants, although the level of dependency differs significantly for different immigrant groups and types of businesses. For Korean businesses in Los Angeles, coethnics accounted for only 31 percent of the paid employees, with Mexicans composing almost half (Min 1989: 93). Korean business owners in New York also rely largely on Latino workers, with coethnics accounting for less than 40 percent (D. Kim 1999; Min 1996: 114). For Japanese-owned businesses in New York City, coethnic employees were found to comprise 52 percent of all employees (Hosler 2000: 126).

The businesses owned by Chinese immigrants are known to depend on coethnic employees more extensively than other Asian businesses. Chinese restaurants and garment subcontracting are two major Chinese-owned businesses in the post-1965 era (Kwong 1987; Zhou 1992). In the Chinese community in New York, these two businesses, both concentrated in Manhattan Chinatown, almost entirely depend upon Chinese employees (Kwong 1987; Zhou 1992). Chinese-owned businesses in Queens, New York City, are more diverse than those in Manhattan's Chinatown. According to my survey of Chinese immigrants in Queens conducted in 1997–1998, coethnic employees comprised 61 percent of all employees of Chinese-owned businesses.

Contemporary Chinese immigrant businesses are more similar to the pre-1965 Chinese and Japanese businesses than contemporary Korean immigrant businesses in that they depend mainly on coethnic employees. However, the owner–employee relations in contemporary Chinese-owned businesses seem to be far from the kind of ethnic solidarity researchers described as existent in those in the earlier Asian immigrant businesses. Both subcontracted immigrant garment factories and small Chinese restaurants, the two major Chinese immigrant businesses in the post-1965 period, run for small profit margins; they succeed mainly because they cut operation expenses. This means that coethnic employees working for Chinese-owned restaurants and garment factories are vulnerable to exploitation. Several researchers have indicated that Chinese workers employed in coethnic firms were subjected to exploitation and therefore that they were very conscious of their class interests (Kwong 1987; Sanders and Nee 1987).[4] In fact, Chinese employees of Chinese restaurants and garment factories in New York City's Chinatown staged demonstrations against the owners several times (Kwong 1987; Light and Wong 1975; Lin 1998). Thus, the owner–employee relations in contemporary Chinese-owned businesses are characterized by class conflict as much as by ethnic ties.

In terms of the lack of conflict between the business owner and the employees, contemporary Korean immigrant businesses are closer to the earlier Asian businesses than contemporary Chinese immigrant businesses are. That is, Korean immigrant businesses lack the class conflict inherent in Chinese immigrant businesses. As discussed elsewhere (Min 1996: 213–215), the substantially lower level of employer–employee conflict in Korean immigrant businesses than in Chinese immigrant businesses seems to be due mainly to the differences in business structure and the socioeconomic background of new immigrants between the two Asian immigrant groups.

On the one hand, Korean immigrants are far more entrepreneurial than Chinese immigrants; there are far more businesses in the Korean community compared to the population size. On the other hand, the Chinese community annually receives a much larger number of immigrants than the Korean, and immigrants from mainland China, who include many illegal residents, in particular, are severely handicapped for employment in the general labor market. While the immigration of people of Chinese ancestry from mainland China, Taiwan, Hong Kong, and other Asian countries has increased greatly during recent years, Korean immigration has dropped substantially during recent years, falling in 1993 to half of that in 1987, the peak year of immigration (U.S. Immigration and Naturalization Service 1980–1998). Thus, while there is a great demand for ethnic employees in the Korean community, there is an oversupply of ethnic employees in the Chinese community, especially in Chinatown, where a large proportion of recent immigrants from mainland China settle.

Chinese immigrant workers employed by coethnic firms are more vulnerable to exploitation by their employers than Korean immigrant workers, not only because of the oversupply of ethnic labor but also because of new Chinese immigrants' lack of class resources. Most immigrants from China, especially those settled in Chinatown, come to the United States with almost no resources and have a severe language barrier. Thus, they have no alternative to low-wage employment in coethnic businesses (Kwong 1987). As widely reported by the media, many people have been brought illegally from China to New York City during recent years, and they are especially vulnerable to exploitation and abuse (Kwong 1997). As most Chinese immigrants employed in Chinese-owned businesses are not able to open their businesses within a short period of time, they are conscious of their class interests as wage earners.

By contrast, most Korean immigrants bring with them a substantial amount of money to the United States (Park et al. 1990: 85). Thus, in most cases, new Korean immigrants work for coethnic businesses mainly to acquire business experiences. Their class resources enable them to avoid exploitation by their coethnic employers and to move into their own businesses quickly. In a 1986 survey of Korean immigrants in Los Angeles, 50 percent of Korean immigrants employed in Korean-owned businesses reported that they planned to change their occupations soon, with the majority planning to start their own businesses. Because most Korean employees of Korean businesses want to start their own businesses,[5] like the earlier Asian immigrants working for coethnic businesses, they take the viewpoint of their employers and thus have little interest in the rights of workers (Min 1996: 214).

Summary

To summarize the preceding accounts, the concentration of the earlier Chinese and Japanese immigrants in small business basically was an involuntary occupational adjustment caused by discrimination and rejection in the general labor market, especially by white workers, although Japanese immigrants' entry into business was slightly more voluntary than that of Chinese immigrants. No doubt, disadvantages for employment in the general labor market have led contemporary Asian immigrants to turn to self-employment in small business. However, contemporary Korean and other Asian immigrants, heavily of middle-class background, choose self-employment in small business mainly because they cannot find occupations in the United States that are commensurate with their educational levels. Thus, contemporary Asian immigrants' occupational adjustment in small business is more voluntary than that of their predecessors.

The second major difference in Asian immigrant business patterns between the two periods is that contemporary Korean immigrants engage in middleman businesses in black neighborhoods more extensively than the earlier Asian immigrants. While only a small number of Chinese immigrants ran the grocery business in black neighborhoods in the pre-1965 period, Korean immigrants have dominated businesses in black neighborhoods in major U.S. cities. Consequently, Korean merchants in black neighborhoods have encountered boycotts, arson, physical violence, and destruction of their stores in the riots, comparable to Jews in the earlier period. It is interesting to note that while the earlier Chinese and Japanese immigrants had conflict mainly with white workers, Korean immigrants have had conflicts mainly with black customers.

The third major difference is related to the differential levels of dependence on ethnic resources and ethnic solidarity. While the earlier

Chinese and Japanese immigrants depended largely on collective or ethnic resources (the rotating credit association) for business capitalization, contemporary Asian immigrants depend mainly on the individual resources, the money brought from their home countries and saved in the United States. This difference in the source of start-up capital is due to the difference in the class background between the earlier (of the farming background) and contemporary (of the middle-class background) Asian immigrants.

For operating businesses as well, post-1965 Asian immigrants depend on ethnic ties less than pre-1965 Asian immigrants. The level of dependency on coethnic employees is substantially lower for contemporary Asian immigrant businesses than for the earlier Asian businesses. Contemporary Chinese businesses depend on coethnic employees to a greater extent than other Asian businesses. But it never reflects ethnic solidarity on the part of Chinese immigrants. In fact, the owner–employee relations in contemporary Chinese-owned businesses are characterized more by class conflict than by ethnic ties. In paternalistic relations between business owners and coethnic employees, contemporary Korean immigrant businesses are more similar to the earlier Asian immigrant businesses than contemporary Chinese immigrant businesses.

Notes

1. Japanese workers comprised more than 40 percent of the plantation workforce in Hawaii in the early twentieth century. But almost all of them worked as field hands and mill laborers with whites monopolizing mill engineering and supervisory positions. Moreover, Japanese workers received lower wages than white workers. See Takaki (1989: 132, 141).

2. The contract system was an arrangement in which the landowner agreed to pay the farmer a set amount of money for planting and harvesting a crop. By contrast, the sharecrop system allows the farmer to receive a certain percentage of the crop's profit.

3. Bonacich (1972), Bonacich and Modell (1980), and other scholars (Light 1980; Light and Bonacich 1988: 17–18) refer to immigrant and ethnic groups with high concentration in commercial occupations as "middleman minorities." However, I believe the term "trading minorities" should be used to refer to immigrant and minority groups that concentrate in commercial occupations in various societies and that "middleman minorities" should be reserved for the

immigrant and minority groups that play an intermediary economic role in societies with extreme ethnic stratification.

4. Zhou (1992) did not agree with this exploitation thesis. She claimed that Chinese employees working for Chinese businesses attained economic rewards from their investments in human capital comparable to those working for the general economy.

5. Korean single women, foreign students' wives, and illegals neither have financial resources nor plan to start their own businesses in the near future. Thus, they are somewhat vulnerable to exploitation by Korean business owners. But the shortage of coethnic employees in the Korean immigrant community still protects them from labor exploitation.

References

Ablemann, Nancy, and John Lie. 1995. *Blue Dreams: Koreans Americans and the Los Angeles Riots.* Cambridge, MA: Harvard University Press.

Arnold, Fred, Urmil Minocha, and James Fawcett. 1987. "The Changing Face of Asian Immigration to the United States." In *Pacific Bridges: The New Immigration from Asia and the Pacific Islands.* New York: Center for Migration Studies.

Asbury, Herbert. 1933. *The Barbary Coast.* New York: Knopf.

Blalock, Herbert. 1967. *Toward a Theory of Minority Group Relations.* New York: John Wiley & Sons.

Bonacich, Edna. 1972. "A Theory of Middleman Minorities." *American Sociological Review* 37: 583–594.

Bonacich, Edna, and John Modell. 1980. *The Economic Basis of Ethnic Solidarity: Small Business in the Japanese American Community.* Berkeley and Los Angeles: University of California Press.

Capeci, Dominic, Jr. 1985. "Black-Jewish Relations in Wartime Detroit: The Mash, Loving, and Wolf Surveys and Race Riots of 1943." *Jewish Social Studies* 5: 221–242.

Chan, Sucheng. 1991. *Asian Americans: An Interpretive History.* Boston: Twayne.

Chang, Edward. 1996. "Jewish and Korean Merchants in African American Neighborhoods: A Comparative Perspective." In *Los Angeles—Struggle toward Multiethnic Community: Asian American, African American and Latino Perspectives,* edited by Edward Chang and Russell Leong. Seattle: University of Washington Press.

Cheng, Lucie, and Yen Espiritu. 1989. "Korean Businesses in Black and Hispanic Neighborhoods: A Study of Intergroup Relations." *Sociological Perspectives* 32: 521–534.

Cohen, Nathan. 1970. *The Los Angeles Riots: A Sociological Study*. New York: Praeger.

Daniels, Roger. 1962. *The Politics of Prejudice: The Anti-Japanese Movement in California and the Struggle for Japanese Exclusion*. Berkeley and Los Angeles: University of California Press.

Eitzen, D. S. 1971. "Two Minorities: The Jews of Poland and the Chinese of the Philippines." In *Majority and Minority: The Dynamics of Racial and Ethnic Relations*, edited by N. R. Yetman and C. Hoy Steele. Boston: Allyn and Bacon.

Fairlie, Robert, and Bruce Meyer. 1996. "Ethnic and Racial Self-Employment Differences and Possible Explanations." *Journal of Human Resources* 31: 757–793.

Glenn, Evelyn Nakano. 1983. "Split Household, Small Producer and Dual Wage Earner: An Analysis of Chinese-American Family Strategies." *Journal of Marriage and the Family* 45: 35–46.

Gold, Steven J. 1989. "Differential Adjustment among New Immigrant Family Members." *Journal of Contemporary Ethnography* 17: 408–434.

Hacker, Andrew. 1992. *Two Nations: Black and White, Separate, Hostile, Unequal*. New York: Scribner's.

Hing, Bill Ong. 1993. *Making and Remaking Asian America through Immigration Policy, 1850–1990*. Stanford, CA: Stanford University Press.

Hosler, Akiko. 2000. *Japanese Immigrant Entrepreneurs in New York City: A New Wave of Ethnic Business*. New York: Garland.

Ichioka, Yuji. 1988. *The Issei: The World of the First Generation Japanese Immigrants, 1885–1924*. New York: The Free Press.

Jo, Moon Ho. 1992. "Korean Merchants in the Black Community: Prejudice among the Victims of Prejudice." *Ethnic and Racial Studies* 15: 395–411.

Kim, Claire Jean. 2000. *Bitter Fruits: The Politics of Black-Korean Conflict in New York City*. New Haven, CT: Yale University Press.

Kim, Dae Young. 1999. "Beyond Co-Ethnic Solidarity: Mexican and Ecuadorian Employment in Korean-Owned Businesses in New York City." *Ethnic and Racial Studies* 22: 583–607.

Kim, Illsoo. 1981. *New Urban Immigrants: The Korean Community in New York*. Princeton, NJ: Princeton University Press.

Kim, Kwang Chung, ed. 1999. *Koreans in the Hood: Conflict with African Americans*. Baltimore: The Johns Hopkins University Press.

Kim, Kwang Chung, and Won Moo Hurh. 1985. "Ethnic Resources Utilization of Korean Immigrant Entrepreneurs in the Chicago Minority Area." *International Migration Review* 19: 82–111.

Kim, Kwang Chung, Won Moo Hurh, and Marilyn Fernandez. 1989. "Intra-Group Differences in Business Participation: A Comparative Analysis of Three Asian Groups." *International Migration Review* 23: 73–95.

Kim, Kwang Chung, and Shin Kim. 1999. "The Multiracial Nature of Los Angeles Unrest in 1992." In *Koreans in the Hood: Conflict with African Americans*, edited by Kwang Chung Kim. Baltimore: The Johns Hopkins University Press.

Kurokawa, Minako, ed. 1970. *Minority Responses: Comparative View of Reactions to Subordination.* New York: Random House.

Kwong, Peter. 1987. *The New Chinatown.* New York: Hill & Wang.

———. 1997. *Forbidden Workers: Illegal Chinese Immigrants and American Labor.* New York: The New Press.

Light, Ivan. 1972. *Ethnic Enterprise in North America: Business and Welfare among Chinese, Japanese, and Blacks.* Berkeley and Los Angeles: University of California Press.

———. 1979. "Disadvantaged Minorities in Self-Employment." *International Journal of Comparative Sociology* 20: 31–45.

———. 1980. "Asian Enterprise in America: Chinese, Japanese, and Koreans in Small Business." In *Self-Help in Urban America*, edited by Scott Cummings. Port Washington, NY: Kennikart.

———. 1984. "Immigrant and Ethnic Enterprise in North America." *Ethnic and Racial Studies* 7: 195–216.

Light, Ivan, and Edna Bonacich. 1988. *Immigrant Entrepreneurs: Koreans in Los Angeles, 1965–1982.* Berkeley and Los Angeles: University of California Press.

Light, Ivan, Hadas Har-Chvi, and Kenneth Kan. 1994. "Black/Korean Conflict in Los Angeles." In *Managing Divided Cities*, edited by Seams Duan. Keele: University of Keele Press.

Light, Ivan, Jung-Kwuon Im, and Zhong Deng. 1990. "Korean Rotating Credit Associations in Los Angeles." *Amerasia* 16: 35–54.

Light, Ivan, and Elizabeth Roach. 1996. "Self-Employment: Mobility Ladder or Economic Lifeboat." In *Ethnic Los Angeles*, edited by Roger Waldinger and Mehdi Bozorgmehr. New York: Russell Sage Foundation.

Light, Ivan, and Angel Sanchez. 1987. "Immigrant Entrepreneurs in 272 SMSA's." *Sociological Perspectives* 30: 373–399.

Light, Ivan, and Charles Wong. 1975. "Protest or Work: Dilemmas of the Tourist Industry in American Chinatown." *American Journal of Sociology* 80: 1342–1368.

Lin, Jan. 1998. *Reconstructing Chinatown: Ethnic Enclave, Global Change.* Minneapolis: University of Minnesota Press.

Loewen, James. 1971. *The Mississippi Chinese: Between Black and White.* Cambridge, MA: Harvard University Press.

Massey, Douglass, and Nancy Denton. 1987. *American Apartheid: Segregation and the Making of the Underclass*. Cambridge, MA: Harvard University Press.

McWilliams, Carey. 1944. *Prejudice*. Boston: Little, Brown.

Min, Pyong Gap. 1984. "From White-Collar Occupations to Small Business: Korean Immigrants' Occupation Adjustment." *Sociological Quarterly* 25: 333–352.

———. 1987. "Factors Contributing to Ethnic Business: A Comprehensive Synthesis." *International Journal of Comparative Sociology* 23: 195–218.

———. 1988. *Ethnic Business Enterprise: Korean Small Business in Atlanta*. Staten Island, NY: Center for Migration Studies.

———. 1989. "Some Positive Functions of Ethnic Business for Immigrant Community: Koreans in Los Angeles." Final report submitted to the National Science Foundation.

———. 1990. "Problems of Korean Immigrant Entrepreneurship." *International Migration Review* 24: 436–455.

———. 1995. "The Entrepreneurial Adaptation of Korean Immigrants." In *Origins and Destinies: Immigration, Race, and Ethnicity in America*, edited by Silvia Pedraza and Rubén Rumbaut. Belmont, CA: Wadsworth.

———. 1996. *Caught in the Middle: Korean Communities in New York and Los Angeles*. Berkeley and Los Angeles: University of California Press.

Min, Pyong Gap, and Mehdi Bozorgmehr. 2000. "Immigrant Entrepreneurship and Business Patterns: A Comparison of Koreans and Iranians in Los Angeles." *International Migration Review* 34: 707–738.

Min, Pyong Gap, and Andrew Kolodny. 1994. "The Middleman Minority Characteristics of Korean Merchants in the United States." *Korea Journal of Population and Development* 23: 179–202.

Miyamoto, S. F. 1939. *Social Solidarity among the Japanese in Seattle*. Seattle: University of Washington Press.

Modell, John. 1977. *The Economics and Politics of Racial Accommodation: The Japanese of Los Angeles, 1900–1942*. Urbana: University of Illinois Press.

Palmer, Mabel. 1957. *The History of Indians in Nahal*. Natal Regional Survey, Vol. 10. Cape Town: Oxford University Press.

Park, In-Sook, James Fawcett, Fred Arnold, and Richard Gardner. 1990. "Korean Immigrants and U.S. Immigration Policy: A Predeparture Perspective." Papers of the East-West Population Institute No. 114. Honolulu: East-West Center.

Park, Kyeyoung. 1996. "Use and Abuse of Race and Culture: Black-Korean Tension in America." *American Anthropologist* 98: 492–499.

Rinder, Irwin. 1959. "Strangers in the Land: Social Relations in the Status Gap." *Social Problems* 6: 253–260.

Sanders, Jimy, and Victor Nee. 1987. "Limits of Ethnic Solidarity in the Enclave Economy." *American Sociological Review* 52: 745–767.

———. 1996. "Immigrant Self-Employment: The Family as Social Capital and the Value as Human Capital." *American Sociological Review* 61: 231–249.

Saxton, Alexander. 1971. *The Indispensable Enemy: Labor and Anti-Chinese Movement in California.* Berkeley and Los Angeles: University of California Press.

Shibutani, Tamotsu, and Kian Kwan. 1966. *Ethnic Stratification: A Comparative Approach.* New York: Macmillan.

Siu, Paul. 1987. *The Chinese Laundryman: A Study in Social Isolation.* New York: New York University Press.

Takaki, Ronald. 1989. *Strangers from a Different Shore: A History of Asian Americans.* Boston: Little, Brown.

Tseng, Yen-Feng. 1995. "Beyond 'Little Taipei': The Development of Taiwanese Immigrant Businesses in Los Angeles." *International Migration Review* 29: 33–58.

U.S. Immigration and Naturalization Service. 1980–1998. *Statistical Yearbook.* Washington, DC: U.S. Government Printing Office.

Weitzer, Ronald. 1997. "Racial Prejudice among Korean Merchants in African American Neighborhoods." *The Sociological Quarterly* 38: 587–606.

Wilson, William. 1987. *The Truly Disadvantaged: The Inner City, the Underclass, and Public Policy.* Chicago: University of Chicago Press.

Wong, Bernard. 1998. *Ethnicity and Entrepreneurship: The New Chinese Immigrants in the San Francisco Bay Area.* Boston: Allyn and Bacon.

Wong, Charles C. 1977. "Black and Chinese Grocery Stores in Los Angeles Black Ghetto." *Urban Life* 5: 439–464.

Wong, Jade Snow. 1950. *Fifth Chinese Daughter.* New York: Harper and Brothers.

Yoon, In-Jin. 1997. *On My Own: Korean Business and Race Relations in America.* Chicago: University of Chicago Press.

Zhou, Min. 1992. *Chinatown: The Socioeconomic Potential of an Urban Enclave.* Philadelphia: Temple University Press.

Zhou, Min, and John Logan. 1989. "Returns on Human Capital in Ethnic Enclaves: New York City's Chinatown." *American Sociological Review* 54: 809–820.

AUTHOR INDEX

SUBJECT INDEX

ABOUT THE CONTRIBUTORS

Andrew A. Beveridge is professor of sociology and director of the M.A. in Applied Social Research Program at Queens College, City University of New York. He is engaged in a number of projects and has published widely concerning demographic trends and changes, including the convergence of development patterns in the New York City and Los Angeles metropolitan areas, and changing patterns in New York City. He serves as a demographic consultant and analyst for the *New York Times*. He has testified on demographic issues in numerous civil rights cases.

Nancy Foner is professor of anthropology at the State University of New York at Purchase. She has written extensively about immigration to New York and West Indian migration. She is the author or editor of nine books, the most recent being *From Ellis Island to JFK: New York's Two Great Waves of Immigration* (Yale University Press, 2000), the winner of the 2000 Theodore Saloutos Book Award of the Immigration and Ethnic History Society; *Islands in the City: West Indian Migration to New York* (University of California Press, 2001); and a completely revised and updated edition of *New Immigrants in New York* (Columbia University Press, 2001).

Steven J. Gold is professor and associate chair in the department of sociology at Michigan State University. He is coeditor of *Immigration Research for a New Century: Multidisciplinary Perspectives* (Russell Sage Foundation, 2000) with Ruben Rumbaut and Nancy Foner and the author of three books: *Refugee Communities: A Comparative Field Study* (Sage, 1992), *From the Worker's State to the Golden State: Jews from the Former Soviet Union in California* (Allyn and Bacon 1995), and *Ethnic Economies* with Ivan Light (Academic Press, 2000). Routledge/University of Washington Press will publish his book *the Israeli Diaspora* in 2002.

Charles Jaret is professor of sociology at Georgia State University. His main areas of interest are in race and ethnic relations, urban sociology, and immigration. His publications include *Contemporary Racial and Ethnic Relations* (1995), "Poverty, Race, and U.S. Metropolitan Social and Economic Structure" (*Journal of Urban Affairs* [1999]), and "Suburban Expansion in Atlanta: 'The City without Limits' Faces Some" (*Urban Sprawl,* edited by Gregory Squires 2002).

Pyong Gap Min is professor of sociology at Queens College and the Graduate Center of the City University of New York. He is the author of three books, including *Caught in the Middle: Korean Communities in New York and Los Angeles* (1996), the winner of the 1997 National Book Award in Social Science by the Association for Asian American Studies and a cowinner of the 1998 Outstanding Book Award by the Asia and Asian America Section of the American Sociological Association. He is the editor/or coeditor of four books, including *Religions in Asian America* (2002) and *The Second Generation* (2002).

Susan Olzak is professor of sociology at Stanford University, where she does research on social movements, protest, and conflict in various countries, including the United States, South Africa, and Germany. She is the author of *The Dynamics of Ethnic Competition and Conflict* (1992). She recently published "The Ecology of Tactics" in the *American Sociological Review* and "Status in the World System and Ethnic Mobilization in the *Journal of Conflict Resolution.* In 2000–2001, she was a fellow at the Netherlands Institute for Advanced Study. While there, she completed research for a forthcoming book, *The Global Dynamics of Ethnic Mobilization* (Stanford University Press).

Dorothee Schneider is a native of Germany who was educated at both German and American universities. She currently teaches the history and sociology of immigration in the United States at the University of Illinois at Urbana-Champaign. Her published work has focused on German-speaking immigrants to the United States in the nineteenth and twentieth centuries and the history of naturalization and U.S. citizenship of immigrants. She is working on a book about the social history of naturalization and citizenship of immigrants in the twentieth-century United States.

Suzanne Shanahan is assistant professor of sociology at Duke University. She is a comparative historical sociologist whose work focuses on the relationship between collective identity, social inequality, and political mobilization. Her current work includes a recently completed book manuscript that explores the relationship between political sovereignty and social classification in Western Europe and North America, research on international adoption policy and children's rights, and an ongoing collaborative project with Susan Olzak that examines the effects of immigration on racial collective conflict in post–Civil War urban America.

Min Zhou is professor of sociology and chair of the Asian American Studies Interdepartmental Degree Program at the University of California, Los Angeles. Her main areas of research are immigration and immigrant adaptation, ethnic and racial studies, Asian Americans, entrepreneurship and ethnic economies, and the community and urban sociology. She is the author of *Chinatown: The Socioeconomic Potential of an Urban Enclave* (1992), coauthor of *Growing Up American: How Vietnamese Children Adapt to Life in the United States* (1997), and coeditor of *Contemporary Asian America: A Multidisciplinary Reader* (2000).